Teaching Comedy

Edited by
Bev Hogue

Modern Language Association of America
New York   2023

© 2023 by The Modern Language Association of America
85 Broad Street, New York, New York 10004
www.mla.org

All rights reserved. MLA and the MODERN LANGUAGE ASSOCIATION are trademarks owned by the Modern Language Association of America. To request permission to reprint material from MLA book publications, please inquire at permissions@mla.org.

To order MLA publications, visit www.mla.org/books. For wholesale and international orders, see www.mla.org/bookstore-orders.

The MLA office is located on the island known as Mannahatta (Manhattan) in Lenapehoking, the homeland of the Lenape people. The MLA pays respect to the original stewards of this land and to the diverse and vibrant Native communities that continue to thrive in New York City.

Options for Teaching 61
ISSN 1079-2562

Library of Congress Cataloging-in-Publication Data

Names: Hogue, Bev, editor.
Title: Teaching comedy / edited by Bev Hogue.
Description: New York : Modern Language Association of America, 2023.
Series: Options for teaching, 1079-2562 ; 61 | Includes bibliographical references.
Identifiers: LCCN 2022061503 (print) | LCCN 2022061504 (ebook) |
  ISBN 9781603296144 (hardcover) | ISBN 9781603296151 (paperback) |
  ISBN 9781603296168 (EPUB)
Subjects: LCSH: Comedy—Study and teaching. | Comedy in popular culture. |
  Comic, The, in literature.
Classification: LCC PN1922 .T43 2023 (print) | LCC PN1922 (ebook) |
  DDC 809.917—dc23
LC record available at https://lccn.loc.gov/2022061503
LC ebook record available at https://lccn.loc.gov/2022061504

Teaching Comedy

Contents

Acknowledgments ix
Introduction: "Defender of the Faith" and the
   Comedy Teacher's Conundrum 1
     Bev Hogue

Part I: Contextualizing Comedy as a Key to Culture

Comedy across Cultures: A Layered Approach to Cultural Studies,
   Critical Thinking, and Community Engagement 13
     Jay Friesen

A Right to Be Hostile: Aaron McGruder's *The Boondocks* at a
   Historically Black College or University 21
     Christopher B. Field, Charles Edward Bowie,
     Michelle D. Wise, and Samantha A. Morgan-Curtis

Charles W. Chesnutt, Joel Chandler Harris, and the
   Minstrel Show Legacy 30
     Stephen Casmier

Blackface in the Comedy Class 38
     Meenakshi Ponnuswami

No Laughing Matter: Immigrant Cartoons of the
   Late Nineteenth and Early Twentieth Centuries 46
     Peter Conolly-Smith

Humor and Intercultural Empathy: Teaching Comedic
   Films of Intercultural Encounter 55
     Iñaki Pérez-Ibáñez and Megan M. Echevarría

Laughing Prejudices Away: Teaching Diversity through
   Jokes in Contemporary Ethnic American Women's Poetry 64
     Mayy ElHayawi

Dark Laughter and Sexual Trauma in Paula Vogel's
   How I Learned to Drive 73
     Miriam Chirico

Who's Stupid? Teaching Histories with
  Gentlemen Prefer Blondes   82
  James Zeigler

Intercultural Critique of Subalternization:
  Parody in Okot p'Bitek's *Song of Lawino*   90
  Lorna Fitzsimmons

Diverse Political Comedy Television in the Classroom   99
  Kimberly Tolson

Translating Trevor: Relatability and the Loss of
  Aesthetic Appreciation for a Joke   105
  Vivian Nun Halloran

Laughing at Belief: The Risks and Rewards of
  Satire in the Classroom   113
  Jeffrey Galbraith

Calvin and Hobbes in the English Foreign
  Language Classroom   121
  Joy Katzmarzik

Part II: Communicating with Comedy throughout the Curriculum

From Plato to Python: Designing an Introduction
  to Humor Course   133
  Paul Benedict Grant

For Better or for Worse: A Marriage of
  Humor and Comedy   141
  Mary Ann Rishel

Transitioning with Laughter: Comedy in the
  First-Year Seminar   150
  Jess Landis

Stand-Up Comedy, Central Questions, and Databases   159
  Jared Champion

Nick Sousanis's *Unflattening* in a Developmental
  Writing Course   168
  Christopher Burlingame

Comedy in the First-Year Writing Classroom Laura Biesiadecki	176
Consume, Converse, Create: Stand-Up and Sketch Comedy in the Classroom Mariann J. VanDevere	184
Using Comics to Teach Analytical Writing Lisa Smith	193
Teaching Long-Form Analytical Writing Using *YouTube* Aaron Duplantier	201
Absurdist Television in the Writing Classroom Eric Kennedy and Jade Lennon	208
Mrs. Maisel, Amy Sherman-Palladino, and a Pretty, Perfect Pilot Jeffrey M. Cordell	216
Learning through Failure: Workplace Comedy in the Professional and Technical Communication Classroom Shelly A. Galliah	224
A Formalist Approach to the Comic Anja Müller-Wood	234
Mankind, the First English Comedy: A Long-Overlooked Teaching Option Richard Obenauf	242
Using Comic Insults as an Approach to Shakespeare Andy Felt	251
Performing Equivocating Sententiousness in Shakespeare's *Othello* Ameer Sohrawardy	258
The Changing of the Joke: Restoration Libertine Sex Comedies Tiffany Potter	266
Modern Chivalry and Satire: Why Teach a Post–Revolutionary War Novel? Janice McIntire-Strasburg	275

Comedy versus Satire in Eighteenth-Century Contexts   282
   Aaron R. Hanlon

The Sincerest—and Most Fun—Form of Flattery:
   Imitation as Analysis of Eighteenth-Century Comic Texts   290
   Deborah J. Knuth Klenck

The Importance of Failing at Teaching
The Importance of Being Earnest   298
   Helena Gurfinkel

How to Laugh for the Future   306
   David Ritchie

Part III: Resources   313

Afterword: Teaching Comedy during COVID-19   319
   Bev Hogue

Notes on Contributors   323

Acknowledgments

Many thanks to Jaime Cleland, Susan Doose, Curtis Mayo, and the Marietta College Faculty Publishing Group, but most of all to the students who laughed—and to the ones who didn't and made me wonder why.

Bev Hogue

Introduction: "Defender of the Faith" and the Comedy Teacher's Conundrum

In May of 1945 Sergeant Nathan Marx finds himself in a bit of a pickle: the US Army expects him to transform raw recruits into faceless cogs in a fighting machine, but three of those recruits want Sergeant Marx to treat them as family, members of a community of faith. He'd been marching east across Germany, developing an "infantryman's heart, which, like his feet, at first aches and swells but finally grows horny enough for him to travel the weirdest paths without feeling a thing," when fighting had ended in Europe, causing Sergeant Marx to be sent back stateside to serve out his remaining time training recruits at Camp Crowder, Missouri (Roth 161). As the only Jewish officer on the scene, Sergeant Marx gets drawn, reluctantly, into an awkward position: mediating between Jewish recruits and the US Army. Though he at first attempts to maintain distance from the demands of the Jewish privates Fishbein, Halpern, and Grossbart, Marx finally admits that, "like Karl and Harpo, [he] was one of them" (165). Accepting his role as "one of them" requires Marx to take on the responsibility of educating the army about what it means to be Jewish in Middle America in 1945.

These attempts at education are often comical, as when Sergeant Marx asks Corporal LaHill to announce the Shabbat service but LaHill mangles the message by inviting recruits to celebrate "the Jewish Mass" (Roth 167). Later, after Grossbart writes a letter to his congressman complaining about nonkosher food in the mess tent—and forges his mother's signature on the letter—Captain Barrett calls on Sergeant Marx to explain the situation, but Marx struggles. "Jewish parents, sir—they're apt to be more protective than you expect," he explains (175), a message Captain Barrett reinterprets for his superior officer on the phone: "Sir—Marx, here, tells me Jews have a tendency to be pushy" (176). Here Sergeant Marx illustrates a conundrum every teacher of comedy eventually faces: How can we instruct others about comic conventions without reinforcing harmful stereotypes?

When I teach Philip Roth's 1959 short story "Defender of the Faith," I have to remind students of the relevant historical context. By May of 1945 fighting had ended in Europe but continued for a short time in the Pacific; Auschwitz had been liberated in January of that year, and while the story never directly mentions death camps or crematoria, Roth would have expected his readers to be familiar with the horrors of the Holocaust, which would make Grossbart's complaints pale by comparison. Indeed, when Grossbart compares his own problems to the Nazis' persecution of Jews, Marx tells him, "This is the Army, not summer camp" (Roth 174). Roth touches only tangentially on Sergeant Marx's war experiences, leaving the Holocaust as an unspoken horror shadowing the plot. And so I pose the question: If Roth wanted to write a story about the persecution of Jews during World War II, why choose comedy?

But here we face another conundrum: in my experience, students don't always recognize or respond to the comic elements in Roth's story. They read right past Sergeant Marx's calling himself a "straight man" (Roth 180) and claiming metaphorical kinship to the Marx brothers (165); further, students are unlikely to perceive the comedy in Marx's attempts to explain the finer points of Jewish family life. And so I, like many teachers of comic texts, stand in Sergeant Marx's shoes, trying to explain jokes about Jewish mothers without reinforcing stereotypes about Jewish mothers. Similarly, I can show students Nazi propaganda posters portraying Jews as sneaky, cheating, money-loving traitors, and I can ask students to examine how these stereotypes loom behind Roth's characterization of Grossbart, but I can't always make them perceive how Roth comically undermines those stereotypes. "Defender of the Faith" reminds us that comedy can build community, ease personal and shared pain, and enhance connections among cultures, but every time I teach the story I struggle with the same questions: Will students accept the invitation to connect, or will they feel further alienated? Will explaining the jokes kill the comedy? And why choose to teach a comic text that requires so much contextualization?

Anyone who teaches comic texts struggles at some point with questions like these, and this collection attempts to provide some answers. When comedy dominates popular culture so thoroughly that it's difficult to distinguish spoofs from truths, when identities and relationships form and fumble on a foundation of comic memes, when the powerful and the powerless wield comedy alternately as weapon or shield, it's time to take comedy seriously. A field that ranges from Aristophanes to *The Onion* by way of Shakespeare, Charlie Chaplin, and *The Simpsons* offers a wide range of areas for inquiry open to a variety of methodologies, and this volume offers a variety of resources for teachers interested in bringing comedy into the classroom. Here teachers will find passionate arguments for the value of comic texts, theoretical foundations for teaching them, practical methods for contextualizing them, and resources for further exploration. Essays in this volume range in style from theoretical treatises to breezy meditations, and while comic moments abound, readers should be prepared to do some intellectual heavy lifting. While many of the essays focus on specific texts and contexts, they also suggest ways to adapt activities to meet the needs of other classes. Most of the essays are aimed at teachers of undergraduates, but high school and graduate school instructors will also find much to engage their attention. Contributors draw on years of reading and teaching, but space limitations require that essays focus closely on limited topics and tasks, which may elide some complexities of classroom dynamics. If nothing else, teachers who have come face-to-face with the challenges of teaching comic texts will find herein kindred spirits exploring thought-provoking concepts and offering practical suggestions for applying them in the classroom.

But why teach comedy at all? And what qualifies as a comic text? Let's face it: comedy isn't easy. Students steeped in stand-up comedy and memes may register for a comic literature class on the assumption that comedy is necessarily a popular culture phenomenon, but then they see Shakespeare on the syllabus and realize the class is no joke. Or perhaps the word *comic* will suggest comic books and students will expect to indulge in familiar fandoms only to find on the syllabus distinctly unfunny graphic texts engaged in philosophical exploration or social critique. As several essays in this volume explain, cartoons, comic books, and other graphic texts share with comedy a concern for subverting cultural norms and holding up to the world a fun-house mirror that may be distinctly unfunny.

Comedy can range from the refined to the ribald, and texts considered *comic* may be difficult or archaic or controversial or, dare I say it, dull, and no matter how much historical and cultural context we provide, some students just won't get the joke—or maybe they'll get the joke but find it offensive, which raises a different set of issues. Further, our colleagues and fellow scholars may wonder why we're devoting valuable class time to frivolous pursuits instead of serious literature, as if comedy were incapable of illuminating the human condition. Given these difficulties, how can we defend our faith in comedy?

Many scholars throughout the ages have attempted to define comedy and defend its worth, but most definitions remain unsatisfactory, and every defense is subject to attack. Comedy springs from simple country people—except when it's developed by sophisticated city dwellers. Comedy exalts vice—except when it subjects the vicious to ridicule. Comedy arouses or anesthetizes the emotions, dulls the mind or demands intellectual engagement, celebrates folly or shines a light on truth. When Matthew Bevis asserts that "the study of the comic involves a consideration of 'that which is laughable,'" he admits that "the 'laughable' may or may not lead to laughter, and that, if it does, this laughter can be hard to gauge" (4). Because comedy is so highly contingent on context and audience response, so subject to change through the ages and resistant to translation across cultures, it's hardly surprising that scholars' understanding of comedy's nature and purpose shifts and shimmies like a drunken procession marching through a staid, solemn campus library.

But defining and theorizing comedy have long been very serious endeavors, dating back to Plato, who equated laughter with vice, and Aristotle, who found comedy instructive despite its origins in carnivalesque revels involving sexual license and excess. Three influential theories of humor have long vied for supremacy: the superiority theory, which characterizes humor as a contest in which participants contend for superiority; the relief, or release, theory, in which laughter provides a safe release of troublesome thoughts and repressed feelings; and the incongruity theory, in which humor springs from the surprising juxtaposition of unexpected elements. The ultimate inadequacy of any of these theories has inspired others to suggest variations or to develop new theories that seek to unify all other theories; for instance, Henri Bergson's theory of mechanical inelasticity suggests that comedy arises when people act in a machine-like manner (10), but Bergson also highlighted the social function of laughter, which arises in group settings and may provide the glue that holds the group together (6). More recently, Dan O'Shannon proposed a model of comedy focused on audience perception (24), and Todd McGowan argues that comedy arises from a specific type of incongruity: the surprising "intersection of lack and excess" (14). In 2010 A. Peter McGraw and Caleb Warren proposed the benign violation theory, arguing that laughter arises when a moral norm is violated in a safe context (1147).

But what makes a context safe for comedy? Mercurial mores make any attempt at universal definitions of comedy fraught with danger, especially for those caught up in the battle to distinguish the acceptable from the offensive. Recent public debates over, for instance, rape jokes or blackface comedy demonstrate that cultural perceptions of comedy are constantly under construction by groups of workers following competing blueprints.

We see this kind of conflict in Umberto Eco's 1980 novel *The Name of the Rose*, which effectively dramatizes long-standing controversies related to comedy's nature and purpose. In the novel, monks at a fourteenth-century monastery are shaken by a series of brutal murders inspired by attempts to control a dangerous text, Aristotle's lost treatise on comedy, which is offered as a reward to members of the powerful inner circle but serves up fatal punishment when eager readers lick their fingers to turn pages sticky with poison. A series of intense informal debates between William of Baskerville, an outsider charged with solving the murder mystery, and Jorge of Burgos, the blind librarian, aptly summarizes the controversies swirling about comedy through the centuries. William describes laughter as "good medicine" (Eco 131), while Jorge sees laughter as "something very close to death and to the corruption of the body" (96). For William, laughter "serves to confound the wicked and to make their foolishness evident" (133), while for Jorge laughter only "foments doubt" (132). William supports his argument with frequent references to Aristotle, who "sees the tendency to laughter as a force for good, which can also have an instructive value" (472). But this reliance on Aristotle disturbs Jorge mightily, for while he believes that laughter is "weakness, corruption, the foolishness of our flesh, . . . the peasant's entertainment, the drunkard's license," he feels that comedy can be dismissed as long as it serves as frivolous entertainment for simple people (474); however, when a great thinker like Aristotle deigns to take comedy seriously, he elevates entertainment to art and undermines the priest's authority, for, Jorge explains, "on the day when the Philosopher's word would justify the marginal jests of the debauched imagination, or when what has been marginal would leap to the center, every trace of the center would be lost" (475). In other words, comedy may seem like a silly distraction for simple people, but it carries a potentially poisonous power—to critique community values, undermine authority, satirize sacred beliefs, and make room for the marginalized to approach the center.

Essays in this volume examine these conflicts and controversies from a variety of angles, but part 1, "Contextualizing Comedy as a Key to Culture," pays special attention to comedy as a conduit for marginalized voices while recognizing the obstacles that may prevent those voices from being heard. This cluster of essays begins with Jay Friesen's "Comedy across Cultures: A Layered Approach to Cultural Studies, Critical Thinking, and Community Engagement," an overview of comedy's ability to connect students with diverse communities, followed by a series of essays dealing with specific types of communities or texts. Readers may approach essays in any order, but this cluster moves from issues concerning race to ethnic stereotypes to gender, political diversity, and religion and concludes with an essay on comic texts in the EFL, or English as a foreign language, classroom. In "*A Right to Be Hostile:* Aaron McGruder's *The Boondocks* at a Historically Black College or University," Christopher B. Field, Charles Edward Bowie, Michelle D. Wise, and Samantha A. Morgan-Curtis show how a collection of comic strips can help African American students tackle the challenges of developing individual agency; the authors' emphasis on understanding context reappears throughout the collection, particularly in essays that examine comic texts from the distant past or from cultures students might be unfamiliar with. In "Charles W. Chesnutt, Joel Chandler Harris, and the Minstrel Show Legacy," for instance, Stephen Casmier examines how understanding the plantation school myth promulgated by Joel Chandler Harris helps students recognize how Charles W. Chesnutt's stories comically undermine that myth. Meenakshi Ponnuswami's "Blackface in the Comedy Class" argues that teaching the history of blackface can help students understand the roots of contemporary racism. Similarly, in "No Laughing Matter: Immigrant Cartoons of the Late Nineteenth and Early Twentieth Centuries," Peter Conolly-Smith presents a method for using historical cartoons to help students understand how comedy can reinforce ethnic stereotypes.

Other contributors examine how comedy can subvert stereotypes and create understanding. In "Humor and Intercultural Empathy: Teaching Comedic Films of Intercultural Encounter," Iñaki Pérez-Ibáñez and

Megan M. Echevarría describe a method for using comic films to inspire cross-cultural empathy. Mayy ElHayawi provides a clear model for using poetry to inspire understanding in "Laughing Prejudices Away: Teaching Diversity through Jokes in Contemporary Ethnic American Women's Poetry," while Miriam Chirico's "Dark Laughter and Sexual Trauma in Paula Vogel's *How I Learned to Drive*" tackles more troublesome territory, demonstrating how incest-related comedy in *How I Learned to Drive* can alert students to gendered messages aswirl in popular culture. Gender stereotypes also take center stage in James Zeigler's "Who's Stupid? Teaching Histories with *Gentlemen Prefer Blondes*," which argues that historical context can help students question cherished stereotypes about stupidity.

Several essays in part 1 deal with the role of parody and satire in creating opportunities for interpersonal understanding. In "Intercultural Critique of Subalternization: Parody in Okot p'Bitek's *Song of Lawino*," Lorna Fitzsimmons shows how parodic elements of a Ugandan poem can build bridges between cultures. Kimberly Tolson argues in "Diverse Political Comedy Television in the Classroom" that satirical comedy can defuse students' prejudices and empower more open discussions; meanwhile, in "Translating Trevor: Relatability and the Loss of Aesthetic Appreciation for a Joke," Vivian Nun Halloran explores the advantages and challenges of viewing American culture through the perspective of an outsider—Trevor Noah. In "Laughing at Belief: The Risks and Rewards of Satire in the Classroom," Jeffrey Galbraith tackles the challenge of teaching satirical comedy that may make students question their religious beliefs. Part 1 concludes with Joy Katzmarzik's "*Calvin and Hobbes* in the English Foreign Language Classroom," which affirms that studying American newspaper comic strips can open doors for non-native speakers of English seeking to understand American language and culture.

The wide variety of texts and emphases in part 1 suggests that comedy can illuminate culture while an understanding of cultural contexts can help students understand comedy, but those concerns are deeply intermingled with comedy as a mode of communication and education. Those who want to delve more deeply into specific types of courses or genres of comedy will find further options in part 2, "Communicating with Comedy throughout the Curriculum." How can comic texts help students think or write more clearly? Can a long-overlooked comic text bring a past era alive for students? What methods can help students engage with Shakespearean language? These and similar questions motivate essays in this part. Readers may focus on the topics most relevant to their own fields, but they may also find helpful pedagogical methods in essays far outside those fields.

Comedy theory comes to the forefront in the two essays about designing courses focused on comedy: "From Plato to Python: Designing an Introduction to Humor Course," by Paul Benedict Grant, and "For Better or for Worse: A Marriage of Humor and Comedy," by Mary Ann Rishel. While Grant and Rishel promote different methods for introducing students to the complexities of comedy, they agree on the necessity of humor theory and offer practical approaches to designing a comedy course.

Using comedy in the first-year or writing classroom is the focus of the next cluster of essays. In "Transitioning with Laughter: Comedy in the First-Year Seminar," Jess Landis shows how comedy can engage first-year seminar students as they make the transition to college-level thinking and writing. A method for helping writing students ask compelling questions and develop convincing answers lies at the center of Jared Champion's "Stand-Up Comedy, Central Questions, and Databases," while Christopher Burlingame's essay, "Nick Sousanis's *Unflattening* in a Developmental Writing Course," describes a technique for using a graphic text to subvert students' expectations of the writing classroom. Similarly, Laura Biesiadecki's "Comedy in the First-Year Writing Classroom" argues that comedy can build first-year students' confidence, while Mariann J. VanDevere's "Consume, Converse, Create: Stand-Up and Sketch Comedy in the Classroom" explores how comedy can enhance critical thinking skills. Two essays address methods for improving students' analytical writing skills: "Using Comics to Teach Analytical Writing," by Lisa Smith, and "Teaching Long-Form Analytical Writing Using *YouTube*," by Aaron Duplantier. In "Absurdist Television in the Writing Classroom," Eric Kennedy and Jade Lennon explain how engaging with the irrational can help students construct rational arguments.

Several essays argue that close attention to form and structure in comic texts can help students develop effective writing strategies or enhance their understanding of literature. In "Mrs. Maisel, Amy Sherman-Palladino, and a Pretty, Perfect Pilot," Jeffrey M. Cordell invites students to step into the shoes of the marvelous Mrs. Maisel to pay close attention to comic beats and structures. In "Learning through Failure: Workplace Comedy in the Professional and Technical Communication Classroom," Shelly A. Galliah shows how analyzing comic communication failures can equip students to improve their technical and professional writing skills. Anja Müller-Wood's "A Formalist Approach to the Comic" argues that focusing on form and structure can help students effectively engage with texts they find difficult (in this case, Renaissance drama).

Other essays in part 2 suggest approaches to teaching specific texts or genres. In "*Mankind*, the First English Comedy: A Long-Overlooked Teaching Option," Richard Obenauf offers an alternative to *Everyman* as an entrée into understanding medieval thought. Andy Felt's "Using Comic Insults as an Approach to Shakespeare" outlines a method for making students comfortable with Shakespeare's language, while Ameer Sohrawardy's "Performing Equivocating Sententiousness in Shakespeare's *Othello*" describes an approach to helping students understand comic sententiousness in a very serious play. In "The Changing of the Joke: Restoration Libertine Sex Comedies," Tiffany Potter considers methods for teaching those sexy Restoration plays that students in the Me Too era may well find offensive. Satirical texts may prove especially challenging when students lack the historical context to understand what is being satirized, a problem examined by Janice McIntire-Strasburg in "*Modern Chivalry* and Satire: Why Teach a Post–Revolutionary War Novel?" Similarly, Aaron R. Hanlon, in "Comedy versus Satire in Eighteenth-Century Contexts," explains that students have become so accustomed to seeing comedy and satire intertwined that they need help understanding noncomedic forms of satire common in the eighteenth century. In "The Sincerest—and Most Fun—Form of Flattery: Imitation as Analysis of Eighteenth-Century Comic Texts," Deborah J. Knuth Klenck argues that imitation can be a valuable tool to help students understand eighteenth-century comedy.

Two essays explore how the very difficulty of teaching comic texts makes these texts especially valuable in developing students' understanding of themselves and their cultures. In "The Importance of Failing at Teaching *The Importance of Being Earnest*," Helena Gurfinkel employs queer pedagogy to suggest that a failure to achieve predetermined outcomes can open space for creativity and understanding. David Ritchie's essay, "How to Laugh for the Future," further asserts that comedy, like history, may be a foreign country but is nevertheless well worth visiting despite the sometimes uncomfortable border crossing.

For those instructors determined to incorporate comedy despite potential pitfalls, part 3 provides an annotated list of resources for further reading. During the time this collection was being assembled, we all inhabited the uncomfortable environs of the COVID-19 pandemic. An afterword titled "Teaching Comedy during COVID-19" argues that comedy remains relevant and essential even in difficult times.

Despite all our well-planned activities and methods, those of us who teach comedy in any context may, at some point, find ourselves facing the wreckage of all our plans and feel like William of Baskerville at the end of *The Name of the Rose*, when he stands before the ruins of the massive library after a fire has incinerated thousands of irreplaceable texts representing centuries of human thought and creativity and mourns the loss of all that learning now reduced to ashes. In the end William reminds himself that "the mission of those who love mankind" is not simply to pursue endless accumulation of facts but to "*make truth laugh*," his final affirmation of the value of studying comedy (Eco 491). It is my fervent hope that this volume will equip us to make truth laugh, to defend our faith in comedy so that we might stand with Sergeant Marx in the liminal space between cultures and use comedy as a threshold toward communication and understanding.

Works Cited

Bergson, Henri. *Laughter: An Essay on the Meaning of the Comic*. Translated by Cloudesley Brereton and Fred Rothwell, MacMillan, 1928.

Bevis, Matthew. *Comedy: A Very Short Introduction*. Oxford UP, 2013.

Eco, Umberto. *The Name of the Rose*. Translated by William Weaver, Harcourt Brace Jovanovich, 1980.

McGowan, Todd. *Only a Joke Can Save Us: A Theory of Comedy*. Northwestern UP, 2017.

McGraw, A. Peter, and Caleb Warren. "Benign Violations: Making Immoral Behavior Funny." *Psychological Science*, vol. 21, no. 8, 2010, pp. 1141–49.

O'Shannon, Dan. *What Are You Laughing At? A Comprehensive Guide to the Comedic Event*. Bloomsbury, 2012.

Roth, Philip. "Defender of the Faith." 1959. *"Goodbye, Columbus" and Five Short Stories*, by Roth, Modern Library, 1995, pp. 159–200.

Part I

Contextualizing Comedy as a Key to Culture

Jay Friesen

Comedy across Cultures: A Layered Approach to Cultural Studies, Critical Thinking, and Community Engagement

E. B. White observed one of the pitfalls of overexplaining comedy, likening it to a lousy science experiment: "Humor can be dissected, as a frog can, but the thing dies in the process, and the innards are discouraging to any but the pure scientific mind" (qtd. in McGraw and Warner i). As a university instructor hoping to avoid a similar fate, I designed a second-year course for the Department of Modern Languages and Cultural Studies, Comedy across Cultures, that took a layered approach to engage students. Central to creating a course that avoided dissecting and killing comedy, I reasoned, was constructing a class that involved students on multiple levels that sparked students' imaginations about how cultures experience comedy rather than tediously dissecting humor around the globe.

This essay summarizes the strategies I used in Comedy across Cultures, strategies that used comedy's unique qualities to create a vibrant classroom. I consider three features that contributed to the success of the course. First, I discuss how comedy worked as a hook to attract students who were unfamiliar with the field of cultural studies and conceivably nervous about enrolling with little prior knowledge. Next, I describe how using comedic case studies from around the world was an effective way to study cultures. Last, I reflect on how partnering with local nonprofits for

13

service learning placements benefited students by allowing them to apply their learning in meaningful contexts beyond the campus walls.

Comedy across Cultures got its place in the university calendar by winning a department competition. The goal of the competition is to inspire new topics for a onetime course, one that attracts a diverse cross section of students. Such courses can help advertise a department. The Department of Modern Languages and Cultural Studies is a department that many students on campus may not know much about and, accordingly, it benefits the department to offer courses that have widespread appeal and that inspire students from other majors to try one of the department's courses as an elective. However, persuading students in unrelated areas of study (e.g., engineering or biology) to take one of the department's courses proves more difficult than persuading students in arts and humanities fields. For students unfamiliar with cultural studies (and unsure if they might succeed in such a course), it can be intimidating to enter a classroom with those who, notionally, have more experience. From the outset, then, one of the goals of offering this course was to connect with nontraditional students, lower their inhibitions, and overcome potential registration barriers. Accordingly, depicting the course as something students were already knowledgeable about was critical. Fundamentally, I worked on the premise that comedic tastes are something everyone is an expert about, insofar that everyone is an expert about what they enjoy. Unlike appreciating opera, for instance, evaluating comedy is something nearly everyone has invested considerable time doing, and making students aware of their latent knowledge was essential.

While I used posters and social media to advertise the course, I also visited classes and spoke with students. The aim was to make students recognize how much they already knew about comedy and, perhaps more importantly, how they could mobilize this knowledge in an academic course on the subject. I started each pitch with a common question that could have come from many cultural studies textbooks: How does cultural identity influence differences between American and British humor? Students were often challenged by and unsure of how to answer this question. This is not a typical question asked, for instance, in a biology classroom, and many students seemed hesitant to respond. This tactic was deliberate, and I strategically transitioned to something more relatable. I asked students to stick with me as I played a clip from the pilot episode of the American sitcom *The Office*. In the clip, the character Dwight becomes frustrated when he reaches for his stapler and finds that Jim, one of his coworkers, has suspended it in Jell-O ("Pilot" 00:14:47–16:04). Many students had binge-watched the series on *Netflix* and were devotees of the series; there were very few who were not familiar with it. In any case, the hook succeeded, and students began to answer follow-up questions more readily. Using comedic preferences as a disarming tactic was the entry point to student participation and conversation about cultures of comedy.

With guards lowered and interest piqued, I offered a piece of trivia for what many consider a blockbuster show: many prominent critics thought the American version of *The Office* was an early flop. I shared the sentiments of the former president of the Television Critics Association, Scott D. Pierce: "The American version casts Steve Carell . . . who's every bit the idiot the British boss was. But Carell doesn't capture the weird charm, the subtlety and the vulnerability—and the show doesn't have any of those." I then noted that the American version of the show needed cultural tweaking in order to be successful. For many students, this revelation seemed to illuminate a point of entry into the course. Students recognized that they had a knowledge base from which to engage in cultural studies, a wealth of personal experience to draw on. I then played a clip from the pilot episode of the British version of the show, which also involved a stapler in Jell-O ("Downsize" 00:13:17–15:13), and students began to recognize subtle differences between the tone and pace of the comedy. More importantly, we had shared an experience that demonstrated how each student could discuss cross-cultural distinctions in comedy, provided that the setup was thoughtfully introduced. I exploited the fun, accessible, and subjective qualities of humor as an inroad into a more academic topic—British and American comic sensibilities—that at first seemed unapproachable and esoteric.

Yet the differences between British and American comic sensibilities are minute compared with the culture gap students encounter elsewhere. Thoughtfully planning the course meant creating a format where students were able to scaffold their learning in a manner consistent with how they were recruited. Structuring the course, then, included finding models where analogous cultural gaps were bridged. After considering different options, patterning the class after an introductory comparative literature course seemed a natural fit. Most of these introductory courses are a survey of world literature that moves from region to region and explores how universal literary themes find radically different forms of expression around the globe. Comedy across Cultures adopted a similar strategy: each week, the class investigated a style or instance of comedy from a different part of the world.

Those who study comedy know that analyzing comic texts is especially tricky. In the class, the notion of comedic ambiguity—that comedy is based on the slippage between expectation and outcome—worked as an orienting principle. It encouraged students to appreciate that each text we explored would be influenced by our own cultural biases, and we would strive to provide the context and understanding necessary to study them more meaningfully. While this is a difficult task at the best of times, analyzing humor adds another layer of uncertainty. Not only does comedy play on ambiguity, it often purposefully subverts cultural expectations, language, and norms, frequently meaning that to get a joke, audiences often require a high level of cultural understanding. The comparativist Marshall Brown made the case that humor is perhaps one of the most demanding areas to study:

> It behooves us to be mindful that humor translates worse than anything else. (The English translators of Freud's study of humor had to find substitute jokes.) That is true interculturally and interdialectically. One guy's joke is another man's slur. But the arrow points both ways. If each culture . . . has a way of making meaning, they also all have to deflate meaning. (256)

What Brown highlights is the intrinsic ambiguity of studying comedy. In the context of a second-year undergraduate course, students need to be provided with analytical tools and, further, construct opinions based on examples shown in class as well as those they encountered independently. Fittingly, each week was divided into halves. The first half of each week aimed to give students the tools and context required for the second half, which looked at an example of comedy in greater depth. Comedy as social activism, for instance, was the focus of the first half of one week that later explored how satirical sketch comedy is mobilized as a form of direct action.

Course flow is crucial when examining disparate cultures and, to maintain this flow, the course took students on a journey that would allow them to tell a story about where they had traveled and what they had learned in each place. One such journey involved tracking the genre of stand-up from culture to culture. South Africa, with its turbulent political past, has not always had a thriving comedy landscape; however, in recent years, a burgeoning stand-up scene has developed (Garrison). Stand-up, an American invention, has its roots in performances that traverse cultural and ethnic boundaries, much like the melting-pot mentality for which the United States is known. This style, then, translates to similar cultural contexts while also picking up cultural nuances along the way. Trevor Noah, a famous South African stand-up and the outgoing host of *The Daily Show*, was discussed to demonstrate how stand-up is an important means of national identity formation. Noah jokes about growing up with a mixed racial background in South Africa: "My mum could walk with me but if the police showed up, she'd have to let go of me and drop me and pretend I wasn't hers, because we weren't supposed to exist as a family. It was horrible for me, I felt like I was a bag of weed" (qtd. in "Trevor Noah"). Considering Noah in class was instrumental in addressing the historical and cultural makeup of South Africa and how comedy offered a nuanced avenue to explore this makeup. The underlying concepts of stand-up and comedy styles, however, were the connective tissue that provided the necessary links to explore other cultures.

Japanese comedy, in contrast to South African comedy, is far more esoteric for North American students. "It's a different world," said the preeminent humor scholar Christie Davies (qtd. in McGraw and Warner 99), speaking about how poorly humor from other parts of the world traveled to Japan and vice versa. The difficulty of finding an entry point into Japanese comedy became especially apparent when the class studied *rakugo*, also known as "sitting comedy." When compared with the comedic forms found in many other places in the world, *rakugo* is more reliant on storytelling that requires intricate knowledge of cultural norms and idiosyncrasies. Stand-up evolved in the multicultural milieu of the United States and was exported abroad as a result of America's cultural hegemony, whereas *rakugo* developed during a monocultural period in Japan and is rarely found outside its borders. When students considered the comedic styles jointly, they saw how comedy comes to reveal cultural outlooks more generally. Japan is a high-context culture, such that the meaning of language (e.g., comedy) is highly implicit, and audiences are required to "read between the lines" (Nishimura et al. 786). The comedy researchers Peter McGraw and Joel Warner surmised that Japan's comedy culture is unlike what many of my students would relate to: "The country is so homogeneous, so unified in its history and culture, that most zingers don't need set-ups at all. . . . Folks get right to the punch line" (103). Which is fine if one is enmeshed in the culture. But what, I asked students, if a person lacked high-context social capabilities or found themselves in a new and unfamiliar context? Furthermore, how might this lack affect the work of our community partners?

While not everyone has the skills necessary to be a comic, undergraduate students can facilitate sessions and activities that use comedy as a tool for community building. The final stage of the course asked students to apply their learning to practical situations. Students were by now acutely aware that, while nearly all cultures appreciate humor, they all do so in culturally specific ways. To mobilize their knowledge, students partnered with two local nonprofits, The Learning Centre Literacy Association and the Edmonton Mennonite Centre for Newcomers, through the university's service learning program. Both organizations work extensively with immigrants integrating into the local culture, and the goal was to support these nonprofits by developing comedically sensitive programming.

The experiential component of the course was optional; in total, eight students (four at each organization) spent twenty hours each in placements. Anyone teaching newcomers about a new culture needs to find a delicate balance between being sufficiently accessible to engage multiple and diverse cultural backgrounds while simultaneously offering enough specificity to explain something about the local community. Initially, students were instructed to spend time in one of the organization's programs in order to become acquainted with the makeup of the groups' demographics, familiarize themselves with each organization's objectives, and develop relationships with participants. During class time, I familiarized students with Dan Butin's notion of postmodern service learning. Butin reasons that the benefits students accrue when working in the community come from the unpredictability of the environment, which forces students to reflect on the incongruity between what is taught in class and what occurs in real-world situations. A natural affinity exists between comedy and this style of experiential learning. Take, for example, Butin's definition of his model, thinking carefully about how, when the language of service learning is removed, the description might equally apply to various notions of comedy: "[It] is focused on how [it] creates, sustains, and/or disrupts the boundaries and norms by which we make sense of ourselves and the world" (91). I made the case to students that the tactics we used in the classroom—using humor to disrupt the boundaries of what we understood about cultures—was how students ought to think about their community placements. Applying this strategy to community engagement, we realized that comedy has the power to make local culture more accessible.

For those students with community placements, the final project was to create and facilitate an activity that used comedy as a tool to assist in community inclusion. Students were given two guiding principles. First, the activity should be accessible and inclusive, meaning that students were to use low-context humor—like slapstick, simple word games, and comics geared toward English-language learners—rather than high-context and culturally nuanced humor. Second, students were encouraged to use comedy to create moments of reflective disruption, meaning that, ideally, their activities should produce instants of laughter that signaled the humorous incongruity between expectation and outcome, thereby allowing students to intervene and use the break as a teachable moment about local culture.

When I reflect on students' community projects, the successful projects adhered to the above strategies. One project, designed for recent adult immigrants with basic to moderate language skills, was a take on the telephone game, where a sentence is whispered person-to-person and, when the message arrives at the last person, the result is almost always a funny mutation of the original meaning. Crucially, the sentences used were about Canadian culture—for instance, "The beaver is Canada's national animal" or the Canadian classic, "'I'd like a double-double, please."[1] Another student adapted heads-up, a game popularized on Ellen DeGeneres's talk show. For this activity, the student created cards with caricatures of famous Canadians, which participants strapped to their foreheads. Based on descriptions provided by other participants, they attempted to guess the identity of the person. As the student correctly reasoned, the game was a success because the funny caricatures worked on multiple levels: the amusing drawings were comically engaging and allowed even those who did not know the celebrity to practice their English. Moreover, as a summary activity, the student then offered context on why the person was culturally significant. Ultimately, the effective projects understood that comedy could create opportunities for discussion, and cultural sensitivity to what styles of comedy resonated across cultures allowed students to more thoughtfully design these opportunities.

Like telling a well-timed joke, teaching comedy hinges on one's ability to set up, deliver, and transition through course materials. What the experience of teaching a course on comedy across cultures has elucidated for me is that the topic is malleable and can be widely accessible and narrowly focused at the same time. Comedy is a topic nearly everyone has an individual taste for; when comedic taste is framed as a sort of personal expertise, educational doors open for students who might not ordinarily take a course in the social sciences. As I learned from past experiences teaching world literature, it is clear that teaching about foreign culture requires well-thought-out transitions. Tracing the genre of stand-up from North

America to South Africa to Japan, for example, offers the connective tissue necessary for students to make thought-provoking leaps between cultures. However, what was most distinctive about this course was its community focus. One of the benefits of using comedy is that it invites conversations about conceptual and contextual slippage. When poorly considered, comedy is a challenging barrier for newcomers; however, when thoughtfully considered, it is a potent tool for inclusion. A comedy course does not need to suffer the same fate as a dull scientific dissection, so, to paraphrase E. B. White, let's dissect some frogs.

Note

1. A *double-double* is a uniquely Canadian term, originating from the coffee chain Tim Hortons, which means that the coffee should contain two creams and two sugars.

Works Cited

Brown, Marshall. "Multum in Parvo; or, Comparison in Lilliput." *Comparative Literature in an Age of Globalization*, edited by Haun Saussy, Johns Hopkins UP, 2006, pp. 249–61.
Butin, Dan W. "Service-Learning as Postmodern Pedagogy." *Service-Learning in Higher Education: Critical Issues and Directions*, edited by Butin, Palgrave Macmillan, 2005, pp. 89–104.
"Downsize." Directed by Ricky Gervais and Stephen Merchant. *The Office (UK)*, season 1, episode 1, BBC, 9 July 2001.
Garrison, Laura Turner. "Inside South Africa's Young Comedy Scene." *Vulture*, 25 May 2011, www.vulture.com/2011/05/inside-south-africas-young-comedy-scene.html.
McGraw, Peter, and Joel Warner. *The Humor Code: A Global Search for What Makes Things Funny*. Simon and Schuster, 2015.
Nishimura, Shoji, et al. "Communication Style and Cultural Features in High/Low Context Communication Cultures: A Case Study of Finland, Japan and India." *Proceedings of a Subject-Didactic Symposium in Helsinki*, vol. 8, 2008, pp. 783–96.
Pierce, Scott D. "NBC Is Off Target with *The Office*." *Deseret Morning News*, 24 Mar. 2005, p. C10.
"Pilot." Directed by Ken Kwapis. *The Office (US)*, season 1, episode 1, NBC, 24 Mar. 2005.
"Trevor Noah: Best Jokes of New *Daily Show* Host." *BBC News*, 30 Mar. 2015, www.bbc.com/news/world-africa-32114264.

Christopher B. Field, Charles Edward Bowie,
Michelle D. Wise, and Samantha A. Morgan-Curtis

A Right to Be Hostile: Aaron McGruder's *The Boondocks* at a Historically Black College or University

Aaron McGruder's *A Right to Be Hostile: The Boondocks Treasury*, a collection of eight hundred comic strips from his syndicated daily comic *The Boondocks* (1996–2006), takes its title from one strip where the protagonist of the series, ten-year-old Huey Freeman, tells his grandfather, Granddad, "I got a *right* to be hostile, man. . . . My people's been *persecuted*!!" (McGruder 57). Granddad responds, wondering whether his grandson will "find justice" in making himself "miserable" (57). Huey considers this retort for one panel before turning away in the last panel and walking off while thinking, "I hate *wisdom*" (57). This scene perfectly encapsulates the tone of *The Boondocks*, which makes it a fitting scene for the title of the collection. In "The Vengeance of Black Boys: How Richard Wright, Paul Beatty, and Aaron McGruder Strike Back," Howard Rambsy II argues, "McGruder's comic strip exposes audiences to the saga of a young black boy who defiantly and comically confronts troubling oppositions" (651). In this case, the "troubling opposition" is the institutionalized racism that Huey believes is leading to African Americans being "persecuted" paired with his grandfather's contention that Huey cannot internalize all the anger and resentment that stems from this perceived persecution.

As teachers at a historically Black college or university (HBCU), an institution of higher learning with a historical mission of serving a population of predominantly African American students, we see this type of opposition daily. We see the young, bright, slightly older Huey Freemans of the world enter our classrooms dealing with the same social inequities that Huey perceives. As *The Boondocks* shows, however, that sense of inequity can be harnessed and channeled into productive means of expression. To borrow Huey's thought, it can lead to "wisdom" and agency rather than internalized feelings of bitterness and helplessness. In this essay we provide a mixture of practical approaches we have utilized to explore the idea of racial agency through *The Boondocks* as well as relevant theoretical frameworks that instructors can employ. While we are teachers at an HBCU, and our lessons work well for students in our classrooms, we believe that these lessons and theoretical frameworks are also relevant in classrooms at institutions that are not HBCUs, as McGruder's comedy helps break down racial barriers, allowing students to see the relevance of the text to their own lives.

The Boondocks in a Black Comics and Graphic Novels Course

Even though it has been over a hundred years since Booker T. Washington gave his speech at the Atlanta Cotton States and International Exposition in 1895 and since W. E. B. Du Bois offered his vociferous rejection of that speech in *The Souls of Black Folk* in 1903, instructors at HBCUs still find themselves wrestling with the legacies of these two titans of Black intellectualism. Every day we hear from our students, who have not yet heard of the concepts of assimilation and double consciousness, how they feel alienated from the majority-white society around them. This is why, when Charles and Christopher first conceived of their Black Comics and Graphic Novels course—a course they coteach as a philosophy and English course and that focuses on comics that predominantly feature Black characters or that were written or drawn by Black creators—they agreed that they needed to include *The Boondocks* as a text that would allow students to examine Black agency through the concepts of disclosure and double consciousness.

Disclosure is a fundamental concept in a comics course. In *Introduction to Phenomenology*, Robert Sokolowski defines the "disclosure of truth" as

> the display of a state of affairs. It is the simple presencing to us of an intelligible object, the manifestation of what is real or actual. Such a presence could occur immediately during our normal experience and

perception: we walk up to the car and are surprised to see that the tire is flat. We need not have been anticipating the tire as flat; our experience of it as such is not an attempt to confirm or disconfirm a proposition that we have been entertaining. (158–59)

In other words, "[a]n intelligible object, a state of affairs, is presented to us, the object or the situation simply unfolds" (159). Disclosure, then, with special attention to the disclosure of truth, becomes important when dealing with *The Boondocks* because the text attempts to vocalize, or depict, the irrefutable, underlying truth of the matter. When it comes to *The Boondocks*, though, many readers will approach it as a disclosure of comedic relief. Comedy is certainly part of the text. And while some readers are put off by its attempt at humor, we want to suggest that there is more that is disclosed in *The Boondocks*—that is, the connection between its characters and its readers. Both share the same world context. In other words, the world that the characters in *The Boondocks* inhabit is also the world of the reader. Thus, the underlying truths disclosed to Huey are also disclosed to us, the readers.

The Boondocks introduces readers to the life of a young African American male, Huey Freeman, who is struggling to come to terms with the way the world is structured. Readers see how life unfolds for Huey. As readers, some of us may share Huey's sense of discovery, nodding our heads in agreement with his resistance to the status quo. Thus, one idea we emphasize to students is that while *The Boondocks* is a comic strip, its importance extends beyond its humor. It is a disclosure of truth.[1] One might ask, a disclosure of what sort of truth? In this case it is the disclosure that the world unfolds for every individual in unique ways, that life takes place in a world that is already there, one that is composed of structures that assist and impede an individual's development.

A great deal of how the world unfolds for Huey in *The Boondocks* situates the reader in the political, social, and cultural life of Black America. For instance, when he first meets his new teacher, Mr. Petto, Huey says, "Public educational facilities such as this are the cornerstone of the institutionalized racism that continues to oppress black people. Not only will I refuse to succumb to your brainwashing—I will dedicate myself to the eventual elimination of this abomination to the high pursuit of learning" (McGruder 27). Huey's words indicate that he is someone who understands that the world he now inhabits is one that already existed prior to his arrival. Rather than be oblivious to the world around him, he understands that he has a relationship with it and that his relationship is one of resistance. This resistance takes different forms (political, social, and cultural). Delving deeper into Huey's comments and examining the world context, the reader is led to a hermeneutic moment concerning nonintegrated educational institutions. A previous strip reveals that this school has not previously had a Black student and that Mr. Petto has never meaningfully engaged with Black people. In one strip, Mr. Petto claims, "I don't know anything about black people. What if I say the wrong thing? The school will get sued—I'll lose my job" (25).

In addition to using McGruder's *Boondocks* to teach students about the ways in which comics can disclose certain truths about the world, we use it to teach students about the disclosure of truth about humanness, or what it means to be a person with a distinct ethnicity in a specific world context. What Huey shows readers about humanness is that human life is political (and, one might say, necessarily so). This is revealed in Huey's awareness of a world context composed of institutions and structures that tend to maintain and legitimate white identity. Huey's response to Mr. Petto highlights the political nature of human life. This political nature can take many forms. Huey chooses the mode of political resistance. In other words, he attempts to express his own power against a power that bears down on him and his people in exploitative and oppressive ways.

Humanness, as McGruder's *Boondocks* shows, is irreducible. That is, one cannot live in the mode of political resistance forever. One must find moments of levity or else be driven into a self-induced apathy. This is apparent in the scene referenced at the beginning of this essay, when Huey claims he has "a *right* to be hostile" (McGruder 57). While Huey does not relinquish an awareness of cultural and political persecution, he finds levity in his recognition of his grandfather's "wisdom," the levity of an inside joke shared with the audience over a disclosure of truth that acknowledges the reality of systemic racial discrimination and that Huey's self-induced apathy will not hasten the glacial pace of addressing inequity.

Two additional aspects of humanness—the social and the cultural—are disclosed as readers follow Huey. Huey shows that sociality is a necessary dimension of human life: readers see his relationships with his close family (his grandfather and his younger brother, Riley) and with others in his family's new neighborhood. These social interactions expose readers to the cultural dimensions of human life. In the social sphere, Huey educates others about Black culture and life. At the same time, he is also educated by others. In one strip, Huey finds himself feeling ashamed that he forgets to celebrate Kwanzaa, yet he is reminded of the celebration by Cindy, a Caucasian girl at his school whom he perceives as clueless with respect to such cultural customs. Thus, the social and cultural dimensions of humanness go hand in hand. Yet they are not divorced from the political. What McGruder's *Boondocks* discloses to readers is that to be human is to engage simultaneously in the social, cultural, and political dimensions of life.

Another idea that is integral to this course is double consciousness, the idea that African Americans are constantly caught between an African identity that is rooted in a sense of forced estrangement from the original cultures of the African continent and an American identity, which often attempts to subvert and minimize the African identity. Many of our students have felt this contradiction in developing a sense of self because they are forced to straddle between their African and American selves. One strip from *The Boondocks* allows us to easily introduce this concept to our students. When Riley, Huey's younger brother, is watching rap videos with Granddad, Granddad sees the "[n]ice cars, nice clothes, beautiful women . . . champagne, jewelry, everything they could want" and wonders why all the rappers appear to be angry (McGruder 37). However, he quickly answers his own question when he looks over at Riley and sees Riley watching the video with a similar expression of anger, and Granddad exclaims, "(Sigh) . . . Never mind" (37). This strip works well to illustrate double consciousness because McGruder successfully satirizes the idea of Black success in America. Younger Black audiences see the excesses of capitalism in these videos and equate them with success. At the same time, Riley's expression of anger indicates an unhappiness at being estranged from that success. However, the part that Riley seems to miss consciously yet still internalize subconsciously is the unhappiness of the rapper. Though the rapper has achieved what many would see as success, this success has still not brought fulfillment and contentment, indicating that McGruder is satirizing the prepackaged idea of success that rap videos offer to Black audiences, as these audiences see contradictory messages about Black access to, attainment of, and satisfaction with the American dream of monetary success.

The Boondocks in an Introductory Film Course

Piggybacking on the success of the comic strip, Cartoon Network developed *The Boondocks* as an animated series (*Boondocks*). In an introductory film course, students are introduced not only to cinematic language and filmic techniques but also to theoretical approaches to analyzing films.

One methodology that is often overlooked is adaptation theory. The goal of this section is to show the importance of including adaptation theory in an introductory film course using *The Boondocks* as an example that illustrates the importance of sound in adaptation theory.

Students are already familiar with film adaptations of novels; however, they do not always realize all that is involved in adapting a text for the screen. It is useful to establish a definition of adaptation theory and to then familiarize students with several film adaptation theorists found in James Naremore's influential collection, *Film Adaptation*, such as Robert Stam, Dudley Andrew, and Andre Bazin. While most students might understand that adaptation is "a transition, a conversion, from one medium to another," it may be necessary to explain to students that, "in the process of adaptation, some form of *transformation* occurs through interpretation" (Jones 392). Transformation is of key importance for adaptation theorists. While there are several approaches to consider with adaptation theory, our focus here is on analyzing the use of song in *The Boondocks*.

Since the first talkie was released in 1927, sound has been an integral aspect of film. Furthermore, sound enabled filmmakers to create soundtracks that reflected the content of their films. According to Maria Pramaggiore and Tom Wallis, "[S]ome film theorists have argued that cinemagoers fail to recognize sound as a unique cinematic element, distinct from the visual image, with physical properties and aesthetic possibilities of its own" (248). As a television series, *The Boondocks* relies on the use of sound effects, such as breaking glass and screeching cars, and songs to engage viewers. The opening song for the show, which remains unchanged throughout the series, is "Judo Flip," by Asheru. This song, with its references to aggressive forms of building and creating, sets the tone by introducing one of the show's key themes: rebellion. When these lyrics are combined with the show's visual images, it becomes apparent that this is a story about the anger that African Americans experience in the face of white oppression.

The opening sequence is a good place to begin a discussion of adaptation theory because it combines both auditory and visual images to transform a static comic strip into a new text. Students can pinpoint the incorporation of music as a strategic difference between the printed comic strip and the animated series. The series provides viewers with an immersive experience that combines lyrics with beats, rhythms, and imagery. When students realize this key difference, they can analyze the show through the lens of adaptation theory and recognize the value of such an approach.

The Boondocks in a First-Year Writing Course

Like many instructors of first-year writing courses, Samantha seeks to teach the skill sets necessary for conducting research and constructing academic arguments. Rather than succumb to the idea of the monolithic research paper, she scaffolds her assignments and makes research a required component. For her most recent *Boondocks* assignment, she had students choose three consecutive strips, identify the argument being made about the topic in the strips, and then analyze the argument being made. Because of the time that had passed since the strips were published, students had to conduct research in order to understand the context and content of the strips. Samantha first provided students with a sample reading of three strips that originally appeared 4–6 August 2004. The strips focus on a disagreement between Granddad and Riley. After Riley refuses to take out the garbage, Granddad orders him to view the film *Catwoman*, a punishment that fits within McGruder's evisceration of pop culture's representation and exploitation of African Americans. Riley, Huey, and Granddad all concede that viewing the film is a punishment. Huey questions the harshness of the sentence, and the final panel shows Riley, who posits himself as a "gangsta," on the phone with someone we assume is from Child Protective Services, yelling, "Well, I say it does constitute child abuse, lady!!" ("Boondocks").

These strips were published mere weeks after *Catwoman* entered theaters in July 2004. Most of the traditionally aged students in the course were born between 2000 and 2002 and had fond memories of watching this film on cable television. However, after reading a review (Honeycutt), students reconsidered the film—comparing Patience Phillips, played by Halle Berry, to the representations of Harley Quinn in *Suicide Squad* (another villain whose representation remains complicated but not as derivative as Berry's Catwoman) and numerous other stronger if still sexualized representations of women characters in the DC and Marvel comic universes. These women take up space on quests to save humanity from dastardly villains bent on destruction. Berry's character seeks to overturn the machinations of a make-up maven who punishes older women for using products to keep them looking young. The misogyny oozes from the screen.

Samantha's most recent class was made up entirely of African American students. With the exception of one student, all were eighteen or nineteen and had come to college full-time immediately after high school. These students initially complained about the use of the comic strips instead of the animated series—many did not know that an original comic strip existed. After reviewing the basic vocabulary for comic strips—*panel, speech bubble, text box*, and so on—and the process of analyzing a visual text with written components (they had begun the semester reading memes as twenty-first-century emblems), students delved into the text.

Students' primary response was amazement. They repeatedly found that the comics dealt with topics overwhelmingly pertinent to students' lived experiences: what is "good hair," what defines Blackness, the one-drop theory, racial identity, and more. The research required students to contextualize such historic moments as MTV's Rock the Vote, 9/11, the Dixie Chicks, and the 1990s discussion of marijuana. Students noted how surprisingly contemporary the arguments in the text were and that the popular culture references required the most investigation.

This assignment reminded Samantha that too often we seek to teach history as something that ended in the 1970s, which compels students to see themselves as removed from history. Using a medium such as comic strips allows students to access more recent history in a genre that suits their experience. *The Boondocks* works well for Samantha's students because the issues raised in the text validate and are validated by students' experiences. For other students, these comics can introduce and humanize these topics. For twenty-first-century students, close reading and analysis necessitate familiarity with texts that incorporate various media.

Though our context is limited to English and philosophy classrooms at an HBCU, the versatility of McGruder's comic strip and the animated series makes it possible to introduce them in other classrooms and at other institutions. These texts can be taught in a wide range of courses—from first-year writing classes to upper-division courses typically offered for majors and minors—and can be integrated into any classroom setting that is dedicated to increasing recognition of and appreciation for individual and cultural diversity through texts that utilize incisive social commentary and that satirize American societal mores.

Note

1. For a more thorough discussion of the concept of disclosure, see Sokolowski, *Introduction* and *Phenomenology*.

Works Cited

Andrew, Dudley. "Adaptation." Naremore, pp. 28–37.
Bazin, Andre. "Adaptation; or, The Cinema as Digest." Naremore, pp. 19–27.

The Boondocks. Created by Aaron McGruder, Adelaide Productions / Sony Pictures, 2005–14.

"The Boondocks." *GoComics*, 2022, www.gocomics.com/boondocks.

Honeycutt, Kirk. "'Catwoman': THR's 2004 Review." *The Hollywood Reporter*, 23 July 2019, hollywoodreporter.com/movies/movie-news/catwoman-review-movie-2004-1226110/.

Jones, Matthew T. "Fiend on Film: Edwin S. Porter's Adaptation of *Dreams of the Rarebit Fiend*." *International Journal of Comic Art*, vol. 8, no. 1, 2006, pp. 388–411. *EBSCOhost*, search.ebscohost.com.

McGruder, Aaron. *A Right to Be Hostile: The Boondocks Treasury*. Three Rivers, 2003.

Naremore, James, editor. *Film Adaptation*. Rutgers UP, 2000.

Pramaggiore, Maria, and Tom Wallis. *Film: A Critical Introduction*. King, 2011.

Rambsy, Howard, II. "The Vengeance of Black Boys: How Richard Wright, Paul Beatty, and Aaron McGruder Strike Back." *The Mississippi Quarterly*, vol. 61, no. 4, 2008, pp. 643–57. *JSTOR*, www.jstor.org/stable/26476885.

Sokolowski, Robert. *Introduction to Phenomenology*. Cambridge UP, 2000.

———. *Phenomenology of the Human Person*. Cambridge UP, 2008.

Stam, Robert. "Beyond Fidelity: The Dialogics of Adaptation." Naremore, pp. 54–78.

Stephen Casmier

Charles W. Chesnutt, Joel Chandler Harris, and the Minstrel Show Legacy

According to important African American literary scholarship, Charles W. Chesnutt's 1899 short story "The Passing of Grandison" is "a clever burlesque" about a freed slave who escapes back into slavery (Foster and Andrews 581). When I first read it, I found it absurdly funny. It involves the zany efforts of a lazy son of a slave owner to woo a Southern belle by liberating one of his father's slaves. First, he takes the preternaturally loyal slave to the North, but the terrified man refuses to go free. So he hauls the man to Canada, hiring men to kidnap and abscond with him into the freedom he seems to dread. The son then returns home to marry his sweetheart. One week later the bedraggled slave returns to the plantation, after having reversed the route of the Underground Railroad by "keeping his back steadily to the North Star" (Chesnutt 601). This absurd image is so overwhelming that it nearly occludes the story's ending, which presents the same slave and his entire family sailing off into freedom on a boat while the youth's angry father stands on the shore, shaking his fist "impotently" (602). The outrageous humor, historical context, and deceptive style of this story were so irresistible that I decided to teach it after I became a professor of African American literature. Yet I quickly discovered that students didn't find the story funny.

I hadn't reckoned with the difficulty of conveying the subtleties of the story's burlesque humor. Students tended to focus so much on the slave Grandison's dogged, seemingly self-hating loyalty to his master that they missed the story's message. I came to realize that students today—steeped in the very serious discourses of identity and social justice—increasingly rebuff the lavish use of the N-word and the dishonest antics of Grandison. He is a man who keeps secrets and seems ashamed of his identity—behaviors and attitudes that are anathema to students. They often read the story as an archaic, racist, and humorless artifact, though serious scholars consider Chesnutt an important writer and "The Passing of Grandison" a significant work. Indeed, my own scholarly research focuses on the novels of the late-twentieth-century African American writer John Edgar Wideman, who cites Chesnutt as a significant influence and a major figure of African American literature in his essay "Charles Chesnutt and the WPA Narratives: The Oral and Literate Roots of Afro-American Literature." Chesnutt's stories, Wideman observes, "altered the traditional frame" that had hitherto denigrated African American identity (62). To enable students to grasp this significance and the workings of the story's humor, I realized that I needed to create lessons that would explore the story's satiric elements, situate the story within its literary context, and encourage close readings of its remarkable stylistic components.

Teaching Humor: Irony, Satire, Parody, and Burlesque

Chesnutt's story performs an ironic burlesque of the ubiquitous racial propaganda of minstrel show caricature and what critics have called plantation or southern school writing. This school of writing often used humor to gentrify and sentimentalize the memory of slavery. Paradoxically, satirizing this type of tradition can act as a Trojan horse of racist propaganda if one fails to understand how the humorous elements of parody and burlesque work, says the media scholar Beth E. Bonnstetter in an article on satire in film. The result, she says, could instead reify "racist, sexist, classist, heterosexist, or otherwise hegemonic ideas" (18).

To surmount this problem, students must first read "The Passing of Grandison" as a parody of plantation school writing, which is humorously unmasked as the actual subject or "true hero" of the story (Bakhtin 51). In his landmark essay, "From the Prehistory of Novelistic Discourse," Mikhail Bakhtin examines this particular element in the lampooning of the sonnet by the seventeenth-century novel *Don Quixote*: "In a parody on the sonnet, we must first of all recognize a sonnet, recognize its form, its specific style, its manner of seeing, its manner of selecting from and evaluating the world—the world view of the sonnet as it were.... It is precisely style that is the true hero of the work" (51). Students must be made aware that the story is largely about the absurdity of plantation school writing and minstrel show performance. Next, they must equally confront the pitfalls of reading the "clever burlesque." The unforgiving caricatures of this genre offer few clues on how to assess characters, asserts Kenneth Burke in his groundbreaking study of comedic forms, *Attitudes toward History*: "The writer of burlesque makes no attempt to get inside the psyche of his victim. Instead, he is content to select the externals of behavior, driving them to a 'logical conclusion' that becomes their 'reduction to absurdity.'... He deliberately suppresses any consideration of the 'mitigating circumstances' that would put his subject in a better light" (54–55). In this light, Chesnutt's story performs as a burlesque of American entertainment and its racist obsessions, reducing "to absurdity" the worldview of its constructs. It subjects everything in its grasp to absurd ridicule, necessarily avoiding, for instance, the representation of any of the serious or internal thoughts of some of its black characters about their enslavement and abject oppression. Indeed, if brought to light, these thoughts would be reduced "to absurdity" as equal opportunity victims of the story's uncompromising humor.

Teaching Context: The Uncle Remus Stories and the Minstrel Show

In my lessons I first establish a contextual baseline by turning to two works by Joel Chandler Harris, "Some Advice to a Colored Brother" and "Intimidation of a Colored Voter," stories first collected in his *Legends of the Old Plantation* (1881). I present them as examples of "the racist interpretation of [the] white writers of the Plantation School" that an anthology of African American literature, *Black Writers of America*, asserts Chesnutt's work challenges (Barksdale and Kinnamon 324). Harris is still famous for his Uncle Remus folk tales, which inspired the popular Disney movie *Song of the South* (1946) and the infamous Disney World theme ride Splash Mountain. Yet Harris's use of eye dialect renders his stories nearly impossible for students to decipher, let alone find funny. Eye dialect represents the speech of a character through nonstandard, phonetic spellings. A major characteristic of plantation school writing, the use of eye dialect once elicited condescending laughter from readers, helping construct a sense of white superiority over black people. I project slides with quotations from Wideman's essay about speech in Chesnutt's fiction. One of these quotations asserts that "[b]lack speech in the form of Negro dialect entered American literature as a curiosity, a comic interlude, a short-hand for perpetuating myths and prejudices about black people" (Wideman 60). Another quotation argues that this stylistic technique "implied lazy, slovenly pronunciation if not the downright physical impossibility of getting thick lips around the King's English. Malapropisms, far-fetched words . . . were all proof positive of the infantilism, carnality, instability and illogicality of black folk" (60).

In Harris's "Intimidation of a Colored Voter," Uncle Remus steps into a newsroom, upset about an upcoming election. He says, "Man down dar on de street ax how I gwine vote dis time, en I des runned up yer fer ter ax you all gentermens ef deyer a gwinter be n'er 'lection in de Nunited States er Georgy" (240). Remus's problem: His boss orders him to vote his way ("w'en dat de case, w'at a ole n— like me gwine do?") and his wife says he won't "git no gravy on my grits" if he doesn't vote hers (241, 242). Remus concludes that he can't upset his boss and that he won't live without gravy on his grits, so he concocts a scheme to sit out the election. Eye dialect works similarly in Harris's "Some Advice to a Colored Brother." This time, Remus confronts a scoundrel, William Henry Haddem, who has been called before a grand jury for theft. Remus cleverly eyes the man and surmises that he stole the money and that the all-knowing white jury would sagely see through the simpleminded ruse. He orders the man to return the money and take the next train out of town.

I expand this lesson on nineteenth-century humor, describing Remus and Haddem as familiar figures from the minstrel stage: the Southern Sambo and Zip Coon. I reinforce this audiovisually with a clip from Marlon Riggs's *Ethnic Notions*, an indispensable documentary on the role of humorous racist stereotypes in fomenting racial oppression.[1] The documentary enables students to see and hear what once passed for humor. An actor plays Zip Coon, a character described by the scholar J. Stanley Lemons "as a high-stepping strutter with a mismatched vocabulary" (102), who gives a speech in the same dialect as Remus and Haddem: "Transcendentalism is dat spiritual cognoscence ob psychological irrefragibility, connected wid conscientient ademtion" (*Ethnic Notions* 12:15–12:24). Meanwhile, the bitter narration of the actress Esther Rolle characterizes these once familiar figures:

> In the North . . . a new character appeared beside the Southern Sambo: Zip Coon. . . . A dandy, and a buffoon, Zip Coon's attempts to imitate whites mocked the notion of racial equality. Together Zip Coon and

Sambo provided a double-edged defense of slavery: Zip Coon, proof of blacks' ludicrous failure to adapt to freedom; and Sambo, the fantasy of happy darkies in their proper place. (12:09–12:49)

This makes clear that the two Uncle Remus stories invoke both tropes. Haddem is lawless, and Remus doesn't understand democracy. Neither is prepared for freedom.

Teaching Burlesque through Close Reading: "The Passing of Grandison"

Finally, I use close reading techniques to show how the style of the text and its rendering of voice become the substance of the story's ironic play. Although most students see Grandison as sadly over-loyal to his master, I excavate through the deceptive layers of the work's style. The story never tells readers what Grandison thinks (which would also be subjected to parody if conveyed) though it allows readers to access the minds of every other character (with the exception of the one I discuss below). The reader only knows Grandison by his outward actions and his dialogue, rendered through unmediated direct speech and in the eye dialect of plantation school writing. Grandison thus seems to epitomize the absurd Southern Sambo, or the "happy dark[y] in [his] proper place."

For example, after Dick Owens hatches his plan, he asks his father if he could take his "body-servant," Tom, on a trip North (Chesnutt 594). His father, Colonel Owens, rejects that servant and recommends Grandison, whom he avows is "abolitionist-proof" (596). As proof, he asks Grandison if he is better off than "poor free negroes," and Grandison responds, "Well, I sh'd jes' reckon I is better off, suh, dan dem low-down free n—s, suh!" (594). The use of the N-word throughout the text often triggers students. It seems to arrive without irony, qualification, or mediating interpretation. Then, the scene, with its play of power between the all-powerful and the powerless, borders on the perverse after the colonel asks Grandison what he would do if approached by an abolitionist. He responds with a combative anger that would present one of the funniest moments of the text if readers suspect there is any irony or hidden motive behind his words. He retorts:

> "I would n' low none er dem cussed, low-down abolitioners ter come nigh me, suh, I'd—I'd—would I be 'lowed ter hit 'em, suh?"

> "Certainly, Grandison," replied the colonel, chuckling, "hit 'em as hard as you can. I reckon they'd rather like it. Begad, I believe they would! It would serve 'em right to be hit by a n—!" (595)

The text never reveals here what Grandison actually thinks, though it presents the colonel brazenly betraying an abject taboo of Southern society. Since the early days of slavery and the slave codes, the death penalty awaited any black person who struck a white man. The colonel's willingness to compromise these values presents the absurdity of burlesque at its most extreme—if one understands the context.

I end my lesson on Chesnutt's story with an exercise in close reading, asking students to look at the story's first sentence: "When it is said that it was done to please a woman, there ought perhaps to be enough said to explain anything; for what a man will not do to please a woman is yet to be discovered" (591). I then ask, Why does the story begin with a passive construction and with such unclear nouns and pronouns? What was done to please a woman? What woman? What man? Who is telling this story? Who is in control?

Stylistically, it follows that Dick is the "man" (he is named after that sentence) and that Charity is the "woman." Both seem to be the protagonists of the story, though neither is mentioned in the title (pay attention to the title is my first directive). The "it" in "it was done to please a woman" thus seems to refer to Dick's scheme. Yet Dick's act doesn't end the story. Instead, the story ends as Grandison and his family escape to freedom, which means that "it" refers to their escape. And the impressed woman who has controlled everything—who has controlled the entire narrative—must be someone the story casually refers to three times—Betty, Grandison's wife. Yet the text never allows her to act or speak. As with the hidden thoughts of Grandison, readers have no access to Betty's inner thoughts or desires. Yet, by ignoring her, the reader becomes just like the slave owner, just like Colonel and Dick Owens, just like consumers of plantation fiction, and just like the raucously laughing audiences of blackface minstrel shows. Such a lack of curiosity about the interior life of a character mirrors the banal cruelty of the society critiqued by the text and explored in literature by theorists such as Richard Rorty. So, when students of the Me Too and Black Lives Matter era suddenly realize that they have missed the clues, have failed to imagine the inner thoughts of Betty, and have read the text like Southern antebellum patriarchs, they come to a disturbing revelation: The burlesque text had toyed with their own racist and sexist "world view" (Bakhtin 51), revealing it was not as progressive as they had imagined.

Such a reading explores the deep humor of Chesnutt's text, a text in which the absurd delusions and blind dangers of white supremacy and a society trapped within its own fictions are the true heroes of its burlesque style. I hope that this newfound understanding of "The Passing of Grandison" leads students to reread works such as the Uncle Remus stories and all literature (or even to rethink their enjoyment of theme park rides) through the lens furnished by Chesnutt and his characters, who cannot ignore the absurd worldview of their dangerous masters. Instead, their absurdist sense of humor subverts it. This speaks to privilege and builds healing self-awareness. This way of seeing renders the self-inflicted antics and blind self-deceptions of people with immense power over the lives of others both outrageous and grimly funny. It enables readers to imagine Grandison and Betty as moving things around rather than merely being moved by power. Projecting what lies behind the unrepresented thoughts of Grandison and Betty—their razor-sharp intelligence, their relentless disingenuousness, their guile, their sardonic wit, their knowledge of fools, their brilliant strategic manipulation of their masters' ignorance, their ludic play with the roles assigned by plantation fiction and minstrel show tropes, their forcing of the text's narration to keep their secrets, the steely resolve and brilliance of Betty, and the fact that Grandison does not emit one single honest tone or perform one straightforward gesture—is what moved me to so much to laughter when I first read the story. This is the strategic humor that I hope students will learn to appreciate in reading "The Passing of Grandison."

Notes

I'd like to thank the students in my fall 2019 course Writing of the African Diaspora for their contributions to this essay.

1. I also make this entire documentary available to students for viewing. As an audiovisual collection of powerful American artifacts, it conveys the relentless and demeaning attacks against African Americans in the popular media that masqueraded as humor and "harmless fun" while buttressing segregation and oppression in the era following the Supreme Court *Plessy v. Ferguson* ruling. Providing a background that many students are not aware of, it ultimately reveals the deadly power behind "harmless fun" such as blackface makeup.

Works Cited

Bakhtin, Mikhail M. "From the Prehistory of Novelistic Discourse." *The Dialogical Imagination: Four Essays*, edited by Michael Holquist, translated by Caryl Emerson and Holquist, U of Texas P, 1983, pp. 41–83.

Barksdale, Richard, and Keneth Kinnamon. "Charles W. Chesnutt." *Black Writers of America: A Comprehensive Anthology*, edited by Barksdale and Kinnamon, Macmillan, 1972, pp. 324–28.

Bonnstetter, Beth E. "Mel Brooks Meets Kenneth Burke (and Mikhail Bakhtin): Comedy and Burlesque in Satiric Film." *Journal of Film and Video*, vol. 63, no. 1, 2011, pp. 18–31. *JSTOR*, www.jstor.org/stable/10.5406/jfilmvideo.63.1.0018.

Burke, Kenneth. *Attitudes toward History*. 1937. 3rd ed., U of California P, 1984.

Chesnutt, Charles. "The Passing of Grandison." Gates and Smith, pp. 591–602.

Ethnic Notions. Directed by Marlon Riggs, Signifyin' Works, 1986.

Foster, Frances Smith, and William L. Andrews. "Charles Chesnutt." Gates and Smith, pp. 580–82.

Gates, Henry Louis, Jr., and Valerie Smith, editors. *The Norton Anthology of African American Literature*, vol. 1, 3rd ed., W. W. Norton, 2014.

Harris, Joel Chandler. "Intimidation of a Colored Voter." Harris, *Uncle Remus*, pp. 238–42.

———. "Some Advice to a Colored Brother." Harris, *Uncle Remus*, pp. 266–70.

———. *Uncle Remus and His Friends: Old Plantation Stories, Songs, and Ballads with Sketches of Negro Character*. Houghton Mifflin, 1892.

Lemons, J. Stanley. "Black Stereotypes as Reflected in Popular Culture, 1880–1920." *American Quarterly*, vol. 29, no. 1, 1977, pp. 102–16.

Rorty, Richard. "The Barber of Kasbeam: Nabokov on Cruelty." *The Ordering Mirror: Readers and Contexts: The Ben Belitt Lectures at Bennington College*, edited by Phillip Lopate, Fordham UP, 1993, pp. 198–220.

Wideman, John Edgar. "Charles Chesnutt and the WPA Narratives: The Oral and Literate Roots of Afro-American Literature." *The Slave's Narrative*, edited by Charles T. Davis and Henry Louis Gates, Jr., Oxford UP, 1985, pp. 59–77.

Meenakshi Ponnuswami

Blackface in the Comedy Class

Many responses to the spate of blackface scandals in 2019 focused on public ignorance about minstrelsy. Rhae Lynn Barnes, for example, argued that "[p]eople have perpetuated blackface because we don't teach minstrel history"; "[i]f these people had ever been exposed to it in a safe classroom environment," she reasoned, "they would know better" (qtd. in Haygood). In a similar vein, Ibram X. Kendi designed a syllabus of thirty-eight books to supplement an anti-racist reading list that Ralph Northam's aides created to reeducate the Virginia governor after he confessed to using "a little bit of shoe polish" in his youth (qtd. in Kendi). Kendi recommended books on history, politics, incarceration, health, housing, and more. Notably absent from his comprehensive list, however, were works about American comedy: indeed, few articles about the blackface scandals reference the extensive scholarship on American comic traditions and the performance history of blackface. This essay explores how comedy has contributed to the longevity and persistence of blackface and considers how teaching the history of blackface affects students' understanding of contemporary racism. I focus on a unit I teach on blackface in my course Ethnic Comedy, which I have offered since 2014 at Bucknell University, a small, predominantly white college in Pennsylvania.

I created Ethnic Comedy imagining that the study of laughter would help students transcend the paralysis and polarization of our cultural conversation about race. However, I have come to believe that we underestimate the power of blackface images to persist in the racial imaginary and to stimulate laughter that objectifies and dehumanizes African Americans. I agree with Barnes that teaching the history of minstrelsy has the potential to transform some racist practices, and I am confident my students benefit from my course's multiethnic focus and our readings about ideology, form, and laughter. However, I argue here that exposure to blackface comedy reinforces cultural norms and stereotypes more than it disrupts them, and that instructors handling these materials should pay close attention to content, context, and pedagogical style.

Before developing Ethnic Comedy, I taught the history of blackface in courses on performance, race, and identity that explored how bodies were racialized in British and American contexts. These courses traced the impact of medieval and early modern racial imagery, particularly in Shakespeare's *Othello* and *The Merchant of Venice*, on a range of modern performance texts. Blackface was ubiquitous in British and American ethnographic show business, including minstrel shows, the circus, so-called freak shows, vaudeville, early cinema, mid-century animation, and early television. Students came to see that blackface was commonplace, unconcealed, and beloved throughout the nineteenth and twentieth centuries, enshrined in popular culture in ways that are still staples of contemporary racism.

Comic forms of blackface were especially influential in the transmission and perpetuation of racism. This thesis shapes my module on blackface in Ethnic Comedy. Introducing students to the role of minstrelsy in disseminating racist imagery, the module anchors a three-week section on African American comedy. In the first week, which focuses on blackface, students study the origins of minstrelsy in the nineteenth century and follow its development into the twentieth, first in vaudeville and black popular theater (the Chitlin' Circuit), and then in early film and mid-century animation and television. We also consider the current proliferation of blackface on white supremacist websites. The second week examines the 1960s and 1970s, including the stand-up comedy of artists such as Bill Cosby, Richard Pryor, and Eddie Murphy and sitcoms such as *Julia* and *The Jeffersons*. In the final week, using Pryor's work as a springboard, students watch Dave Chappelle, Chris Rock, Wanda Sykes, and Paul Mooney before proceeding to excerpts from contemporary stand-up, sitcoms, and films such as Spike Lee's *The Original Kings of Comedy* and

Bamboozled and Tyler Perry's *Madea* series ("Tyler Perry's Madea"). The three-week section explores how African American comedians struggled against the legacy of minstrelsy even when they were obliged to work within its confines; how they designed separate, secret, and sustaining forms of comedy for black communities; and how they eventually rewrote the script of American comedy as a whole.

At the outset of the first week, to frame the history of blackface in ways that emphasize its destructive legacy and tenacity, I screen Marlon Riggs's powerful 1987 documentary film *Ethnic Notions*. Before watching this film, students complete a homework assignment that asks them to google "blackface on college campuses." After reading reports about students using blackface, they post their search results on a community *Google Doc*, which all students read before watching Riggs's film. It is depressing to see that this simple exercise yields new results every year, but it enables students to approach *Ethnic Notions* with a sharp awareness of its relevance. Riggs's documentary emphasizes the political usefulness of blackface images as instruments of punishment and control: antebellum depictions of happy-go-lucky "darkies" on idyllic plantations offered a defense of slavery, while brutal images of the post–Civil War period sustained the emergence of Jim Crow. The film thus underscores minstrelsy's role in preserving white supremacy and terrorism. Both its narrative content and its style demonstrate that blackface caricature was a tragedy with devastating consequences; the images it depicts are often comic, but its gravity discourages laughter.

After viewing *Ethnic Notions*, students read excerpts from histories of blackface and view examples of vaudeville performances and mid-century animated films such as "Scrub Me Mama with a Boogie Beat," which features grotesque, watermelon-eating Sambos; snoring Uncle Toms; and a stereotypical, scrubbing Mammy. In the 1932 Betty Boop short "I'll Be Glad When You're Dead, You Rascal You," which opens with a recording of a live performance of the eponymous hit by Louis Armstrong and his band, the revered singer's face morphs into a blackface-style animated cartoon of a cannibal, the contemptuous implication being that black expressive culture, and black people, are always already savage.

Students are often unprepared for the raw impact of the images, animation, and acting they encounter in *Ethnic Notions*. However, black and white students respond to these materials in measurably different ways. The cumulative impact of this unit can be chilling and traumatic for many African American students, for whom these images are not simply vestiges of an ugly past but also visceral reminders of the immediacy of racist violence.[1] As George Yancy reminds us, blackface worked "through both the consumption and the negation of black humanity"; it was "historically grounded in white supremacy and as such, an act of epistemological and ontological terror."

Many nonblack students, however, experience the images primarily as curiosities and relics. Most do signal shock, distress, and anger, but the animated films invariably also produce uneasy laughter. In class discussions and written responses, students try to process not only their guilt at being amused by a form of entertainment that they know is hateful but also their surprise that the images are so familiar and recognizable. Stephen Johnson describes experiencing a jolt of identification when he first saw blackface, despite being a white Canadian raised in rural Ontario: "It was not *recognition* as some distant cultural memory, or an image or two from early television—it was more immediate, more visceral than that. I recognized it as present in the fabric of my own personal, familial, and local culture, inextricably intertwined into my life" ("Persistence" 5). Ideally, such cognitive dissonance would translate into teachable moments in which students could explore difficult questions of complicity and hegemony. However, I believe comic blackface is so deeply entrenched in the cultural unconscious that it resists such efforts, leaving students with indelible impressions that imprint themselves on the materials they watch in later weeks. Despite the solemnity of *Ethnic Notions* and our extensive historical readings, the comic impact of the old blackface images overwhelms student perceptions of all black comedy. Unable to draw a clear line of contrast between racist and anti-racist comedy, they end up seeing even stereotype-defying, black-authored contemporary comic performances as simply a new form of blackface.

To anticipate and redirect such reactions, it is useful for instructors to familiarize themselves with the complex theory of white desire in blackface. A dominant version of this theory, developed in the mid-1990s, examines what Mel Watkins calls the "salutary aspect of the apparent fascination and attraction that has impelled white mimicry of blacks" (ix). Eric Lott's influential *Love and Theft* argues that early minstrelsy was characterized by "the dialectical flickering of racial insult and racial envy, moments of domination and moments of liberation" (18). "Even in expropriation," Lott contends, "there was a strong white attraction to the material" (20). W. T. Lhamon, Jr., similarly describes the "construction of cross-racial selves for fun and profit" (275) as part of a long "history of white mimicry of black carnivalesque" (276), arguing further that blackface "responded to [racial] anxieties . . . by *enacting* miscegenation" (276). In this view, blackface offered whites "a mask which allowed deep expression of emotions of loss and longing" (Stowe and Grimsted 83) and a "deep yearning" for "preindustrial man" (80–81). Lott does acknowledge that minstrelsy "finally divested black people of control . . . over their own cultural representation" (18), and even William Stowe and David Grimsted grudgingly concede that "[t]he minstrel image of the Black probably reinforced Negro social exclusion" (80). But these approaches sideline the damaging influence of blackface on African Americans and instead applaud the creative, anarchic, and liberating potential of blackface for white audiences.

Although such theories exonerate blackface, they can offer instructors a starting point from which to theorize the continuing popularity of blackface at white parties and the uncomfortable laughter of white students studying blackface in a comedy class. By enacting white love, desire, and self-liberation, blackface serves as a constitutive element of white power, solidarity, and community building. As Yancy argues, "[B]lackface is a form of 'white knowing' (in reality, of white unknowing), of white projection, and of stipulating through performance what it means to be black by way of lies about what it means to be white." Werner Sollors further notes that all comedy entails differentiation and empowerment, because "laughing at others is a form of boundary construction and can be cruel" (132): "The community of laughter itself is an ethnicizing phenomenon," he argues, "as we develop a sense of we-ness in laughing with others" (132).

But if in-group comedy builds solidarity through laughter, can it help non-white comedians "develop a sense of we-ness" with white audiences? As my white students' uncomfortable laughter suggests, the legacy of white blackface implicates all black comedians who address mainstream or majority-white audiences. Ralph Ellison astutely notes that "[t]he comic point is inseparable from the racial identity of the performer": a black comedian's "self-humiliation" enables a powerful cathartic release for white audiences as the performer, "by assuming the group-debasing role for gain[,] not only substantiates the audience's beliefs in the blackness of things 'black,' but relieves it, with dreamlike efficiency, of its guilt" (103–04). In other words, black comedians who address majority-white audiences always perform in, within, and against blackface.[2] It is important for students to recognize the complex strategies of these comedians' self-affirmation and self-denial.

Yancy argues that "[t]o face blackface . . . we must address the structure of whiteness that drives it." In the final section of this essay, I recommend texts and strategies that help students contextualize the history and continuing presence of blackface. My first recommendation is Mel Watkins's deeply thoughtful history of African American comedy, *On the Real Side*, which documents the work of African American comedians in overcoming the legacy of minstrelsy. Watkins's invaluable history offers comprehensive biographies of key performers, explanations of the historical contexts in which their work evolved, and discussions of key concepts, including double consciousness, tricksterism and inversion, audience reception, and cultural influence.[3]

To explain how blackface is, in Yancy's terms, "a form of 'white knowing'" and "white projection," it is essential to select readings and viewings that explore its centrality in the structure of whiteness. In literary studies classes, where information about blackface precedes an extensive syllabus of complex literature by African American writers, such as the anti-lynching drama of the interwar era, or texts of the Harlem Renaissance or Black Arts movement, students can see clearly not only how minstrelsy impeded African American struggles for self-determination but also how black artists have overcome minstrelsy's powerful legacy. Comedy classes should likewise juxtapose blackface history against the history of black popular (Chitlin' Circuit) comedians, as in-group laughter has long been acknowledged as a way "to build group solidarity and to critique the dominant cultural framework" (Gillota 6).

Spike Lee's feature film *Bamboozled* is another valuable asset in helping students understand the whiteness of blackface in comedy. This 2000 satire sharply critiques how white supremacy undergirds the entertainment industry and threatens to colonize African American self-perception. Under pressure from his white boss to generate a hit show, the black television executive Pierre Delacroix revengefully produces a minstrel show that ends up becoming a commercial success. *Bamboozled* was criticized for its allegedly outdated view of minstrelsy (Maurice 193), but it unpacks complex questions about African American comic performance and identity: the search for authenticity in the shadow of the minstrel mask, the rich beauties of actual black performance arts hidden in the Chitlin' Circuit and on the street, and the artistry of the minstrel show itself, which is performed skillfully and authentically as a tribute to the talents of black performers and comedians through the ages. Critically, the film demonstrates how central blackface continues to be to white identity and success, particularly in its depiction of Delacroix's boss Dunwitty, whose pursuit and colonization of authentic blackness is both sincere and driven by a desire for power. In Dunwitty, students can see what Yancy calls "the white face that refuses to see itself in its own monstrous creations": the contemporary manifestation of the white artists and businessmen who created blackface for fun, profit, and what Lott calls "love."

Can such efforts to teach minstrelsy in comic contexts enable students to recognize and deconstruct ingrained habits of racialized seeing and believing? As news reports repeatedly affirm, blackface comedy remains powerfully entrenched in white culture and consciousness, undergirding a bridge that spans college parties, white supremacist websites, and the halls of government. I believe it is crucial to acknowledge and contest its continuing influence. However, as Bambi Haggins puts it, the problem for the teacher of ethnic comedy is always this: "I know what I'm laughing at, but I don't know what you're laughing at" (205). Just as Dave Chappelle was appalled to see a white cameraman laughing the wrong way after watching his pixie sketch (Haggins 228–30), I fear my students' exposure to blackface comedy often leaves the structures of racism intact and unchallenged despite my best efforts to control and redirect their responses.

Notes

1. Because students may have strong reactions after viewing blackface in class, instructors may wish to reach out to any students who are subsequently absent.

2. This approach is relevant to understanding the historical use of blackface comedy by white-aspiring immigrants, which similarly involved layers of impersonation and interlocution. The minstrel tradition's "Americanization of immigrant groups on the American stage," as Joyce Flynn argues, "took place through the filter of the negative portrayal in blackface" (qtd. in Mahar 184). This has important implications for contemporary cross-racial comedy by nonblack ethnic minorities.

3. For other important discussions of this material, see Brooks; Haggins; Colbert; and McMahon.

Works Cited

Bamboozled. Directed by Spike Lee, New Line Cinema, 2000.
Bean, Annemarie, et al., editors. *Inside the Minstrel Mask: Readings in Nineteenth-Century Blackface Minstrelsy*. Routledge, 1996.
Brooks, Daphne A. *Bodies in Dissent: Spectacular Performances of Race and Freedom, 1850–1910*. Duke UP, 2006.
Colbert, Soyica Diggs. *The African American Theatrical Body: Reception, Performance, and the Stage*. Cambridge UP, 2011.
Ellison, Ralph. "Change the Joke and Slip the Yoke." *Shadow and Act*, by Ellison, Random House, 1964, pp. 100–12.
Ethnic Notions: Black People in White Minds. Directed by Marlon Riggs, California Newsreel, 1987.

Gillota, David. *Ethnic Humor in Multiethnic America*. Rutgers UP, 2013. *JSTOR*, www.jstor.org/stable/j.ctt5hjctg.

Haggins, Bambi. *Laughing Mad: The Black Comic Persons in Post-Soul America*. Routledge, 2007.

Haygood, Wil. "Why Won't Blackface Go Away? It's Part of America's Troubled Cultural Legacy." *The New York Times*, 7 Feb. 2019, www.nytimes.com/2019/02/07/arts/blackface-american-pop-culture.html.

"I'll Be Glad When You're Dead, You Rascal You." 1932. *YouTube*, uploaded by Boing Boing Video, www.youtube.com/watch?v=aUcUhLg_0-0. Accessed 6 June 2022.

Johnson, Stephen, editor. *Burnt Cork: Traditions and Legacies of Blackface Minstrelsy*. U of Massachusetts P, 2012.

———. "The Persistence of Blackface and the Minstrel Tradition." Johnson, *Burnt Cork*, pp. 1–17.

Kendi, Ibram X. "The Anti-Racist Reading List: Thirty-Eight Books for Those Open to Changing Themselves, and Their World." *The Atlantic*, 12 Feb. 2019, www.theatlantic.com/ideas/archive/2019/02/antiracist-syllabus-governor-ralph-northam/582580/.

Lhamon, W. T., Jr. "'Ebery Time I Wheel About I Jump Jim Crow': Cycles of Minstrel Transgression from Cool White to Vanilla Ice." Bean et al., pp. 275–84.

Lott, Eric. *Love and Theft: Blackface Minstrelsy and the American Working Class*. 20th anniversary ed., Oxford UP, 2013.

Mahar, William J. "Ethiopian Skits and Sketches: Contents and Contexts of Blackface Minstrelsy, 1840–1890." 1996. Bean et al., pp. 179–220.

Maurice, Alice. "From New Deal to No Deal: Blackface Minstrelsy, *Bamboozled*, and Reality Television." Johnson, *Burnt Cork*, pp. 191–222.

McMahon, Rashida Z. Shaw. *The Black Circuit: Race, Performance, and Spectatorship in Black Popular Theatre*. Routledge, 2020.

The Original Kings of Comedy. Directed by Spike Lee, MTV Productions / Latham Entertainment, 2000.

"Scrub Me Mama with a Boogie Beat." 1941. *YouTube*, uploaded by reelblack, 22 Sept. 2019, www.youtube.com/watch?v=FUYarKCTvIk.

Sollors, Werner. *Beyond Ethnicity: Consent and Descent in American Culture*. Oxford UP, 1988.

Stowe, William F., and David Grimsted. "White-Black Humor: Review Essay." *The Journal of Ethnic Studies*, vol. 3, no. 2, 1975, pp. 78–96.

"Tyler Perry's Madea." *Lionsgate*, www.lionsgate.com/franchises/tyler-perrys-madea. Accessed 29 Nov. 2022.

Watkins, Mel. *On the Real Side: A History of African American Comedy from Slavery to Chris Rock*. Lawrence Hills, 1999.

Yancy, George. "Why White People Need Blackface." *The New York Times*, 4 Mar. 2019, www.nytimes.com/2019/03/04/opinion/blackface-racism.html.

Peter Conolly-Smith

No Laughing Matter: Immigrant Cartoons of the Late Nineteenth and Early Twentieth Centuries

When my students first examine late-nineteenth- and early-twentieth-century cartoons featuring immigrants (often depicted alongside Uncle Sam), they have questions: Why are the immigrants so small? Why are they wearing such strange clothing? Who's the guy with the white beard? While my arts and humanities courses are hardly the place to teach them the full scope of immigrant history their questions invoke—issues of prejudice, assimilation, race, and ethnicity—I have found that immigrant caricatures are an effective means through which to introduce students to such complex material. Widely available on the Internet—including from the Library of Congress's *Prints and Photographs Online Catalog* (loc. gov/pictures)—late-nineteenth and early-twentieth-century immigrant caricatures were rendered according to a visual code of representation so consistent that their stereotypes and meanings were instantly recognizable to readers at the time. The purpose of this essay is to offer strategies to enable students to interpret such caricatures, place them in their historical context, and perhaps answer the most difficult of their questions: But are they funny?

Introducing Uncle Sam

One reason students don't recognize the humor in these cartoons is that, to contemporary observers, late-nineteenth- and early-twentieth-century ethnic stereotypes are signifiers without referents. Long gone from the visual landscape of urban America are the ape-like Irish and beer-bellied Germans of the funny pages of yore. Having no real-life model on whom to pin such caricatures, students do not know what to make of them. Indeed, even visual personifications of America, like Uncle Sam, are so old-fashioned that most students do not recognize them.

For this reason, I suggest beginning with Uncle Sam, the most famous embodiment of the United States, known for his lanky legs, red-and-white striped trousers, blue cutaway, star-rimmed top hat, and trademark beard. When viewing images of Uncle Sam, students quickly agree that he is late-nineteenth-century America's self-image incarnate: a white man who literally wears the flag and whose initials are the same as his country's (kudos to the student who catches this detail). Another important point is that his height is an expression of his prowess: Uncle Sam is almost always the tallest figure in any group composition, a fact particularly relevant in images that juxtapose him with immigrants. With only minimal coaxing, students are able to arrive at such insights simply by looking at, describing, and then analyzing the way in which Uncle Sam tends to be portrayed.

Immigrant Groups

Students become more interested still when they consider Uncle Sam in relation to immigrants. For this, it helps to first review the portrayal of immigrants of different national origins, a task ideally suited for group work. Each group is assigned a different immigrant group and asked to brainstorm what that group—for instance, the Irish, the Germans, or the Chinese—has in common in terms of its portrayal in nineteenth-century immigrant cartoons. The exercise can be further refined by having students break down their observations by the physical characteristics, sartorial choices, occupations, and pastimes associated with each group. Students are given sufficient time for this exercise, after which each group reports back to the class. In all likelihood, students will have caught on to some of the basic visual tropes: for example, the Chinese, clad in dress-like garments, their hair in pigtails, are feminized, the shape of their eyes and the color of their skin grotesquely exaggerated; the Germans are portrayed as beer-bellied but generally likable buffoons; the Irish, as ape-like, whiskey-drinking thugs; Italians, as stiletto-wielding criminals; and so on.

After we have established the conventional representation of different groups of immigrants and the attendant issue of ethnic (i.e., culturally based) stereotypes in broad terms, the next step—perhaps reserved for a separate day and requiring students to conduct some advance research—is a closer examination of one or more immigrant groups. The goal is to provide specific information on one group that also relates meaningfully to broader aspects of the immigrant experience. Thus, the Chinese, the only numerically significant non-white immigrant group of the nineteenth century (for obvious reasons, since African slaves were not considered immigrants), raise the important issue of racial prejudice, especially when one considers the culmination of their nineteenth-century experience, the 1882 Chinese Exclusion Act, which barred the future admission of Chinese laborers through the mid–twentieth century. The treatment of Germans, to cite a different example, was in many ways the opposite: white, northern European, frequently Protestant, the Germans, though sometimes disdained for their occasionally radical politics, did not suffer the viciousness of visual portrayal to which the Chinese were subjected—at first. Yet even this generally favored immigrant group experienced the brunt of cartoonists' venom with the onset of World War I, especially after the United States entered the war in 1917. At that point, what had been an overall benign (if slightly ridiculous) portrayal of the German as convivial beer monster, often clad in clogs and smoking a pipe, was replaced by the intensely negative portrayal of the sinister wartime Hun, evidence that cartoon portrayals could flip at a moment's notice under the right (or wrong) historical circumstances.

Case Study: The Irish

While each immigrant group is thus of interest in its own right, and the choice of which groups to focus on may vary depending on an instructor's particular goals, I have found the Irish to be of particularly rich potential for several reasons: first, the Irish were among the earlier of mass migrations to the United States. Arriving throughout the first half of the nineteenth century, their numbers spiked in particular during the successive potato famines of the mid- to late-1840s. The Irish are thus an example of the immigrants from northern and western Europe who dominated American immigration prior to the 1890s. As such, they are useful to help establish the basic periodization of immigration history into a pre-1890 period and a post-1890 period that was dominated by immigrants from southern and eastern Europe, who began outnumbering all other immigrant groups around the turn of the century, and whose arrivals resulted in backlash policies that culminated in the immigrant restriction laws of the 1920s. Examining the Irish, in other words, sets up a great deal of relatively dense history that is relevant also to the experiences of other immigrant groups.

Second, the Irish are of interest as an immigrant group whose visual stereotype was one of the earliest and most clearly articulated. Irishmen were commonly portrayed as "hirsute, muscular laborer[s], with cheek whiskers, a broad upper lip, and button nose" (Linneman 29). The cartoon Irishman's patched cutaway, dented top hat, and heavy brogue made him instantly recognizable as Irish. That he was uneducated and therefore stupid was an equally important part of the stereotype.

Finally, the Irish also help illustrate two important categories of analysis in immigrant studies: ethnicity and race. To wit: the host society's hostility toward the Irish was based on ethnic (read: cultural) resentment, especially their near-exclusive Roman Catholicism, which made them important outliers in the WASP-dominated society of nineteenth-century America. Students will find it hard to grasp the intensity of anti-Irish prejudice in the first half of the nineteenth century, so examples will help, including the many caricatures that sought to tarnish the Irish by visual association with, and juxtaposition to, African Americans (see, e.g., Nast). Students marvel at the portrayal of the Irish as "white negroes," which in turn yields rich conversations about the social construction of race—what it meant to be "black" in nineteenth-century America or, for that matter, to be "white" (Pieterse 211–15). Yet the very fact that the Irish were cast as "*white* negroes"—that they may have been black in construct but were in fact white—offered an escape hatch. Indeed, the host culture's contempt for the Irish, though framed in quasi-racist terms, was in the end based on ethnic factors: their religion, their brogues, their penchant for drink. Thus, the Irish could, if they wanted, rid themselves of the stigma attached to their identity by choosing to assimilate. Being white, all the Irish had to do in order to be absorbed into mainstream (read: white) American society was to unlearn or at least temper their ethnic distinctiveness—lose their brogues, moderate their religiosity, consume whiskey less ostentatiously, and downplay other markers of their otherness—which, over time, is exactly what they did. This in turn explains why humor based on Irish or other white ethnic stereotypes rarely registers with today's students. Through the process of assimilation, the Irish simply "disappeared," as did most other nineteenth-century European immigrants as they became accepted as no-longer-ethnic Americans. The fact that most European immigrants were white is key here: it was the color of their skin, the fact that their differences were ethnic, not racial, that allowed for their gradual absorption and disappearance into white American society.

Race versus Ethnicity

The above points are complex and best arrived at by means of carefully guided discussion. Having established them, the stage is set for further visual analysis that can now juxtapose multiple immigrant groups and incorporate Uncle Sam too. A particularly telling example that explicitly thematizes both Irishness and the distinction between ethnicity and race is a cartoon from the 1860s, at which time the Irish were only just beginning their gradual process of assimilation. Entitled "The Great Fear of the Period: That Uncle Sam May Be Swallowed by Foreigners," this three-part cartoon shows, first, a stereotypical Irishman facing an equally stereotypical Chinese man. Between them they hold the prone body of Uncle Sam, recognizable by his trademark striped trousers and waistcoat, his feet in the Chinese man's mouth, his head in the Irishman's. We are literally witnessing the cartoon's title: "Uncle Sam . . . Be[ing] Swallowed by Foreigners." But rather than suggest that the two groups shown pose equal threats to America, the cartoon's unfolding narrative establishes a pecking order. The second image shows the Chinese man's rapid progress as he reaches Uncle Sam's thighs, while the Irishman remains stuck where he was previously. The third image, finally, shows the Chinese man fulfilling the title's "great fear": he has fully swallowed all of Uncle Sam's body and, what is more, is now in the process of swallowing the Irishman. The message is clear: both the Irish and the Chinese pose a threat to the nation—both are shown attempting to devour Uncle Sam—but the greater menace is posed by the Chinese, who threaten to destroy not only Uncle Sam's WASP America but also the country's Irish immigrant population, a population that is neither Anglo-Saxon nor Protestant but is, importantly, white. Ethnic differences may have been objectionable, in other words, but racial differences were more objectionable by far. This conclusion is also borne out by history, as the Chinese were soon to be legally excluded from further immigration, while the once despised Irish succeeded in establishing themselves as a quintessential American immigrant group.

Scenarios of Welcome, Scenarios of Exclusion

The same was true for later groups of European immigrants, including Italians and Jews, who began immigrating to the United States in the later nineteenth century. They, too, experienced a quasi-racial hazing similar to that of the Irish (Pieterse 215–18) but then also gradually found acceptance as white ethnics—often at the expense of non-white others. Still, their increasing numbers post-1890 did stoke nativist fears that ultimately yielded restrictionist policies, a historical trajectory that can be traced through cartoons showing scenarios of Uncle Sam contemplating arriving immigrants. For this final unit, groups of students again take responsibility for different cartoons, such as those suggested below, then report back for a last group discussion.

The 1880 cartoon "Welcome to All!" is the most positive in its portrayal of immigrants (Keppler). Uncle Sam stands with outstretched, welcoming hands at the top of a gangplank, framed in the doorway of a barge—the "U.S. Ark of Refuge"—while immigrant couples line up in orderly procession, awaiting their turn to embark. Following the cartoon's biblical conceit (which casts Uncle Sam as Noah and the United States as a promised land), each immigrant couple is of mixed gender. Students recognize each couple's national origin based on their stereotypical physical and sartorial portrayals: the pug-nosed Irishman with his stout wife, now first in line—what better sign of their arrival?; the Russians in their distinctive headgear, he with cap, she in babushka; the picturesque Italians, she barefoot, wearing a peasant dress; the jovial Germans, fair-skinned and well-fed, he smoking his pipe, she in clogs; and so on. It is only at the end of the line that the two-by-two pattern breaks. At the rear (and significantly so) we find two single men, smaller in size, their features distinctly darker when compared with the others: a Chinese man in pigtails (whose 1882 exclusion was imminent at the time of this drawing) and a bearded, turbaned Middle Easterner.

Thus did turn-of-the-century cartoons perpetuate the national and racial pecking orders developed over the previous decades, in which one's place in the hierarchy of nations (and immigrants) was determined by the lightness of one's skin—the whiter, the better—and was confirmed by one's stature: the taller, the more powerful. Hence, Uncle Sam is by far the largest figure in the image, while the smaller immigrant couples are all approximately the same size, with the exception of the two even smaller and visibly darker men at the back of the line. Size definitely matters here: Uncle Sam is both the largest figure in the image and, in further confirmation of his superiority, stands above all others at the head of the gangplank.

A similar visual dynamic is found in a later, 1891 cartoon, "Where the Blame Lies" (Hamilton). Though visually reminiscent of "Welcome to All!," this cartoon conveys a very different attitude towards its subject. As grim-faced Uncle Sam contemplates the immigrant masses arriving in New York Harbor, turn-of-the-century American society's ills find personification in the individual immigrants, representative of their groups, here helpfully labeled as "Russian Anarchists," "Italian Brigands," and so on. Again, Uncle Sam is the largest figure in the image. And, again, his superiority finds further expression in the fact that he is standing on a pedestal, elevated far above the crowd of immigrants below. The immigrants are portrayed as teeming masses, exclusively male; their numbers are innumerable, their appearance fearsome.

Taking the principle that size matters to its logical conclusion, an even later cartoon, "The Only Way to Handle It" (1921), rendered immigrants so small—tiny, now, in comparison with Uncle Sam—that they were indistinguishable. If the earlier two cartoons already registered a decline in the favor felt toward immigrants over time, this one, which accompanied an article supporting the 1921 Emergency Quota Act, represents that trajectory's culmination. The Emergency Quota Act restricted the number of immigrants from any nation to just three percent of that nation's immigrant population, as reported in the United States census of 1910. This formula drastically reduced immigration overall (from more than 800,000 arrivals in 1920 to approximately 300,000 in 1921) and, further, favored immigrants from northern and western Europe over the more recent immigrants from southern and eastern Europe, whose increasing numbers since 1890 had significantly contributed to immigrants' fall from grace during the intervening years (Dinnerstein et al. 184). The cartoon shows a giant Uncle Sam guarding America's shores (marked "U.S.A.") and facing "Europe" across the sea. A huge funnel bridges the ocean separating the continents. Masses of tiny emigrants clamor around the funnel's wide base in Europe, seeking admission, but only a small number arrive stateside, squeezing through the funnel's narrow neck. Entry is controlled by a solemn-faced Uncle Sam and a "gate" marked "3%." A far cry from the orderly procession of clearly identifiable immigrant couples lined up before the welcoming Uncle Sam of 1880, this portrayal of immigrants as minuscule and indistinguishable does more than merely illustrate the usual size differential; just as importantly, it invokes the specter of immigrant hordes: a veritable sea of humanity (already hinted at in the transitional "Where the Blame Lies") that, if not limited by legislation, threatens to utterly overwhelm America's shores, a popular trope among nativists in favor of the sort of restrictive legislation this cartoon supports, as it is even today.

Many of my students—most of whom are either recent immigrants themselves or descended from the immigrant groups addressed in this essay—are grateful to learn about immigration through immigrant caricatures and cartoons. They are fascinated to learn that today's immigration debate bears many of the same hallmarks of the debates that riveted the nation more than a century ago, including the racial underpinnings of such debates. Having learned to decode nineteenth-century immigrant cartoons, students also quickly pick up on the similarities of these cartoons to today's portrayals of immigrants in words and images. Back then, immigrant cartoons reduced their subjects to their most basic visual signifiers and ordered them according to a scale of size and skin color that was directly proportional to the host society's estimation of their desirability. The humor of these cartoons, such as it was, lay in their subjects' confirmation of the worst stereotypes attributed to them: the Irish were brutes; the Chinese, cannibals; the Germans, bumbling drunks; and so on. As such, the cartoons held interesting, albeit twisted, lessons for immigrants. By holding up the warped mirror of American racism and nativism, these cartoons showed immigrants how they were perceived in the host society's eyes and, therefore, in William Linneman's words, "how not to act" (or dress, or speak) if they wished to hasten their acceptance into American society (38). The fact that this negative logic assumed a white Anglo-Saxon Protestant norm and perpetuated ethnocentrism and racism does, in the end, suggest that my students' initial skepticism toward this brand of American visual humor was right all along: although fascinating as a subject of analysis and discussion, and eminently readable in their semiotics, immigrant cartoons of the late nineteenth and early twentieth centuries are no laughing matter.

Works Cited

Dinnerstein, Leonard, et al. *Natives and Strangers: A Multicultural History of Americans.* Oxford UP, 2003.

"The Great Fear of the Period: That Uncle Sam May Be Swallowed by Foreigners: The Problem Solved." White and Bauer, 1860–69. *Library of Congress*, www.loc.gov/pictures/resource/pga.03047/.

Hamilton, Grant E. "Where the Blame Lies." *Judge*, vol. 19, no. 494, 4 Apr. 1891, pp. 458–59. *Library of Congress*, www.loc.gov/pictures/resource/cph.3g05739/.

Keppler, J. "Welcome to All!" *Puck*, vol. 7, 28 Apr. 1880, pp. 130–31. *Library of Congress*, www.loc.gov/pictures/resource/cph.3b52460/.

Linneman, William. "Immigrant Stereotypes, 1880–1900." *Studies in American Humor*, vol. 1, Apr. 1974, pp. 28–39.

Nast, Thomas. "The Ignorant Vote—Honors Are Easy." *Harper's Weekly*, 9 Dec. 1876. *Library of Congress*, www.loc.gov/pictures/resource/cph.3b05167/.

"The Only Way to Handle It." Funk and Wagnalls, 1921. *Library of Congress*, www.loc.gov/pictures/resource/cph.3a44285/.

Pieterse, Jan Nederveen. *White on Black: Images of Africans and Blacks in Western Popular Culture.* Yale UP, 1992.

Iñaki Pérez-Ibáñez and Megan M. Echevarría

Humor and Intercultural Empathy: Teaching Comedic Films of Intercultural Encounter

Milton Bennett's simple yet powerful statement that "the goal of intercultural learning is empathy, not just tolerance" underscores a key yet elusive element of intercultural competence and a critical challenge for educators in the twenty-first century ("Short Conceptual History" 432). World language educators in particular grapple with how to effectively work with students in the affective domain of intercultural competence. For specialists in linguistic, cultural, and literary analysis, bolstering students' cognitive awareness of cultural difference and equipping them with the necessary linguistic and analytical skills to describe, explain, and analyze cultural products, practices, and perspectives are clearly discernible goals. While not easy tasks, many of us feel capable of working productively toward these outcomes. Changing hearts, however, is not something that world language educators necessarily feel as confident approaching in such a systematic manner.

This essay argues that comedic films are particularly well-suited tools for activating the affective domain of intercultural competence because of the sensory and cognitive power of film, the role of humor in intercultural competence, and the uniquely high potential that the combination of the narrative form, the film medium, and the comedic genre has for eliciting positive empathetic responses in viewers. Using as a theoretical framework Bennett's Developmental Model of Intercultural Sensitivity ("Developmental Approach"), we outline an approach to teaching comedic films of intercultural encounter in which students take on the role of ethnographic field researchers, observing and analyzing the words and behaviors of characters in order to uncover the implicit knowledge and attitudes that inform their communication strategies and behaviors. While watching funny movies for the sake of watching funny movies will likely not help us make noteworthy strides in acquiring intercultural competencies, carefully selected films used purposefully to this end do indeed drive important gains toward this goal. To successfully achieve such gains, a process that involves pre-viewing preparation, guided viewing, individual reflection, debriefing, and collaborative discussion is also essential. Through these scaffolded activities, students analyze how characters respond to cultural difference and assess the impact that continued exposure to cultural difference has on characters' attitudes, perspectives, personalities, and quality of life.

This model allows students to examine intercultural issues from a comfortable comedic and critical distance while also empathizing with characters who unwittingly enter into amusing predicaments and droll situations of light tension that are frequently the result of intercultural ignorance. The combination of empathy and critical distance, both triggered by the use of humor, creates a unique space for broadening our cognitive understanding of and ability to explain and analyze cultural differences as well as our own attitudes and perspectives in the affective domain of intercultural competence. Based on a model designed for use with Spanish-language films in a Spanish-language curriculum in the United States, our pedagogical and critical framework is applicable to films from any language and culture (or from multiple languages and cultures). The primary goal of this essay is to provide educators from various disciplines with useful tools for teaching comedic texts for the purpose of promoting deeper intercultural awareness, understanding, and sensitivity in students.

Popular Films and Humor in Intercultural Training

A number of scholars have demonstrated the benefits of using popular films for developing intercultural competence. Articles by José Vallalba and Rachelle Redmond and by Paula Ross and colleagues focus on these issues in the context of training health-care professionals, and Satish Pandey reports on programs for business professionals. Christine Roell argues that films "contain excellent examples of intercultural communication" (2), and we would add that they also contain equally valuable illustrations of intercultural miscommunication and misunderstanding. According to Roell, films provide opportunities for intercultural training because they "simultaneously address different senses and cognitive channels" and "involve the viewers, appeal to their feelings, and help them empathize with the protagonists" (2). The inherently multilayered nature of motion pictures has often been cited as a reason films are particularly beneficial and motivating for students with different learning styles. However, and more importantly in the context of intercultural training, the simultaneous sensory and cognitive stimulation of the film-viewing experience is often linked directly to the affective reactions that films frequently provoke. These reactions, if properly channeled, can help people empathize not only with the films' characters but also with the broader cultural perspectives and intercultural growth processes that characters convey and substantiate through their words, body language, attitudes, interactions, and overall evolution.

Recent studies also emphasize the role of humor in learning environments as a vehicle for "expanding our students' communicative repertoires and indeed . . . their overall understanding of the language" (Bell and Pomerantz viii). In fact, Guy Cook suggests that the ability to "produce play" with language (which, by definition, includes humorous play) "is a necessary part of advanced language proficiency" (150). Nancy Bell and Anne Pomerantz have demonstrated how the use of humor and playful language can raise learners' language awareness (115). In addition to this clear linguistic benefit, they also highlight the social and interpersonal function of humor in our personal and professional lives: "Conversational joking, humorous refusals, and playful teases, for example, feature just as heavily in the talk of children on the playground, as they do in the talk of adults in the workplace" (viii). Bell and Pomerantz note the extent to which "in our everyday lives we draw on non-serious language" to relate more effectively to others in our interpersonal relations, manage conflicts and difficult situations, "subvert, resist, or critique social norms and conventions (albeit often in a safe or deniable fashion)," and navigate power dynamics (viii).

While we recognize the valid points that these scholars make and do not underestimate the importance of linguistic humor (word play, double meanings, puns, etc.), it is also important to note the equally powerful nonlinguistic elements of humor. In her study of the use of humor in a study abroad setting, Rachel Shively found that most failed humor exchanges were due not to insufficient linguistic knowledge (pronunciation, grammar, or vocabulary) of the target language but to "lack of shared knowledge," the interlocutor not finding the topic amusing or funny, lack of cues marking the utterance as playful, or the interlocutor's desire to keep the conversation serious (938). All these causes relate much more closely to intercultural competence (especially insufficient cultural knowledge and limited intercultural sensitivity) than to any kind of implicit or explicit knowledge about or mastery of the linguistic system.

An Ethnographic Approach to Interculturality in Film

An ethnographic approach to teaching comedic films of intercultural encounter, consisting of the application of Bennett's Developmental Model of Intercultural Sensitivity to character analysis, achieves multiple learning outcomes related to language proficiency, film analysis, critical thinking, and intercultural competence. By comedic films of intercultural encounter, we refer to comedic films in which characters from two or more cultures enter into close contact and, as a direct result of that physical and psychological proximity, must contend with and negotiate cultural differences. Spanish-language examples of such films include Sebastián Borensztein's *Un cuento chino* (*Chinese Takeaway*), Emilio Martínez Lázaro's *Ocho apellidos vascos* (*Spanish Affair*) and *Ocho apellidos catalanes* (*Spanish Affair 2*), Patricia Ferreira's *Thi Mai, rumbo a Vietnam* (*Thi Mai*), Borja Cobeaga's *Fe de etarras* (*Bomb Scared*), and Ignacio García Velilla's *Perdiendo el norte* (*Off Course*). At times, the cultures in question coexist within the same country. Some of these cultures have long histories and strong claims to their own unique national identities, while others are the result of more recent global migratory patterns. These films provide the added benefit of illustrating multiple modes of cultural diversity within a single country. In some cases, the films present characters who do not conform perfectly to all of their own culture's norms and conventions, highlighting what at times is a subtle but quite significant facet of the human experience of culture and intercultural growth.

The Developmental Model of Intercultural Sensitivity

Bennett's Developmental Model of Intercultural Sensitivity conceptualizes the process of achieving intercultural competence as a journey along a continuum of six stages. Bennett characterizes the first three stages (denial, defense, and minimization) as ethnocentric, reflecting a largely monocultural mindset, and identifies the last three stages (acceptance, adaptation, and integration) as ethnorelative, corresponding to an intercultural mindset. In the initial stages of the ethnocentric side of the continuum, people progress from a complete lack of interest in or awareness of cultural differences and alternative worldviews (denial) to a view of superiority of one culture over another (defense in the case of viewing one's own culture as superior, reversal in the case of idealization of the target culture). In the last stage of ethnocentrism (minimization), the individual emphasizes commonalities and universal principles among cultures, often to the point of acute underestimation of cultural differences. On this ethnocentric side of the continuum, limited exposure to and reflection on cultural differences and worldviews constrain the individual's response to the experience of cultural diversity and limit the possibility of developing intercultural sensitivity.

Once we cross the threshold and enter the ethnorelative stages of the continuum, the experience of culture becomes more nuanced, reflective, and positive. At this point a fundamental shift toward a more dynamic conceptualization of cultural difference and its varied manifestations in concrete behaviors and attitudes occurs: the ethnorelative perspective necessarily conceives of "cultural reality as consensual and mutable," and within this mindset "people are seen as dynamic co-creators of their realities" (Bennett, "Developmental Approach" 185). Individuals at the initial stage of this side of the continuum demonstrate acceptance, recognizing and appreciating cultural differences. For the accepting individual, "difference is perceived as fundamental, necessary, and preferable in human affairs" (184). This stage is followed by adaptation, when we acquire the ability "to act ethnorelatively" (186), adjusting our approach to events depending on the culture in which we are immersed (cognitive shift) and modifying our behavior based on those principles (behavioral shift). In the adaptive stage, we have the "ability to shift into two or more rather complete cultural worldviews" (185). The most advanced stage is integration, characterized by "the application of ethnorelativism to one's own identity" and one's ability to "construe" oneself "in various ways" (186). At this stage, the subject is able to judge cultural phenomena not as good or bad but as relative to the cultural context. According to Bennett, "As the culmination of intercultural sensitivity, the stage of Integration suggests a person who experiences difference as an essential and joyful aspect of all life" (186).

Preparatory Phase

To be able to use this framework as a tool for analyzing characters, students complete a series of pre-viewing preparatory activities that scaffold their subsequent work as film analysts and ethnographic field researchers. These activities include working with terminology and analytical tools from literary, film, and cultural studies as well as readings and discussions about the Developmental Model of Intercultural Sensitivity.

Study of key terms from literary and film studies hones our attention on the techniques used in the films to construct and convey different layers of meaning. Purposeful exposure to and discussion about these concepts as powerful artistic tools that shape the way viewers consume and process the representation of culture empowers students to discern, extract, question, analyze, and discuss meanings constructed in the films with greater autonomy. In the case of the films we focused on, which are mentioned above, key terms included *hyperbole, irony, satire, parody, caricature*, and *mise-en-scène*. These tools and discursive strategies are central to understanding and analyzing how the films confront culture and cultural difference and how they represent and poke fun at characters' intercultural shortcomings (i.e., their lack of cultural knowledge and literacy and limited intercultural awareness and sensitivity).

To appreciate more deeply the importance of nuance and connotation when communicating about diversity and cultural studies, students create semantic maps using words and images and then work collaboratively, comparing and discussing their understanding of specific words. The films selected dictate which semantic groupings are most relevant and useful. One semantic grouping of high relevance to many comedic films of intercultural encounter that relates to patterns of behavior among groups of people includes words such as *pattern, tendency, generalization, universality, standard, stereotype, bias,* and *prejudice*. Another semantic group particularly useful in the context of intercultural sensitivity focuses on communicating about difference, for example: *different, dissimilar, distinctive, atypical, unique, particular, personal, eccentric, peculiar, outlier, weird, anomalous, divergent,* and *aberrant*.

Finally, and most importantly, we examine and discuss the key features and distinguishing characteristics of the two broad categories of ethnocentrism and ethnorelativism as outlined in the Developmental Model of Intercultural Sensitivity as well as the specific details that define each of the three stages that fall within those respective categories.

Viewing Phase

In preparation for each individual film-viewing experience, students conduct structured research activities to ensure that they possess sufficient basic understanding of cultural references to be able to appreciate and enjoy each film's culture-based and culturally specific humor. While viewing each film, students take notes on various elements used to create meaning and to represent culture and intercultural sensitivity. At this stage, students act as field researchers, focusing attention on visual, acoustic, linguistic, and relational cues and what they reveal about the cultures represented and how various cultural actors relate to one another. Provided with guidelines on specific areas of focus, students hone in on visual subtleties in facial expressions, eye contact, body language, physical contact and distance between characters, hair, makeup, wardrobe, physical environments, climate, geography, configurations of space, food, color, and light, searching for patterns, interrelations, connections, and disconnections. Similarly, they pay close attention to audio cues, including volume, tone, noise, and music, making note of how these acoustic elements contribute to the ideas and sentiments at play throughout the narrative. Students also make note of linguistic patterns and the importance of dialogue and linguistic comprehension (or lack thereof) throughout the film. Finally, they focus on interpersonal relations and the ways in which characters behave and respond to one another, considering additional factors that configure personal identity (gender, age, race, etc.) and that often influence interpersonal dynamics and the cultural appropriateness of behaviors.

Postviewing Phase

After viewing the film, students write individual reflections in which they discuss the situations and predicaments they found most striking and the characters and situations with which they identified and sympathized most. In class, students work collaboratively, bringing together their individual insights and beginning to make sense of the film, the way it is constructed, and the ways in which it represents culture and cultural practices, making inferences about the values that might motivate observed behaviors. They engage initially in a large group, instructor-led debriefing session to clarify any blatant points of confusion, incomprehension, or miscomprehension and to begin sharing hypotheses about the beliefs that observed behaviors might reveal. They then participate in a series of structured small group discussions about cultural similarities and differences, distinguishing between patterns of behavior and stereotypes and making and testing hypotheses about the phase of intercultural sensitivity that specific characters appear to illustrate. Specific topics are selected with the purposeful intent to create space for students to relate their own experiences, if they wish to do so, or to actively contribute without sharing personal experiences. After these discussions, students choose one character to focus on, view the film again, and write an essay analyzing the stage or stages of intercultural competence displayed by the character throughout the film.

Intercultural Metacognitive Awareness and Affect

These activities are designed as an initial step toward promoting intercultural metacognitive awareness and intelligence, ultimately setting up students to successfully continue their intercultural growth beyond the confines of a course experience. These activities prepare students to engage reflectively and productively with cultural diversity and with the notion of difference itself. This approach to comic film affords students repeated pleasurable exposures to cultural differences and promotes sustained self-reflection on students' own assumptions about culture and cultural diversity in a comfortable, nonthreatening, and amusing environment. Students enjoy the luxury of regulating their personal involvement with characters and the target culture from a safe and critical distance. The process of enjoying the comic relief present throughout the films combined with collaborative analysis of characters' actions and reactions serves to reasonably normalize the ethnocentric tendencies and attitudes that are often present in classroom settings. Inscribing that normalization in a clear continuum that leads to positive, attractive, and satisfying ethnorelative attitudes equips students with powerful coping skills and motivates them to further develop their intercultural competencies and identities.

Works Cited

Bell, Nancy D., and Anne Pomerantz. *Humor in the Classroom: A Guide for Language Teachers and Educational Researchers*. Routledge, 2016.

Bennett, Milton J. "A Developmental Approach to Training for Intercultural Sensitivity." *International Journal of Intercultural Relations*, vol. 10, no. 2, 1986, pp. 179–96.

———. "A Short Conceptual History of Intercultural Learning in Study Abroad." *A History of U.S. Study Abroad, 1965–Present*, edited by William Hoffa and Stephen C. DePaul, Forum on Education Abroad, 2010, pp. 419–49.

Cook, Guy. *Language Play, Language Learning.* Oxford UP, 2000.
Un cuento chino. Directed by Sebastián Borensztein, Pampa Films / Tornasol Films, 2011.
Fe de etarras. Directed by Borja Cobeaga, Mediapro, 2017.
Ocho apellidos catalanes. Directed by Emilio Martínez Lázaro, Lazona Films / Kowalski Films / Telecinco Cinema, 2015.
Ocho apellidos vascos. Directed by Emilio Martínez Lázaro, Lazona Films / Kowalski Films / Telecinco Cinema, 2014.
Pandey, Satish. "Using Popular Movies in Teaching Cross-Cultural Management." *European Journal of Training and Development,* vol. 36, nos. 2–3, 2012, pp. 329–50.
Perdiendo el norte. Directed by Ignacio García Velilla, Antena 3 Films / Aparte Producciones / Telefónica Studios, 2015.
Roell, Christine. "Intercultural Training with Films." *English Teaching Forum,* vol. 48, no. 2, 2010, pp. 2–15.
Ross, Paula T., et al. "Using Film in Multicultural and Social Justice Faculty Development: Scenes from *Crash.*" *Journal of Continuing Education in the Health Professions,* vol. 31, no. 3, 2011, pp. 188–95.
Shively, Rachel L. "Learning to Be Funny in Spanish during Study Abroad: L2 Humor Development." *Modern Language Journal,* vol. 97, no. 4, 2013, pp. 930–46.
Thi Mai, rumbo a Vietnam. Directed by Patricia Ferreira, Atresmedia Cine y Levinver, 2018.
Vallalba, José A., and Rachelle E. Redmond. "*Crash*: Using a Popular Film as an Experiential Learning Activity in a Multicultural Counseling Course." *Counselor Education and Supervision,* vol. 47, no. 4, 2008, pp. 264–76.

Mayy ElHayawi

Laughing Prejudices Away: Teaching Diversity through Jokes in Contemporary Ethnic American Women's Poetry

A joke can be the venom that poisons a society with allegations of supremacy and pretexts of aggression—or the antidote that heals a culture, helping it overcome delusions of inferiority and presumptions of submissiveness. Throughout history, self-directed humor and humor directed at others have been used as a defense against the threats posed by ethnic diversity—the multidimensional social complexity that has been historically tied to power-seeking conquests, labor-chasing enslavements, and turmoil-fleeing migrations. The process of assigning the self and the other to specific groups and attributing to those groups certain positive or negative characteristics—presumed to be shared by all members of that group—has been unconsciously or consciously performed to respond to ethnic heterogeneity, accelerate comprehension of differences, and facilitate treading into unfamiliar cognitive, social, and cultural territories. The act of highlighting and intensifying stereotypes through ethnic jokes—whether those jokes are structured in the form of stable texts that can be tailored in response to societal and cultural demands (canned jokes) or performed spontaneously in response to ongoing interaction (situational or interpersonal joking) (Fine and Wood 303)—has provided dominant and minority groups with the weapons and shields necessary for protecting their group identity and collective consciousness from intruding outsiders or oppressive insiders.

Paradoxically, the laughter induced by the ironic deviations from the ordinary meanings of sociocultural life, traditional logic, language, and emotions (Zijderveld 299) has been utilized by dominant ethnic groups as a control mechanism for enforcing superiority (Boskin and Dorinson 97) and by minority groups either as a survival tool kit for turning ostensible "weaknesses into strengths" and "criticism into ironic self-congratulation" (Mintz 125) or as "a weapon of liberation" to "expose naked emperors and reduce their prestige" (Lowe 442; La Fave 244). Such humor, which is triggered by the unexpected shifts, abnormal drifts, double meanings, false logic, and mention of the unmentionables, not only reveals the underlying dynamics of ethnic diversity but also creates a fertile catalyst for challenging norms, subduing biases, deconstructing perceptions, and constructing new spaces where the voiced and the voiceless can be equally heard. Taking into consideration the rapid increase of racial and ethnic minorities in US higher education institutions and the dire need for addressing students' unintentional misconceptions and prejudiced preconceptions, this essay focuses on how contextualizing, deconstructing, and reconstructing humorous racial encounters in a selection of ethnic American women's poems can help undergraduate students see through traditional divisions, embrace differences, preach and practice ethnic diversity, and comprehend the dynamics of cultural intelligence and coexistence in a transcultural world.

Ethnic Humor in the Classroom: From Alienation to Integration

In his book *Distinction*, Pierre Bourdieu defines jokes in the following terms: "a joke is the art of making fun without raising anger, by means of ritual mockery or insults which are neutralized by their very excess and which, presupposing a great familiarity, both in the knowledge they use and the freedom with which they use it, are in fact tokens of affection, ways of building up while seeming to run down, of accepting while seeming to condemn" (180). Investigating ethnic humor in the classroom not only serves as an exceptional key for comprehending the ways in which groups perceive and judge one another (Apte 132) but also explains "the motivation of individuals to create and consume ethnic humor" and highlights the role "this kind of humor plays in intragroup cohesion and intergroup relations" (Shifman and Katz 844). On the one hand, ethnic humor can dissect the racial environment, probe into the wear and tear of the national fabric, identify the cracks in collective identity, and link them back to an embedded legacy of oppression and ongoing practices of vilification and subjugation. On the other hand, joking creates "comfort in group life and bolsters group relationships through a shared history" (Fine and Wood 310). Creating a community of laughter "can channel anger, celebrate survival," unite "diverse groups," and offer "a venue for alternative articulations of selfhood and community" (Andrews 4). It can also act as a conflict-alleviating strategy and provide "a mode of communication and conciliation" (Lowe 442). The tensions arising from the sensitivity of the topic and the possibility of triggering further controversial questions and heated debates are warded off by laughter, which, as Gary Alan Fine and Christine Wood maintain, "is a physical, emotional, and seemingly uncontrolled depiction of consensus" (310). Even if laughter disappears, there remains the hope, as Martin Grotjahn puts it, "that we may laugh even more merrily and with greater inner freedom when we have understood laughter better" (vii).

Contextualization, Deconstruction, and Reconstruction

To enable students to comprehend the metaphoric structure of jokes and the dense layers of meaning created by minority voices in order to delineate their dilemmas, fears, and aspirations, teachers can follow a model that involves contextualization, deconstruction, and reconstruction. Using reliable sources, including images, videos, and recordings, to stimulate students' prior knowledge of the historical, social, and cultural backgrounds in which jokes are embedded will help students "build mental models of historical eras" and situate the poets' experiences within their proper contexts (Baron 532). History, as Gail Gehrig argues, "is presented not only as information about the past, but also as a bridge to give members of dominant and minority groups a point of mutual identification" (63). Hence, to help dominant-group students focus on the psychology of prejudice and the evils of racism, the contextualization stage should also include a consideration of the first waves of European immigrants to the Americas: "Once dominant-group students have learned to identify their own groups as past minorities, they find it more difficult to dismiss the concerns of current minorities" (63). Nevertheless, to avoid relegating the evils of racism and oppression to the past or overlooking "the systemic and systematized ways that minority groups are often ignored, exploited, and oppressed on a daily basis," contextualization should establish a link between past atrocities and present prejudices (Johnson 13).

The next stage in teaching diversity through jokes is the deconstruction of the ethnic-gender dichotomies that have consistently feminized minority-group men, hyperfeminized minority-group women, and framed both as objects to be positioned, defined, and controlled by the white male subjects. "Racist meanings," as George Dei and colleagues maintain, "become historically produced through processes of contextualization, de-contextualization and re-contextualization, so by de-constructing them, we de-centre the hierarchal oppositions in which they are framed" (74). Refuting the "assumptions, expectations and contradictions that privilege Whiteness in relation to the racialized *other*" (74)—by investigating the social dynamics of humorous racial confrontations—will help students break free from the vicious circle of racially scripted self-fulfilling prophecies. Moreover, deconstructing the dichotomous master narratives of white supremacy and ethnic inferiority—which have been consciously and unconsciously standardized, assimilated, and internalized by both the oppressors and the oppressed "as 'intra-psychic' disciples and relational scripts" (74)—will pave the way for reconstructing the ethics and dynamics of ethnic diversity and transcultural agency.

The aim of the final stage is to help students perceive the immense potentials of diversity and the indispensability of cross-cultural pollination in their globalized translocal mode of living and belonging, where dividing the world "between the West and the rest; between locals and moderns, between a bloodless ethic of profit and a bloody ethic of identity; between 'us' and 'them'" can no longer be tolerated (Appiah xxi). Free-practice activities—for example, activities that ask students to imagine their lives without the invaluable contributions of ethnic minorities or to conceptualize what the future would be like if all human beings were only bound up with a collective global-centric obligation to create a better future—can help students integrate the taken-for-granted services and sacrifices of non-white groups into their conception of amalgamated intergroup relations and their perception of transcultural interdependence. Activities may also ask students to reconstruct racial encounters in jokes by creating alternative ways for building characters, narrating events, and resolving conflicts, which would open students' minds to the potentials of productive negotiation, mutual understanding, and coexistence. To give a clearer view of how ethnic humor can be effectively incorporated in undergraduate courses, the remainder of this essay focuses on the analysis of racial jokes in poems written by African American, Latin American, and Arab American women.

Ethnic American Women Poets

Feeling trapped between two worlds and accepted fully in neither, feminized in the patriarchal culture of the homeland and hyperfeminized in the majority-white, masculinized hostland, burdened with a legacy of oppression and marginalized in microcosmic and macrocosmic spheres, many ethnic American women poets have utilized subversive incongruities to renegotiate their gender and racial agency. In her poem "Still I Rise," Maya Angelou—the African American poet, author, director, and civil rights activist who has been heralded as one of America's literary giants and national treasures—humorously subverts the alleged binary oppositions that have robbed black people of their liberty, humanity, and dignity. Angelou's African American female persona rebelliously teases the reader by posing a series of rhetorical questions: "Does my sassiness upset you? / Why are you beset with gloom?," "Did you want to see me broken? / Bowed head and lowered eyes?," "Does my sexiness upset you?" Reconstructing the social realities of the oppressors and the oppressed, Angelou's poem is a celebration of the possibility of turning unspeakable racial injustices into an uncrushable dignity, unquenchable zeal for survival, and indomitable determination to thrive.

Contextualizing Angelou's poem in class using excerpts from her autobiography, *I Know Why the Caged Bird Sings,* or by showing parts of her 1968 television series *Blacks, Blues, Black!* paves the way for deconstructing the black-white dichotomy of "the powerless against the powerful, the poor against the rich, the worker against the worked for and the ragged against the well-dressed" (Angelou, *I Know* 25). Exploring humor in Angelou's "Still I Rise" helps students understand her sense of voice, agency, and empowerment: "You may kill me with your hatefulness, / But still, like air, I'll rise." Like a phoenix growing out of the ashes of subjugation, humiliation, terror, and torture, African Americans will continue to rise, blessed and entrusted with "the dream and the hope of the slave."

The mythical resilience of ancestors and their exquisite ability to overcome all adversaries are similarly conjured up by the Mexican American poet and novelist Alma Villanueva in her poem "To Jesus Villanueva with Love," which centers on the figure of the poet's grandmother, Mamacita. While involved in the rituals of reminiscence, assortment, and fortification, which aim at strengthening her Chicana identity and cleansing her value system of the self-degrading toxicants necessary for surviving in a racist hostland, Villanueva recounts her grandmother's humorous encounter with a customs officer while crossing the border from Mexico to the United States:

> [T]he U.S. customs officer
> undid everything you so
> preciously packed, you
> took a sack, blew it up
> and when he asked about
> the contents of the sack,
> well, you popped it with
> your hand and shouted
> AIRE MEXICANO. (54)

Outwitting the US official, whose prejudiced preconceptions have intensified the baggage-checking procedures and disregarded the traveler's pregnancy, has turned Mamacita into "the supernatural ancestor/woman warrior who struggled against a destructive dragon, the United States customs officer who guarded the gates of a strange, dangerous and wonderful land" (Morales 126). The Spanish punch line crystallizes the grandmother's insistence on preserving her cultural identity even if all her "preciously packed" items are suspected and scrutinized. Contextualizing the racialization of Mexican Americans and linking Mamacita's checkpoint encounter to current racist practices enables students to deconstruct the ethnic and racial myths that have branded Mexicans and Mexican Americans as inferior others. Reframing Mamacita's story within the context of preserving cultural identity helps students perceive how holding to one's values is necessary for overcoming the influences of oppression when "our identities are created for us and are positioned only in ways that define us in relation to our oppressor" (Dei et al. 75).

In her poem "How to Translate a Joke," Emtithal Mahmoud—the young Darfuri refugee and Yale University graduate who was selected as one of the BBC's one hundred most inspirational women of 2015 and became a goodwill ambassador for the United Nations High Commissioner for Refugees in 2018 (Mahmoud, "Slam")—investigates the politics and dynamics of gender and racial oppression by exploring the multiple layers of a popular joke. To teach a man how to find a date in a village market, the village playboy flirts with three women selling honey, flowers, and sugar. The first "swoons, gives him honey / and a kiss," the second "melts, gives him flowers / and a kiss," and the third "practically dies, / Gives him sugar, / And kisses him twice." In an attempt to practice the playboy's teachings, the man walks to a woman selling dairy and asks her, "*Do you have any milk, cow?*" (Mahmoud, "How" 37).

In the second part of the poem, Mahmoud elaborates how the popularity of the joke in different languages and cultures, the laughter it induces in multiple settings, the systemized objectification of those deemed inferior others, and the silence of the four women bond female grievances worldwide and trigger a series of upsetting realizations. First, such racist and sexist humor leaves little room for questioning ethnic and gender injustices; less room for humanizing, identifying, or empathizing with the victims of such injustices; and even less room for feeling guilty about actively practicing or passively witnessing prejudices against the victimized. The market, audience, schoolyard, or other men keep cheering even when "the girl's hair [is] a bracelet around his wrist" (Mahmoud, "How" 41). Second, patriarchal despotism and gender violence are not "a *third world* problem" (39). Mahmoud feels as unsafe on the streets of New York, Philly, and Indiana as on the streets of Nepal, India, Sudan, and Egypt. Third, versions of the joke may differ—depending on cultural, social, and historical contexts—yet the cycle of oppression, resistance, and submission is consistent in all versions. The man may be searching for a date, a wife, or an answer, yet the cow in the punch line will continue to be regarded as the silent, marginalized other. If she dares to challenge the established sociocultural order of ethnic-gender racism, she will be unjustifiably condemned, while the aggressor will be safely acquitted.

Unlike the triumphant female voices in Angelou's and Villanueva's poems, who could tease, outwit, and defy their oppressors, the butt of Mahmoud's joke—the man searching for a date—locks his victims in a cycle of systematic violation and suppression. In the last part of the poem, Mahmoud reconstructs the joke by rewriting the endings of the four encounters. The man looking for a date "leaves with an unwilling woman," the girl selling honey "gives him her eyes, / her arms, her silence" ("How" 39), the girl selling sugar "practically dies" (39), and the girl selling flowers is stripped of "her thorns," stuck "in a bouquet," broken and "trampled in the market" (39–40). In the second version of the joke, the women remain silent, yet the scenes are tragic rather than humorous, alerting readers to the "normalizing spheres of influence" that "silently constitute the oppressed minorities and shape their social reality" (Dei et al. 73–74).

These poems help students identify how racial humor and gender irony have been utilized to subvert prejudiced presumptions. Each poem challenges misconceptions within contexts of playfulness and laughter, allowing students to revisit histories, rethink normative values, and see societal roles anew. When these jokes are contextualized, students are able to perceive how ethnic minority groups have been agonizingly sewn into the fabric of American society. Meanwhile, the deconstruction of appropriate incongruities and the reconstruction of the ironic renderings of ethnic and gender biases enable students to see through traditional divisions, embrace differences, and comprehend the dynamics of cultural intelligence and coexistence in a transcultural world.

Works Cited

Andrews, Jennifer. *In the Belly of a Laughing God: Humour and Irony in Native Women's Poetry*. U of Toronto P, 2011.
Angelou, Maya. *I Know Why the Caged Bird Sings*. Random House, 1970.
———. "Still I Rise." *Poetry Foundation*, 2022, www.poetryfoundation.org/poems/46446/still-i-rise.
Appiah, Kwame Anthony. *Cosmopolitanism: Ethics in a World of Strangers*. W. W. Norton, 2006.
Apte, Mahadev L. *Humor and Laughter: An Anthropological Approach*. Cornell UP, 1985.
Baron, Christine. "Using Embedded Visual Coding to Support Contextualization of Historical Texts." *American Educational Research Journal*, vol. 53, no. 3, 2016, pp. 516–40.
Blacks, Blues, Black! Created by Maya Angelou, KQED, 1968.
Boskin, Joseph, and Joseph Dorinson. "Ethnic Humor: Subversion and Survival." *American Quarterly*, vol. 37, no. 1, 1985, pp. 81–97.
Bourdieu, Pierre. *Distinction*. Harvard UP, 1984.
Dei, George J. Sefa, et al. "Theorizing Power: Rupturing Dichotomies." *Counterpoints*, vol. 244, 2004, pp. 59–80.
Fine, Gary Alan, and Christine Wood. "Accounting for Jokes: Jocular Performance in a Critical Age." *Western Folklore*, vol. 69, nos. 3–4, 2010, pp. 299–321.
Gehrig, Gail. "Strategies for Teaching Greater Tolerance of Cultural Diversity." *Teaching Sociology*, vol. 19, no. 1, 1991, pp. 62–65.
Grotjahn, Martin. *Beyond Laughter*. McGraw-Hill, 1957.
Johnson, Brian C. "Guidelines for Teaching Diversity." *Counterpoints*, vol. 474, 2015, pp. 11–20.
La Fave, Lawrence. "Ethnic Humor: From Paradoxes toward Principles." *It's a Funny Thing, Humour*, edited by A. Chapman and H. Foot, Pergamon, 1977, pp. 233–59.
Lowe, John. "Theories of Ethnic Humor: How to Enter, Laughing." *American Quarterly*, vol. 38, no. 3, 1986, pp. 439–60.

Mahmoud, Emtithal. "How to Translate a Joke." *Sisters' Entrance*, by Mahmoud, Andrews McMeel, 2018, pp. 37–43.
———. "Slam from Sudan: How Emtithal Mahmoud Shook the World." Interview by Alison Flood. *The Guardian*, 2 July 2018, www.theguardian.com/books/2018/jul/02/emtithal-mahmoud-emi-interview-slam-poet-activist-sudan.
Mintz, Lawrence E. "The Rabbi versus the Priest and Other Jewish Stories." *Jewish Humor*, edited by Avner Ziv, Transaction Publishers, 1998, pp. 125–34.
Morales, Alejandro. "Terra Mater and the Emergence of Myth in 'Poems' by Alma Villanueva." *Bilingual Review*, vol. 7, no. 2, 1980, pp. 123–42.
Shifman, Limor, and Elihu Katz. "'Just Call Me Adonai': A Case Study of Ethnic Humor and Immigrant Assimilation." *American Sociological Review*, vol. 70, no. 5, 2005, pp. 843–59.
Villanueva, Alma. "To Jesus Villanueva with Love." *Blood Root*, by Villanueva, Place of Herons, 1977, pp. 52–54.
Zijderveld, Anton C. "Jokes and Their Relation to Social Reality." *Social Research*, vol. 35, no. 2, 1968, pp. 286–311.

Miriam Chirico

Dark Laughter and Sexual Trauma in Paula Vogel's *How I Learned to Drive*

Some time before the sexual misconduct accusation drove Louis C.K.'s career to a swift halt, C.K. riffed briefly about pedophilia on *Saturday Night Live*. In the cold opening that in retrospect seems correlated to his larger transgressions, he offered a comic anecdote of the creepy sex offender who pursued everyone in the neighborhood except for C.K.; "he didn't like me," C.K. quips, pretending to feel left out; "I felt a little bad" ("Louis C.K. Monologue" 6:00). As he continues the monologue, he invites the audience to consider the intensity of the pedophile's sexual desires by drawing a comparison to his own love for chocolate candy: "If somebody said to me, 'if you eat another Mounds bar you will go to jail and everyone will hate you,' I would stop eating them" (8:05), he reasons, thus logically implying that the pedophile must lack this ability to regulate his aberrant longings. As we watch C.K. maneuvering this comic bit, as he struggles to cast pedophilia in a humorous light, it is crucial to consider the push-pull dynamic with the audience; the audience's nervous yet tolerant laughter reveals much about the nature of dark humor. For C.K.'s comedic routine operates on two levels: first, C.K.'s anecdote showcasing the sexual predator's inability to change even under threat of imprisonment posits that pedophilia is a psychiatric disease; and second, the humor drawn from C.K.'s routine, such as his self-impersonation of joyfully indulging in Mounds bars, entices the audience to lower their guard and to laugh at something criminal and morally repugnant. Many criticized the skit as going too far in trying to elicit sympathy for sex offenders, but that is precisely the risk of morbid humor. Black comedy, also known as dark comedy, trolls in ambiguous and unsettling areas; the anxious laughter it provokes is the sound of audiences adjusting or loosening their ethical boundaries.

Twenty years before C.K.'s monologue, Paula Vogel examined the same topic in comedic form. Her play *How I Learned to Drive*, which earned her a Pulitzer Prize, considers an incestuous relationship between a teenage girl and her older uncle, narrated as a series of flashbacks from the woman's perspective many years later. The controversial aspect of Vogel's work lay in her sympathetic portrayal of the pedophiliac character, Uncle Peck, depicting how he empowers his young niece through their driving lessons, and in her hinting at psychological reasons for his illicit behavior. In handling such inherently troubling material, Vogel relied on nonnaturalistic techniques to lessen the impact of Peck's sexual predation: first, the events are performed in reverse chronological order so that Peck's crude encounter with his niece, L'il Bit, delayed until the play's end, does not define him. Second, three actors—listed in the cast as Male Greek Chorus, Female Greek Chorus, and Teenage Greek Chorus—adopt different roles, ranging from family members to high school classmates. This Brechtian multirole technique reminds the audience that the play is a representation of events that have already occurred; the moment Uncle Peck masturbates himself against his eleven-year-old niece, a member of the Greek chorus stands in for L'il Bit. Third, L'il Bit is not presented as a child but as a thirty-five-year-old woman who both narrates and participates in scenes from her past. Consequently, the play is understood as a character's reconstruction of the events rather than as a living through of the events, a process that provides L'il Bit with control over her own life.[1] However, a significant distancing device that is overlooked is Vogel's deployment of humor, both in the main character's tonal perspective and in comedic scenes. Vogel incorporates humor to engage the audience with the topic of child sexual abuse without the blinders of moral indignation. Her use of dark comedy encourages audiences to lower their ethical threshold long enough to engage earnestly in a societal failing.

This essay focuses on teaching *How I Learned to Drive* and on how to make explicit the discordant tones of dark humor—a form many college students are already well familiar with from television shows such as *Curb Your Enthusiasm, Breaking Bad,* and *South Park*. Vogel's dark comic sensibility appears in many of her plays: "Maybe it's a survival strategy," she explains, "Some people say that this comes from Jewish genes." Carl Vogel, her brother who died of AIDS-related complications, shared this dark humor, as evidenced by his instructions regarding his funeral: "Well, I want a good show, even though my role has been reduced involuntarily from player to prop" (qtd. in Mansbridge 146). The laughter in Vogel's play, like her brother's blithe comments about his own death, are perspectival choices that alter how one approaches a sensitive topic. As a category, dark comedy traffics in the unhappier side of life; it laughs at death, disease, and depression; it jokes about actions such as rape and murder; and it scoffs at social or moral taboos, such as incest, suicide, or in this case pedophilia. Humor is known for pushing boundaries and often offending people, but dark comedy deliberately courts the possibility of upsetting others by poking fun at serious or sacred topics. An audience's resistance to joking about a topic demarcates what makes us uncomfortable or what we cannot face, as C.K. discovered in his audience's unwillingness to cross conceptually a moral boundary. Vogel's intention with *How I Learned to Drive* is not much different than C.K.'s in asking people to analyze the dynamic between an abuser and the victim: "I sometimes feel that being in that kind of mind set of victimization causes almost as much trauma as the original abuse. And so in many ways I think I felt that it's a mistake to demonize the people who hurt us, and that's how I wanted to approach the play" (qtd. in Griffiths 107). Vogel uses dark humor to invite audience consideration of sexual trauma.

 I strongly recommend providing students with a content or trigger warning ahead of time. It is important that students are aware that the play involves a child sexual offender and his niece, so that students might prepare themselves for class discussions, particularly in the light of the play's comic framing of the topic (see Levin's valuable discussion of trigger warnings in literature classes). Most of my students choose to engage in the play's moral ambiguities, but I have encountered students whose past experiences prevented them from attending class. I cannot discount their reaction to the play, as reliable studies have shown that as many as one in three girls is abused before the age of eighteen and that thirty-four percent of people who abuse a child are family members; nor can I assume that those who willingly explore the play have *not* suffered such abuse. The play, controversial when produced off-Broadway in 1997, may prove even more divisive to teach following the increased exposure of Catholic priests' sexual abuse against children and the Me Too movement's public revelations, but that does not mean such topics should be avoided in class. In fact, Manhattan Theater Company's choice to revive the play on Broadway, with the same actors as in the original production, speaks to the cast's belief that audiences need to engage with such "deeply damaging relationships caused by . . . trusted authority figures" (Vogel et al.). Since public perception regarding child sexual offenders is myopically negative, based on stereotypes of "dirty old men" and "stranger danger," teaching *How I Learned to Drive* encourages an open-minded consideration of a character who cares about his niece but whose behavior is criminal. Vogel's oft quoted description of the play is key to this paradox: "My play dramatizes the gifts we receive from the people who hurt us" ("Through the Eyes").

To begin discussion of the play, I state my own stance as someone who deplores child sexual abuse and violence against children; I explain the difference between the terms *pedophile* and *child sexual offender* (Wurtele), and I provide students with a clear definition of *sexual abuse* as the wrongful touching of another individual for the purpose of sexual gratification. Furthermore, I ensure students are familiar with the current state laws regarding the legal age of consent, which can be easily found on the Internet (Glosser et al.). Comparing the various state laws concerning statutory rape offenses not only provides a clear frame to discuss Peck's actions, as his actions are unmistakably criminal, but also illustrates the social constructivist nature of laws that differ from state to state—and even over time. Vogel's characters reveal this ambiguity regarding statutory rape when Grandmother defends herself against potential criticism of her young marital age: "it was legal, what Daddy and I did! I was fourteen and in those days, fourteen was a grown-up woman" (Vogel, *Mammary Plays* 17). The instructor should use the societal ambiguity in the construction of laws as a conduit toward asking students to consider the moral ambiguity governing the sexual relationship between the uncle and his niece. The play delves into complicated societal mores, the domain of dark comedy.

As a literary form, dark comedy flippantly recasts tragic subjects in a humorous light through the use of narrative voice and point of view. These elements are typically the domain of fiction, not drama, yet *How I Learned to Drive* manipulates tone and perspective by situating L'il Bit as the onstage narrator. By reading aloud her opening monologue with students, I ensure that we take our direction from L'il Bit's tone and its emotional coolness, so indicative of dark comedy. L'il Bit is a sardonic narrator from the outset, taking the audience into her confidence, admitting how she is "very old, very cynical of the world" (Vogel, *Mammary Plays* 7). It's important to guide students into hearing the facetious attitude that L'il Bit takes toward her own story, found, for example, in her reference to Canadian whiskey as "a constant companion in [her] dorm room" or her jesting description of men's obsessive fascination with cars: "Long after he's squeezed down the birth canal but before he's pushed his way back in: The boy falls in love with the thing that bears his weight with speed" (46). On the one hand, her laughter may be understood as a posture, the sign of a grown-up woman looking at men not as predators but as puerile. On the other hand, it is fair to read L'il Bit's tone as a mask—that is, her wryness is the resulting attitude of a young girl who has been forced to grow up too soon. As a young victim of sexual abuse, she has learned how to be seductive and adopt certain behaviors to feel in control when circumstances are not normal. L'il Bit assumes responsibility for her sexual involvement with Uncle Peck, particularly in how she rewards him romantically as an incentive to stop him from drinking. Some students may (rightly) resist her decision to take ownership in this affair and see her behavior toward her uncle as the maladaptive behavior a victim develops in an abusive relationship. These students interpret the joking voice as an act, a pose to hide her divided self. As she acknowledges, using language similar to survivors of sexual abuse, she no longer resides in her body but in her head (90), and one could argue that her comic voice and her sexuality exist in separate spheres of her divided consciousness. A fertile discussion could follow the question, "What does L'il Bit's sardonic tone represent: power over her circumstances or shame?"

After establishing L'il Bit's wry perspective as prohibiting sentimentality, we work to consider the play's treatment of sexuality, particularly sexual objectification and gender formation of girls and young women.[2] Students readily pick up on the family's bawdy sexual references in the nicknames originating from a humorous appraisal of genitalia, such as "Big Papa," "Uncle Peck," and even "Lil Bit," and on the grandfather's belittling L'il Bit's aspirations to go to college: "What does she need a college degree for? She's got all the credentials on her chest" (Vogel, *Mammary Plays* 17). Students, sensitive to the body shaming L'il Bit experiences from her family and her high school classmates, readily point out these scenes of sexual objectification; they mention the classmates who discount that her breasts are real and gawk at her in the gym shower or the young man who only wishes to dance with L'il Bit because of the persuasive power her breasts have over him. In addition, it is worth underscoring the scene's sci-fi parody: Vogel's tongue-in-cheek portrayal of men's fascination with breasts is evidenced in the high-pitched beeps, like those of a homing beacon, emanating from L'il Bit's breasts. Similarly, in the opening scene, "[s]acred music, organ music, or a boy's choir" (12) begins to play when L'il Bit opens her shirt for her uncle, hyperbolically showcasing Peck's ecstasy by equating the view of L'il Bit's breasts with a celestial ensemble. Calling attention to the humor of these scenes does more than just illustrate an overlooked joke; Vogel is deliberately connecting this sexual objectification by others—ridiculous though it may seem—to L'il Bit's growing awareness of herself as attractive to men. As uncomfortable as it is to acknowledge the power of the objectified, students must be nudged toward seeing this dualism in the play. L'il Bit understands how her allure lies in the physical attractiveness of her breasts, by which she is objectified, yet which conversely gives her power, as when she barters her sexual appeal in exchange for curtailing Uncle Peck's alcoholism. She demonstrates her insight regarding the manipulable nature of male desire when she sardonically quips that the automobile is the "boy's first love," a love that falls somewhere between "a mother's tits, but before a woman's breasts" (46). The play is structured, as Joanna Mansbridge notes, to provide the audience with the pedophile's point of view as well: "Vogel brings into often uncomfortable focus the implications of the 'Lolita' myth—the myth of a female sexuality that is both innocent and cunning, available and active—placing this myth in direct tension with the stigmatized pedophile" (127). Through a humorous treatment of male longing, from high school adolescents to Uncle Peck, Vogel highlights female sexuality for what it is: sought after and objectified as well as powerful and seductive.

Dark humor's utility comes to the fore in Vogel's attack on hypocrisy. In the production notes to the piece (*Mammary Plays* 5), Vogel advises directors to use music suggestive of cultural pedophilia in order to emphasize societal complicity—for instance, "You're Sixteen" (Johnny Burnette, 1960), "Little Surfer Girl" (The Beach Boys, 1963), or "This Girl Is a Woman Now" (Gary Puckett and the Union Gap, 1969). In playing these songs to students or in sharing the lyrics in class, I demonstrate how society replicates an ideology about the magical transformation of adolescent girls into womanhood, even though in the play the only character who is shown to act on this belief is Uncle Peck. Though the lyrics of these older songs may strike some students as depraved because of the emphasis on the untouched and childlike beauty of young girls, I ask students to consider how today's music inculcates behavioral mores within a generation, and I even ask students to bring song lyrics to class.[3] Vogel's directorial recommendation to "have fun" (5) with the music selections for the production is meant to showcase society's own waggish—rather than critical—attitude toward the frank desire for underage women embedded in the lyrics. The sound design's darkly humorous ploy exposes the public's hypocrisy in condemning sexual abuse while simultaneously condoning illicit attitudes toward women's sexuality in popular culture.

A similar plot operates in a monologue called "A Mother's Guide to Social Drinking" (Vogel, *Mammary Plays* 24–30), which is reminiscent of stand-up with its direct address to the audience. The speech uses dark humor to indict societal attitudes that proscribe women's behavior and establish unequal gender norms. I ask students to consider the speech as social indoctrination—that is, how L'il Bit's mother, played by a member of the Greek chorus, provides biased instruction to L'il Bit and to other young women on how they should comport themselves to avoid being sexually compromised. "A Mother's Guide to Social Drinking" acts as a contrapuntal frame to a scene between Uncle Peck and L'il Bit: he has invited L'il Bit to a restaurant to celebrate earning her driver's license and encourages her to drink to the point of intoxication. The mother's wry commentary to girls to avoid becoming intoxicated in social situations is doubly ironic because, first, it goes unheeded, and, second, the mother grows tipsy herself. She comically advises young girls to "[s]tay away from *ladies'* drinks" by listing colorful, sexually provocative drinks, "black Russians, red Russians, melon balls, blue balls," as examples, and she warns against ordering drinks with "sexual positions in the name like Dead Man Screw or the Missionary" (24). She warns of how men drug women through their alcoholic drinks and that women must be caretakers of their own virtue by wearing girdles "so tight that only a surgical knife or acetylene torch can get it off" (29). She cheerfully recommends ways a woman should ensure self-control, such as dunking her head in water to sober up, "because a wet woman is less conspicuous than a drunk woman" (27), a direct echo of Florence King's jibe at southern propriety: "to a Southerner it is *faux pas*, not sins, that matter in this world" (12). The incongruity between the mother's jovial patter and Peck carrying an incapacitated L'il Bit to the car could not be more unsettling; it is clear that L'il Bit cannot defend herself from her uncle, yet Vogel lures the audience into laughter at the mother's lighthearted proscriptions encouraging women to protect their virtue. The comedy of this scene serves a specific purpose, as it does for many other southern women writers: "Black humor," Barbara Bennett notes, "serves as a powerful vehicle for questioning and attacking the social structures behind those values that limit or restrict the roles of women" (64). The audience's laughter is caused by the mother's tipsy words but is directed at Uncle Peck's control over L'il Bit. Consequently, their laughter at this dangerous situation signals their acceptance, for, as Vogel reminds us, "comedy is complicity" ("Through the Eyes"). It's hard to indict Uncle Peck's behavior when we all seem to be in on the joke.

Vogel's play problematizes the traditional victimization paradigm vis-à-vis child sexual abuse; she refrains from resting blame entirely on Uncle Peck's shoulders and challenges audience members to examine their own attitudes toward sexuality. The play asks them to focus attention on the transaction of power embedded in family incest. It asks them to consider pedophilia and delay their immediate condemnation of the abuse in order to hear L'il Bit's story. Comedy may be the ideal zone for treading such tricky waters; the humorous tone cues the audience to laugh at lighthearted cultural references or L'il Bit's saucy narrative, thereby lessening the blinkered disapproval one feels toward Peck. Without siding with Uncle Peck, Vogel acknowledges that any progress on matters regarding sexual abuse involves examining multiple dimensions: "In this time of political correctness," she expresses, "you have to go against the grain. If audiences don't embrace both sides of an issue, there can be no real political dialogue" (qtd in. Drukman). Dark comedy gets past unilateral thinking and opens up an issue for true debate. Vogel uses dark comedy as an exploratory tool that encourages an audience to consider and redress sexually exploitative relationships.

Notes

1. As scholars have pointed out, L'il Bit's control over her own narrative enables her to resist the traditional victimization paradigm. Mansbridge analyzes the play as an enactment of memory retrieval, whereby L'il Bit gives "shape to her memories and forms them into a newly made self . . . [due to] the reparative possibilities of performance" (126). Griffiths argues that "L'il Bit acknowledges a traumatic event but also asks us to recognize her capacity of creating meaning from this experience and her response to it" (98).

2. An APA task force report on the sexualization of girls enumerates four conditions or indicators of sexualization, including "sexuality is inappropriately imposed upon a person" (APA Task Force 1).

3. Smiler and colleagues compare trends in song lyrics from the 1960s to the early twenty-first century, documenting how women were more likely to sing

about dating and love, while men were more likely to objectify others, especially women. Their article provides sample lyrics used for coding their research as an example of sexual standards embedded in songs.

Works Cited

APA Task Force on the Sexualization of Girls. *Report of the APA Task Force on the Sexualization of Girls*. American Psychological Association, 2010, www.apa.org/pi/women/programs/girls/report-full.pdf.

Bennett, Barbara. *Comic Visions, Female Voices: Contemporary Women Novelists and Southern Humor*. Louisiana State UP, 1998.

Drukman, Steven. "A Playwright on the Edge Turns toward the Middle." *The New York Times*, 16 Mar. 1997, sec. 2, p. 6.

Glosser, Asaph, et al. *Statutory Rape: A Guide to State Laws and Reporting Requirements*. Office of the Assistant Secretary for Planning and Evaluation, U.S. Department of Health and Human Services, 15 Dec. 2004, aspe.hhs.gov/sites/default/files/migrated_legacy_files//42881/report.pdf.

Griffiths, Jennifer. "Sympathy for the Devil: Resiliency and Victim-Perpetrator Dynamics in Paula Vogel's *How I Learned to Drive*." *Contemporary Women's Writing*, vol. 7, no. 1, Mar. 2013, pp. 92–110.

King, Florence. *Southern Ladies and Gentlemen*. 1975. Reprint ed., Griffin, 1993.

Levin, Kate. "'The Course of Her Whimsical Adventures': 'Fantomina' and Trigger Warnings at a Women's College." *Pedagogy*, vol. 18, no. 3, Oct. 2018, pp. 550–65.

"Louis C.K. Monologue - SNL." *YouTube*, uploaded by Saturday Night Live, 17 May 2015, www.youtube.com/watch?v=yzh7RtIJKZk.

Mansbridge, Joanna. *Paula Vogel*. U of Michigan P, 2014. Michigan Modern Dramatists.

Smiler, Andrew P., et al. "From 'I Want to Hold Your Hand' to 'Promiscuous': Sexual Stereotypes in Popular Music Lyrics, 1960–2008." *Sexuality and Culture*, vol. 21, no. 4, Dec. 2017, pp. 1083–105.

Vogel, Paula. *The Mammary Plays:* How I Learn to Drive, The Mineola Twins. Theatre Communications Group, 1998.

———. "Through the Eyes of Lolita: Pulitzer Prize–winning Playwright Paula Vogel Is Interviewed by Arthur Holmberg." *American Repertory Theater*, 18 Sept. 1998, americanrepertorytheater.org/media/through-the-eyes-of-lolita/.

Vogel, Paula, et al. "How They Learned to Drive. And Why They're Driving Again." Interview conducted by Laura Collins-Hughes. *The New York Times*, 25 Feb. 2020, www.nytimes.com/2020/02/25/theater/how-i-learned-to-drive-broadway-vogel.html.

Wurtele, Sandy K. "University Students' Perceptions of Child Sexual Offenders: Impact of Classroom Instruction." *Journal of Child Sexual Abuse*, vol. 27, no. 3, 2018, pp. 276–91.

James Zeigler

Who's Stupid? Teaching Histories with *Gentlemen Prefer Blondes*

It's funny that in Anita Loos's *Gentlemen Prefer Blondes* the protagonist Lorelei's ridiculous ignorance is not ultimately the target of the novel's mockery. Composed entirely of Lorelei's diary entries, which are rife with laughable grammar, misspellings, confusion, and errors, the narrative really punches up at male chauvinism. Lorelei proves to be no more opportunistic than the novel's parade of male suitors who appraise her sex appeal and pursue her as an illicit mistress or trophy wife. They underestimate her unconventional intelligence, and so might we without careful reading. While the men seek to objectify and control her, she manipulates their physical attraction to make them pay her way. Usually, her way involves going where she likes to entertain herself whether or not her benefactors approve of her plans. The seemingly transactional nature of her arrangements may suggest that she trades in sex, but ambiguity in all the novel's episodes means it's possible she may only monetize her allure. In any event, she remains impressively uneducated and yet possesses a discerning control over her admirers. Lorelei appreciates that diamonds add luster to her looks, but her diary also shows her uncanny understanding of how precious gems make excellent capital. Just three years before Virginia Woolf famously instructed an audience of wealthy women about the value of possessing "a room of one's own," Loos prepared a comparable lesson with this fictional, ribald diary of a woman raised poor in parochial Little Rock, Arkansas, who has grown up to realize that diamonds are a girl's best friend for good reason. They are a dependable investment. Different from the resolution of the more famous film adaptation from 1953 starring Marilyn Monroe, in the original 1925 novel Lorelei's ambition and social intelligence finally launch her career overseeing a film production company that takes over the grounds of her new father-in-law's estate. In the end, she has married the rich son of a wealthier father, but she negotiates for creative control, emerging in the final journal entry of the novel as an unexpected example of the new woman of the 1920s: an authoritative and savvy boss of a professional enterprise.

The novel's invitation to revel in women's liberation is also risky. This comedy about gender roles is complicated by a signature consideration in the study of satire: the distinction between mention and use. To expose sexist tropes to scrutiny, the novel must invoke them. Putting sexism into evidence for the purpose of critique risks replicating it by accident. If Lorelei's errors occasion laughter at her expense rather than at the stereotypes her character illustrates, then these mentions of sexist preconceptions cross over into use for comic effects that participate in sexist bigotry. Presented with familiar negative conceits about women, sexist readers may be able to read a text such as *Gentlemen Prefer Blondes* in order to confirm rather than challenge their biases. Loos's characterization of Lorelei hazards interpretations that concentrate on observing that her apparent stupidity is no impediment to her defining features: the brilliance of her looks and her compulsive greed, which together make her rich with other people's money. Such readings may seem to hew close to the text. Lorelei is indisputably ignorant and materialistic. She does exploit her sexuality to gain wealth and influence. Plus, her glaring errors are frequently amusing. However, to regard her intelligence failures and selfishness as innate or even typical expressions of her sex without subjecting the men to identical scrutiny would be a misogynistic interpretation that polices women for offenses that are afforded to men without penalties (Manne 33).

Drawing on my experience teaching *Gentlemen Prefer Blondes* several times in an American literature course that surveys writing from the end of the US Civil War to the present, I offer an account of the novel's curricular value. My lesson plans build on the risky intricacy of the novel's critique of sexism in order to develop instruction on different ways to contextualize literature historically.

Gentlemen Prefer Blondes in Literature Surveys

Gentlemen Prefer Blondes has proven especially rewarding for addressing a challenge when teaching survey courses in literature at the university level. Such courses introduce students to a representative sampling of influential texts in various genres and media across a long period of time. Addressed to English majors, education majors, and students satisfying a general education requirement in the humanities, my course includes units on the American Renaissance, realism, modernism, and postmodernism. Literary Histories of Stupidity is the course's provocative subtitle. The required readings concern the representation, evaluation, and consequences of being intelligent or not. Moving expeditiously through representative texts from different periods tends to emphasize the succession of literary examples to the neglect of the historical circumstances in which the texts were composed, published, and received. One challenge, then, of teaching surveys is to check the forward momentum of chronological order in order to supplement the account of literary history with insight into social conditions that contribute to the significance of the assigned readings.

By countering the built-in emphasis on literature's progression across time, the survey provides a chance to examine the importance of historical context in the discipline of literary studies. In other words, a liability inherent to surveys can be repurposed for metacognitive benefit: learning to reflect on how we think about and formulate history when we study it. However, with much literature to cover in limited time, asking students to think about historiography is a tall order. *Gentlemen Prefer Blondes* can help. It provides for efficient practice with multiple perspectives toward historical contexts. My survey course focuses on three: literary history, social history, and reception history. Examining *Gentlemen Prefer Blondes* in relation to these historical frameworks also enriches the treatment of the novel. Each provides a different orientation to the challenge of adjudicating between, on one side, the novel's satire of patriarchal gender norms in each of its episodes and, on the other side, the comic resolution of the narrative in which Lorelei attains wealth and standing without having appreciably redressed her ignorance. Another way to pose this dilemma is that it is hard to know what to think of Lorelei's character. Consider her the "quintessential gold-digger," as the *Sex in the City* author Candace Bushnell does in her introduction to the 1998 reissue of *Gentlemen Prefer Blondes* (xiv), and Lorelei is held to a higher standard than are her men suitors. Blaming her for expressing her sexuality in that way is now called "slut shaming." My students' familiarity with the anti-bullying edict not to "slut shame" has frequently helped in class discussion. At the same time, Lorelei's success at the resolution of the narrative is not a good reason to regard her as a role model for women who seek sexual equality at work, home, and everywhere else. Instead, the book's attention to equality between women and men relies on our reading around Lorelei to arrive at the novel's holistic ridicule of sexism.

Three Kinds of History: Literary, Social, Reception

Gentlemen Prefer Blondes is an instructive and fun choice for introducing students to stylistic innovations that distinguish literary modernism. Most notably, the epistolary form of the novel mimics the stream-of-consciousness narration found in canonical works by James Joyce, William Faulkner, Woolf, and others. *Gentlemen Prefer Blondes* begins with an entry dated 16 March:

> A gentleman friend and I were dining at the Ritz last evening and he said that if I took a pencil and a paper and put down all of my thoughts it would make a book. This almost made me smile as what it would really make would be a whole new row of encyclopediacs. I mean I seem to be thinking practically all of the time. I mean it is my favorite recreation and sometimes I sit for hours and do not seem to do anything else but think. (Loos, *Gentlemen* 3)

Pretending to hold a diary, we read Lorelei's thoughts as she recorded them, which is not the same as inhabiting the consciousness of, for example, Molly Bloom as her thoughts race in the last chapter of Joyce's *Ulysses*. Still, the unruly grammar and idiosyncratic spelling of Lorelei's diary participates in the modernist tendency to create an impression of immediate connection with the interior life of a character.

I include *Gentlemen Prefer Blondes* in a constellation of modernist texts: Charlie Chaplin's film *Modern Times*, Henry James's *Turn of the Screw*, T. S. Eliot's "The Love Song of J. Alfred Prufrock," Nella Larsen's *Passing*, and James Cain's *Double Indemnity*. These texts represent individuals struggling with feelings of alienation that distress their psychologies and confound their perceptions. Lorelei is different. The content of her interior monologue is unstrained. A punch-line moment of the novel comes when she spends time in Vienna and participates in a single session of psychoanalysis with "Dr. Froyd." Shocked by her unrestrained impulsiveness, he counsels her "to cultivate a few inhibitions and get some sleep" (Loos, *Gentlemen* 118–19). Her consciousness is a program of action, and the diary's style echoes that mentality and records its consequences.

My polemical introduction to the novel's resourcefulness for social history (i.e., the context in which it was written and first read) is to ask students how many have read *The Great Gatsby*. It is still assigned reliably in many high schools. With several hands in the air, I grin and declare that *Gentlemen Prefer Blondes* will simply be better. I then acknowledge that the preference is no doubt personal, that their having read *Gatsby* is, well, good, but that I'm sincere in my conviction that *Gentlemen Prefer Blondes* has superior explanatory power for our consideration of the Roaring Twenties. Lorelei's glamorous travels from New York to Paris, London, and Vienna display an elite cosmopolitan culture and undermine its pretensions not with tragic failure but with Lorelei's immunity to discriminating between cultivated taste and conspicuous consumption.

The understated social history that is important for appreciating the novel's significance for its original audience is the suffragette movement in the United States. In the summer of 1920, white female citizens finally secured the right to vote. Lorelei never speaks of suffrage, and neither does her friend Dorothy. The record of their conversations is never political. But the unwitting transcription of Dorothy's wry remarks about Lorelei's mercenary flirtations provides a foil with at least two levels of significance. Dorothy's insights bring into relief Lorelei's brilliant scheming and her obliviousness to moral offense. In the storyworld of *Gentlemen Prefer Blondes*, Dorothy teases Lorelei, and those jokes, while funny, also function for us as straight lines that show how other people foolishly assume that Lorelei is unintelligent. Dorothy witnesses how Lorelei's unlikely schemes work. Moreover, her difference from Lorelei's aspiration to join the wealthy provides the novel with the perspective of an ostensibly middle-class woman enjoying a vacation while her enterprising friend seeks a permanent position among the wealthy. In other words, Dorothy is a self-possessed and independent person whose fortunes will depend on the stability of civil institutions shared and coordinated by citizens who vote. Lorelei, in contrast, endeavors to accumulate so much fortune that she will escape any degree of dependence on other people. The happy irony of the book's conclusion is that when Lorelei achieves this dream she becomes devoted to people who depend on her.

Reading Bushnell's introduction against Loos's 1963 preface, "The Biography of a Book," is a useful introduction to reception history. Sharing selections from an article such as Jason Barrett-Fox's study of Loos's rhetorical strategy of indirect feminist critique could add an academic contribution to the history of how the novel has been interpreted since its original publication. However, the most influential chapter so far in the reception history of *Gentlemen Prefer Blondes* is the film from 1953. Indeed, this Hollywood musical's reputation overshadows the novel. Most of my students begin our course knowing something about the movie and nothing of the book. Whether screened in its entirety or in a limited selection of clips, the film is a reliable prompt for further discussion of both the novel's form and its representation of women. I ask students to write in class and then talk about how faithful the film is to the original and what big decisions were required for the adaptation.

In the "Diamonds Are a Girl's Best Friend" song and dance production, Marilyn Monroe's Lorelei is a professional entertainer whose performance is a metafictional play within the film (*Gentlemen* 01:08:50–01:14:20). Her singing and choreography replicate her offstage behavior to the distress of the suitor in the audience whom she will finally marry. With numerous handsome young men dancing in tuxedos while vying for her affections, Monroe's Lorelei commands the men's movements while voicing her impassioned fixation on diamonds instead of them. Students have been quick to note that Monroe's bombshell Hollywood iconicity amplifies the insinuation that Lorelei is promiscuous. We have speculated about whether the visual medium of film fails to convey the force of the book's satirical targeting of sexism. But we have also acknowledged that this adaptation of an epistolary novel to a Hollywood musical involves a clever transmission of Lorelei's authority. As the novel progresses through successive diary entries that follow Lorelei's longer episodes of international travel, her enjoyment and prosperity resonate with the genre in which she writes. The epistolary mode puts her in charge; she may be laughably uninformed, but she's also an authority who commands our attention. As it has for my students each time I teach *Gentlemen Prefer Blondes*, observing the agency of Lorelei singing and dancing in the film has helped me appreciate the intelligence of Loos's choice to use the epistolary form to make us work to realize the regard for Lorelei that she ultimately warrants in the story.

The Conclusion of *Gentlemen Prefer Blondes*

For all the incisive satirical fun of this epistolary and episodic novel, the resolution of the plot prioritizes comedy over satire. In the end, adversity has been overcome and the protagonist is rewarded with standing that engenders a harmonious community. The final diary entry catalogs how Lorelei's new relatives and many employees are happy as a result of their shared involvement in the movie business that she has created with her in-laws' wealth and property:

> So Henry says that I have opened up a whole new world for him and he has never been so happy in his life. And it really seems as if everyone I know has never been so happy in their lives. . . . And Henry's sister has never been so happy since the Battle of Verdun, because she has six trucks and 15 horses to look after and she says that the motion picture profession is the nearest thing to war that she has struck since the Armistice. (Loos, *Gentlemen* 163–64)

The film ends in a double wedding for Lorelei and Dorothy. In the novel, Lorelei's final success is more than romantic. Secure with affluence that she applies to her dream of making movies, she becomes generous. Her final entry shares her satisfaction that everyone around her is happy, and she acknowledges her responsibility for continuing to lead the movie enterprise for the sake of others. She still misunderstands plenty and remains comically naive about facts that are accessible to other characters and to us. The above description of her unnamed sister-in-law is a good example. Lorelei's innocence in the passage contributes to the novel's critique of sexism. She characterizes her sister-in-law with a factual description. Nothing in the passage suggests that Lorelei questions or judges the appropriateness of her sister-in-law's unconventional appearance or unusual preferences for work. The diary registers that her sister-in-law's satisfaction at work recalls her happy memories of taking part in one of the deadliest battles of the First World War. Estimated fatalities exceeded 300,000 (Bidou). Description without judgment, the passage leaves us to wonder at social norms that inhibit women from enjoying masculine customs and occupations except in the midst of a catastrophic emergency.

Discussion of the novel's conclusion in my classes has reliably seized on the gender of Henry's sister, which also amplifies the potential significance of minor characters in general. As described earlier in the novel, her apparel and manner, like her physical labor with trucks and horses, communicate her "female masculinity," as Halberstam terms it (1–5). Inconsequential to the progress of the narrative, Henry's sister is important to the comic resolution of the novel's satire of sexism because she demonstrates that women need not emulate Lorelei or the more moderate femininity of her cisgender friend Dorothy. The influence of traditional gender norms is obvious; conventional expectations make it possible for us to read Henry's sister as uncommon. Mediated through Lorelei's diary, her sister-in-law's masculine distinction is also unobjectionable. Featured in Lorelei's catalog of her happy associations, Henry's sister adds to the novel's complaints about sexism a critique of the "privileged reservation of masculinity for men" (Halberstam xii).

Coming at the end of the narrative after Lorelei has cashed in with her social intelligence, her sister-in-law's happiness serves to remind us that the diary has exposed sexism but that Lorelei has also exploited it for her own ends. In the end, her greed may be sated, but she has advanced her career and the happiness of everyone around her by monetizing her appearance according to exclusive beauty standards. No matter how cultivated, such means are fundamentally unearned. Henry's sister and most other people lack this capacity. Students in my classes have cited these facts to express frustration that the narrative may encourage more pleasure at Lorelei's success than indignation at the unjust and arbitrary means available to her. Even lacking a proper name, Lorelei's sister-in-law affords us consolation that the novel ends with a marginal figure starting work who will develop a distinct, nonsexist story of her own. A preference for whatever tale she may engineer is at least invited by this smart book.

Works Cited

Barrett-Fox, Jason. "Rhetorics of Indirection, Indiscretion, Insurrection: The 'Feminine Style' of Anita Loos, 1912–1925." *JAC*, vol. 32, nos. 1–2, 2012, pp. 221–49.
Bidou, Henri. "Battle of Verdun." *Encyclopedia Britannica*, 14 Feb. 2019, www.britannica.com/event/Battle-of-Verdun.
Bushnell, Candace. "Introduction to the Liveright Paperback Edition." Loos, *Gentlemen*, pp. xi–xvi.
Cain, James. *Double Indemnity*. 1936. Vintage Books, 1992.
Eliot, T. S. "The Love Song of J. Alfred Prufrock." 1915. *The Waste Land and Other Poems*, by Eliot, Harcourt Brace Jovanovich, 1934, pp. 1–9.
Gentlemen Prefer Blondes. Directed by Howard Hawkes, Twentieth Century-Fox Film, 1953.
Halberstam, Jack. *Female Masculinity*. Duke UP, 1998.
James, Henry. *The Turn of the Screw*. 1898. Dover, 1991.
Larsen, Nella. *Passing*. 1929. Dover, 2004.
Loos, Anita. "The Biography of a Book." 1963. Loos, *Gentlemen*, pp. xvii–xxiv.
———. *Gentlemen Prefer Blondes*. 1925. Liveright, 1998.
Manne, Kate. *Down Girl: The Logic of Misogyny*. Oxford UP, 2018.
Modern Times. Directed by Charlie Chaplin, United Artists, 1936.
Woolf, Virginia. *A Room of One's Own*. 1928. Mariner, 2005.

Lorna Fitzsimmons

Intercultural Critique of Subalternization: Parody in Okot p'Bitek's *Song of Lawino*

During the coronavirus crisis, parody is going viral—Internet users are posting parodies not only for comic relief but also to express serious health or political concerns, thus affording educators many opportunities to foster student engagement with the parodic in other cultures and eras—in this case, with the Ugandan writer Okot p'Bitek's partial parody of Henry Wadsworth Longfellow's *The Song of Hiawatha* in his poem *Song of Lawino*. *Song of Lawino* is an important example of intercultural critique, and learning to understand p'Bitek's parody provides a valuable opportunity for students to engage with the issue of race relations. My comparatist approach to teaching these texts draws on a problem-based learning framework informed by health and environmental humanities and postcolonial cultural studies. It also considers the translation process as a source of humor.

P'Bitek (1931–82) earned university degrees in law and social anthropology and lectured at several universities. He was also a performer and the director of the National Theatre of Uganda, with expertise in traditional songs. He composed this poem in the late 1940s in the Acholi language, under the title *Te Okono Obur Bong Luputu: Wer pa Lawino* (*Lawino's Thesis: The Culture of Your People You Don't Abandon*), and later translated it into English (Taban lo Liyong, *Defence* x, xiv). Its main character is a woman, Lawino, who is married to a westernized man named Ocol. Lawino's song voices her disagreement with her college-educated husband's ways and those of others who imitate Westerners, a condition she ridicules as deathly. Through his skillful characterization of Lawino, p'Bitek creates a sardonic critique of the impact of westernization on Ugandan society. Today, the poem is widely recognized as one of the major works of African literature of the twentieth century. It is a required text in the Ugandan educational system (Finnström 35) and increasingly taught elsewhere.

In many African countries, health issues may require an environmental and political framework because "health and disease are seen as caused not by germs, but by tensions and aggressions within social interrelations as well as by the malevolence of supernatural forces" (Okwu 21). In p'Bitek's hands, the concept of spirit influence, which Longfellow romanticizes in *Hiawatha*, is ironized as part of a social critique. Some representations of deathly states in *Song of Lawino* are expressions of resistance to subalternization ("the continual processes of minoritization and/or marginalization" [Sarker 818]). I suggest that engagement of this theme in p'Bitek's poem can cultivate awareness of choices for healthier pathways at the individual and collective levels (Stewart and Swain). Cross-cultural death studies strengthens respect for difference, locally or globally, improving the quality of life and possibly even saving lives.

Parody, in Linda Hutcheon's terms, is "a form of imitation, but imitation characterized by ironic inversion" and often associated with satire (6). It has an ancient history of classroom application to develop students' writing and critical thinking skills. In the nineteenth and twentieth centuries, the parodic gained more repute. Launching political critique to express resistance became a common goal of parodists in postcolonial culture (Ball; Devisch). In recent years, educators have used parody to teach social and political issues, such as freedom of expression (Paddon). Parody "can offer a safe space in which difficult tensions and conflicts can be explored, and in which new and challenging insights can be generated," David Buckingham argues (49). It is currently conceptualized as "a tool to teach and learn across content areas" (Bintz 511).

Activating Prior Knowledge and Applying New Information

Following a session on *Song of Hiawatha*, I teach *Song of Lawino* as a partial parody of Longfellow's epic using a five-step problem-based learning format, with flexible and compulsory scaffolding (Schmidt et al.; Simons and Klein). Core competencies in focus are critical and reflective thinking, communication, collaboration, problem-solving, cultural awareness, and application of learning. The first step is to activate students' prior knowledge of *Song of Hiawatha* and parody and then to facilitate their assimilation of new information. Students form small groups and share what parody means to them. I scaffold by discussing Hutcheon's definition, which sets the stage for engaging p'Bitek's ridicule of Ugandans' imitation of white people. I then call on volunteers to recite a couple of parodies of *Song of Hiawatha* (Moyne), which the groups discuss. We follow that with laptop searches for parodies of *Song of Hiawatha* on *YouTube*, attending to issues of race in particular. Several of those videos serve to illustrate the technique of inversion applied to racial identity. The groups' discussion of the videos facilitates application of new information about parody.

The Problem

How does p'Bitek use parody of *Song of Hiawatha* to criticize subalternization? In the previous session, we discuss the problem of subalternization in relation to the stereotypes and racist implications of Longfellow's poem—Alan Trachtenberg, for example, mocks Hiawatha as "the most congenial of all the white man's Indians" (52). Since the relevance of this issue to many students' lives is palpable, sharing personal experiences about it in small groups can foster empathy, motivate deeper engagement with the texts, and stimulate more meaningful modeling of solutions. Positive student responses suggest that this problem meets the "good problem" criteria in problem-based learning, which specifies that "a problem should: (i) be authentic; (ii) be adapted to the students' level of prior knowledge; (iii) engage students in discussion; (iv) lead to the identification of appropriate learning issues; (v) stimulate SDL [student-directed learning]; and (vi) be interesting" (Schmidt et al. 795).

Critical Contextualization

Anticipating that students will comprehend the problem of subalternization in various ways, I scaffold by discussing some of the published criticism on relationships between the two poems. Recalling that "Okot used to recite lines containing 'Minihaha' [sic]," Taban lo Liyong, who knew the author, argues that "*Wer pa Lawino* was modelled after *Song of Hiawatha*. . . . Longfellow's Indian Prince Hiawatha challenged Lawino in a deep way. He . . . brought out the spirit of Acholi or black cultural nationalism in Lawino" ("From *Wer*" 94–95). Jahan Ramazani argues that, whereas Longfellow writes of the "native American" from the perspective of an ethnographer, p'Bitek "reverses Longfellow's imperial perspective on 'childlike' oral culture by singing and writing from 'within' it" (145). Ngũgĩ wa Thiong'o observes that "Lawino . . . castigates her husband for abandoning the ways of his people, comparable to a Minnehaha castigating a Hiawatha" (43). He concludes that p'Bitek's writings are "not derivatives. They are a synthesis forged in resistance" (43).

Author-Translator as Jester

Discussion of that criticism encourages students to draw parallels between the two works, usually starting with the titles and main characters. The parody is more perceptible, though, when engaging the several versions of p'Bitek's poem, which I approach, as a fourth step, using the concept of the author-translator as jester. Harry Garuba and Benge Okot refer to the relationship between the Acholi and English versions of this work as "lateral textuality rather than one of original and translation" (315). Lo Liyong, who retranslated *Wer pa Lawino* as *The Defence of Lawino*, has argued that

> Okot did not translate *Wer pa Lawino* into *Song of Lawino*. He wrote two books: *Wer pa Lawino* (a very deep, philosophical book in Acholi, a book of morals, religion, anthropology, and wisdom) and a second light book, *Song of Lawino*. In *Song of Lawino*, Okot the jester—the cultural critic of the whiteman, the whitewoman, and their African imitators—is in the fore. ("On Translating" 88)

Discussing this tonal shift primes students to recognize p'Bitek as a parodist. An example of this shift is the deeper use of desacralization for comic effect in *Song of Lawino* (Nwosu 77). "Clean Ghost" is used for the Holy Ghost in both versions, but the phrase "Ten Instructions of the Hunchback" used for the Ten Commandments in *Song* is more literally translated from *Wer pa Lawino* as "God's Messages Ten," according to lo Liyong's translation (Okot p'Bitek, Song 84; Taban lo Liyong, *Defence* 64). As noted in *Song of Lawino*, "The name of the Christian God in Lwo is *Rubanga*. This is also the name of the ghost that causes tuberculosis of the spine, hence Hunchback" (94). The first version and its two translations are as follows:

> Ki Dekalogu, Or pa Rubang'a apar.
> (Okot p'Bitek, *Wer* 98)
>
> And the Dekalogu,
> The Ten Instructions of the Hunchback.
> (Okot p'Bitek, Song 84)
>
> The Decalogue and God's Messages Ten.
> (Taban lo Liyong, *Defence* 64)

Students are usually interested to learn that p'Bitek "lost his Christian commitment" during his law studies (Heron 3).

Collaborative Comparison

When p'Bitek revised *Wer pa Lawino* as *Song of Lawino*, he omitted chapter 14 (Taban lo Liyong, "On Translating" 88). Lo Liyong's translation of it provides evidence with which an important parallel between *Hiawatha* and the Acholi and English versions of p'Bitek's poem can be drawn: all three works treat death as a culminating theme. The next step, therefore, is group members' collaboration to compare passages from the three works, with each student completing a worksheet. I designed the worksheet to develop perspective-taking and evidence-based argumentation skills. My experience supports problem-based learning findings that such compulsory scaffolding may enhance students' performance (Simons and Klein).

The worksheet guides students to identify and discuss explicit or implicit evidence of the cognitive, emotional, social, and physical states of the dying, or departing, characters represented in these passages, starting with *Hiawatha*. Longfellow's poem, which has twenty-two chapters, features death from famine in the antepenultimate chapter and the departure of the hero, Hiawatha, for the "Land of the Hereafter" (248), in the final chapter. *Wer pa Lawino* details death from famine in its final stanzas: emphasis is placed on the scarcity of food and the need not to waste it, a key theme in environmental humanities (Okot p'Bitek, *Wer* 150–51; Taban lo Liyong, *Defence* 106–07). P'Bitek's description of hunger, an engaging resource for health humanities discussions, is still relevant; many Ugandans continue to suffer from food insecurity (Okori et al.).

Song of Lawino represents deathliness in the penultimate chapter, but, omitting *Wer pa Lawino*'s somber chapter on famine, it uses humor in a way that seems to parody *Song of Hiawatha*, satirizing the racial bias with which the Anglo-American writer concludes his epic. The penultimate chapter of *Hiawatha*, titled "The White Man's Foot," envisions the coming of "the people with white faces" (Longfellow 235), sent by "the Creator" with his "message" (236). When some white Christians arrive, Hiawatha welcomes them and values their "wisdom" (246). That sentiment is inverted in *Song of Lawino*. It draws to a close with the penultimate chapter of *Wer pa Lawino*, in which the speaker, Lawino, issues an ironic set of commandments that Ocol should follow to recover from his westernized condition, which she mocks as a moribund one (Okot p'Bitek, *Wer* 117–20). Students usually zero in on Lawino's prescription, which requires Ocol not to abandon the food of his people, but rather to discard his westernized habits and possessions: throw away his sunglasses, be cleansed and scratched free of that which he has heard in church or read in books, and clear his mouth of the contemptuous language he has learned from white people (118–19). The author empowers the female speaker with "sarcastic English" to satirize the adoption of Western ways (Taban lo Liyong, "On Translating" 89). Whereas Hiawatha accepts white hegemony (Nurmi 253), Lawino holds the trappings of white culture up to ridicule.

The worksheet also guides students to relate the textual evidence to their personal experience and to propose and choose between alternatives to some of the actions represented in these poems. Questions on chapter 12, "CEGU DOG GANG' WOKO KI OKUTU" ("My Husband Has Become a Slave to European Culture through Reading Their Books"; Okot p'Bitek, *Wer* 135; Taban lo Liyong, *Defence* 94), help students relate the theme of spirit influence to the issue of cyberbullying. Lawino laments Ocol's figurative emasculation and death caused by reading Western books (Okot p'Bitek, Song 113). The translation of this chapter's title in *Song of Lawino*, "My Husband's House Is a Dark Forest of Books," prepares for the metaphorization of Western print media as malicious spirits:

> Ka irii i ot pa cwara nonono
> Lwak cen ma gibedo i bung'-wa ni,
> Cen pa lwaki coo ki mon Munni
> Ma gidang'ng'e ka igudu buk mo-ni
> Cen ma kec pa lu-coo bukki
> Donyo woko i wii
> Ci itoo la-cung'u lapan cwara Ocol. (Okot p'Bitek, *Wer* 138–39)

> If you stay
> In my husband's house long,

> The ghosts of the dead men
> That people this dark forest,
> The ghosts of the many white men
> And white women
> That scream whenever you touch any book,
> The deadly vengeance ghosts
> Of the writers
> Will capture your head,
> And like my husband
> You will become
> A walking corpse. (Okot p'Bitek, Song 115)

This scene of domineering spirit influence, set in Ocol's house, in the penultimate chapter of *Song of Lawino* (antepenultimate of *Wer pa Lawino*), parallels the intrusion of Hiawatha's dwelling near the end of *Hiawatha*. During the famine, malign entities enter Hiawatha's wigwam, resembling the ghosts who enter it in chapter 19. The ghostly "Famine and the Fever" intimidate the languishing Minnehaha (Laughing Water) as they gaze on her and make sounds. Analyzing the power imbalance represented in these scenes and comparing the subjugation of the ill Native American woman to that of the Ugandan man facilitates students' solution modeling, while cultivating interpersonal and cultural sensitivity.

Figuratively emasculated by his Western ways, Ocol seems a parody of Minnehaha: a feminized figure subjected to malignance inside the dwelling. Westernization enters Africans' heads and homes, turning the dwelling into a forest of evil spirits and the body of men into that of women, or the dogs of white people (Okot p'Bitek, Song 115). Lawino's bitter recognition of this inverts her, as a Minnehaha, into a hero, a defiant Hiawatha, and the latter's admiration of the "Pale-face" into disdain (Longfellow 240, 241).

Finally, the worksheet asks groups to create a debate between Longfellow and p'Bitek on reviving Ocol, which prepares for subsequent essay writing. Dynamic scaffolding with Frantz Fanon's and Homi Bhabha's critiques of the psychological impact of colonialism serves to broaden the discussion.

As René Devisch observes, "[P]arody allows the subaltern to somehow level down centre/periphery dichotomies into a virtual communal equality" (392). In *Song of Lawino*, p'Bitek turns elements of Longfellow's epic into politicized parody that mocks effects of Western influence on

Ugandans while generating a productive critical distance from African assumptions about the ontology of spirit influence. By engaging *Song of Lawino*'s figurations of death, students can learn choices for living.

Works Cited

Ball, John Clement. *Satire and the Postcolonial Novel: V. S. Naipaul, Chinua Achebe, Salman Rushdie.* Routledge, 2015.
Bhabha, Homi. "Of Mimicry and Men: The Ambivalence of Colonial Discourse." *October*, vol. 28, spring 1984, pp. 125-33.
Bintz, William P. "Writing Parodies across the Curriculum." *The Reading Teacher*, vol. 64, no. 7, 2011, pp. 511-14.
Buckingham, David. "Pedagogy, Parody and Political Correctness." *Teaching Popular Culture: Beyond Radical Pedagogy*, edited by Buckingham, Routledge, 1998, pp. 45-62.
Devisch, René. "Christian Moderns: Parody in Matricentric Christian Healing Communnes of the Sacred Spirit in Kinshasa." *The Postcolonial Turn: Reimagining Anthropology and Africa*, edited by Devisch and Francis Nyamnjoh, Langaa Research and Publishing Common Initiative Group, 2011, pp. 367-404.
Fanon, Frantz. *Black Skin, White Masks.* Translated by Charles Lam Markmann, Pluto Press, 1986.
Finnström, Sverker. *Living with Bad Surroundings: War, History, and Everyday Moments in Northern Uganda.* Duke UP, 2008.
Garuba, Harry, and Benge Okot. "Lateral Texts and Circuits of Value: Okot p'Bitek's *Song of Lawino* and *Wer pa Lawino*." *Social Dynamics: A Journal of African Studies*, vol. 43, no. 2, 2018, pp. 312-17.
Heron, G. A. Introduction. Song of Lawino *and* Song of Ocol, by Okot p'Bitek, Waveland Press, 2013, pp. 1-33.
Hutcheon, Linda. *A Theory of Parody: The Teachings of Twentieth-Century Arts Forms.* U of Illinois P, 2000.
Longfellow, Henry Wadsworth. *The Song of Hiawatha.* 1855. Floating Press, 2009.
Moyne, Ernest J. "Parodies of Longfellow's *Song of Hiawatha*." *Delaware Notes*, vol. 30, 1957, pp. 93-108.
Ngũgĩ wa Thiong'o. *Globalectics: Theory and the Politics of Knowing.* Columbia UP, 2012.
Nurmi, Tom. "Writing Ojibwe: Politics and Poetics in Longfellow's *Hiawatha*." *The Journal of American Culture*, vol. 35, no. 3, 2012, pp. 244-57.
Nwosu, Maik. *The Comic Imagination in Modern African Literature and Cinema: A Poetics of Laughter.* Routledge, 2016.
Okori, Washington, et al. "Logit Analysis of Socioeconomic Factors Influencing Famine in Uganda." *Journal of Disaster Research*, vol. 5, no. 2, 2010, pp. 208-15.
Okot p'Bitek. Song of Lawino *and* Song of Ocol. Waveland Press, 2013.
———. *Wer pa Lawino.* East African Publishing House, 1969.
Okwu, Austine S. O. "Life, Death, Reincarnation, and Traditional Healing in Africa." *Issue: A Journal of Opinion*, vol. 9, no. 3, 1979, pp. 19-24.

Paddon, Anna R. "Parody as Free Expression: A Unit for Magazine Classes." *Journalism Educator*, vol. 46, no. 2, 1991, pp. 42–45.

Ramazani, Jahan. *The Hybrid Muse: Postcolonial Poetry in English*. U of Chicago P, 2001.

Sarker, Sonita. "A Position Embedded in Identity: Subalternity in Neoliberal Globalization." *Cultural Studies*, vol. 30, no. 5, 2016, pp. 816–38.

Schmidt, Henk G., et al. "The Process of Problem-Based Learning: What Works and Why." *Medical Education*, vol. 45, no. 8, 2011, pp. 792–806.

Simons, Krista D., and James D. Klein. "The Impact of Scaffolding and Student Achievement Levels in a Problem-Based Learning Environment." *Environment Instructional Science*, vol. 35, no. 1, 2007, pp. 41–72.

Stewart, Kearsley A., and Kelley K. Swain. "Global Health Humanities: Defining an Emergent Field." *The Lancet*, vol. 388, no. 10060, 2016, pp. 2586–87.

Taban lo Liyong, translator. *The Defence of Lawino*. By Okot p'Bitek, Fountain Publishers, 2001.

———. "From *Wer pa Lawino* to *Song of Lawino* with Loss." *World Literature Written in English*, vol. 36, no. 1, 1997, pp. 93–109.

———. "On Translating the 'Untranslated': Chapter 14 of 'Wer pa Lawino' by Okot p'Bitek." *Research in African Literatures*, vol. 24, no. 3, 1993, pp. 87–92.

Trachtenberg, Alan. *Shades of Hiawatha: Staging Indians, Making Americans, 1880–1930*. Hill and Wang, 2004.

Kimberly Tolson

Diverse Political Comedy Television in the Classroom

Many students hope that their education will help them succeed in the world outside the classroom, and teaching political comedy can engage students in topics that are relevant to their daily lives. Instructors can offer a positive and engaging classroom experience for their students that not only enables healthy discussion but also entertains and informs on the subject matter. And this approach doesn't have to tackle current issues head-on. Instructors can use comedy to help students engage in thoughtful and dynamic political discussions through issues that touch their own lives.

For this practical approach to teaching political comedy from the periphery, I like to use current, on-the-air comedians and their shows in my classroom. There are several reasons for this. First, this comedy is available to anyone. Despite being aired on different platforms, the shows that I mention in this essay are available on *YouTube* and can be easily streamed in the classroom. Second, platforms like *Netflix*, *Hulu*, and *Amazon* have gained a lot of traction and popularity in recent years, so they are recognizable to students. Third, these platforms offer the kind of diversity that allows for unique points of view that were previously restricted to seasoned white male comedians on prime-time television shows like *The Late Show* or *The Tonight Show*.

Comedy presents a strong method for discussing politics in the classroom. Approaching politics through comedy seems to help students realize that they don't have to be defensive about their ideas; instead, they can consider a new idea while laughing, which feels different emotionally. Staci Beavers's article "Getting Political Science in on the Joke: Using *The Daily Show* and Other Comedy to Teach Politics" discusses other benefits of using humor in the classroom, making "a serious case for humor as a critical tool in improving pedagogy": according to Beaver, comedy has the potential to capture students' interest, motivate the learning process, foster classroom relationships, encourage student engagement, and improve retention (415–16).

The two shows that I present in this essay as examples for fostering classroom discussion are *Full Frontal with Samantha Bee* (TBS) and *Patriot Act with Hasan Minhaj* (*Netflix*). While instructors can use just about any episode from either show, I'd suggest finding one that brings in politics in a roundabout fashion. There is a big difference between having a conversation where two sides aren't listening to each other, fully entrenched in their preexisting beliefs, versus having a conversation with eager, open-minded individuals who know little about sponsored content on *Instagram* (Bee's episode ["Big Little Lies"]) or fast fashion (Minhaj's episode ["Ugly Truth"]). Bee's episode "Big Little Lies" is only about seven minutes long but covers a plethora of problems with sponsored content, which many students are likely exposed to on a daily basis. While it might seem unrelated to politics at first, students will find the connections to governing bodies, legislation, and regulation after viewing the episode and discussing the implications. Similarly, Minhaj's episode "The Ugly Truth of Fast Fashion" includes a great deal of nuanced political topics as part of its twenty-nine-minute discussion of clothing. Both of these episodes are heavy on the comedy, allowing students to enjoy the jokes, jabs, and slights while engaging with serious and relatable conversations.

Because the topics in my selected episodes are not featured in the news on a regular basis, students might be uncertain about how they feel regarding sponsored content or fast fashion. Humor is a great way to enter those meaningful conversations. Equipping students with the context and techniques to unpack the comedy, though, is what will help them be engaged. As Beavers states, "Instructors who use such comedy [like Jon Stewart's *The Daily Show*] must provide students with the tools they need to 'get' the jokes and appreciate the humor while keeping the overarching objective of building critical-thinking skills firmly in mind" (417). In what follows, I provide a more specific road map to preparing the classroom for a discussion grounded in a political comedy television episode.

Before screening a selected television episode in class, I prepare by watching the episode several times, taking notes on what I want to bring up in class discussion. I break down suggested analysis into several parts: basic critical thinking topics, basic analysis topics, key words and phrases for discussion, purpose and audience analysis questions, and comedy questions.

To maintain full participation, I encourage students to focus on one element of the episode. I assign this element ahead of time and inform students what they are paying attention to by printing and passing out little slips of paper with their assigned topic: students must meet in small groups after the screening to discuss the given topic with their peers before reporting back to the class as a whole, or they must complete a short, written reflection in their journals and individually contribute to the conversation following the screening. For example, if I give one group of students the topic of audience, those students must watch the episode with attention to who the intended audience is and how they came to that conclusion. In their small group discussions, students share their thoughts and conclusions. They receive immediate feedback and consider other perspectives in a smaller, less intimidating situation than a large group discussion.

If I require students to be individually responsible for their own thematic key word or phrase, I hold a class discussion following the screening in which students listen to their peers' comments to find the right segue to comment on their assigned word or phrase. Often, I have to get the ball rolling, but then students can address their individually assigned word or phrase and contribute to the conversation freely. Because I know what the key words or phrases are, I can transition more easily from topic to topic; similarly, because students know what their key word or phrase is, they feel better prepared to engage in class discussion than they otherwise would. I find it's easier to ask students to contribute to the conversation when they know ahead of time what I'll be asking of them. Also, I can keep track of who has spoken, encouraging the more reserved students to chime in on the topic with their angle.

It is also vital to have a brief discussion prior to watching the episode. I ask students to make some predictions of what will be addressed in the episode based on its title or name recognition of the host. This discussion allows us to reflect more thoughtfully after the screening and in large group discussion: what did they expect to learn, what did they actually learn, and what assumptions needed to be corrected. Finally, if the episode uses strong language, I announce this before the screening. I also encourage students to analyze why that language is used and how it relates to the comedy—for example, by indicating the target audience.

Discussions of the episode can fall into several categories. Critical thinking topics include pathos, ethos, logos, purpose, and audience. Stylistic and analysis topics include prompts related to the episode's use of comedy, its tone, its source material, the metacommentary it offers, its style and presentation, critical responses to its content, and its relevance. The remaining topics are briefly discussed in what follows.

Key words and phrases: Each student can focus on a thematic key word or phrase from the episode. For "Big Little Lies," these words and phrases can include *sponsored content, Instagram influencers, advertisers, transparency,* and *consumer protection,* among others. In "The Ugly Truth of Fast Fashion," thematic key words and phrases might include *fast fashion, shopping culture, legacy brands, democratization of fashion, dynamic assortment,* and *greenwashing.*

Purpose: Both Bee's and Minhaj's episodes have three major purposes: to inform, to persuade, and to entertain. I ask students how Bee and Minhaj achieve these goals and with what degree of success: How does each episode inform the audience on the topic, major players, and research? Who does that information affect, and why is it relevant? How does each episode persuade us to question our assumptions and to make better decisions? How does each episode entertain us with the use of graphics and humor?

Audience: I ask students several questions to get them thinking about who the host's intended audience might be: Who produces and airs the show? Who is Samantha Bee? Who is Hasan Minhaj? Where have they worked? What topic do they address in the episode? What kinds of jokes do they make? Are you part of the target audience? Further breakdown of the intended and secondary audiences might include the following: age, political ideology, gender, race, ethnicity, and financial status.

Comedy: I ask students to identify the jokes in the episode (the punch line and setup), determine any preexisting knowledge or information needed to understand the joke or who its target audience might be, and then explain if and, if so, how the joke works in context. I ask students to pay attention to the jokes they responded to and explain why those jokes connected or failed to connect with them. I also ask them what their favorite joke was and to explain why.

It is important to screen episode choices regularly, since comedy can fall flat or be read as stale when it's years old and no one cares who Kirstie Alley is or why Bill Cosby is the butt of the joke. It is also helpful to research and understand the comedians' references. Contextually speaking, Minhaj's episode requires more preexisting cultural knowledge than Bee's does. Minhaj references Billie Eilish and child labor ("Ugly Truth" 11:35), which requires an understanding of who Billie Eilish is and how she recorded her music while she was still a minor. It also requires a cultural awareness of child labor in countries where our clothes and electronics are produced. Bee, on the other hand, references "Brahs" and jokes about the rat from the 2007 film *Ratatouille* ("Big Little Lies" 1:55, 2:22). Her humor requires a general cultural knowledge, referencing texts that are not as current as those referenced by Minhaj. In contrast, at the end of "The Ugly Truth of Fast Fashion," Minhaj refers to Greta Thunberg, a current political figure in youth progressivism (28:17). Some students might have seen her in the news, but others won't know the young Swedish climate change activist. Instructors may have to spend some time explaining references to students, but this may also be an opportunity for students to bring their own knowledge to the table and to explain certain references to the instructor.

While I've briefly analyzed episodes from Bee's and Minhaj's shows, the format and approach I have presented can lead to meaningful and considerate conversations with students using any political comedy episode. There are many other shows, such as John Oliver's *Last Week Tonight* (HBO) or Wyatt Cenac's *Problem Areas* (HBO), that present political issues using humor and that would stimulate strong classroom conversation.

Overall, my goal in showing political comedy is to foster a classroom that encourages critical thinking and effective learning. Analyzing the comedy, language, terminology, and appeals used are ways to achieve that goal. Greg Lukianoff and Jonathan Haidt delineate three things that are necessary for critical thinking: "curiosity, open-mindedness, and intellectual humility" (247). Critical thinking also requires students to "ask questions, seek understanding, and practice the habits of good thinking . . . practice ongoing self-reflection and self-awareness . . . strive for a strong sense of community marked by collaboration, empowerment, and intentional openness and respect for the thinking of others" (247). I use humor to puncture that seemingly impenetrable topic of politics because that topic allows students to practice all these good critical thinking habits that will transfer to every aspect of their lives.

Works Cited

Beavers, Staci L. "Getting Political Science in on the Joke: Using *The Daily Show* and Other Comedy to Teach Politics." *PS: Political Science and Politics*, vol. 44, no. 2, 2011, pp. 415–19. *Cambridge Core*, https://doi.org/10.1017/S1049096511000266.

"Big Little Lies: *Instagram*'s Sponsored Content Problem." *YouTube*, uploaded by Full Frontal with Samantha Bee, 31 Oct. 2019, www.youtube.com/watch?v=O_vfyEpyB4A.

Lukianoff, Greg, and Jonathan Haidt. *The Coddling of the American Mind: How Good Intentions and Bad Ideas Are Setting Up a Generation for Failure*. Penguin Books, 2018.

"The Ugly Truth of Fast Fashion." *YouTube*, uploaded by Netflix Is A Joke, 25 Nov. 2019, www.youtube.com/watch?v=xGF3ObOBbac.

Vivian Nun Halloran

Translating Trevor: Relatability and the Loss of Aesthetic Appreciation for a Joke

Trying to make sense of the current immigration policies and debates in the United States with a group of undergraduates in fifteen weeks or less is a daunting task made somewhat more palatable by the prospect of assigning a variety of relevant online materials featuring comics flexing their humor muscle to critique the inhumane treatment that refugees, asylum seekers, and would-be immigrants receive at the nation's southern border. In an era when late-night shows make their content freely available on *YouTube*, it makes sense to include immigrant comics among the chorus of first-person narratives and historical material about the nation's changing attitudes toward new citizens; their satiric and informative takes on the latest news, such as John Oliver's evidence-based, systematic takedowns of policies like having toddlers appear at immigration court proceedings without adult guardians ("Immigration Courts") or Trevor Noah's segment discussing the negative reaction to the Trump administration's decision to separate migrant families in different detention centers ("Trump"). Such performative texts entertain students who are learning about the historical context surrounding the circumstances critiqued in the comedy bits, thus lending an air of much-needed levity fueled by each performer's righteous indignation. Though none of the courses discussed here were explicitly engaged in the teaching of composition, my choice to include video clips of comedy performances and news parodies as part of the required viewing materials reflects my commitment to showcasing the importance of changing one's writing or rhetorical style to reach multiple audiences, each of which is a distinct stakeholder of the text. In what follows I detail my experience teaching Noah's memoir, *Born a Crime: Stories from a South African Childhood*, three times during the 2018–19 academic year in two distinct introductory-level courses—one each for the departments of English and American studies—at my institution, a residential four-year flagship campus of one of the state's university systems. Despite my best efforts to frame this principle of adapting one's prose or rhetorical style to suit a particular audience, my students had trouble detecting the humor in an excerpt of Noah's stand-up comedy at the Apollo when asked to consider the self-deprecating anecdote I'll call the "Black Hitler" joke in light of his written explanation of the lack of stigma surrounding the dictator's name in South Africa in *Born a Crime* (95). The joke's premise is that Noah refreshed his knowledge of German by watching online tutorials and listening to German speeches while he slept, but he did not check whose speeches he had downloaded. Subsequently in Cologne, Noah orders a sandwich at a café. His accent, emphatic yelling, and heil salute while ordering frighten the shop employee, who suffers cognitive dissonance watching a black man ordering lunch while emulating the führer's political speeches.

There are several reasons why teaching Noah's *Born a Crime* in the undergraduate literature and American studies classrooms is a pleasure. For one thing, Noah's prose is startlingly beautiful, witty and poignant in its simultaneous invocation of empathy for the child's emotional response to difficult situations while also maintaining the adult narrator's critical distance and objective perspective. A didactic element is built into the memoir's dynamic structure, which intersperses chapters focused on personal recollections with short interchapters that either recount relevant historical events that contextualize the rise and development of South Africa's apartheid system or else elucidate some of the aspects of apartheid that would otherwise be unfamiliar to many readers, such as how South Africans invoked the black/white color line to differentiate among various Asian populations in the country. Noah points out that "Chinese people were classified as black in South Africa," while "at the same time, Japanese people were labeled as white" (74). This artificial distinction maintained the racial logic of apartheid without elucidating the cultural or historical calculus that led to this alignment of Asian nations.

Noah's book will have an impact on today's students not only because of its didactic elements and beautiful, poignant prose but also, more importantly, because the memoir easily meets that most elusive of criteria: relatability. Students recognize the host of *The Daily Show* and are familiar with his stand-up, since Noah is still on the college campus comedy circuit. This recognition and assumed relevance of Noah as a cultural icon meets the first definition of what constitutes the *relatable*, in Rebecca Mead's definition of the term. However, in students' responses to written assignments, I observed a different dimension of relatability in students' reactions to reading the memoir that prompted me to try to translate the relationship between Noah's understated humor on the page and his more explicit attempt to get laughs from a live audience so that students would get the joke rather than take all his statements literally.

Before outlining the specific instance of relatability that I found so troubling in my students' writing, I will clarify the contexts in which I have taught *Born a Crime*. As mentioned, I taught this book three times during the 2018–19 academic year in two courses offered through different departments at my institution: English and American studies. Each class was fully online, and the student population was entirely made up of students enrolled in my residential campus. All students were nonmajors, and most were seniors. *Born a Crime* was one of three book-length texts I assigned in my semester-long, online, introductory American studies course in the fall of 2018. The other two were young adult novels written by immigrants. The class topic was "A Nation of Immigrants." I taught the memoir again during a condensed half-semester course focused on the same topic during the first eight weeks of the spring semester of 2019. This time, though, *Born a Crime* was one of only two assigned book-length texts; the other was a graphic novel in translation. My rationale for including *Born a Crime* was to challenge and deepen my own and my students' familiarity with this late-night show host and comedian as a person who was born and raised in a different country and thereby to cast his critique of contemporary American politics and popular culture as that of an outsider, like his fellow comedian and late-night show host, John Oliver.

The English course in which I taught Noah's book was also an online introductory-level world literature course offered during the spring semester of 2019. The topic was "Global Stories of Current Events." *Born a Crime* was one of five books assigned for this semester-long class, which also included two nonfiction books, one each by a Mexican woman and a Nigerian man, and a short story collection by a Nepalese author. *Born a*

Crime was scheduled to be read beginning in the tenth week of the semester, or two weeks after the end of my American studies course. Between the fall and spring, I decided to broaden the scope of comics included in my presentation of the memoir to include more gender and linguistic diversity that directly related to the topics Noah raises in his memoir. To this end, I assigned two videos by the German-speaking, Swiss-born vlogger Tama Vakeesan, whose family immigrated from Sri Lanka (Vakeesan, "Making Fun" and "What Does It Take"). Her videos use visual puns, emojis, and other visual gags to comment on and give expression to her featured guests' discussions of their immigrant experiences. In his memoir and his early stand-up, Noah often mentions that his father is Swiss, so giving students a sense of what immigration looks like both in Switzerland and through Swiss humor in German (which they access through subtitles) helps them get an idea of what part of Noah's life could have sounded like.

Assignments and the "Black Hitler" Joke

To emphasize the pedagogical function of quizzes in my class, I call them close reading exercises. In both of my American studies classes, there were ten assigned close readings during the semester. These assignments were designed to meet three different learning outcomes for the class:

> World Cultures: Students will explain how immigration policies incorporate different cultural beliefs, values, perspectives, and practices into a dominant society.
> Arts and Humanities: Students will interpret varieties of aesthetic expression by analyzing written texts and works in literature, the visual arts, music, and other performing arts.
> Diversity in the United States: Students will analyze how cultural practices and artifacts represent the communities that produced them and how they serve to create, refine, and blend cultures.

In the fall of 2018, the week's close reading asked the following question: "Based on your reading of chapter 15 of *Born a Crime*, explain what Noah means by the following: 'The name Hitler does not offend a black South African because Hitler is not the worst thing a black South African can imagine' (95)." According to the *Canvas* analytics for this question, 92% of students gave a satisfactory answer that earned a score in the top third of the points available, while only 8% of respondents earned scores in the lower third of points. No students earned scores in the middle. Most students recalled that Noah suggested that Cecil Rhodes was a much more reviled figure whose actions and ideology laid the foundation for the indignities black South Africans suffered under apartheid. That is an accurate representation of the material students read, and, thus, their responses conveyed comprehension. In this version of the class, I assigned a clip of Noah's *Live at the Apollo* stand-up performance where he makes his "Black Hitler" joke ("Daily Show's Trevor Noah"), but I did not ask about it, and no students mentioned it in connection to the question in the close reading. This became my baseline for expectations of how students would interpret this passage in subsequent courses.

In the spring of 2019, I decided to explicitly connect the Apollo video to students' reading of the memoir in a variation of the question asked above. This time, I asked students not only to explain what Noah means by the statement in his memoir but also to contrast this statement with his claim, made in his *Live at the Apollo* stand-up performance, that his accent when he's speaking German sounds like Hitler. In the previous close reading, I had asked students to compare a specific element from the Apollo performance with some part of the assigned reading that resonated with the excerpt chosen. That meant that by the time they faced this question the following week, I had firmly established the connection in their minds between Noah's stand-up act and his memoir writing. This time around, the point value was higher and the revised question had the increased difficulty of adding a comparative element to the initial question: only 52% of students' answers scored in the top third of points available; 22% of student responses earned scores in the middle third of scores; and 26% of answers scored in the lower third of points available. Again, the nature of the task I asked students to perform was different in both cases, but what was most surprising to me was that students' references to the "Black Hitler" joke from the Apollo performance conveyed their absolute conviction that Noah's account of sounding uncannily like Hitler when ordering food in Germany was accurate, despite the fact that students had read about how Noah's ability to learn multiple languages besides English as a child had helped him navigate the racism he encountered as a mixed-race person. The comment I most frequently wrote when explaining point deductions for this answer was the following: "Excellent analysis on the first part. The second—it's just a joke. He doesn't actually sound like Hitler. He just says that to shock his audience into laughter." Upon reflection, it occurred to me that students interpreted the joke literally because they had never tried to watch online content in a language other than English and thus assumed that Hitler's speeches were the only examples of the language one could find in that space. Another possibility might be that their frames of reference for online tutorials, whether cooking demonstrations, makeup tutorials, or video game playthroughs, depend on the viewer's ability to replicate exactly what they see on screen to arrive at a comparable result. This is speculation, but it could explain why these young people were more likely to accept the joke's claims at face value rather than recognize the irony that made the joke funny.

My world literature class also featured close readings, but they only met the following learning outcome: Students will identify and analyze the specific cultural, intellectual, and historical contexts through which these literary genres interpret and communicate a concern with the social problems afflicting particular countries. I used the same comparative wording of the question for the close reading in my world literature class later in spring 2019, with similar results: 37% of students earned scores in the top third of possible points; 37% of answers scored in the middle third; and 26% of answers scored in the lower third of possible points. Once again, I found myself commenting the following: "He doesn't actually sound like Hitler. He just said this for laughs." While there were other reasons to explain the lowest scores in both the world literature class and the American studies class, such as not answering the question at all or not addressing both the memoir and the Apollo clip, by and large the most frequent source of point deductions for this question was the fact that students didn't get the joke.

The Cost of Being Relatable

My overall approach to using comedy clips, including bits from Noah's stand-up days and his political comedy in *The Daily Show* alongside clips from other high-profile immigrant comics, in these two courses was to make students aware of how prevalent the topic of immigration is as fodder for popular culture texts. This chorus of immigrant voices supplements, echoes, augments, and complicates Noah's own critiques of the dehumanizing way the US government treats immigrants. My goal in having students read his memoir alongside his stand-up comedy was for them to learn to alternate rhetorical registers in order to interpret these various texts about identity, belonging, and how hard it can be to fit in. However, I found that the memoir had an unforeseen dampening effect on how students interpreted the stand-up comedy: rather than recognize the humorous situation as a joke that stretched the truth for effect, they assumed that Noah's self-deprecating humor was a factual representation of the comic's own shortcomings. Because the artistry in the crafting of a joke as an aesthetic object meant to elicit laughter from the audience was self-referential, like the memoir, students did not appreciate it. According to John Morreall, "Humor tends to be aesthetic, then, to the extent that the cognitive shift is enjoyed for its own sake, playfully, and not for any boon that it signals. Humor is aesthetic to the extent that it is not mixed with self-interested pleasures" (72). My students' conflation of the confessional style of memoir writing with the self-referential material from a stand-up show as both literally and objectively true, then, means that assigning the two texts together decreased their ability to undertake the "cognitive shift" necessary for them to recognize the performance of either as inherently aesthetic and, thus, significantly different than everyday experiences of people recounting events from their own lives. Their sense of the material being relatable made it difficult for them to experience the humor.

In Mead's lamentation against what she considers "the scourge" of the acceptance of the concept of relatability into written parlance, she zeroes in on the term's paralytic dimensions. Mead suggests that the term *relatable* serves as a shortcut that leads to passivity rather than as a starting point for exploring the significance of a given person's identification with an event, circumstance, person, or character: "But to demand that a work be 'relatable' expresses a different expectation: that the work itself be somehow accommodating to, or reflective of, the experience of the reader or viewer. The reader or viewer remains passive in the face of the book or movie or play: she expects the work to be done for her." While my students did not think Noah's South African childhood paralleled their own childhoods, their written analysis of his life writing assumed he was in earnest for the entirety of the text. This may have more to do with another relatable aspect of undergraduate life: the foreign language requirement. My students' responses when asked to analyze Noah's stand-up comedy routine in the light of a passage from the memoir showed that a large number of students were unable to recognize that each text—the recorded performance and the written one—placed different demands on them as participatory audience members. In trying to achieve this goal by substantially changing the nature of the question so as to affirm the enduring shock value of making jokes about Hitler across the registers of race and ethnicity, I ultimately missed an opportunity to convey a useful historical lesson about the lasting negative impact that Cecil Rhodes has had in South Africa and related nations. Appealing too much to relatability has its downsides.

Works Cited

"The Daily Show's Trevor Noah Was Born a Crime." *YouTube*, uploaded by Live At The Apollo, 11 Jan. 2022, youtu.be/Aryhj4LaDx0.

Mead, Rebecca. "The Scourge of 'Relatability.'" *The New Yorker*, 1 Aug. 2014, www.newyorker.com/culture/cultural-comment/scourge-relatability.

Morreall, John. *Comic Relief: A Comprehensive Philosophy of Humor*. Wiley-Blackwell, 2009.

Noah, Trevor. *Born a Crime: Stories from a South African Childhood*. John Murray, 2016.

Oliver, John. "Immigration Courts: Last Week Tonight with John Oliver." *YouTube*, uploaded by LastWeekTonight, 2 Apr. 2018, www.youtube.com/watch?v=9fB0GBwJ2QA.

"Trump Gets Blasted for Breaking Up Migrant Families." *YouTube*, uploaded by The Daily Show with Trevor Noah, 18 June 2018, www.youtube.com/watch?v=-gQeWTuWMn8.

Vakeesan, Tama. "Making Fun of Migration Stereotypes." *Swissinfo.ch*, 7 Dec. 2017, www.swissinfo.ch/eng/tama-s-tales_making-fun-of-migration-stereotypes-/43735670.

———. "What Does It Take to Feel Swiss in Switzerland?" *Play SWI*, Swiss Broadcasting Corporation, 31 Aug. 2017, play.swissinfo.ch/play/tv/politics/video/what-does-it-take-to-feel-swiss-in-switzerland?id=43474438.

Jeffrey Galbraith

Laughing at Belief: The Risks and Rewards of Satire in the Classroom

The humor of satire represents a particular challenge for teaching comic texts. This observation became increasingly evident to me upon taking a position at an evangelical Christian college. The libertine wit of Restoration comedy proved a hard sell, suitable only for advanced English majors (*why are they so mean?*). More challenging was the fact that many of my favorite satires ridiculed aspects of religious belief whose value I actually wanted my students to affirm. The relation between Samuel Richardson's novel *Pamela* and Henry Fielding's parody *Shamela* illustrates the dilemma I encountered. Whereas *Pamela* seeks to edify its readers through the main character's claim to moral purity, a satire like *Shamela* exposes the hypocrisy that lurks behind such religiously motivated positions. My classes, I discovered, consisted of students whose individual temperaments, family contexts, or faith history inclined them equally to readerly modes of attachment as to modes of disenchantment. Earnestness and sincerity, often as not, shared space with skepticism. Satire sparked a range of affects, which made it as welcome as it was feared. These circumstances required dedicating time at the beginning of the semester to building trust with students, working to develop the class into a community that was comfortable with the sting of disagreement. We needed to learn how to disagree, which also meant learning how to extend hospitality to one another in instances of giving and taking offense. To that end, I developed an in-class exercise that focuses on short satirical news articles, often no more than a paragraph long, which can be found online at websites like *The Onion*. Designed to ease students into the risks of interpretation, the exercise can be adapted to composition and general education literature courses as well as to courses in the English major. In what follows, I describe the exercise with reference to satires that address or take aim at forms of Christian belief. The satires discussed suggest how religiously minded students might be encouraged to reflect on, and charitably embrace, conflicting interpretations of being in the world.

In graduate school, when my cohort began teaching the university's first-year composition class, it was not uncommon to hear colleagues express frustration with outspoken evangelical students. I understood their frustration, knowing from personal experience how certain church cultures view the classroom as an arena of conflict. Some students from these cultures, at least the ones that come readily to my mind, may be on guard against professors whom they perceive as godless, suspicious that postsecondary education has become a form of indoctrination that erodes honest faith. They often refuse to engage fully in discussion-based classes, particularly when the goal is to question received wisdom in pursuit of thicker, more complex readings. While I encountered these students in part-time work at a state university and other secular schools, I now regularly encounter them at my current institution as well—an odd fact, since professors voluntarily sign a statement of faith, ink our names to a community covenant, and rub shoulders with students in local churches.

If one is tempted to dismiss these students as willfully blind to the demands of critical thinking, the history of satire suggests that their siege mentality is not without warrant. Believers have long served as the butt of the joke, and the extent to which a society's satirists feel free to laugh at religious belief is often considered the measure of modernity. Such was the message that circulated in the wake of the *Charlie Hebdo* massacre of 2015, after Islamic terrorists stormed the offices of the satirical weekly newspaper in Paris, killing twelve people and injuring eleven more. As we reeled with horror from the murderous attack, many scholars and pundits rehearsed the view that satire represents the freedom of expression on which modern liberal democracy depends. Ridicule aimed at Islam was no different from the satirical forms of critique that developed during the age of the Enlightenment. The cartoonist Charb scourged Muslims in the same way that Ben Jonson sent up the Puritans in *Bartholomew Fair* or Voltaire skewered the facile belief in Providence in *Candide* (Turner). To be modern required somehow shrugging it off when one's deep convictions came under attack. Keep calm and carry on.

The problem with this view is that it absolves the satirist of responsibility. In *The Difference Satire Makes*, Fredric V. Bogel explains that "we . . . frequently refuse to see the satiric voices within texts as compromised, partial, in problematic relation to their own aggression and to their satiric objects" (66). Such refusals appeared frequently in responses to the Paris massacre, as John Clement Ball notes in the article "Capital Offenses: Public Discourse on Satire after Charlie Hebdo." Invoking Dustin Griffin's conception of satire as "a rhetoric of inquiry and provocation" (64), Ball argues for taking a more measured view of "the risks and perils of satire's unstable power in our heterogeneous societies" (300). This approach resonates with the insights of Talal Asad following the Danish cartoon controversy of 2005. In the volume *Is Critique Secular?*, Asad raises a question concerning life in pluralist societies that is instructive for my purposes here. Stating that "Critique is no less violent than the law—and no more free," he muses, "What does this do to the way one is asked to—and actually—lives?" (134). Asad's question has special significance for the satire classroom, where critique, at its extreme, may take the form of ridicule laced with scorn. "It is not the secular claim to truth that worries me," he explains, "but what critique may do to relationships with friends and fellow citizens with whom one deeply disagrees" (134). Now more than ever, we find ourselves in communities fractured by deep disagreements. These circumstances provide a challenge for teaching satire, since satirists insist on making the implicit explicit. But the challenge also represents an opportunity. How might we use satire to come to a greater awareness of our disagreements while at the same time learning to live peaceably in the midst of conflict? How might we form bonds capable of spanning the fractures, without obscuring them from view? The answer requires creating a space that is hospitable to reflection on the beliefs and convictions that define and divide us.

The exercise I use gives students practice in identifying some of the basic elements of satire, which I designate, loosely following tradition, as vehicle, technique, and target. My initial attempts at teaching satire tended to ask too much of students. While I wanted to push bravely into the weeds of irony, I underestimated the risks involved in interpretation. Students wanted in on this laughter, which gives special status to an in-group of knowing readers, but they feared not getting the joke. My solution was to lower the stakes by breaking interpretation into its component parts. I use the term *vehicle* to refer to the kind of writing the satire is imitating. What does the piece sound like? Where have you heard or seen something like this before? The techniques of satire should be understood as consisting of how, or to what end, the satirist uses the vehicle. Ironic reversal, *reductio ad absurdum*, and exaggeration are useful starting points. Generally, students have a good understanding of the target, or satiric object, though discussion usually raises possibilities that students struggle to hold in tension. The exercise itself comprises the following steps: First, I provide the image of a satirical news article, often from the "News in Brief" section of *The Onion*, which we then read aloud. Next, I break students into groups with the task of identifying vehicle, technique, and target. After five minutes or so, we discuss what they came up with. The exercise does not depend on arriving at a single, fixed interpretation. Sometimes I select the satire based on relevance to the day's assigned reading. If the subject is comedy, we may talk about why humor works in certain contexts but not in others. Often, I also give students a chance to create their own instances of a particular technique.

I model the exercise with an article whose absurdity is obvious from the outset. A favorite is "Grizzly Bear Catches Spawning Michael Phelps in Jaws." The vehicle is a news report, resembling both the tragic accident story and the report of an athletic event. The satire creates irony by describing an aquatic athlete in terms of the salmon swimming upstream to reproduce, literalizing the idiom that a person "swims like a fish." The satire tweaks convention by sexualizing Phelps's prowess in the water, describing him as "the sexually mature Olympian." Students also notice how the swimmer is humorously dehumanized. The bear, upon seizing its prey, is reported to have "gorged on the protein-rich 18-time Olympic gold medal winner." When pressed to identify a target, students might talk about how sports figures may be viewed in dehumanized terms. I make the point that media depictions of victims tend toward a similar objectification.

The satirical news article, often readily available online, offers a useful way to explore interpretive issues related to religious belief. I have in mind two examples that work in this way. The first is "Local Church Full of Brainwashed Idiots Feeds Town's Poor Every Week." According to the lede, "Sources confirmed today that the brainwashed morons at First Baptist Assembly of Christ, all of whom blindly accept whatever simplistic fairy tales are fed to them, volunteer each Wednesday night to provide meals to impoverished members of the community." The clash of perspectives is striking. How can these church members be exemplary in a moral sense and yet also idiotic? Some students read the article as a punitive satire. They point to the so-called bias of the liberal media in the description of one participant as a "mindless sheep who adheres to a backward ideology and is incapable of thinking for herself." A bracketed editorial insertion adds further insult, when a church member explains that "it's fun to work alongside all the members of our [corrupt institution of propaganda and lies] who come out each week." I am quick to note, however, that *The Onion* does not usually use satire as a scourge. More plausibly, the satire stages the conflict between Christian and atheistic perspectives. The article raises the issue of how to value acts of altruism that derive from motivations that one objects to or does not wish to support. The satire works as a plague, so to speak, on both of the houses involved. The targets include those who too readily dismiss the church's actions and those who, in response, too quickly claim the position of victim.

My second example points to the conflict inherent in religious pluralism. Since the 2016 election, *The Onion* has frequently targeted evangelical belief in the figure of the former vice president Mike Pence. In these satires, the target comes off as a simpleton whose bumbling ignorance is amusing rather than alarming, given the position he holds. Typically, the humor derives from reducing evangelical belief to hypermoralism ("Mike Pence Asks Waiter to Remove Mrs. Butterworth from Table until Wife Arrives") and blithe naivete ("Mike Pence Assures Detained Children That They Will Have Safe, Sanitary Conditions in Heaven"). The satire I have in mind constructs a scenario in which Pence considers competing claims to religious truth. In "Mike Pence Struggling to Reckon with Vision of Prophet Muhammad Revealing That VP Destined to Become Next President," Pence learns that his dream of becoming president will one day come true, but the vision he receives comes from a false prophet. "I'm not a huge supporter of Islam," Pence says casually, "but on the other hand, I really liked what Muhammad was saying. Hmm, this is a toughie . . ." Characterized as "weigh[ing] his desire for political power against his strict commitment to Evangelical Christianity," Pence realizes that his desire (tied to Islam) and his commitment (Christianity) are "seemingly unable to coexist in the vision of the future brought forth by the sacred prophet and founder of Islam." The punch line comes when self-interest weakens the politician's resolve: "I mean, Islam and Christianity are actually kind of similar when you think about it, right?" More interesting for my purposes is the possibility signaled by the word "seemingly" in the description of the two religions as "seemingly unable to coexist." Islam and Christianity have vied with each other historically, but what if their coexistence is only seemingly, rather than necessarily, at odds? The challenge is how to reconcile the exclusive interpretive claims of these religions with the pragmatic work of constructing a more peaceful future. It is worth asking students to identify the barriers that prevent religious communities from embracing change while considering the extent to which such barriers are real or only imagined.

Whereas the future of religious communities remains a pressing issue for democratic societies, satirists are typically more concerned with religion's orientation toward the past. When satirists want to expose modern hubris or folly, religious tradition often provides critical distance on the current moment. But satire also depicts the religious believer as comically backward or out of place in the present age. My last two examples briefly sketch this problematic relation between religion and modernity. In the first, the modern age itself provides the delusion, in the tradition of Alexander Pope's *The Rape of the Lock*. While Pope's mock-epic exposed the distorted values of the fashionable world, *The Onion* applies a similar critique to haute couture in the news brief "Karl Lagerfeld Horrified by Uninspired, Garish Tunnel of Light Coming toward Him." The article, which concerns the afterworld experience of the iconic designer Karl Lagerfeld, appeared on the day of his death in February 2019. In the satire, the designer is disgusted, rather than relieved, by his encounter with transcendence, sounding like a snarky judge on *Project Runway*: "Maybe it was *haute* a thousand years ago, but now it looks hopelessly outdated. It's just tacky, really, to have a light that's so all-encompassing and transcendent in this day and age. It's like a caricature of Heaven." The satire shows how a commitment to the modern, figured here as artistic innovation, can corrupt one's view. The satire suggests that Lagerfeld's aesthetic judgment is more of a caricature than the image he deplores. I recently used this story when adapting the satire exercise for an exam. The humor proved engaging for students, and the assessment worked well for measuring the extent to which students had honed their interpretive skills.

In my final example, satire ridicules religious belief for being out of step with the times. The article "Archaeologists Discover Fully Intact Seventeenth-Century Belief System in Ohio Congressman" inverts the scenario in which a politician appeals to their religious views by creating a faux-naif sense of awe that such beliefs continue to exist at all. News of an archeological discovery serves as the vehicle for targeting the "archaic opinions" of Congressman Jim Jordan. The satire employs the technique of describing the abstract in terms of the material, turning Jordan's opinions into relics from a premodern age. Details such as the fact that "the congressman's belief system . . . could deteriorate rapidly if examined too much" contain multiple gibes, invoking the criticism of religion as irrational while suggesting that Jordan's beliefs are as fragile as mammoth remains exposed to air by a receding glacier. When an expert registers amazement that the belief system "shows absolutely no signs of decay," readers may even detect a faint allusion to Catholic saints whose flesh is reported to have remained magically free from corruption in the grave. The satire is keenly efficient in delivering its blow. Faith is a museum piece, it says, with no place in the modern world.

When the satire exercise is used to build a community of trust, the classroom becomes a space capable of deep reflection. Religious students can discuss the critique that belief unfits a person for modern life without taking offense, noting that such critique possesses a history that merits its own scrutiny. In this, I do not wish to defang satire's rhetoric of inquiry and provocation or somehow inoculate students against secular disenchantment. Satire remains a risky enterprise, yielding outcomes that are hard to predict. My goal is rather to increase the transformative potential of the classroom by inviting more students into the discussion. Critical thinking need not imperil one's deeply held religious beliefs. As classroom practice has shown, we must relinquish the illusion that it should.

Works Cited

"Archaeologists Discover Fully Intact Seventeenth-Century Belief System in Ohio Congressman." *The Onion*, 15 June 2017, theonion.com/archaeologists-discover-fully-intact17th-century-belie-1819580026.

Asad, Talal. "Reply to Judith Butler." *Is Critique Secular? Blasphemy, Injury, and Free Speech*, by Asad et al., Fordham UP, 2013, pp. 131–39.

Ball, John Clement. "Capital Offenses: Public Discourse on Satire after Charlie Hebdo." *Genre*, vol. 50, no. 3, 2017, pp. 297–318.

Bogel, Fredric V. *The Difference Satire Makes: Rhetoric and Reading from Jonson to Byron*. Cornell UP, 2001.

Griffin, Dustin H. *Satire: A Critical Reintroduction*. UP of Kentucky, 1994.

"Grizzly Bear Catches Spawning Michael Phelps in Jaws." *The Onion*, 5 Jan. 2016, theonion.com/grizzly-bear-catches-spawning-michael-phelps-in-jaws-1819578500.

"Karl Lagerfeld Horrified by Uninspired, Garish Tunnel of Light Coming toward Him." *The Onion*, 19 Feb. 2019, www.theonion.com/karl-lagerfeld-horrified-by-uninspired-garish-tunnel-o-1832730087.

"Local Church Full of Brainwashed Idiots Feeds Town's Poor Every Week." *The Onion*, 3 Jan. 2014, theonion.com/local-church-full-of-brainwashed-idiots-feeds-town-s-po-1819575966.

"Mike Pence Struggling to Reckon with Vision of Prophet Muhammad Revealing That VP Destined to Become Next President." *The Onion*, 14 Sept. 2018, theonion.com/mike-pence-struggling-to-reckon-with-vision-of-prophet-1829058208.

Turner, Gustavo. "Ben Jonson, like Charb of Charlie Hebdo, Sought to Reduce Zealots." *Los Angeles Times*, 16 Jan. 2015, www.latimes.com/entertainment/la-et-cm-ca-satire-turner-20150118-story.html.

Joy Katzmarzik

Calvin and Hobbes in the English Foreign Language Classroom

Although teaching graphic novels is on the rise, there is often not enough time in high school curricula to include an entire graphic novel for discussion in the classroom. Newspaper comic strips, however, can add depth and variety to sequences taught in the EFL (English as a foreign language) classroom: their brevity and ineluctable humor make them a popular medium of international communication for non-native speakers all over the world. As such, they are a particularly appropriate in the EFL classroom.

In this essay, I carve out the characteristics innate to newspaper comic strips that make them a beneficial medium for the EFL classroom and offer some useful ways to include newspaper comic strips in the EFL classroom at different levels of language education: as a way to practice language skills and as a medium for teaching about culture.

Why are newspaper comic strips a beneficial medium for the EFL classroom? Since the shift in pedagogy from teaching literacies (i.e., "rule-governed forms of language" [Cazden et al. 61]) to teaching multiliteracies ("understanding and competent control of representational forms that are becoming increasingly significant in the overall communications environment, such as visual images and their relationship to the written word" [61]), comics have secured their rightful place in the classroom:

today's media-saturated world is filled with images students need to learn to read and work with. However, newspaper comics are more than images: as a hybrid art form consisting of image and text, the comic is "not a simple coupling of the verbal and the visual, but a blend, a true mixture" (Harvey 9). Thus, for learners of English, the picture takes over the function of scaffolding: it supports the message but does not take away any of the content. Since readers comprehend the image before they are able to process the content cognitively, they quickly gain an overview and an immediate approach to the matter (Sofos and Kron 115). Moreover, as the illustrations in comic strips are often drawn in a simplified and abstract way, they help readers focus on the gist of the comic strip and present complex issues in an easily comprehensible way (Koch 318).

The genre of newspaper comic strips (also known as "funnies") presents an especially effective way of teaching English to non-native speakers. Strips usually consist of about four panels that tell a short and often humorous story that frequently appeals to a young audience. The general narrative framework is mostly kept simple: there is a small cast (between two and six characters) with (slightly) exaggerated character traits (Sofos and Kron 116). Usually, the aim of the series is not to establish a coherent plot but to tell disconnected individual stories held together by a common set of characters. Thus, as there is no progressive plotline, each comic strip can narratively stand on its own and function as a unit in the EFL classroom.

In this essay I mostly draw on examples of one particular comic strip series I find especially useful: *Calvin and Hobbes*, created by the cartoonist Bill Watterson. The series ran in newspapers from 1985 to 1995 and revolves around two characters, six-year-old Calvin and his stuffed tiger, Hobbes, who are named after the theologian John Calvin and the philosopher Thomas Hobbes. Whenever Calvin and Hobbes are on their own, Hobbes turns into a real tiger, whereas for every other character, Hobbes appears only as a stuffed tiger. The series is useful because the visuals are carefully drawn and offer an easy approach to learners and because it deals with a broad range of topics.

Because analyzing comics requires a unique vocabulary, it may be helpful to provide students with a word bank before they start reading. A glossary that includes some useful terms can be found in figure 1.

Practicing Language Skills

Teaching English means equipping students with a communication tool. The most basic aim is to enable them to apply their language skills in

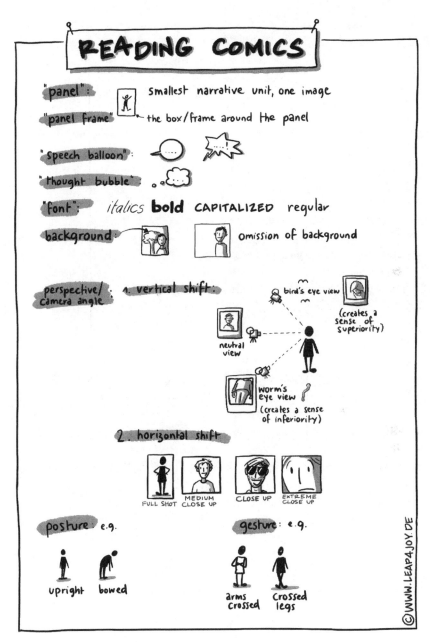

Figure 1. Glossary created by the author

everyday situations: the first main goal postulated in the EFL curriculum for the German state of North Rhine–Westphalia is to develop systematic functional communication skills—among others, speaking, reading comprehension, and writing skills (Ministerium 12).

In that respect, newspaper comic strips present an authentic use of language: they mostly render short dialogues between characters in which characters use spoken language and direct speech, at times accompanied by short narrative passages (in narrative boxes). Because of their spatial limitations, newspaper comic strip characters do not use very many words. That focused use of language makes it easy for foreign language learners to understand the gist. Moreover, the depiction of the characters, setting, facial expressions, and so on visually supports the text.

This simple use of language with the provided visual scaffolding opens several options for concrete language practice in classrooms. One option is to present students with a comic strip with blank speech balloons and ask students to fill in the text. This exercise allows students to practice creative writing and to experiment with linguistic register, characterization, and, depending on students' level, expressing emotions. For this exercise, instructors may want to provide students with the following word bank: *panel, posture, gesture, facial expressions,* and *speech balloon*.

In this exercise students read the postures and gestures of the characters and develop their own interpretation of the short visual story. It is important to remind students that it is not about guessing the "right" answer but about creating a story that is in unison with the images. For this exercise it is not necessary for students to be familiar with the cast of the series; familiarity can even make things more difficult for students, as it makes them more eager to find the one right solution.

The exercise encourages students to find adequate phrasal expressions for emotions expressed in the images. They use short phrases to express the given emotions and to try to make sense of the situation. Here, they also practice employing the appropriate linguistic register (e.g., formal versus informal language). In *Calvin and Hobbes,* Calvin uses a different register to address his teacher Mrs. Wormwood than he does when addressing his friend Hobbes, which is something students should keep in mind when they fill in the speech balloons.

In addition, this exercise allows students to practice their characterization skills. Students are usually expected to do a characterization by reading a prose text and using the information given in the text. However, reading a character's emotion by reading their postures, gestures, and facial expressions is much closer to the experience of everyday life and creates a bridge for students who do not have much experience reading and analyzing literature, encouraging them to put themselves in the shoes of the character.

For students, this is a profitable exercise, as it is a simplified and guided version of a creative writing assignment. Although the comic strip is only a short sequence, the character must act coherently, and the actions must make sense. I practiced this with my students as they lent words to a *Calvin and Hobbes* comic strip. The results were surprising: they were imaginative, and all the words fit the story. Those students who were not familiar with *Calvin and Hobbes* were especially unprejudiced in their creative writing, whereas those students who knew the series struggled more to find words that would fit the characters' actions.

For the medium to be used effectively, it is important to choose a comic strip that provides enough visual information to offer students some narrative signposts (such as props, setting, or visible emotions). If the images only show two heads with speech balloons, students will find it harder to contextualize the comic strip.

Another exercise might present students with various panels and ask students to bring the panels into a logical order. This exercise allows students to practice prepositions of time and adding elements of causality to a narration. For this exercise, instructors may want to provide students with a word bank that includes words such as *panel* and *protagonist* as well as useful phrases to describe narrative coherence, including adverbs of time, such as *when*, *while*, *as soon as*, and *before*, and linking words, such as *thus* and *because*.

Students often consider not only subjects at school but also individual learning units within one subject as disconnected, and they struggle to link their knowledge to broader and more abstract concepts. This form of disconnected knowledge is often reflected in students' language, as is often revealed in class tests, when students simply reproduce knowledge and summarize disconnected facts instead of using connecting phrases.

Since newspaper comic strips consist of clearly defined narrative units in the form of panels, they are a good medium to practice narrative thinking: the teacher can provide students with the individual panels of a comic strip in a random sequence. As students try to bring the panels into a logical order, they practice looking beyond the individual panels toward an overarching narrative. For this purpose, the comic strip does not necessarily need to include text. In one *Calvin and Hobbes* comic strip, for example, Watterson uses nineteen panels as snapshots to visually tell a story of confusion: as Calvin is running late for school, he forgets his lunch box at home. As he returns home through the backyard to fetch it, his mother leaves their house through the front yard with Calvin's lunch box. When Calvin eventually arrives at school with his lunch box, he realizes that he forgot his books at home (Watterson, *It's a Magical World* 141). In this example, the unchanging angle plays an important role in supporting the narration: Calvin's home is on the left-hand side of the page, whereas the bus and the school are on the right-hand side, indicated by the bus in the thirteenth panel, driving to the right, and Calvin's mother driving Calvin to school in the fifteenth panel. This helps students recreate the plot.

As students work in pairs to develop a narrative, they discuss and reflect on their panel arrangement. They practice the use of temporal adverbs as they agree on a chronological sequence of the panels. Thus, they have to communicate in English and express in English their reasons for their choice of panel arrangement. They use appropriate adverbs to justify and explain their sequence—for instance, "Because Calvin has no lunch in his hands, this panel must come before this panel."

Once students agree on a sequence, they can present their result in class, using the respective linking words. The beginnings of sentences can also be given to students to explain the comic strip—for example, "Calvin is late for school. When Calvin arrives at the bus stop, . . ." This exercise can be adjusted depending on the group of learners: for instance, instructors can also provide students with words that should be used to form sentences, such as *while*, *after*, and *before*. As students work in pairs and discuss their process together, they reflect on the narrative process and practice their communication skills in terms of literary narration.

A third method to practice language skills is to ask students to write out the comic strip as a story. In that exercise, students practice summarizing events, writing complete sentences, and establishing a shift in narrative viewpoints. The word bank for this exercise might include words such as *narrative perspective* and *first-person narrator*.

This exercise can be on the easier side or it can be made more difficult. The most basic exercise is to ask students to write a summary. As the narration is partly carried through images rather than text, students have to come up with their own phrases and expressions to summarize the plot and cannot rely on phrases used in a narration. Adapting the comic strip into prose can also be used to practice a shift in the narrative viewpoint: students can be asked to write out the comic strip from one character's perspective. In doing so, students not only practice establishing a change in perspective and empathizing with a character but also learn to describe a situation from multiple angles. For this purpose, Sunday newspaper strips might be more useful, as they are longer than the dailies (which usually consist of only four panels).

Practicing Cultural Studies

Comic strips can be used not only to improve language skills. They can also be used for cultural studies and can allow students to practice intercultural competence. Texts and cultures form an "interplay," as Wolfgang Hallet, a leading scholar in the field of foreign language acquisition, postulates (qtd. in Decke-Cornill and Küster 245). As such, the EFL classroom should always represent a real or virtual intercultural and communicative space. Consequently, Ansgar Nünning demands a broader variety of texts be used in the EFL classroom, including popular culture texts (152).

Good newspaper comic strip artists are able not only to create humor but also to address topics of cultural relevance. These comically exaggerated interventions in cultural affairs are often thought-provoking and can serve well to initiate a discussion. The seemingly nonserious approach appeals to younger learners and prompts them to respond to questions raised and to provocations. As such, comics can help create an interdisciplinary approach to different subjects (Koch 318), mediating between different languages and different fields in the humanities.

Calvin and Hobbes touches on various topics of cultural relevance. The series discusses and questions, for instance, the value and quality of literature and the arts. In one comic strip, Calvin explains to Hobbes the stereotypical difference between high and low art. Pointing at a painting, Calvin describes it as "[s]piritually enriching" and "[s]ublime." The painting is then juxtaposed with a comic strip, which Calvin characterizes as "[v]apid" and "[j]uvenile." A painting of a comic strip is, on the other hand, "[s]ophisticated" and "[p]hilosophically challenging." But in answer to a question posed by Hobbes—What if one were to "draw a cartoon of a painting of a comic strip"?—Calvin responds that this would be "[s]ophomoric" and "[i]ntellectually sterile" (Watterson, *Homicidal Psycho Jungle Cat* 152).

I used the beginning of this comic strip as an introduction to a graphic novel adaptation of Shakespeare's *Hamlet* and to raise the question of whether comics can be considered an art form. Students commented on the dichotomy between high and low art that Calvin suggests. We entered a vibrant discussion as students reflected on the relationship between paintings and comic strips as two forms of art.

The series touches on other culturally relevant topics that are beneficial for classroom discussions: in one comic strip, Calvin takes a moment for "personal reflection" around Christmas, "a time to spread the joy of material wealth . . . A time to glorify personal excess of every kind!" (Watterson, *It's a Magical World* 158). Here, he raises the question of the true meaning of Christmas and what modern consumerism has made out of it.

Another recurring theme in the comic strips is Calvin's ambiguous relationship to nature: on the one hand, Calvin is a consumer child who hates being in nature because something's "always stinging you or oozing mucus on you. Let's go watch TV" (Watterson, *Something* 32). On the other hand, Calvin's best friend Hobbes is a wild tiger, and through his eyes Calvin also questions the way humans subdue nature: when Calvin tells Hobbes that "Mom wants to know if we'd like to go to the zoo today," Hobbes replies, "Can we tour a prison afterward?" (Watterson, *There's Treasure Everywhere* 19). As Hobbes turns the table and assigns the role of the captives to humans, he sheds a new light on social issues. Because of the brevity of the comic strip, the comic strip is not only humorous but also thought-provoking.[1] The comic strips mentioned serve well to initiate a discussion about the way humankind treats nature.

Other culturally relevant topics touched on in *Calvin and Hobbes* include Calvin's questionable notion of morality, which he always adjusts to his present needs; his antipathy toward the institution of school (as represented by his disillusioned teacher Mrs. Wormwood); and his addiction to mass media. These topics are both entertaining and thought-provoking and can help students regard issues from a different angle, initiate a discussion, or add depth to a discussion. A simple search on *Google Images* will unearth a broad variety of *Calvin and Hobbes* comic strips; for further study, simply browse any of the published collections of Watterson's comic strip series. I recommend later publications starting from 1990 as they deal with a broader range of cultural topics. Because the compilations consist of individual comic strips, they are an easy and entertaining read, and the strips offer plenty of material for discussion.

Of course, there are additional ways to incorporate newspaper comic strips in the EFL classroom: because the study of literature plays an essential part in the EFL classroom, students could also be asked to practice creative writing by adapting part of a literary story into a comic strip.[2]

Newspaper comic strips in general and *Calvin and Hobbes* in particular can benefit the EFL classroom on various levels: they can be used as a creative medium to teach basic language skills, or they can be used to introduce topics of cultural relevance. In all instances, comic strips serve as a humorous initiation for vivid and engaged classroom discussions. In this sense, comic strips transform conventional EFL teaching from routine practices and rote memorizations into a lively exercise of the performance of language for practical usage in an English-speaking country.

Notes

1. Hobbes criticizes zoos again when Calvin shows him a beautiful butterfly he caught in a glass. Hobbes replies, "If people could put rainbows in zoos, they'd do it" (Watterson, *It's a Magical World* 51).

2. For further studies in creating comics, see Comer, which describes the creative writing project the author employed with her students.

Works Cited

Cazden, Courtney, et al. "A Pedagogy of Multiliteracies: Designing Social Futures." *Harvard Educational Review*, spring 1996, pp. 60–92.
Comer, Kathryn. "Illustrating Praxis: Comic Composition, Narrative Rhetoric, and Critical Multiliteracies." *Composition Studies*, vol. 43, no. 1, 2015, pp. 75–104.
Decke-Cornill, Helene, and Lutz Küster. *Fremdsprachendidaktik: Eine Einführung*. Narr, 2014.
Harvey, Robert C. *The Art of the Funnies: An Aesthetic History*. UP of Mississippi, 1994.
Koch, Corinna. "English-Physics, Francais-Histoire, Espanol-Arte: Comics als Ausgangspunkt für fachübergreifenden und fachverbindenden Unterricht." *Vernetzter Sprachunterricht: Die Schulfremdsprachen Englisch, Französisch, Griechisch, Italienisch, Latein, Russisch und Spanisch im Dialog*, edited by Michael Frings et al., vol. 4, Ibidem Press, 2017, pp. 317–29.
Ministerium für Schule und Bildung des Landes Nordrhein-Westfalen. "Kernlehrplan Englisch für die Sekundarstufe I Gymnasium in Nordrhein-Westfalen." *Qualitäts- und UnterstützungsAgentur–Landesinstitut für Schule*, 2019, www.schulentwicklung.nrw.de/lehrplaene/lehrplan/274/gesk_e_klp_2021_07_14.pdf.
Nünning, Ansgar. "Kultur." *Metzler Lexikon Fremdpsrachendidaktik: Ansätze, Methoden, Grundbegriffe*, edited by Carola Surkamp, J. B. Metzler, 2010, pp. 151–52.
Sofos, Alivisos, and Friedrich W. Kron. *Erfolgreicher Unterricht mit Medien*. Logophon, 2010.
Watterson, Bill. *Homicidal Psycho Jungle Cat: A* Calvin and Hobbes *Collection*. Andrews and McMeel, 1994.
———. *It's a Magical World: A* Calvin and Hobbes *Collection*. Andrews and McMeel, 1997.
———. *Something Under the Bed Is Drooling: A* Calvin and Hobbes *Collection*. Andrews and McMeel, 1990.
———. *There's Treasure Everywhere: A* Calvin and Hobbes *Collection*. Andrews and McMeel, 1996.

Part II

Communicating with Comedy throughout the Curriculum

Paul Benedict Grant

From Plato to Python: Designing an Introduction to Humor Course

Courses on comic texts tend to be good fun for teachers and students alike. Specialists in the subject enjoy bringing their research into the classroom, while students respond positively to a course based on subject matter that they may have previously considered to be outside the province of academic study; consequently, enrollment and participation levels are generally high. That enthusiasm may wane a little in the early stages as students realize that humor is a serious business and that the subject is as challenging and as demanding as any other on the curriculum; but most students can be counted on to stay the course, apply themselves, and reap the rewards.

Those rewards are rich and various, for few subjects are as fascinating or strike as unerringly and insightfully at the heart of human behavior. Beyond its primary purpose to amuse, humor functions in myriad ways—to cajole, console, insult, persuade, ostracize, express superiority, expose stupidity, hypocrisy, or prejudice. The questioning, curious mind that is by nature unwilling to settle for superficial readings and shallow assessments—the mind compelled to look beneath the surface of the laugh in order to investigate the complex nature of that laughter—finds much to feed on. Comic texts teach us to be sensitive to subtleties, that there is no such thing as an innocent, burden-free joke, that they are all freighted with meaning; teaching comic texts is a way to pass on these lessons—and have fun while doing so.

Since 2007 I have taught a self-designed English course called An Introduction to Humor. Interdisciplinary in nature, it explores the various ways in which humor functions in a wide range of comic texts from classical antiquity to the present, in relation to topics such as transgression, iconoclasm, sexuality, gender, ethnicity, class, culture, politics, and religion. In the course of a single semester, students travel from the humor theory of Plato to the madcap antics of Monty Python and beyond. It has been a thought-provoking trip, and I would like to share my experiences with other instructors who may be considering taking a similar journey as they design their own introductory courses to teaching comic texts. Faced with the prospect of putting together such a course, instructors may feel overwhelmed: how do they draw up a workable blueprint that will cover all the necessary ground and, simultaneously, keep themselves and their students satisfied and engaged? Unquestionably, the challenges that we face as educators vary according to specific situations and contexts; it is also true that several factors affect the success of any course—class size and student expectations, to name only two. But what follows is tried and tested. It is also, crucially, adaptable: instructors can apply this course blueprint to their own particular situation, retaining the structure while modifying the content—the comic texts themselves—as they see fit, so as to achieve the maximum benefit for themselves and their students.

Choosing Texts

One of the first issues that I encountered when designing the course was in choosing the required texts. Teachers of comic texts would benefit enormously from a single, one-stop book that includes all the major humor theories (if only in abridged form), illustrative examples from primary texts, and a comprehensive bibliography of secondary sources. In lieu of such a book, I decided to design my own book of readings that incorporated all of the above. This decision required advance planning and copyright clearances, but the advantages outweighed the extra work involved: it brought the required material together under one cover at a cost that did not prove prohibitive to the university or the students; and it provided a kind of template that I could—and did—adapt for future courses.

I divided my book of readings into two sections. The first, introductory section was devoted to a survey of humor theory. All courses on comic texts should start with such a survey; to bypass the theoretical aspects of humor and simply plunge in would be an ill-considered decision. Admittedly, this makes for rather dry reading right out of the gate, so one runs the risk of turning students off before things are fully underway; but no proper, serious analysis of the subject can begin without it. As mentioned, pleasure is humor's raison d'être, but the number of thinkers who have attempted to limn humor's complexities attests to the fact that humor is a serious business at heart, and it is as well to pass this lesson on to students at the outset. This approach is not a matter of bowing to critical convention by ticking the so-called theory box; it has practical advantages. A grounding in humor theory, however rudimentary, provides students with the critical vocabulary required to analyze comic texts insightfully and move beyond impressionistic, evaluative responses that do not lead to deeper reflection. The lesson is clear: instructors ignore humor theory at their peril. Extracts from the three traditional and prevailing theories of humor—the incongruity, superiority, and relief theories—can be found in many academic anthologies, but many of these are out of print, so I decided to draw on a book that I was familiar with from my research in humor studies: John Morreall's excellent anthology *The Philosophy of Laughter and Humor*. In reader-friendly prose, with helpful introductions and summaries, Morreall presents generous extracts from the traditional theories of humor, including those of Plato, Aristotle, Thomas Hobbes, Immanuel Kant, Søren Kierkegaard, Henri Bergson, and Sigmund Freud. Having secured permissions, I included these extracts in my book of readings.

I wanted the second section of my book of readings to contain a selection of primary texts that served to illustrate the humor theories contained in the first section, so that students could apply their newfound knowledge. I listed the texts under genres such as parody, farce, satire, wit, and black humor, choosing a selection of poems, short stories, extracts from plays and novels, and transcriptions of stand-up routines (such transcriptions have become readily available in recent years, in print and online). Personal preference dictated some of my choices, but I strove for variety, aware that not everyone would share my tastes. Comedians covered in 2007 included Woody Allen, Lenny Bruce, Bill Hicks, and Rick Mercer. Some texts proved popular; some did not. But within the parameters that I had set, the course could be modified to account for this inevitability:

in subsequent years I changed the texts from time to time to keep things fresh.

Although the book of readings is the main reference point for my students and the source of essential course information, it is supplemented by other texts. As a companion to the book of readings, I always assign a comic novel so that the class can engage in two to three weeks of in-depth, extended critical analysis. I would suggest choosing a novel whose humor presents particular challenges, because controversial comic content always generates discussion. For this reason, Vladimir Nabokov's *Lolita* has been a favorite of mine in the past; other novels that I have taught include Ken Kesey's *One Flew Over the Cuckoo's Nest*, Joseph Heller's *Catch-22*, Chuck Palahniuk's *Fight Club*, and Brett Easton Ellis's *American Psycho*. All these novels have been successfully adapted for film, and the movies are of interest in themselves, so I would recommend watching them in order to compare and contrast the different comic effects that can be achieved in this medium.

Mention of movies brings me to an important aspect of the course that is worth highlighting here—namely, the use of audiovisual material. In addition to movies, and in keeping with the interdisciplinary nature of the course, the class analyzes many other forms of comic texts during the semester: sitcoms, sketch shows, animation, music videos, and stand-up. Doing so allows us to discuss issues relating to performance and theatricality—for instance, timing and delivery, the influence of a live audience, and manufactured moments versus spontaneous improvisation. Predictably, perhaps, this has proven to be one of the most popular aspects of the course. Comedians covered have included Larry David, Jerry Seinfeld, Ricky Gervais, Richard Pryor, Chris Rock, Amy Schumer, Sarah Silverman, Bill Burr, Katt Williams, Dave Chappelle, and Weird Al Yankovic. I line up my examples beforehand in order to maximize the learning moments: whatever we watch or listen to in class relates directly to the particular subject or genre that we are examining in that specific class. It is fun to watch these clips, but they have to serve a structural purpose.

Learning Management Systems

I recommend that instructors set up a page for their course in advance of term (e.g., on *Brightspace* or *Moodle*), a meeting place to post all their class material and as many links as possible so that students can take advantage of the wealth of available material. Be creative in seeking links that illuminate or illustrate points that you cover in class, and bring in as many topical, popular culture references as possible.

Library Reserves

Increasingly, students are not using their university libraries and are missing out on the many benefits of paying visits to libraries; instructors can help reverse this trend by placing several primary and secondary sources on library reserve. Anyone working in this field knows that there is a vast amount of print material available on comic texts: overviews as well as genre-specific and author-specific texts. Explore the catalog and encourage your students to do the same. Reserved texts can include not only books but also CDs, DVDs and Blu-rays, and so on.

Test Case: Roberto Benigni's *La vita è bella*

In bringing this brief essay to a close, I thought it might be useful to present a test case so that instructors can see the way in which I approached teaching a comic text using the full range of materials available. I have chosen a work that I have taught many times with positive results: the writer, director and actor Roberto Benigni's feature film *La vita è bella* (*Life Is Beautiful*).

I slot Benigni's movie into the course under the category of black humor. I begin the section by defining the term; this is tricky, because it has, alas, become a kind of catchall for humor that is regarded as edgy or controversial. To summarize: Black humor is a mode of writing in which things that are usually treated seriously—death, sickness, violence, war—are treated humorously. Its hallmarks are a combination of horror and hilarity, grotesque imagery, disparity between form and content, and, on occasion, an emphasis on verbal play. From a philosophical point of view, black humor offers none of the assurances of traditional comedy, where the incongruities of life are resolved (the kind of cozy resolutions that close Shakespeare's comedies); instead, it presents images of disorder and instability that reflect an underlying belief in a meaningless universe; Samuel Beckett's absurdist plays are perhaps the most obvious cases in point, and a brief summary of *Waiting for Godot* or *Endgame* has proven useful.

Black humor was given its name by the surrealist André Breton in the introduction to his *Anthologie de l'humour noir* (*Anthology of Black Humor*; 11–17), a book that is available in English translation. In his introduction, by way of explaining what he means by the term, Breton quotes from Freud's famous theory of humor (16–17), as presented in *Jokes and Their Relation to the Unconscious* and his shorter essay "Humour." Since I include extracts from both of these works in the book of readings, my students are already familiar with them. For Freud, humor functions as a safety valve for expelling negative emotions (e.g., fear or pity) and as a means of evading or displacing unpleasant facts that we would rather not consciously explore. Key to Freud's theory is the concept of gallows humor, laughter in the face of death. By way of illustration, he uses an example of a criminal who cracks a joke en route to the gallows, asking for a scarf for his throat so as not to catch cold—an example of someone using humor to rise above perilous circumstances. Freud believes that at the root of this jesting lies a desire to return to the realm of childhood, so that life is seen as nothing but a game for children.

Life and literature furnish many funny examples of Freud's theory of humor, and I always devote some class time to a selection of these before proceeding to our main text, *Life Is Beautiful*. From Mercutio's making light of his fatal injury in Shakespeare's *Romeo and Juliet* to Dorothy Parker's witty poem "Resume" to Oscar Wilde's alleged remark on the disgusting decor of the Parisian boarding room in which he lay dying—"My wallpaper and I are fighting a duel to the death. One or the other of us has to go" (Henley)—there is no shortage of examples from which to choose. There are also several movies and sitcoms that treat death in the same lighthearted fashion, which students will enjoy watching: in *Weekend at Bernie's*, *Little Miss Sunshine*, and an episode of John Cleese's *Fawlty Towers* titled "The Kipper and the Corpse," corpses are manically manhandled; and in *Monty Python's The Meaning of Life* the Grim Reaper comes calling during a dinner party whose obnoxious guests have died as a consequence of consuming salmon mousse that has itself expired.

On a much more serious, moving, and somber note: the ultimate test of humor in the face of death would seem to have been the Nazi concentration camps. The testimony of camp survivors such as Victor Frankl supports Freud's claims regarding the sense of liberation that humor affords. As Frankl records in his memoir *Man's Search for Meaning*:

> Humor was another of the soul's weapons in the fight for self-preservation. It is well known that humor, more than anything else in the human make-up, can afford an aloofness and an ability to rise above any situation, even if only for a few seconds. . . . The attempt to develop a sense of humor and to see things in a humorous light is some

kind of a trick learned while mastering the art of living. Yet it is possible to practice the art of living even in a concentration camp, although suffering is omnipresent. (42–43)

I use Frankl's testimony to transition into Benigni's *Life Is Beautiful*, which treats of the same subject matter. Freud's theory of humor, with its roots in childhood games, has particular relevance to Benigni's story, for the fable concerns a father who, in order to keep his young son ignorant of the terrible circumstances in which his family finds itself, draws on his comedic talents to turn their incarceration into a children's game. By such means, he shields his son from the horror of what is taking place. He dies in the process, but his son survives to narrate the story as an adult and to celebrate his father's legacy: his belief that life *can* be beautiful has not been broken.

If class time permits, I suggest watching this movie in one sitting, although I realize that this might not be possible. It is very much a movie of two halves (the first establishes the father's comedic character, the second explores how he applies this to the situation in the camp), so it is not difficult to choose an appropriate time for intermission. *Life Is Beautiful* proved popular with both audiences and critics, being nominated for seven Academy Awards and winning three Oscars, one for best foreign language film, in 1999. Because of its unusual (and, for some, controversial) treatment of its subject matter, it generated much comment and several academic essays. Prior to showing the movie in class, I placed a selection of these essays, along with the published screenplay (Benigni and Cerami), on library reserve. I also provided a DVD so that students could watch the movie again in their own time, at their own pace, and with fewer distractions. If students decided to write an essay on *Life Is Beautiful* as part of their course evaluation, they were required to use the screenplay as their source text, to use quotations from the critical essays, and to reference Freud's theory from the book of readings: this ensured that they had researched the subject with sufficient seriousness and did not produce superficial, sensationalist interpretations, by which I mean writing that mimics the journalistic style of movie reviews—an ever-present danger in the age of the blog. This approach was doubly important given the gravity of the material.

In my experience, students often have emotional reactions to *Life Is Beautiful*, which confirms their commitment to this comic text and, by extension, their involvement and investment in the course. Students left the class with an increased awareness of what comedy is capable of doing and with clearer insight into why it matters so much, not only to the lives of fictional characters but also in students' own lives. There is no stronger justification for courses of this nature. I hope that my experiences have been helpful to those embarking on such a course, and I wish you success in your own important endeavors to bring comic texts into the classroom.

Works Cited

Benigni, Roberto, and Vincenzo Cerami. *Life Is Beautiful*. Translated by Lisa Taruschio, Faber and Faber, 1999. Screenplay.

Breton, André, editor. *Anthology of Black Humour*. 1939. Translated by Mark Polizzotti, Telegram, 2009.

Ellis, Brett Easton. *American Psycho*. Vintage Books, 1991.

Frankl, Victor. *Man's Search for Meaning: An Introduction to Logotherapy*. Translated by Ilse Lasch, Hodder and Stoughton, 1964.

Freud, Sigmund. "Humour." *The Standard Edition of the Complete Psychological Works of Sigmund Freud*, edited and translated by James Strachey, vol. 21, Hogarth, 1981, pp. 159–66.

———. *Jokes and Their Relation to the Unconscious*. 1905. Edited and translated by James Strachey, Penguin Books, 1983. Vol. 6 of *The Standard Edition of the Complete Psychological Works of Sigmund Freud*.

Heller, Joseph. *Catch-22*. Simon and Schuster, 1961.

Henley, Jon. "Wilde Gets Revenge on Wallpaper." *The Guardian*, 1 Dec. 2000, www.theguardian.com/world/2000/dec/01/classics.books.

Kesey, Ken. *One Flew Over the Cuckoo's Nest*. Viking, 1962.

"The Kipper and the Corpse." Directed by John Howard Davies and Bob Spiers. *Fawlty Towers*, season 2, episode 4, BBC, 1979.

Little Miss Sunshine. Directed by Jonathan Dayton and Valerie Faris, Big Beach Films, 2006.

Monty Python's The Meaning of Life. Directed by Terry Jones, Celandine Films / Monty Python Partnership, 1983.

Morreall, John, editor. *The Philosophy of Laughter and Humor*. State U of New York P, 1987.

Nabokov, Vladimir. *Lolita*. Putnam, 1958.

Palahniuk, Chuck. *Fight Club*. W. W. Norton, 1996.

La vita è bella. Directed by Roberto Benigni, Miramax, 1997.

Weekend at Bernie's. Directed by Ted Kotcheff, Gladden Entertainment, 1989.

Mary Ann Rishel

For Better or for Worse: A Marriage of Humor and Comedy

Teaching comedy can lead down a long prickly path given the complexity of comedy's definition, genre, and purpose. Compounding this complexity, theorists often conflate *humor* with *comedy*, at times using them loosely as synonyms, at other times transmogrifying them into distant relatives. To date, both have been characterized as "anything amusing," an all-purpose, all-points-bulletin description that carries no substance. With this quandary in mind, and with distinctions still much debated, early in my writing seminar on humor and comedy, my students and I establish working definitions, which become a platform for easing into critical analysis. Definitions, however, require a theory of their own, and in the first two weeks of the course, I begin by introducing the three most cited theories of humor to date: superiority; release, or relief; and incongruity. The first two theories have strong advocates; however, current humor scholarship gravitates toward incongruity theory, citing the other two theories as subsets. Students may choose to support these definitions of humor, to modify them, or to propose new ones. As for research in humor studies as a science, I briefly acknowledge it, but I do not include it in the syllabus as it is best assigned to psychology, computational linguistics, cognitive science, and neurophysiology.

The Joke Molecule: Elements and Identifiers

Since my course is a writing seminar, it requires five papers, each with opportunities for revisions, and I supplement the main assignments with brainstorming exercises that are not graded. To understand how humor works as text, as a first-day exercise, and before any discussion of definitions of *humor* and *comedy*, I ask students to write a two-page, two-part thought paper. For the first part of this assignment, students select their favorite joke and describe why they like it. Then, using a large computer screen, we post their responses and cluster underlying concepts. A favorite joke might remind them of their first kiss, a winning goal, or a monster chemistry exam.

Take as an example the following joke: "The world is flat!! – Class of 1491." Students generally agree to the basic elements that make this joke amusing, such as the fifteenth century's preconceived assumptions, but as they explore it from a conceptual perspective, they find that its humorous impact is premised on sophisticated epistemological knowledge. We discuss how its punch line requires comprehension of epistemologies and how anyone not familiar with theories of reasoning would miss its satiric humor. Questions for discussion might include the following: What elements create the humor in your favorite joke? What extratextual knowledge does your joke require?

During our third session, I introduce current scholarship on incongruity theory, focusing on the joke molecule proposed by Salvatore Attardo and Victor Raskin in their *General Theory of Verbal Humor*. Under the category of knowledge resources, Attardo and Raskin maintain that a joke molecule is made up of the following linguistic elements: script opposition, logical mechanism, situation, target, narrative strategy, and language. Script opposition in particular presents itself as a central element of humor, where a joke is fully or partially compatible with two different and opposed scripts that meet at a clash point. This clash point almost always appears as a punch line—that is, the instant when the playful incongruity is recognized and resolved. Returning to our first assignment, for the second part of our thought paper, students now extend their analysis of the joke they selected by applying the theory presented in the Attardo-Raskin humor molecule. Questions for discussion are as follows: Does analyzing your favorite joke using the Attardo-Raskin theory reveal more complexities than you found in your initial analysis? If so, what are they? If not, why not?

For example, with our "Class of 1491" joke, my class discusses the information required to get the joke, which includes the methodologies that make up an epistemology. We parse out character and voice, where the joke's subtext pokes fun at those who trust the prevalent truths of their current knowledge and where it indicates that knowledge is truth only within its specific empirical context. The text conveys a double satire. Both we and the characters are satirized. The satire of the overly confident students in the joke—and the receivers of the joke—reminds us that the truths we now hold can be reconfigured to form new truths as new evidence is discovered. This exercise leads to an introduction of comedy as narrative.

Longer Comedic Narratives

Because of textual limitations in the one-line joke molecule discussed in Attardo and Raskin's general theory of verbal humor, and acknowledging the complexity of humor, Attardo realized the need for adding additional contexts to the theory to accommodate longer, more sophisticated comic narratives ("Multiple-Level Analysis" and "Analysis"). Since Attardo and Raskin's general theory introduces but does not detail elements for longer narratives, my class has found it invaluable to borrow theories and methodologies from neighboring disciplines. An objective is to see how larger comedic frames and the elements of the humor molecule merge within a narrative. In a group collaboration, students examine critical theories from fiction, drama, and cinema to strengthen their analyses, supplemented by journal articles by humor scholars that introduce dialogue with or challenges to the general theory. For example, in addition to joke molecules that end in a punch line, humor scholars have proposed that humor in a comedy can appear as structural and thematic threads through jab lines of script oppositions that do not result in a punch line (Chlopicki; Tsakona), nodals that appear as concentrated humor molecules (Holcomb), and enhancers that support the humor by association but are not humorous themselves (Triezenberg). Humor can also present itself as allusions, metaphors, and motifs (Norrick) or cluster as stacks, strands, bridges, combs, lattices, patterns, and sequences (Chlopicki; Ermida). Any number of literary approaches can be used to analyze the literature, from formalism (characterization, plot, setting, voice and mood, point of view, style and theme) to postmodern theory. In addition, theories housed in other disciplines, such as those in gender studies and ethnic studies, offer sociocultural perspectives. Further, by adopting cross-disciplinary theories, students can see how humor molecules join with comedic threads and how that unity creates complex, and even paradoxical, meaning in a comedy.

With the contextual range of a joke molecule thus expanded, joke molecules and comedic threads become two of three major identifiers of a comedy. The third component is its nonhumorous elements, as all comedies are launched from a serious platform. Thus, from this vantage point, my curriculum creates a frame for a deep reading of a comedy by applying these three methodologies: humor molecules, comic elements, and a nonhumorous foundation. The goal is to have students envision the tripart webbing by providing them practice in analyzing these vectors of humor through crosshatched triangulations.

With these humor and comedy methodologies in place, our focus turns to literature, drama, and film. A rich source for analysis has been Charlie Chaplin's film *The Gold Rush*, where we discuss, for example, two complementary dance scenes, which I call the "Invitation Dance" and the "Potatoes-on-a-Fork Dance" (00:54:16–00:56:00, 01:01:28–01:05:47). During his youth Chaplin knew the indignities of poverty, having been orphaned and left destitute as a child, and, like Chaplin, the Tramp is the ultimate outsider. In the first of these twin dances, Georgia, the dance-hall girl whom the Tramp loves, inadvertently passes by his cabin, and he graciously invites her to visit. During their conversation, she accepts his invitation to a New Year's Eve dinner. The Tramp does not realize she is insincere. After she leaves, the Tramp becomes euphoric with the belief that he is loved, racing around his cabin, leaping on a table, spinning cartwheels, turning over furniture, and standing on his head in pratfalls symbolic of a world turned upside down, each a joke molecule. Then, nearing exhaustion, he tears open a pillow, allowing its feathers to drift over him in a soft embrace, paralleling the gently falling snow outside. Nature itself showers him with kisses. But in keeping with the pathos and irony that embody the Tramp, his dance is interrupted by the sudden return of Georgia, who has forgotten her gloves. She enters to find the Tramp spread-eagle on the floor, covered in debris. His dance has ended in embarrassment. Georgia has caught him foolishly celebrating her unrequited love. Underlying this moment—the Tramp's absolute joy in believing he has found love—is the poignant reality that the beautiful Georgia could never love such a pitiful creature. My class explores the Tramp's psychological need for illusion in order to endure the harsh realities of an existential, but comedic, universe.

In the complementary scene to the Invitation Dance, the narrative expands into a joke topper with the Potatoes-on-a-Fork Dance, which occurs as the Tramp prepares his elaborate New Year's Eve dinner. While waiting for Georgia to arrive, he sees on the table two oversize potatoes. In a burst of imagination, he places each potato on a fork, then transforms the potatoes into an image of magical shoes performing a high-kick dance-hall routine. Each playfully incongruous movement can be understood as a joke molecule: the tilt of his head, the smile, the wobbling bowler hat, the graceful movements of his pathetic body, the potatoes on their forks. As students discuss the comic dimensions of these two dance scenes, they map their critical analyses through jab lines, enhancers, and nodals that reveal themes where illusion is entangled with reality and love with pathos. By parsing, then merging, humor and comic elements, my students develop conceptual frames from the theoretical underpinnings of the two scenes. Questions we ask include the following: What strengths must the Tramp have to overcome the indignities he endures? How does the theme of love provide scaffolding on which the comedy weighs its seriousness? How can the Tramp survive in a world where love is only a comic illusion?

These questions lead to part three of the tripart humor matrix, its nonhumorous and tragic elements, which carry the broader concepts of a philosophy of humor and comedy. Students might be asked to consider the following question: If the Tramp persistently believes that life is filled with possibility and hope, what comic markers rest in existential hopelessness and comedic hope?

Students have the choice to apply these humor-comic frames to other texts, such as Jane Austen's novel *Pride and Prejudice*. A popular topic for Austen's novel addresses epistemological themes, particularly socially constructed thought expressed through hyperextended logic. Among the members of the Bennet family, for example, Mrs. Bennet is the most laughable. Even Austen's narrator satirizes the mother when she describes her, in a joke molecule, as "a woman of mean understanding, little information and uncertain temper" (180). On the surface, Mrs. Bennet does indeed delight us as a ditzy, self-absorbed character lacking in social intelligence, with this personality integrated as a satiric thread throughout the novel. At her first meeting with Mr. Darcy, she is delighted to learn of his enormous wealth. But Mr. Darcy becomes the object of her scorn for snubbing her daughters, and in an imperious joke molecule, Mrs. Bennet says, "[H]e is such a disagreeable man, that it would be quite a misfortune to be liked by him" (186). Yet, while the comic contrast she provides with other members of the family is valid within its frame, the satire does her a disservice, as her place within society carries a serious theme. By examining opposites in her character, students generally agree that Mrs. Bennet understands consequences and that she instinctively knows, as a woman of meager wealth, that she cannot overturn society's strictures. She can only protect her daughters by ensuring their economic futures, and she can only command attention for her plight through comic exaggeration. In a merging of the joke molecule, comic strands, and the serious undercurrent, she says, "Nobody can tell what I suffer! But it is always so. Those who do not complain are never pitied" (232). As a participant of this society, however comic she is, she demonstrates the most common sense. Her comic persona protects her from the society that patronizes her. From readings of early-nineteenth-century culture, the class presents brief reports on how this society was structured and how Mrs. Bennet's status was imposed upon her. Questions for discussion include the following: How does Mrs. Bennet's comic logic satirize the illogical culture in which she lives? Is she deserving of Austen's satire, or is she the satirist?

To raise the critical value in my students' final papers, our course advances our study of comic narratives to higher conceptual arenas by exploring first principles in comic philosophies. This last section of the course sets forth a cognitive domain as progressing from background information to high-value judgment. Roddy Doyle's novel *Paddy Clarke Ha Ha Ha* is a strong choice for critical interpretation because it embraces a comic-tragic philosophy. In this novel, socially constructed Catholic reasoning shapes Paddy's moral conflict as he struggles to survive his brutal culture. Some of my students have argued that this is not a comedy at all but a serious novel with humor that only skims its serious language and fragile logic. In this novel of dark ironies, the Irish idioms in the boys' dialogue are amusing, each a joke molecule, but the novel's undercurrents of cruelty and violence are chilling. The seriousness is driven through silences. Dramatizing a constructed helplessness, this novel narrates a vicious glee for the violence that will haunt these characters as adults. The brutality the boys inflict on each other is also paralleled in Paddy Clarke's family. Interestingly, however, in spite of the novel's violence, its code of honor includes behavior that Paddy Clarke and his friends subscribe to as Catholics. In a scene where the boys find a dead rat in their neighbor's yard, they feel morally compelled to bury it in a proper funeral, but they hesitate to remove it from the ground because the yard and, therefore, the rat belong to the neighbor. They reason that taking the rat would be stealing. Paddy struggles with his moral code in the following passage:

> We were in Donnelly's yard, behind the barn. We'd have to smuggle the rat out.
>
> —Why?
>
> —It's their rat.
>
> Questions like that spoiled everything. (Doyle 73)

Among the serious elements in this novel is the moral anguish Paddy experiences when he discovers faulty reasoning in his previous thinking. His is not a world that invites moral reasoning but a world of stories where the false ones make the most sense. These values are playfully conveyed through the humor molecules as wit and through comic resignation; however, the truth manifests itself as too frightening or too absurd to be humorous. Paddy writes, "Mister Quigley was dead and Missis Quigley wasn't that old, so she must have done something to him; that was what everyone thought. We decided that she'd ground up a wine glass and put the powder in his omelette—I'd seen that in Hitchcock Presents and it made a lot of sense" (Doyle 77). The tripped-up logic in this sentence creates a run of joke molecules leading to Paddy's growing awareness that moral codes have to do with death. The serious theme in this novel announces the inevitability of epistemological absurdities; since the boys can never truly survive this absurdity, they suppress the pain through comedy. As the class concludes their reading of this novel, we ask the following: In what ways does this novel narrate a comic philosophy? This question leads to a broader question: In what ways does comedy offer us a philosophy that differs from nonhumorous literature in its goals, methods, and principles?

A typical assignment, therefore, asks that students consider the following suggestions for developing an academic paper:

> Read or view a literary comedy (e.g., a short story, novel, or film).
> Narrow the topic so that it is manageable for a five-page paper.
> Analyze several representative jokes in the comedy using the elements of a humor molecule.
> Identify a comic jab line, thread, running motif, enhancer, or nodal from the larger narrative.

Analyze the larger context, including nonhumorous elements, by applying a critical or literary theory we have introduced in class. Supplement this with several research articles on that theory.

Extend the analysis to include a high-value theme housed in a conceptual, critical, literary, or philosophical thesis.

Comedy as Theory

Why teach comedy? We celebrate comedy because it operates within a set of life-affirming values, and it has at its heart a moral foundation premised on happiness as a human right. Its philosophy resides in a comic universe where comic markers narrate existential hopelessness and comedic hope. Humor forges the elements of comedy. To this end, comedy can be defined as follows: a narrative composed of tripart webbings of humor molecules, comedic threads, and a serious platform that coalesce into complex networks of philosophies and truth. In an existential world, at the very least, it offers an explanation. In a world of imagination, it offers hope. Comedy, as a tripart structure, introduces an original way of evaluating and valuing a text and thus advances a new interpretative theory. It introduces new ways of seeing. That theory is exciting.

Works Cited

Attardo, Salvatore. "Analysis of Humorous Narratives." *Humor: International Journal of Humor Research*, vol. 11, no. 3, 1998, pp. 231–60.

———. "A Multiple-Level Analysis of Jokes." *Humor: International Journal of Humor Research*, vol. 2, no. 4, 1989, pp. 438–39.

Attardo, Salvatore, and Victor Raskin. *The General Theory of Verbal Humor.* Mouton de Gruyter, 1993.

Austen, Jane. *Her Complete Novels:* Pride and Prejudice. Crown, 1981.

Chlopicki, Wladyslaw. "An Approach to the Analysis of Verbal Humor in Short Stories." *Humor: International Journal of Humor Research*, vol. 10, no. 3, 1997, pp. 333–46.

Doyle, Roddy. *Paddy Clarke Ha Ha Ha.* 4th ed., Penguin Books, 1995.

Ermida, Isabel. *The Language of Comic Narratives: Humor Construction in Short Stories.* Mouton de Gruyter, 2008.

The Gold Rush. Directed by Charlie Chaplin, United Artists, 1925. *YouTube*, uploaded by Jonatan Svensson Glad, 17 Sept. 2016, www.youtube.com/watch?v=a-nyVGSEjyU.

Holcomb, Christopher. "Nodal Humor in Comic Narrative: A Semantic Analysis of Two Stories by Twain and Wodehouse." *Humor: International Journal of Humor Research*, vol. 5, no. 3, 1992, pp. 233–50.

Norrick, Neal R. "Intertextuality in Humor." *Humor: International Journal of Humor Research*, vol. 2, no. 2, 1989, pp. 117–39.

Triezenberg, Katrina. "Humor Enhancers in the Study of Humorous Literature." *Humor: International Journal of Humor Research*, vol. 17, no. 4, 2004, pp. 411–18.

Tsakona, Villy. "Jab Lines in Narrative Jokes." *Humor: International Journal of Humor Research*, vol. 16, no. 3, 2003, pp. 315–29.

Jess Landis

Transitioning with Laughter: Comedy in the First-Year Seminar

Humor can be effective and productive in the classroom as both a practice and a subject of inquiry. Personally, I use it to help students feel more comfortable with one another and to connect with them by dismantling the inherent hierarchy of the classroom. While I like to think myself a regular Joan Rivers in front of the classroom, I have learned that what I find funny is almost never what my traditionally aged students find funny. (This becomes increasingly true as the age gap between us widens.) While I still sneak in the occasional wisecrack of my own, I mostly rely on the texts I teach to deliver the punch lines. Comic texts not only keep students interested but also help first-year students understand expectations associated with academic rigor and engagement. This essay explores the usefulness of teaching comic texts specifically in first-year seminars. Using my own course as a model, I demonstrate how comedy as content, broadly conceived, aids in accomplishing the sometimes disparate social and academic goals of the first-year seminar.

The focus on comic texts in my seminar was born initially of sheer academic selfishness. When choosing a topic for a first-year seminar at my first full-time faculty job, one not in my chosen field, I wanted to hang on to something in my specialty area, which includes gender studies and

Shakespeare. I settled on a general theme of comedy that would allow me to slip in at least one Shakespeare play, determined to help students see Shakespeare in a new light.

Choosing the theme of "Comedy: What Makes Us Laugh and Why?" for the seminar forced me to consider new kinds of texts alongside Shakespearean standbys. I wanted to design a course that broadly appealed to students. In the year I began teaching this course, 2013, comedy was experiencing a cultural moment of importance, and there was increased public interest in discussing it in a critical way. Media outlets were touting comedians like Dave Chappelle, Amy Schumer, and Aziz Ansari as important cultural commentators. Articles about how humor mirrors societal concerns emerged on websites like *Splitsider* and in venerable publications like *Vanity Fair*. Hoping to capitalize on this cultural interest, I added course content about humor theory, stand-up comedy, and film comedy to Shakespeare. The benefits of the theme presented themselves quickly; it spoke to academic learning outcomes by offering plenty of food for thought and to first-year transition goals by promoting bonds and easing anxiety.

Introducing Academic Expectations with Comic Texts

A large majority of US four-year institutions of higher education offer first-year seminars. The purpose of these seminars varies from one institution to the next, but the general aim is "to introduce students to the college experience and teach them how to master it" (Bigger). George D. Kuh, an expert in higher education, asserts that first-year seminars develop "critical inquiry" and "intellectual and practical competencies" (9). The 2019–20 course catalog description of the required First Year Inquiry Seminar at Franklin Pierce University, my institution, states, "Students select one . . . academically-engaging, inquiry-based [topic] based on their interests. Each section, regardless of theme, works on improving students' academic skills . . . [of] information literacy, inquiry and analysis, and career exploration" (*2019–2020 Academic Catalog* 260). While unstated in the course catalog, an unofficial goal of this course is to help students adjust to college life socially by offering them nontraditional, group classroom experiences and direct access to faculty advisors who teach the course.

So, what makes comedy a particularly good theme for this and other first-year seminars? First, it is a complex, interdisciplinary topic with easy access points that is unlikely to intimidate first-year students. Everyone laughs and has seen a comedic movie, television show, or stand-up routine. The theme eases students into the sometimes daunting initiation into academia by encouraging them to look at something familiar and see it through new lenses. The study of humor pulls from a variety of academic fields, including literature, philosophy, media studies, evolutionary biology, and anthropology, making it a broadly appealing topic to students with diverse academic interests.

My course's theme is not unique; similar first-year seminars that investigate comedy exist at other institutions, such as Duke University, Butler University, and Loyola Marymount University. Anthony Ciccone, Renee Meyers, and Stephanie Waldman present a case study of such a course at the University of Wisconsin, Milwaukee, in a 2008 article. They conclude that comedy as a theme for a first-year seminar can "promote . . . the development of complex thinking" (Ciccone et al. 309) and can help students consider and improve their learning practice (313). Introducing humor into the classroom through content or teaching style also encourages students to pay attention. A study measuring student interest in course material when an instructor employed humor found student interest correlated positively with instructors' use of relevant and appropriate humor (Machlev and Karlin 197). The theme can help students be more conscientious learners by asking them to grapple with familiar but difficult content.

However, the comedy often studied in academia may seem inaccessible or boring to students. Sometimes they believe that comedy from past eras is passé and that the more intellectual comedians of today are not relatable. Alleen and Don Nilsen, cofounders of the International Society for Humor Studies, see part of the project of studying humor as "help[ing] students mature in their taste and appreciation. [Instructors] need to educate students to catch onto a multitude of allusions and to have the patience required for reading and appreciating certain kinds of humor" (34). They then point out that "it takes skill and practice, along with a broad, cultural background to understand the full range of humor" (35). First-year students do not always have the experience or exposure to understand, let alone seek out, the kind of critical comedic texts that academics deem worthy of study. Comparison can be a valuable strategy that gets students to recognize and appreciate sophisticated humor.

I want students to think about what is at stake in humor and to develop the skills of inquiry and analysis; the comedic texts are merely vehicles that deliver that lesson. When we encounter references to authors like Molière or P. G. Wodehouse, I offer students similar, more familiar examples, such as the movies *Clueless* or *Animal House*. I am less concerned that they know what Molière wrote than I am that they understand the "so what" behind the comedy. Ellie Fitts Fulmer and Nia Nunn Makepeace claim that comic texts can be useful because they offer students "a way to embrace difficult material" (40). My job as an instructor of first-year students is to introduce challenging, college-level work and transferrable skills that help them feel confident enough to succeed academically. My course on comedy allows them to practice these skills and navigate their transition from high school to college.

Studying Humor to Ease the Transition to College

There are also social benefits of making comedy a theme in first-year seminars. Comedic content helps students manage their transition from high school to college by aiding their social journey. In a literature review for a study of the use of humor in the college classroom, Kristin Trefts and Sarah Blakeslee found that introducing humor into instruction is used "as an aid in teaching sensitive subjects, in reducing classroom tension, to make learning more personable and enjoyable, to mold a collection of individuals into a group, to cultivate spirit, to alleviate stress . . . to motivate and energize . . . [and] to build confidence" (370). Many of these benefits overlap with the orientation goals of first-year seminars. It stands to reason that comedy as a subject of study or as course content would accomplish some of the same goals.

Comedic content alleviates social pressure and promotes bonds between peers. Students realize that their textual reference points are similar and that they have common interests. Amid my lessons about humor, they remind each other of bits, crack each other up, and band together to implore me to show clips of their favorites. Studying humor may also help students ease tension in their lives outside the classroom. Today's students report experiencing a lot of stress and anxiety. A 2018 study by the American College Health Association reported that almost thirty percent of college students feel that anxiety has affected their academic performances (*American College Health Association* 5). Realistically speaking, levels of anxiety may be heightened at the beginning of a student's first year, when first-year seminars are typically offered. Comedic course content and shared positive experiences with peers may offer some relief from the isolation many students feel during their transition to college. In a

2004 study, Gregory Hickman and Garnet Crossland hypothesized that "it seems plausible that humor may play a role as a coping mechanism on the initial adjustment of college freshmen" (226). They measured students' ability to use humor as a coping mechanism in stressful times and found that it "is an important factor in predicting initial indices of college adjustment" (240). Their findings suggest that students' exposure to and usage of humor positively impact their college success. Studying humor, then, may help students feel more empowered when facing their own challenges during this time.

Another transition issue that first-year students face is learning to understand and accept new and diverse ideas and people they may not have encountered before. Humor, as a course theme and as a pedagogical tool, creates an environment in which students may feel more comfortable confronting and discussing these issues. In developing a course on humor for high school students, Taylor Schulze posits that "understanding how humor is socially constructed puts students on the road to developing a greater sense of other cultures' gestures, customs, and value systems" and that "humor alerts students to what is multiple. . . . [It] prepares [them] to meet new situations with flexible attitudes and earnest empathy." Similarly, Nilsen and Nilsen assert that humor can alleviate discomfort when "talk[ing] about cultural difference" (39). Such issues seem particularly important in a first-year seminar, an academic setting meant to help students understand that they will encounter new ideas and different people in a new environment.

Teaching Nontraditional Comic Texts alongside Shakespeare

Here I turn to the details of my own first-year seminar on comedy, including the comic—and related—texts I assign. Although the idea of comedy as a theme appeals to students, they actually find it frustrating at first. They initially want to insist that any text we encounter is funny simply because it is funny. They often do not see value in analyzing jokes and comedy as texts; they do not want to kill the joke. To create student buy-in, it is helpful to assign examples of critical comedy, or comedy that asks its audience to question the status quo. I try to allow the assigned comic texts to lead students to want to think critically about everything from stand-up to Shakespeare. To this end, inquiry-based pedagogy becomes an important tool.

Comedy, critical or not, lends itself to academic inquiry because even jokes themselves can easily be seen as questions ("Why did the chicken cross the road?"). For this reason, individual jokes are the first primary texts we study in class. Presenting a joke as a question opens up discussion about context and rhetorical choices, pushing students beyond their focus on the humorous effect. Sharing strategies for a course on comedy, the English professor Richard F. Hardin advises avoiding the "thudding" question, "Why is this funny?" (80). Instead, he has students look at comic texts through a historical or biographical lens to understand humor in context. His approach is interesting because it is interrogative, requiring students to consider questions beyond the humor itself. It is challenging to get first-year students to understand what is behind questions posed by comedic texts and what is at stake in answering them; offering diverse examples can help.

The texts we discuss comprise a variety of material because of my broad understanding of a *text*. Some of the first substantial texts we read are not comic texts but overviews of theoretical approaches, like Peter McGraw's TED talk on the benign violation theory of humor and Mary Beard's 2014 article "What's So Funny?," which covers several theories of laughter and humor. Even though these readings are not technically academic texts, most students still find them difficult, so we discuss critical reading strategies as we go through their content. These skills then help students adopt a critical eye when approaching nontraditional texts, such as media clips of sketches, stand-up sets, films, and television. These kinds of texts encourage discussion of controversial subjects and expose students to content they will likely encounter in other college classrooms but may not have tackled in high school. For example, we watch Wanda Sykes's or Hannah Gadsby's specials, then talk about inequality based on gender or sexual identity, and we view sketches from *Key and Peele* before discussing the caveats and possibilities of racial humor. This helps students see that jokes on these subjects are possible but that they come with a nuanced set of rules. Students come to see comedy as a tool of social critique. Because we first read theoretical texts, students have frameworks to help them analyze comedy and academic language to discuss it, making them more open to engaging with controversial subjects. The practice they get interpreting these comic texts sets the tone for studying more traditional comedic texts, like those of Shakespeare.

Eventually, the focus of the course turns to conventions of comedy as a genre. I pair Shakespeare's *The Taming of the Shrew* with the film *Ten Things I Hate about You* or Shakespeare's *Twelfth Night* with *She's the Man* by first introducing a unit on comedic films. We discuss general origins of cinematic comedy and then concentrate on the conventions of romantic comedy since the movies mentioned above fall into that genre. Students take guided notes as we watch the films together in order to demonstrate their understanding of these conventions. Then we move into reading the paired play. By the time students get to Shakespeare, they have seen how pop culture and academic discourse exist side by side and produce teleological understandings of each other. I ask students to view the play as an example of early modern pop culture and encourage them to find the joke in the Elizabethan language structures they so often resist. They recognize Julia Stiles's Kat from *Ten Things* in *Taming*'s Katherine and Amanda Bynes's character in *She's the Man* in *Twelfth Night*'s Viola. They become invested in identifying how the film interprets or eliminates elements of the Shakespearean text. Often without realizing it, students engage in real academic inquiry and become more confident in their abilities to understand difficult texts, two important goals for first-year seminars.

This unit is brief; the film viewing and the play take about three weeks of a fifteen-week course, but the impact of the exercise is powerful. Studying Shakespeare's comedy provides opportunities to raise sophisticated topics like the interplay between ontology and gender identity, themes also prevalent in the corresponding movies. Showing the film first creates a familiarity with which students can read the play, but reading the play can also improve interpretations of the films. The English professor L. Monique Pittman's initial experience pairing *Taming* and *Ten Things* revealed interesting student tendencies: "While students were more than willing to dissect the gender trouble readily observable in Shakespeare's sixteenth-century play, my students steadily resisted any serious critique of the recent film version" (144). After reading the play, however, her students more easily identified the "gender trouble" in *Ten Things*, moving them beyond surface reactions and helping them develop a more critical eye.

Reading the films and then the plays helps students transition into burgeoning academics. Assigning Shakespeare in a first-year seminar has added benefits for students' social transition to college. Students in my first-year seminar bond as they groan in unison when the play is assigned and gather outside class to read and help one another understand it. They become an academic community and build bonds. The experience of reading comic texts—modern or historical—boosts students' peer-to-peer interactions, builds academic skills, and engages students through content that interests them.

Works Cited

American College Health Association National College Health Assessment II: Reference Group Executive Summary Spring 2018. American College Health Association, 2018.

Beard, Mary. "What's So Funny? So Many Theories of Laughter, So Many Chortles Left Unexplained." *The Chronicle of Higher Education*, vol. 60, no. 41, 18 July 2014, pp. B6–B9.

Bigger, Jessica J. "Improving the Odds for Freshman Success." *NACADA Clearinghouse of Academic Advising Resources*, 2005, www.nacada.ksu.edu/Resources/Clearinghouse/View-Articles/Advising-first-year-students.aspx.

Ciccone, Anthony, et al. "What's So Funny? Moving Students toward Complex Thinking in a Course on Comedy and Laughter." *Arts and Humanities in Higher Education*, vol. 7, no, 2, 2008, pp. 308–22.

Fitts Fulmer, Ellie, and Nia Nunn Makepeace. " 'It's Okay to Laugh, Right?': Toward a Pedagogy of Racial Comedy in Multicultural Education." *Perspectives on Urban Education*, vol. 12, no. 2, 2015, pp. 38–53.

Gadsby, Hannah. *Nanette*. Directed by John Olb and Madeleine Parry, Guesswork Television, 2018. *Netflix* app.

Hardin, Richard F. "Discussing Comedy—an Interrogative Approach." *CEA Forum*, vol. 41, no. 1, 2012, pp. 78–93.

Hickman, Gregory P., and Garnet L. Crossland. "The Predictive Nature of Humor, Authoritative Parenting Style, and Academic Achievement on Indices of Initial Adjustment and Commitment to College among College Freshmen." *Journal of College Student Retention*, vol. 6, no. 2, Aug. 2004, pp. 225–45.

Key and Peele. Created by Keegan-Michael Key and Jordan Peele, Monkeypaw Productions, 2012–15.

Kuh, George D. *High-Impact Educational Practices: What They Are, Who Has Access to Them, and Why They Matter*. Association of American Colleges and Universities, 2008.

Machlev, Moshe, and Nancy J. Karlin. "The Relationship between Instructor Use of Different Types of Humor and Student Interest in Course Material." *College Teaching*, vol. 65, no. 4, 2017, pp. 192–200.

McGraw, Peter. "What Makes Things Funny." *TEDxBoulder*, 2010, tedxboulder.com/videos/what-makes-things-funny.

Nilsen, Alleen Pace, and Don L. F. Nilsen. "The Straw Man Meets His Match: Six Arguments for Studying Humor in the English Classroom." *The English Journal*, vol. 88, no. 4, 1999, pp. 34–42.

Pittman, L. Monique. "Taming *10 Things I Hate About You*: Shakespeare and the Teenage Film Audience." *Literature/Film Quarterly*, vol. 32, no. 2, 2004, pp. 144–52.

Schulze, Taylor. *"What's So Funny?": Exploring Comedy, Humor, and Laughter. PeterSmagorinsky.net*, www.petersmagorinsky.net/Units/Schulze_2012.pdf. Accessed 7 Sept. 2022.

Shakespeare, William. *The Taming of the Shrew*. Edited by Barbara Mowat and Paul Werstine, Simon and Schuster, 1992.

———. *Twelfth Night*. Edited by Barbara Mowat and Paul Werstine, Simon and Schuster, 1993.
She's the Man. Directed by Andy Fickman, DreamWorks Pictures, 2006.
Sykes, Wanda. *Wanda Sykes: Sick and Tired*. Image Entertainment, 2006.
Ten Things I Hate about You. Directed by Gil Junger, Touchstone Pictures, 1999.
Trefts, Kristin, and Sarah Blakeslee. "Did You Hear the One about the Boolean Operators? Incorporating Comedy into Library Instruction." *Reference Services Review*, vol. 28, no. 4, 2000, pp. 369–77.
2019–2020 Academic Catalog. Franklin Pierce University, www.franklinpierce.edu/academics/FranklinPierceCatalog1920.pdf. Accessed 29 Nov. 2022.

Jared Champion

Stand-Up Comedy, Central Questions, and Databases

Just a couple years ago, I taught a seminar titled Stand-Up Comedy and Social Discourse. My college offered the course as a one-hour honors seminar that met once a week. The course filled up almost immediately with sixteen bright, motivated students. The course culminated with a conference-style colloquium where students presented papers on comedians and listened to a keynote address by Rebecca Krefting. I used the course to develop a method for shepherding students through a paper-writing process that leads to complicated and articulate arguments. This essay outlines the successes, pitfalls, and challenges I discovered while developing this method, which I have found yields strong analytic papers.

In this method, everything stems from the central question: the question provides a map for the entire paper's content, structure, revision, and development. I built much of this step from *The Craft of Research*, by Wayne Booth, Gregory Colomb, and Joseph Williams, which discusses the importance and nuances of an effective research question at length (35–48). In Stand-Up Comedy and Social Discourse, I scaffolded assignment deadlines with concrete benchmarks that began when students created a central question. To help students come up with a central question,

I gave them a sort of Mad Lib–style prompt that looked something like this:

> How does the comedian ___(of your choice)___ shape meaning around ___(A)___ in their special ___(any of the comedy specials from the syllabus)___? Or: How do ___(A)___ and ___(A)___ interact in the material from ___(special of your choice from the syllabus)___ to shape meaning?

For A, students chose from the following list: race, gender, class, labor, place, money, bodies, manhood, womanhood, and power. Once students created a tentative central question, I met with each student to consider the relative advantages of their question as well as potential pitfalls. A student who asked "How does Chris Rock shape meaning around race in his special *Bring the Pain*?" was encouraged to narrow the topic because Rock focuses so heavily on race in the special: a revised question might ask, "How does Chris Rock shape meaning around race and gender in his special *Bring the Pain*?" I credit much of my students' success in this course to their careful revisions of central questions that led to strong papers because the questions afforded the class direction with a clear path to a strong, complicated thesis that would answer the central question.

I also wanted students to engage with critical scholarship, but I wanted to temper the work requirements, given that the course earned students only one credit hour. I relied heavily on Gerald Graff and Cathy Birkenstein's *They Say, I Say*, which will come as no surprise to most instructors. I also leaned heavily on Joseph Bizup's article "BEAM: A Rhetorical Vocabulary for Teaching Research-Based Writing," which reframes the terms *primary sources* and *secondary sources* to a more functional rubric that describes how scholars use sources rather than what the sources are or are not. For Bizup, the common terms *primary* and *secondary* cause students to examine what a source *is* rather than consider how the source might be *used* in the paper. Bizup replaces these categories with the acronyms FEAT or BEAM, which describe how scholars utilize sources in analytic works:

> Fact/Background (F/B): "materials whose claims a writer accepts as fact" (75).
> Exhibit (E): "materials a writer offers for explication, analysis, or interpretation" (75).
> Argument (A): "materials whose claims a writer affirms, disputes, refines, or extends in some way" (75).

> Theory/Method (T/M): "materials from which a writer derives a governing concept or manner of working" (76).

In my own teaching, I have found these terms to be extremely useful for the creation of annotated bibliographies or research plans because, as Bizup argues, the terms help student writers see the options for using materials more clearly: "Writers *rely on* background sources, *interpret* or *analyze* exhibits, *engage* arguments, and *follow* methods" (81). Students responded well to these categories, and it helped many students distinguish between writing arguments *to* comedians and writing arguments *about* comedians, a common struggle for students studying humor.

Students generally tended to understand how to use sources as exhibits and background (though they often relied on sources as background when the same sources proved far more effective as arguments). I found the best work comes from pushing students to use materials as arguments and methods in order to inform their analysis of the exhibit material.

I have found that a few specific sources lend themselves well to use as arguments.[1] Two notable examples are Linda Mizjewski's *Pretty/Funny: Women Comedians and Body Politics* and David Gillota's *Ethnic Humor in Multiethnic America*. Likewise, students often make great use of the following sources, which lend themselves well to use as method sources: Krefting's "The Laughscape of American Humor," from *All Joking Aside: American Humor and Its Discontents* (1–16); Lawrence Mintz's "Standup Comedy as Social and Cultural Mediation"; and Prakash Kona's "Being George Carlin: *Carlinesque* as Performative Resistance."

To make the distinctions in source use clearer for students, I used specific exercises and practices that positioned students as writers from the outset of the course. Once students had functional central questions in place, they then gathered exhibit materials in what I termed "the exhibit database." For the database, I instructed students to write their central question at the top of a *Word* document. Then, students combed through their exhibit material to gather pieces of evidence in the database that could help them answer the central question: quotations, details, observations, and so forth. I recommended that students turn the closed captions on so they could read the material while hearing it. This also helped ensure accurate transcription from the comedy special to the database. The database had just a few basic rules that I still use today:

> Each section should open with a formatted bibliographic entry for the exhibit source.

If students wonder whether or not to include a detail, quotation, or observation in the database, the answer is always "yes."

Students should not simply copy and paste material from an online source. Instead, all entries into the database should be typed out.

Everything that goes into the database should be immediately observable in the exhibit material (the student's specific comedy special in this case). No judgments, evaluations, or interpretations.

The database should be at least as long as the final paper (roughly 250–300 words per page).

For this course, I shared a short sample (the first three entries) from a seven-page database I built for my own project on Christopher Titus's comedy special, *Norman Rockwell Is Bleeding*:

> Titus, Christopher. *Norman Rockwell Is Bleeding*. Directed by Jack Kenny, Deranged Entertainment, 2004.
>
> - The set looks like a living room with no furniture other than the chair featured in Titus's show's black-and-white soliloquies. The set's left side is orderly and neat, but the right side has holes in the wall, molding and tiles ripped from their places, and a picture of a tidal wave hung askew.
> - "63% of American families are now considered dysfunctional. My god. That means we're the majority. We're normal" (Titus 00:01:00–00:01:05).
> - "We actually have no pictures of my dad where he is *not* holding a beer. Weddings, funerals, water skiing, parent-teacher conference" (Titus 00:01:30–00:01:38).

For those considering this method, I should note that the database is especially useful for instructors who teach students who worry more about reaching page-length requirements than about enhancing the paper's quality; students using databases begin the writing process with more material than necessary, so students can direct their energy to quality rather than quantity.

Once students collected a sufficient amount of evidence for the database, we put aside those materials briefly in order to develop a battery of what I refer to as "complicating questions." In this course, the class completed an exercise where each student wrote their central question at the top of a sheet of paper. Students, with their desks arranged in a circle, passed the sheets around the room clockwise. Each student added a complicating question to the sheet in front of them and then passed the paper to the left. By the end, each student had a list of several dozen questions that looked something like this abbreviated version:

Central question:

>How does Michael Che's special, *Michael Che Matters*, address issues of race and gender?

Complicating questions:

>Does Che discuss men differently than women? How?
>How does his material explicitly discuss race and gender together?
>Does his treatment of race and gender change in any way? If so, how?
>How does he address his own race and gender?

I encouraged students to consider the ways the central question for their own paper could be adapted to complicate the arguments their peers set out to answer. For instance, a student considering questions of intersectionality could ask another student to consider intersectionality in their paper as well. In doing so, I hoped students would see themselves not only as scholars with a clear critical lens that transcended a single research project but also as engaging in a conversation where scholarly stakes constantly informed the ebbs and flows of all scholarship, not just their own.

After building a complete list of complicating questions, a full exhibit database, and a central question, students then began crafting paragraphs. Students chose one complicating question that they felt was most likely to help them answer the central question. Then students scoured the database for evidence that might help answer the question. When students answered the complicating question using evidence, they then converted the complicating question into an affirmative claim that would open the paper. For example, if a student hoped to answer the question "How does Nikki Glaser address shame and womanhood in her special, *Perfect*?," they then worked to create an affirmative answer to that question that ultimately served as a claim: "Nikki Glaser addresses shame and womanhood in her special, *Perfect*, through self-deprecating humor that addresses her own shame surrounding her body." The student could then draw on the database to ground this claim in the evidence they used to answer the question.

At this point, students then unpacked or broke down the evidence cited to answer the complicating question. The payoff came when students offered a simple, concise statement that explained how this specific claim and evidence helped answer the larger central question guiding the essay—the "so what," as it's known informally. In the end, the body paragraphs came together to follow a familiar structure. First came the claim, the answer to the complicating question. This was followed by the evidence—that is, where the student found the answer to the question. After the evidence came the analysis, in which the student unpacked the evidence they had just offered, followed by the "so what," where the student explained how the claim and evidence helped answer the central question.

These paragraphs often required a bit of revision, and students sometimes began with evidence followed by a claim. Knowing this, instructors utilizing this method should watch for paragraphs that are particularly short and open with evidence so that students can be coached through revision, which requires drawing the claim to the front and developing the analysis in paragraphs.

Papers were generally choppy and disjointed after this stage, so students needed to develop effective and clear transitions. Over the years, I have found that students struggle to create effective transitions beyond adding introductory clauses. These make for poor transitions because indentations in paragraphs do the same rhetorical work as tired introductory words like *next, then, furthermore,* and so on. I wanted students to understand the ways transitions can complement the argument by guiding the reader's attention through the paper's logic. To do so, I had students use a technique I call a "pocket square," a term I borrow from men's fashion, where a suit and tie includes a matching handkerchief to tie the entire look together. For the papers, students were told to find the key word—the "pocket square"—in the final line of a paragraph and then use this word in the opening line of the next paragraph, a technique that forced students to explain the logical connection between the two paragraphs. This looked a bit like these fictional examples:

> Final sentence of a paragraph: "This shows that Hannah Gadsby's tone in her anti-comedy special, *Nanette*, emphasizes her personal rage by creating contrast with the material's gravity."
> First line in the succeeding paragraph before introducing the pocket square: "Hannah Gadsby delivers her material in a calm, measured pace that helps slowly walk the audience through her personal traumas."
> First line in the succeeding paragraph after introducing the pocket square: "Hannah Gadsby uses her pacing to complement her tone

> by delivering the material in a calm, measured pace that helps slowly walk the audience through her personal traumas."

The pocket square exercise offers students a simple yet effective path to a clear transition that signals not only the introduction of a new idea but also the logical connection to the previous idea (what some might call "flow").

In this course, students wrote the introduction toward the end of the process by following a method I adapted from John Swales and Christine B. Feak's CARS (Create a Research Space) model (331–43). Students brought in their database to class one day later in the semester to workshop the introduction. In class, I had students type their question about two-thirds of the way down a *Word* document. Then, I had students start the paper by using a representative example from their database to establish the question for their readers. Instead of using vague language like "hook the reader's attention," I focused on more concrete instructions: for instance, "Your job is to give an example that highlights the key themes in your central question and then to explain to the reader how this question stems from the example." A representative example is just one way to establish the central question, so I offer students three other concrete methods for creating an effective introduction:

> *Question raised by the exhibit.* This is when students draw entirely from the exhibit (i.e., the primary materials) to show that the question needs to be asked. This model works particularly well with students early in their college career because it only requires a database and critical thought.
>
> *Problem with the scholarship.* In this model, students pair an example from the exhibit with critical work to show that the scholarship needs to be revised to account for the exhibit material. This model worked nicely with the structure of my course because students had an article to pair with any special on the syllabus.
>
> *Knowledge gap.* Students rely entirely on scholarship in this model in order to show that many scholars have danced around this specific topic but have never asked this specific question. This not only is the most sophisticated model but also requires the most research.

Students created generally strong introductions but not without some struggles. Most commonly, students resisted using database material in the introductions because they wanted to save their best material for the body paragraphs. Many created their first drafts by offering general background information about comedy, the comedian, or the social issue rather than evidence that established the question. This allowed for a productive conversation about the ways material can often be used in a paper twice so long as it accomplishes different rhetorical work: in the introduction the material could be background but could then be reused as exhibit material, or evidence, to ground a claim in the body paragraphs, most often in the first paragraph.

Students finished the process by crafting conclusions, and this was deliberate because students tend to write their strongest initial thesis in the first draft of a conclusion. Students are often told that conclusions should "wrap up" their papers, which is mostly true and means that most students will land on a very strong thesis in the first draft. Some of my most rewarding moments in composition classes have been when I found a complex, illuminating thesis in the rough draft of a student's conclusion. However, I also encouraged students to think of their body paragraphs as a microcosm of the entire paper: the biggest claim is the thesis, presented in the introduction; the evidence and analysis are presented in the body paragraphs; and the conclusion should then answer the question, "So what?" To clarify the purpose of a conclusion for my students, I asked them to develop concluding paragraphs that explained the stakes of their essay to an academic audience: Does the paper change how we treat all work by this comedian? The work that deals with the same material? Just this special? In the end, students were able to spell out the stakes rather clearly and to draw their papers neatly to a close.

I still look back on that semester as a favorite. Students created strong papers and engaged with humor and irony in ways that surpassed my expectations. As one final note, though, class discussions took an entirely different tone when students approached comedy specials that discussed social issues they cared deeply about, especially when the comedian offered novel insights. The following are a handful of comedy specials and texts that, when paired, led to particularly fruitful class discussions: Jeff Foxworthy's album *You Might Be a Redneck If . . .* and J. David Thomas's article "Jeff Foxworthy's Redneck Humor and the Boundaries of Middle-Class American Whiteness," Dave Chappelle's *Killing Them Softly* and Bambi Haggins's chapter "Dave Chappelle: Provocateur in the Promised Land" (*Laughing Mad* 178–236), and Maria Bamford's *Old Baby* and Simon Cross's article "Visualizing Madness: Mental Illness and Public Representation."

There are, of course, countless other pairings that might work. I offer these solely as helpful suggestions as I believe they would anchor any syllabus on stand-up comedy. Finally, I hope the method described here helps other instructors guide students through texts, comedic or otherwise.

Note

1. I explain to students that, much like the word *theory* in the sciences, *argument* means something quite different in an academic setting. In fact, an academic argument does not require any disagreement. As I tell students, to use a source as an argument source, they should revise, update, adjust, or add to what the author of the source text has already claimed. If students want to confirm adequate engagement with the source as an argument, they can do so by asking, "If the person I cited read this paragraph, would they learn something new even if that something new is very small?" If the answer is "yes," the student has most likely engaged with the source as an argument source.

Works Cited

Bamford, Maria. *Old Baby*. Directed by Jessica Yu, Netflix, 2017.
Bizup, Joseph. "BEAM: A Rhetorical Vocabulary for Teaching Research-Based Writing." *Rhetoric Review*, vol. 27, no. 1, 2008, pp. 72–86.
Booth, Wayne C., et al. *The Craft of Research*. 3rd ed., U of Chicago P, 2008.
Chappelle, Dave. *Killing Them Softly*. Directed by Stan Lathan, HBO, 2000.
Cross, Simon. "Visualizing Madness: Mental Illness and Public Representation." *Television and New Media*, vol. 5, no. 3, 2004, pp. 197–216.
Foxworthy, Jeff. *You Might Be a Redneck If*.... Warner Brothers, 1992.
Gillota, David. *Ethnic Humor in Multiethnic America*. Rutgers UP, 2013.
Graff, Gerald, and Cathy Birkenstein. *They Say, I Say: The Moves That Matter in Academic Writing*. 4th ed., W. W. Norton, 2018.
Haggins, Bambi. *Laughing Mad: The Black Comic Persona in Post-Soul America*. Rutgers UP, 2007.
Kona, Prakash. "Being George Carlin: *Carlinesque* as Performative Resistance." *Americana*, vol. 9, no. 2, 2010, www.americanpopularculture.com/journal/articles/fall_2010/kona.htm.
Krefting, Rebecca. *All Joking Aside: American Humor and Its Discontents*. Johns Hopkins UP, 2014.
Mintz, Lawrence. "Standup Comedy as Social and Cultural Mediation." *American Quarterly*, vol. 37, no. 1, 1985, pp. 71–85.
Mizjewski, Linda. *Pretty/Funny: Women Comedians and Body Politics*. U of Texas P, 2014.
Swales, John, and Christine B. Feak. *Academic Writing for Graduate Students: Essential Tasks and Skills*. 3rd ed., U of Michigan P, 2012.
Thomas, J. David. "Jeff Foxworthy's Redneck Humor and the Boundaries of Middle-Class American Whiteness." *SAGE Open*, vol. 6, no. 2, 2015, pp. 1–15.
Titus, Christopher. *Norman Rockwell Is Bleeding*. Directed by Jack Kenny, Deranged Entertainment, 2004.

Christopher Burlingame

Nick Sousanis's *Unflattening* in a Developmental Writing Course

In eliminating our stand-alone developmental education classes, my institution was ahead of the national trend of eliminating developmental education departments described by Katherine Mangan in *The Chronicle of Higher Education* in February 2019. However, many of the students we serve still needed additional support the semester after our administration made these cuts. The solution was to add a lab component to our existing Rhetoric I course that would be led by members of our professional staff from the Learning Commons (myself and our coordinator, who previously served as the professional writing and study skills tutor). After a semester of supporting students as both a lab section leader and the professional writing tutor, I was given a chance to teach my own lecture and lab.

    With this opportunity in mind, in my dual roles as lab section leader and professional writing tutor, I had begun to gather student feedback about the strengths of the course as well as areas of concern that would allow us to improve future iterations of the course. In spring 2019, teaching the course was more difficult because my roster was made up almost entirely of students who had failed the course in the fall. Not having David Gooblar's succinct terminology at my disposal at the time because his book, *The Missing Course*, was published only later that year, I approached my teaching with the idea that "[s]tudents are my discipline" (8). My first task was helping students overcome their frustrations of having to take the course again, something I achieved by using an unconventional frame for the course: Nick Sousanis's graphic novel *Unflattening*.

I anticipated resistance to graphic literature because I find that it shares a kinship with comedy in the sense that it is often dismissed as a lesser art form or somehow not as serious as text-only prose or drama. I wasn't sure whether the resistance would come more from the students or from the more traditional and established members of the faculty and staff. Much like studies of the comedic form, the study of graphic literature was slow to assimilate into the broader field of English and is now a more established subfield that blurs the boundaries between literature and visual art, not unlike comedy, which can straddle the emotional spectrum, often finding humor in dark and dramatic places. This kind of slipperiness that graphic literature and comics share with their etymological predecessor, comedy, made graphic literature the perfect vehicle to challenge the seemingly easy, formulaic, and simplistic approaches to teaching writing and literacy, especially with students who had already been confronted with the reality that they had not met the necessary threshold for proficiency.

With its stark and elaborate black-and-white imagery, Sousanis's graphic text argues that society as a whole is trapped in flat (i.e., restrictive and repetitive) thought patterns that interfere with creativity and problem-solving. During the first class, as we picked through the first chapter, students acknowledged that how they had been taught writing had shaped their conceptions of their own writing. Throughout the semester, *Unflattening* became a constant point of reference. Paired with readings, writing experiences from John Warner's *The Writer's Practice: Building Confidence in Your Nonfiction Writing*, and other graphic texts like Elizabeth Losh and colleagues' *Understanding Rhetoric: A Graphic Guide to Writing*, I was able to empower students to begin to view themselves as writers.

Working as a tutor and adjunct instructor for over seven years at my institution, I have provided professional writing tutoring for students across the curriculum and have taught unleveled developmental reading and writing, freshman composition and introductory literature, and upper-level creative writing and literature special topics seminars. Since 2015, every course I've taught has included at least one piece of graphic literature. I have employed it for purposes ranging from providing foundational information about rhetoric to teaching descriptive writing to challenging narrative conventions and structure. My experience as both a tutor and a teacher has helped me recognize how traditional anthologies and canonical texts actually discouraged student engagement and academic progress. My decision to include graphic literature is grounded in research on comics, graphic literature, and pedagogy by Emily Lauer, Sean Connors, Frank Serafini, and Rocco Versaci and in research concerned with students in need of additional support with writing by Victor Villanueva, Holly Hassel and Joann Baird Giordano, and Dolores Perin.

Every decision I made—from determining how to structure the course and sequence the readings to planning out lab activities in order to reinforce lecture concepts to teaching students and myself new ways of providing feedback—came from my own revelatory experiences of reading *Unflattening*. I first encountered Sousanis's book while preparing for my comprehensive exams in my PhD program in literature and criticism, and it quickly became clear to me that Sousanis would be a pivotal figure in my discussion of transgressive fiction in my dissertation. By *transgressive fiction*, I refer to works that were made into films and have achieved cult status and been influential in popular culture, such as *Fight Club*, *Trainspotting*, *American Psycho*, and *Requiem for a Dream*. I mention this because, in trying to define what transgressive fiction is, I experienced some theoretical slippage in trying to apply more traditional frameworks. Sousanis's illustrations and text made me realize that we cannot arrive at new academic discoveries if we are trapped on the same conveyor belts of thought provided by past scholars. We have to be willing to break free and create new pathways, to incorporate explanations that extend beyond Times New Roman type and explicit placement of a three-pronged thesis at the end of a paper's introduction.

This may seem like a long digression, but my lightbulb moment in my doctoral studies coincided with my realization that many of my students had already seen a version of this class and had not fared well. I took this to mean that they were likely to be resistant to having to do the same thing over again, so I needed a way to make the class new for them. But beyond that, my interactions with them as a lab leader and a professional tutor, with whom they were all required to meet as a stipulation of completing the first assignment (a literacy narrative), revealed that most shared preestablished negative biases against all forms of reading and writing.

To resolve both these issues, I knew setting the tone for the course would require an effort to shift students' understanding of what constituted reading and writing. According to the 2016 NCTE statement *Professional Knowledge for the Teaching of Writing*, which replaced the

2004 statement *NCTE Beliefs about the Teaching of Writing*, "In order to provide high-quality writing opportunities for all students, teachers need to understand . . . ways of organizing and transforming curricula in order to provide students with adequate education in varied purposes of writing" as well as "[h]ow to set up a course that asks students to write for varied purposes and audiences" (*Professional Knowledge*). I wanted to ensure that I was clear with students about why I had structured the course the way I did and how the course could lead to marked improvement in their writing. I also wanted to make sure that some of my decisions that likely didn't coincide with their previous experiences of what writing instruction looked like were actually essential to my aim of helping them grow as writers.

During the first class, only three of my seventeen students knew what a graphic novel was. Most of them knew about comics, and some described comedy as pertaining to humor and "silliness," but when I projected images from the first chapter of *Unflattening* on the document viewer, they were not sure where to focus their attention. This kind of disorientation was important to me. We actually dove right into the graphic text before we even said the word "syllabus."

Where should they start reading? How did they connect the word bubbles? What was more important: the pictures or the text? After about ten minutes, we came back together as a group, and I asked them how reading *Unflattening* and processing the imagery made them feel. Some liked it. Some hated it. Some were confused, but all of them had something to say. That was lesson number one: I wanted everyone to feel comfortable discussing the writing of others in a critical, thoughtful, and engaged way. I pointed out that what they were doing so effectively now would be what they would be expected to do in every class. Many nodded with the optimism and good intentions typical of a first class session, but I could tell more than a few were not completely convinced.

Many of the students were operating under a "fixed mindset" (Dweck 48) about what they could and could not do as readers and writers, but a graphic text is, by its nature, more accessible than many other types of literature. If the words don't make sense, students can look at the pictures. If the text makes them feel something, they might consider why or how it produced that effect and how they can incorporate that awareness into their own writing. A student raised her hand. "But this is so weird and creepy," she said. I asked her why, to which she replied, "They don't have faces, and there's no color." I asked her why their not having faces was creepy. She said she didn't know, but another student jumped in and said it was because it made them less human and therefore less relatable. I asked the class why relatability or having a comparable frame of reference matters. We carried on with this conversation, adding new observations, picking out new images and text to discuss, and then my break alarm went off. It was 6:15 p.m. We had been discussing nineteen pages that contain in total fewer than three hundred words for an hour and fifteen minutes. Every single student had contributed.

After their ten-minute break (the lecture for this Monday evening course is nearly three hours long), students came back. While they were taking a break, I had written on the board some key terms about reading and writing expectations for the course, some page numbers, and the phrase "Don't Stay in Line," a reference to the first page of the text (Sousanis 3). I had not explicitly revealed the reason we were doing such a deep dive with this work. I explained to students that I had worked with all of them before and recognized in them, in our previous encounters, some preconceived notions about how they perceived writing and reading and how they perceived themselves as readers and writers.

I suggested that this manner of thinking could limit their potential to be successful in growing as writers who could take what I hoped they learned with me beyond my class. One of the words I pointed to on the board was *flatness*, and we discussed how their attitudes were drawn from a flatness of experience. I had them turn to page 6 and asked what had led them to "a contraction of possibilities" where they "conformed" to a "pattern of one-dimensional thought and behavior" (Sousanis 6). Immediately, a student raised her hand and described her experience with the five-paragraph essay.

From there, we shared horror stories from high school or previous institutions, even negative experiences at our own institution where students were made to feel that there was only one right way to write or read and if they weren't doing that, they were wrong. I promised them they would not have that experience in my class. Some students described being given fill-in-the-blank worksheets for organizing their papers and feeling condescension and ridicule when they asked questions or wanted to go in a different direction. I anticipated some but not all of these experiences. We talked about how this class would attempt to free them from the flatness of their previous experiences and misconceptions about writing. We also addressed how our writing would break the convention of being an isolated activity because we would have regular opportunities for variations of community feedback. This point led me to talk about the lab portion of the class and finally to the syllabus—a couple minutes after the two-hour mark of the first class.

While I explained that the Sousanis excerpt would be the frame from which we'd build the course together, I also pointed out that it would be something that we would need to revisit as we moved through different phases of the writing process, something that would receive additional attention during our fifty-minute lab. Originally, when the lab was conceived of as being taught by someone other than the instructor, the expectation was that that individual teaching the lab would focus on grammar and mechanics and on answering questions that arose in the lecture section. Despite the fact that teaching things like grammar in isolation had not been supported by the NCTE or the four Cs for nearly thirty years, this is how I was expected to teach when I taught the lab in the fall.

That spring, I wanted students to be more engaged and find more value in the lab portion. So, with little oversight, I experimented with what I'd been given. I borrowed and modified from Warner's *The Writer's Practice* and brought in "Walk the Talk" sections from *Understanding Rhetoric* (Losh et al. 32–33, 66–67, 114–15, 148–49, 188–89, 214–15, 254–55, 284–85, 318–19). The lab became a mix of in-class writings that were started and discussed in draft format in class and completed on *Canvas*; microworkshops on everything from multiformat organizational devices to thesis statements, introductions, and half drafts; and question-and-answer sessions intended to clarify or expand on what we started in our lecture earlier in the week.

During labs, whenever we began to discuss a new subject, such as research, drafting, revision, or anything in the writing process, our focus was always on how we could break away from the flatness of thought about how we had done those things or had been taught and told how to do them in the past. Labs became brainstorming sessions where students could share their experiences and work. They were a time for students to show one another how they were working with an explicit focus on when something wasn't working for them so they could try to determine why.

Not everything worked out perfectly. The department required the lab to use the same anthology that had been used in the fall, and I had to find a balance between using enough of the book to justify the students having bought it and supplementing it with things that I believed would be more engaging for them.

I was also expected to give several prescribed assignments: a literacy narrative, a response to two essays about leisure time, and a final research project that was preceded by a presentation about one of the readings. At every opportunity, I challenged students to give me something more, something that went beyond the assignments I was required to give them, and they answered these challenges because they could tell that I was trying to meet their needs.

They experimented. They came to meet with me during my professional tutoring, which also served as forty weekly office hours. They asked questions. Their enthusiasm sparked ideas. The most valuable and enjoyable work we did together stemmed from an alternative way I proposed they thought about their research project, a method borrowed from Warner's book that encourages students to ask the question, "Why Am I So Angry and What Can I Do about It?" (163). We channeled their anger and frustration about their desired topic into narrowing the focus of their research project, following each of the steps provided by Warner. One of the premises that I took from Warner's writing experiences was that, at this stage, students do not need to be bogged down by a desire to label every type of paper. Warner suggests it is better to let them work from familiar frames of reference and then point out how they are actually working with rhetoric without even realizing it. This limits the intimidation factor that students may have experienced in the past and ultimately led my students to produce better results. This assignment fulfills what Hassel and Giordano describe in "Occupy Writing Studies: Rethinking College Composition for the Needs of the Teaching Majority" by recognizing how rhetoric instructors who follow this approach "are well-positioned to develop increasingly better ways of preparing students to meet the rigorous expectations of college-level reading, writing, and thinking" (126).

What I did was not perfect, but it worked. Students really responded to Sousanis's *Unflattening*. They appreciated that I was not going to hold them to the flatness that had held them back before. In my end-of-semester evaluations, one student wrote, "This is my favorite class during this semester. I enjoy the way you teach class, and always willing to help us with the paper. Giving us ideas of how to go about the topic and when what we have doesn't do well with the topic you try to find a way to make it work vs telling us to forget it and start over." And another student added, "He helped me feel more confident in my writing."

My hope was that students would leave my class feeling as though they had found their own identities as writers, that they now had a better understanding of their strengths and limitations and that that understanding would lead to their continued success. Some of my most hesitant students at the beginning of the semester were the ones who ended up taking the biggest risks and experimenting with different sources and ideas. I hope that means they will be able to keep themselves from returning to the limited, flat mindset they entered my course with, but my greatest fear is that our educational system is increasingly demanding and rewarding flatness. How can we lead more people toward unflattening, especially when working with developmental writers?

Works Cited

Connors, Sean. "Designing Meaning: A Multimodal Perspective on Comics Reading." *Teaching Comics through Multiple Lenses*, edited by Craig Hill, Routledge, 2016, pp. 13–29.

Dweck, Carol. *Mindset: The New Psychology of Success*. Ballantine, 2008.

Gooblar, David. *The Missing Course: Everything They Never Taught You about College Teaching*. Harvard UP, 2019.

Hassel, Holly, and Joanne Baird Giordano. "Occupy Writing Studies: Rethinking College Composition for the Needs of the Teaching Majority." *College Composition and Communication*, vol. 65, no. 1, 2013, pp. 117–39.

Lauer, Emily. "Spider-Men in the Composition Classroom." *Transformation: The Journal of Inclusive Scholarship and Pedagogy*, vol. 24, nos. 1–2, 2014, pp. 184–99.

Losh, Elizabeth, et al. *Understanding Rhetoric: A Graphic Guide to Writing*. 2nd ed., Bedford / St. Martin's, 2017.

Mangan, Katherine. "The End of the Remedial Course." *The Chronicle of Higher Education*, 18 Feb. 2019, www.chronicle.com/interactives/Trend19-Remediation-Main.

Perin, Dolores. "Literacy Skills among Academically Underprepared Students." *Community College Review*, vol. 41, no. 2, 2013, pp. 118–36.

Professional Knowledge for the Teaching of Writing. National Council of Teachers of English, 28 Feb. 2016, www2.ncte.org/statement/teaching-writing/.

Serafini, Frank. "Multimodal Literacy: From Theories to Practice." *Language Arts*, vol. 92, no. 6, 2015, pp. 412–23.

Sousanis, Nick. *Unflattening*. Harvard UP, 2015.

Versaci, Rocco. "How Comic Books Can Change the Way Our Students See Literature: One Teacher's Perspective." *English Journal*, vol. 91, no. 2, 2001, pp. 61–67.

Villanueva, Victor. "Subversive Complicity and Basic Writing across the Curriculum." *Journal of Basic Writing*, vol. 32, no. 1, 2013, pp. 97–110.

Warner, John. *The Writer's Practice: Building Confidence in Your Nonfiction Writing*. Penguin Books, 2019.

Laura Biesiadecki

Comedy in the First-Year Writing Classroom

The property damage on my first day of teaching was greater than I had anticipated. After brief introductions I turned the group's attention to the syllabus, which was being projected onto what I thought was the dry-erase board. With clammy palms I grabbed a marker from the podium, uncapped it, and charged toward the projection of my expected learning outcomes—I was going to circle that first point boldly, nobody in the room would notice my hands shaking, and every student would forever remember the call to "create and defend your own arguments through effective rhetorical strategies"! I don't know how I could have been so nervous as to mistake a pull-down projection screen for a dry-erase board, but the marker tip hit the vinyl sheet, and evidence of my mistake was undeniable. In a nervous panic I blurted out one of my favorite lines from *Arrested Development*: "We shan't be telling your mother this, shan't we?" ("Meat the Veals" 9:13). The students had never seen *Arrested Development*, didn't know Tobias Fünke or Mrs. Featherbottom, but they started laughing at the sheer absurdity of their teacher accidentally vandalizing the classroom on the first day. It was impossible not to join them. My horrible mistake became an experience that offered our group a chance to laugh together, and through comedy we were able to avoid the usual two weeks of early-semester tension.

In "Pedagogy of Laughter," Laura L. Ellingson observes that "beginning a course with shared laughter and encouraging students to laugh early and often throughout the term is a better approach to embracing humor in university teaching" (131). My experience with comedy and comedic texts in the first-year writing classroom has been a tremendous success, especially in building my confidence as a young educator during that first semester: the class experience was genuinely enjoyable, and in course evaluations I was thrilled to read responses like "She is funny and is always filled with energy" and "The instructor was a hoot!" But more importantly, several students took note of their ability to better engage with course content when they participated in class discussions and felt comfortable as a member of a scholarly community: "My course instructor created a very welcoming and understanding learning environment"; "[L]arge group discussions were helpful in my understanding of many of these subjects"; "Group discussions contributed the most to my learning." That first group chuckle made for a unique introduction, yes, but it also fostered a feeling of familiarity among students that resulted in better communication and deeper conversation. In revising my syllabus for the spring semester, I chose to replace that first day of social bonding with a full unit on contemporary comedy, looking for a way to facilitate a "welcoming and understanding learning environment" without ruining another projector screen.

In the first weeks of class, students were asked to consider the motivations behind specific marketing techniques and apply those methods to the presentation of their own ideas. Sara Champlin rightfully claims that "students [of advertising] get to learn through real-world examples and creative problem-solving in the context of daily, evolving changes," and the value of a relevant and familiar visual in the classroom cannot be understated (82). After showing students several pictures of comedic billboards and subway advertisements I had seen around campus, as well as the trailer for the first season of *Arrested Development* ("*Arrested Development*"), I was able to point out that many of the rhetorical techniques used in marketing products to potential consumers or viewing experiences to potential audiences were the same persuasive writing techniques I would be teaching them in class. Starting the semester with a critical look at comedy in advertising offered these first-year writers an opportunity to work with content they had seen before and promised a real-world application for lessons they would learn in class.

On the first day of our advertising work, we looked at an advertisement for Tabasco hot sauce: A Tabasco bottle made to look like a fire extinguisher takes center stage, standing larger than life in front of a fire-engine red background. The slogan "BEWARE THE HEAT" in bold white font is situated above the much smaller "Little Bottle Big Flavor" ("Beware"). Not particularly funny, but an opportunity to explore persuasive content as a large group. First, students were asked to summarize the advertisement: What is being sold? Who is the ideal or intended audience for this advertisement? Then they were asked to interpret the advertisement: How is the product being marketed to its intended audience? Which methods are being used? Finally, students were asked to apply analysis to each interpretation: Is the use of this specific marketing technique successfully attracting the target audience? Why or why not? After I had posed these questions to the class and written applicable answers on the board, the group came up with the following analysis: "The Tabasco brand is selling Tabasco sauce to people who like spicy foods by using the color red, the image of a fire extinguisher, and the Tabasco logo. The color red and the fire extinguisher make viewers think of fire and heat, and the Tabasco logo ensures that consumers purchase this particular brand instead of just any old hot sauce." Students were then asked to find and post two advertisements they found funny to the class website. To ensure the censoring of any content that may be triggering, inappropriate, or disrespectful, these images and videos can only be seen by me and the student who submitted them. Advertisement submissions over the past three years have consisted mostly of images and videos from *Snapchat* or *Instagram*, ads that use relevant memes, social media influencers, contemporary designer brands, or cultural references to target potential young millennial or Gen Z consumers.

From the batch of fifty advertisements, I selected three to share with the group during our next class meeting, and students were provided with a worksheet asking them to summarize, interpret, and analyze the ads before we came together for group discussion. They had fun bonding over humor designed for their age group and laughed in disbelief when I didn't recognize a popular *YouTube* celebrity. A benefit of the independently completed worksheet was the establishment of common ground for discussion: through objective summary and interpretation, the class is able to agree on the product being sold, the ideal audience, and the marketing methods and can then move to the more subjective task of analysis. In "You Gotta Laugh," Kristen McDermott observes that "[d]iscussions of puns and language-related humor are a useful place to start, because they allow the focus to be placed on the cognitive work that jokes require . . . and remove the emotional and social packing" (341). At least one of the three student-submitted advertisements was chosen because it was both emotional and social and was included to elicit a wider range of reactions from the class. In this case, the independently completed worksheet allowed for the establishment of common ground: through objective summary and interpretation, the class was able to agree on the product being sold, the ideal audience, and the marketing methods. From there, the group was able to tackle the more subjective task of analysis, asking themselves "Was this method successful?" rather than "Was this advertisement funny?" The practice of summary and interpretation took focus away from the evaluation of content and guided students toward evaluation of method, not only supporting more productive conversation among classmates whose responses to the comedic attempts may have differed but also changing student expectations for the requirements of their first writing assignment.

Successfully writing comedy is incredibly difficult and can seem an impossible task for students with little to no confidence in their ability to write, let alone write well. During the next group meeting, I shared several pages of Mel Helitzer and Mark Shatz's 2016 *Comedy Writing Secrets* and asked students to consider the authors' claim that "[a] key prerequisite to thinking and writing funny is understanding funny" (25). A majority of students in past semesters have agreed with Helitzer and Shatz and confirmed that they had at least some experience trying to "understand funny" through group analysis of several funny advertisements as well as in discussions of Jonathan Swift's "A Modest Proposal" and Leon Rappoport's "What Makes Us Laugh: Humor Theory and Research from Plato and Aristotle to Sigmund Freud" (*Punchlines* 13–30). The prompt for the first assignment challenged students to apply their "understanding [of] funny": "In 1,000-1,500 words, use any number of comedic methods we've explored in class to sell me something. This assignment requires a minimum of three reliable sources and should follow the most recent guidelines for MLA formatting." Though I was worried during the first semester that the prompt's simplicity and intentionally vague instruction to "use any number of comedic methods" might confuse or frustrate students, there were few complaints, and they were resolved with simple clarification questions.

Before students were asked to spend thirty minutes brainstorming or discussing possibilities with peers, I emphasized the importance of creative interpretation and invited each student to experiment boldly and to do so with the understanding that drafting this essay would come with very little risk of failure. For the most part, this first draft was completed independently: we had one in-class writing day and open office hours, but students were encouraged to develop their personal comedic and writing style independently. I received a set of wonderfully unique essays trying to sell me real and invented products, but just as many submissions encouraged me to explore ideas—life philosophies, political ideologies, new strategies for mental health, fad diets, grading systems, and travel plans. The originality of product promotion and rhetorical marketing methods in first drafts was encouraging and progressed to a dynamic collaborative group revision process.

After essays had been submitted, students were assigned the introduction (3–6) and the chapter "All Girls Must Be Everything" (19–26) from Tina Fey's *Bossypants* and asked to highlight examples of Fey's personal information in blue (summary), uses of comedy in yellow, and references to outside sources or content in green (interpretation). During class discussion students shared their chosen highlight colors for two sample paragraphs of *Bossypants*, judged whether there was enough information supplied by passages highlighted in blue, and analyzed the effectiveness of any passages highlighted in green and yellow. A final version was agreed on, with analytical notes in the margins, and posted on our class website as a reference tool. The choice of memoir for this exercise was deliberate. As Ilana Blumberg observes, memoir has the potential to "show students just how much art went into shaping even seemingly straightforward accounts of historical events" (97). Because students knew very little about Fey, her life became a series of unexplored historical events for students, rather than a retelling of old news, and they were able to concentrate on the "art" of Fey's comedic style without getting distracted by any temptation to challenge or contribute to the content.

The assignment was then repeated with the introduction and the chapter "A/S/L" from Issa Rae's *The Misadventures of Awkward Black Girl* (xi–xiii, 1–16), readings similar to the introduction to and chapter from *Bossypants* in that they both present an account of the authors' preteen years, but with a number of significant differences: Rae, the star of HBO's popular series *Insecure*, who was thirty-five at the time, was much more likely to be recognized by the group than was Fey, who was fifteen years older than Rae; students agreed that they are part of Rae's target audience, while they identified the target audience of *Bossypants* as "older women, maybe over 40"; Fey's early years are marked by musings of bodily changes, while Rae's are marked by treacherous navigation of public online chat rooms; *The Misadventures of Awkward Black Girl* explores blackness and black girlhood in different parts of the United States, while the early pages of *Bossypants* are set in "the late seventies . . . a small-eyed, thin-lipped blond woman's paradise" (Fey 9). Students were introduced to a new tone of comedy with *The Misadventures of Awkward Black Girl* and charged with the task of focusing on the art of Rae's memoir without being distracted by their response to arguably much more relatable content. The second iteration of this assignment resulted in a more confident classroom discussion of textual analysis as well as an opportunity to explore rhetoric used in an intersectional text. Working with Brian Huot's assertion that "before students can learn to revise rhetorically, they need to assess rhetorically" (170), these highlighting assignments reinforced the practice of summarizing, interpreting, and analyzing and managed to facilitate a transition of that practice from visual advertisements to long-form nonfiction in preparation for peer review. The next week, students were asked to highlight their own work just as they had highlighted *Bossypants* and *The Misadventures of Awkward Black Girl*, using specific colors to identify the points in which they presented their idea or product for the audience (summary), methods they used to market that idea or product (interpretation), and the resources they had used to bring credibility to the text. They analyzed their own work in the margins, asking themselves whether their marketing methods were effective, and brought to class a fully highlighted and annotated copy of their first draft for peer review. When they broke into small groups, students were able to laugh at one another's work and at themselves—having their humorous essays read by new classmates and friends bolstered their confidence as persuasive writers and storytellers, the class community was strengthened, and the group established a familiarity that allowed for more earnest participation in later units.

However, congenial peer review does not guarantee effective peer review. I paraphrase Amy Tsui and Maria Ng in saying that a number of researchers have found peer comments to be more interesting and informative than teacher feedback and that peer comments encourage a more positive engagement with the writing process (148), but the process of peer review can often be a difficult and unproductive one. Kristen Getchell and Kat Gonso observe that "the peer review process is a complex series of tasks, of giving and receiving, of critiquing and responding, that have become problematically simplified" and acknowledge that students enter peer review with "[d]istrust, apprehension, confusion, reluctance, self-consciousness, cynicism, [and] disengagement" (64). Asking students to highlight their own work before engaging with classmates in peer review was an attempt to address the "problematically simplified" peer review system. By categorizing their sentences, students were able to create a productive self-evaluation of the argument they were presenting to classmates—the highlighting process gave them a sense of which sections of their paper were sufficiently argumentative and which need to be supplemented with more summary or style and also discouraged any fixation on spelling or grammatical errors. Both in the initial review of their own work by student writers and in the review of another student's self-highlighted draft, attention was taken away from the content of the piece and directed toward the structure of paragraphs and method of execution, making it more difficult to respond with empty praise or vague criticism. Instead, reviewers were asked to be more direct in their written feedback, agreeing or disagreeing with the student writer's choice to highlight a certain passage in this or that color, asking for more information when summary was insufficient, or questioning a certain method of comedic delivery. Peer annotations made on the highlighted first drafts focused on responding to the student writer's dissection of their own work rather than to the work itself. Through the application of summary, interpretation, and analysis, most students were able to avoid unhelpful subjective commentary about the success or failure of the paper ("I do/don't like this" or "Not funny to me") and instead made specific comments about the effectiveness of their classmates' comedic efforts. The authors were then able to read that feedback without any sense of personal failing, and they produced incredibly productive draft revisions.

Each first-year writing classroom has the potential to exist as a place of both comfort and challenge for new students. When instructors make space for comedy in lesson plans and in the classroom, the group is able to build and maintain a scholarly community that encourages first-year writers to confidently participate in each stage of the writing process without fear of judgment from themselves or their peers.

Works Cited

"*Arrested Development* (Trailer)." *Netflix*, www.netflix.com/watch/81007174. Accessed 17 Nov. 2022.

"Beware the Heat." *Adicator*, www.adicator.com. Accessed 17 Nov. 2022.

Blumberg, Ilana M. "Traceable Beginnings: Reading and Writing Memoir in the First-Year Humanities Classroom." *Life Writing*, vol. 15, no. 1, 2018, pp. 95–106.

Champlin, Sara. "Why I Teach Advertising: Critical Voices." *Journal of Advertising Education*, vol. 24, no. 1, 2020, pp. 81–84.

Ellingson, Laura L. "Pedagogy of Laughter: Using Humor to Make Teaching and Learning More Fun and Effective." *Teaching with Sociological Imagination in Higher and Further Education: Contexts, Pedagogies, Reflections*, edited by Christopher R. Matthews et al., Springer, 2018, pp. 123–34.

Fey, Tina. *Bossypants*. Little, Brown, 2011.

Getchell, Kristen, and Kat Gonso. "Valuing the Process: Building a Foundation for Collaborative Peer Review." *Teaching English in the Two-Year College*, vol. 47, no. 1, 2019, pp. 63–75.

Helitzer, Mel, and Mark Shatz. *Comedy Writing Secrets: The Best-Selling Guide to Writing Funny and Getting Paid for It*. Writer's Digest Books, 2016.

Huot, Brian. "Toward a New Discourse of Assessment for the College Writing Classroom." *College English*, vol. 65, no. 2, 2002, pp. 163–80. *JSTOR*, www.jstor.org/stable/3250761.

McDermott, Kristen. "You Gotta Laugh: Teaching Critical Thinking via Comedy." *Pedagogy: Critical Approaches to Teaching Literature, Language, Composition, and Culture*, vol. 19, no. 2, 2019, pp. 339–51.

"Meat the Veals." *Arrested Development*, season 2, episode 16, Fox, 3 Apr. 2005. *Netflix*, www.netflix.com/watch/70133709.

Rae, Issa. *The Misadventures of Awkward Black Girl*. Simon and Schuster, 2015.

Rappoport, Leon. *Punchlines: The Case for Racial, Ethnic, and Gender Humor*. Praeger, 2005.

Swift, Jonathan. *A Modest Proposal and Other Satirical Works*. Dover, 1996.

Tsui, Amy B. M., and Maria Ng. "Do Secondary L2 Writers Benefit from Peer Comments?" *Journal of Second Language Writing*, vol. 9, no. 2, 2000, pp. 147–70. *ScienceDirect*, https://doi.org/10.1016/S1060-3743(00)00022-9.

Mariann J. VanDevere

Consume, Converse, Create: Stand-Up and Sketch Comedy in the Classroom

In my introductory writing course, I wanted to highlight the effectiveness of stand-up and sketch comedy as social critiques whereby, through creativity and critical thinking, comedians' performances serve as models for argumentation. I sought to examine these performances with specific attention to race, as humor is often one of the best tools for discussing such sensitive topics, especially within a classroom. Thus, I set out to identify traditional pedagogical practices and apply them to comedy. Ultimately, by asking students to generate their own comedic content, I challenged them to refine their critical thinking skills and to foster the creativity needed to reimagine our worlds and our positions in them.

Working with comedians like Moms Mabley, Richard Pryor, Eddie Murphy, and Wanda Sykes in the first iteration of this course, I attempted to organize the comedic performances chronologically. Initially I was hoping to shape a historical conversation regarding the genre. I quickly discovered that I had assumed students possessed a knowledge base that they did not. So, after a few weeks, I decided to restructure the materials thematically. Doing so required me to think deeply about the foundational basis for stand-up and sketch comedy. I concluded that we must begin by examining stereotypes.

Consume

Early on in the course, students watched a short excerpt from Aziz Ansari's *Dangerously Delicious* (2012). In this clip, titled "Racist Locksmith" on *YouTube*, Ansari offers a humorous opinion on the creation and mobilization of an Asian stereotype. In order for students to identify Ansari's main points, I asked them to reverse-outline the segment. For this activity I modified a compilation of reverse-outlining strategies to best fit my needs.

First, I asked students to identity the thesis or, rather, the main point of Ansari's argument as a whole. In this case, it happened to be the comedian's very first statement, in which he declares, "I just think it's a little silly when sometimes people act as if all the really crazy racism is just in places like South Carolina . . . because I've seen crazy racist stuff happen everywhere" ("Racist Locksmith" 0:00–0:10). Second, I asked students to identify the main point of each paragraph. Last, I asked them to respond to the following questions: How does this paragraph support the overall thesis? What tactics does Ansari use to prove his point?

Since students were applying reverse outlining to a performed text, I was initially uncertain of how to guide them in breaking up the stand-up clip into "paragraphs" and left it open to their interpretations. Most of the students had an intuitive sense of how to do this, while a few struggled. I then realized that further guidance would be useful. I informed students that they could break down the clip into smaller parts by focusing on the moments where they felt or noticed a narrative shift, silences or pauses, or the emergence of a new, but related, point. While this instruction seemed to offer more support, in revamping for the upcoming semester I realized that students could benefit from reinforced scaffolding.

In the spring course, I decided it was best to first model the reverse outline. Using a different stand-up clip, and with input from the class, I modeled a reverse outline on the board. Students were then tasked with completing their own reverse outline for the assigned Ansari clip. After about ten minutes, I asked them to compare and discuss with a partner. As evidenced by the succeeding classroom discussion, students who were uncertain were often guided by their peers, and a thoughtful conversation regarding the reverse outline as a tool further solidified students' investment regarding its utility. This new scaffolding that included modeling proved useful throughout the semester. Students were able to effectively complete reverse outlines for thirty-minute and one-hour comedy specials. Students were able to use their reverse outlines as springboards for constructing arguments in their essays.

As an instructor, I have found that having students reverse-outline stand-up performances has several benefits. First, it highlights the stylistic differences between comedians, which in itself can be a site of exploration in student essays. Second, it inspires and validates different yet equally compelling argumentative styles. Third, reverse-outlining stand-up reveals clear and concise argumentation and can be used as a model for teaching specific writing devices, such as topic sentences. Finally, creating a reverse outline encourages further critical inquiry into the things we consume every day; it illustrates that critical thinking is not something done solely within the walls of a classroom but that it is a crucial life skill. It exemplifies the "so what?" aspect of argumentative essays in a way that stretches students' imaginations and encourages them to dream of their own personal impact on the world.

Sketch comedy was an effective medium for teaching students how to unpack an idea (i.e., how to close-read). In one version of my course, I had students watch a sketch from *The Richard Pryor Show*. While I am not sure if this is the actual name of the sketch or if it is definitely intended to be a parody, it is titled "The Richard Pryor Show—To Kill a Mockingbird" on *YouTube*, where my students and I accessed it. The sketch takes place in 1926 in Beauville, Mississippi. John Witherspoon plays a black man on trial for the alleged rape of a white woman—an allegation that is quickly exposed as flagrantly false. Robin Williams plays a northern liberal Jewish lawyer who defends Mr. Witherspoon and tries to prevent the accused's lynching. Richard Pryor, sans makeup, is the southern white prosecutor determined to render a guilty verdict despite contradicting evidence. The lawyers plead their case in a hot and sweaty segregated courtroom.

I used the Pryor sketch to reinforce close reading skills and to challenge students to articulate the fine details and how they work together to create a complex argument. I assigned the video for homework and asked students to write a one-paragraph response. This reflection could focus on any aspect of the sketch they wanted. It could even center on their feelings about it. For the following class, I instructed them to spend the first five to seven minutes writing an individual response to the following questions or to discuss them with a partner: What is the main point of this sketch? How do you know? While it was important for students to be able to differentiate the many, often interrelated arguments, establishing what each student believed to be the main contention (arguably in this sketch that the judicial system is biased against black men) was important. This exercise forced students to make their own argument in the process, since they were asked to work through the many contentions and decide on the overarching one. The exercise also illustrated the diversity of opinions among students and illustrated how there can be a difference of ideas as long as evidence is used to support a chosen argument.

After reflecting on the questions I asked to ignite close reading, I realized that the "the" in "What is the main point of this sketch?" could potentially cause students to go against their intuition in favor of trying to find the one right answer implied by the way I posed the question. I wanted students to use their own lenses and offer multiple entry points for engaging with the texts. So, in a later version of this course, I instead asked the following questions: What statements or arguments are being made in this sketch? How do you know? While these questions offer more space for diverse opinions and conversations, the phrasing was still a bit abstract. Thus, to alleviate any potential confusion, I modeled the activity using the following as an example of one of the sketch's arguments: "Lynching is a cruel spectacle." My evidence for this argument was the conversation between two white women spectators in the courtroom. The southern belles are debating what they will wear to the lynching, their outfit choices dependent on whether or not attendees will be taking photographs.

When students were stuck and uncertain of how to articulate statements the sketch was making, I switched gears and instead asked them to identify a moment they were drawn to—whether they thought it was funny, strange, offensive, or something else. I then asked them to explain in writing why they were drawn to it and why it conjured up that emotion. Once they answered these questions, they were able to return to the initial questions—What statements or arguments are being made in this sketch? How do you know?—with greater confidence and understanding. Applying the method of close reading to the sketch revealed the richness of the sketch and further enhanced students' self-confidence by assuring them that following their inclinations or emotional responses could lead to serious academic inquiry. Practicing this skill with the sketch served as a model for how students could perform the close reading needed to generate argumentative writing in their assignments.

If I were to teach this course again, I would spend the first few classes going over specific comedic techniques—for example, callbacks, act outs, crowd work, and so on.[1] I believe this would have provided more specific and shared language and potentially connected with and inspired student writing styles. I would also attempt to apply each skill to varying content. For example, I imagine that asking students to unpack an idea presented in stand-up could help them look beyond the rhetorical and focus on tone, movement, gesture, and so on, further enriching their analyses. I would also incorporate more hybrid comedic formats, such as on-the-street interview segments often found on late-night shows. I did incorporate two such segments from *The Chris Rock Show* ("Chris Rock Show—Confederate Flag" and "Chris Rock—Tupac Shakur Boulevard"). These segments led to lively discussions, but I think applying reverse outlining, the unpacking of an idea, or another skill to these on-the-street interviews would further enrich the student writing around it.

Converse

As a young black woman teaching a course titled Race and Comedy at a predominantly white institution, I was a bit nervous about how I would be received. The first time I taught this course, I did not encounter any challenges based on my identity or the materials. However, in the spring semester I was met with some resistance from one white male student. Despite willingly signing up for a class titled Race and Comedy, this student seemed to be convinced that racism was not a real thing. After watching Ansari's "Racist Locksmith," the student claimed that Ansari was being racist toward the locksmith. Despite the lack of textual evidence necessary to support such a claim (Ansari never states the locksmith's race, does not imitate his voice or discuss his appearance), the student attempted to prove his point in a poorly written essay. He later complained about his grade despite the absence of the basics of argumentative essay writing—a clear and concise thesis, strong topic sentences, balance between summary and analysis, and, of course, textual evidence.

Creating an Atmosphere

The following year, I decided that I would spend the first class making this statement: "Racism is real. If we are going to work together this semester, we must all agree that this is true. It is not a productive use of my time or yours to argue whether or not it is real, because it is." I then assigned the first reading, George M. Fredrickson's "The Concept of Racism in Historical Discourse," which serves as the appendix to his book *Racism: A Short History* (151–70). This excerpt defines racism and traces its history through examples from scholarly work and lived experiences. This reading further expanded students' knowledge of racism and supplied us with definitions of racism that undergirded our conversations.

Since we would be discussing several sensitive topics, I thought it would be useful for us to collectively come up with guidelines for communication. These guidelines were meant to help ensure that there was a certain level of respect despite potential differences in opinions, views, and lived experiences. For homework, I asked students to come up with some ideas to meet this mission, and in the following class, they stated their thoughts aloud and I wrote them on the board. Guidelines included the following: If someone makes a statement that is offensive, inform them that the statement is offensive and give them the opportunity to reflect and respond. Ask for clarity when unsure instead of assuming. Be respectful and avoid interrupting or overtalking. Collaborating with students to create these guidelines increased their sense of commitment to engaging in intentional dialogue with their peers. It also led to some great conversations wherein students willingly shared their vulnerabilities.

Early on, I quickly noticed the gap between my knowledge of comedians and students' knowledge. In other words, I did not realize that my students were toddlers when *The Chappelle Show* was one of the top programs on television. While they knew who he was, they weren't as familiar as I thought they might be with such iconic sketches as "The Racial Draft," "Frontline: Clayton Bigsby"—the infamous blind African American who was raised white and was a black white supremacist—or "Racial Pixie." Thus, to contextually situate these sketches, I asked students to construct and present a short bio for each comedian. I asked them to focus on such specifics as where the comedian was from, what they were known for, and conversations and important cultural moments during the height of their careers. This not only helped students better understand the comedic content but also resulted in a deeper level of appreciation for the talent of these comedians.

Facilitating In-Class Conversation

To ensure that students came to class prepared for discussion, I routinely assigned reflection paragraphs for homework. While students were allowed to write about whatever they wanted, I provided general questions such as the following: What, if anything, did you find funny? Why or why not? What aspects of the text were you drawn to and why? I also required them to generate a question at the end of the paragraph that they were interested in posing to their peers. This activity ensured that students came to class with something to contribute.

Since liveness is an important aspect of stand-up comedy, I required a group trip to a stand-up performance. Prior to our trip I asked students to pay attention to how their live experiences differed from the experiences of watching comedy on a screen. I also asked them to be prepared to share their individual experiences with their peers. I noticed that meeting off campus and seeing a show and laughing together increased the bond among us and enriched the classroom and our conversations. In all future renditions of this course, I attempted to have this field trip toward the beginning of the semester so that we could really reap the benefits of deepened relationships.

During the midsemester slump, I would try to include some creative in-class exercises to motivate and inspire our continued studies. One of my favorite activities was asking students to make memes based on ideas and conversations we'd had in class. My students consumed memes often on social media and thus possessed an intuitive understanding of the relationship between texts and images and of how to capitalize on that knowledge in order to produce a funny and often satirical message or critique. I brought in a large stack of magazines, construction paper, scissors, glue, and other fun things. I tasked students with using these arts-and-crafts materials to design an original meme inspired by our classroom discussions on topics such as antiblackness, cultural appropriation, and more. Once students had completed the assignment, I collected all their memes, shuffled them, and passed them out to their peers. Students took turns verbally explaining their classmate's meme, and the creator would chime in at the end to correct, clarify, or contribute to their peer's interpretations of their creative work. Asking students to create visual pieces with their hands was a refreshing change of pace that further solidified my classroom as one that was open to creativity.

Create

For their final assignments, I encouraged students to further develop their critical-creative lens by submitting a comedic project. Students were asked to submit an original stand-up performance, a comedic sketch or short story, or something else of their choosing. As long as students consulted with me beforehand, I remained open to practically any idea. I presented a portion of my original sketch in which I turned comedians into characters who worked together to solve a problem. I presented my sketch to the class and required that students do the same prior to the final submission of their projects.

For their presentations, students needed to come up with one to three specific questions they wanted to pose to their peers for guided support and then present a sample of their project. While students did voice their suggestions verbally, we also started a shared *Google Doc* for feedback, which eased the pressure for presenters as they did not have to remember every bit of information offered them. One student used her friends as models to complete a series of memes about microaggressions. Another student created a satirical advertisement influenced by global antiblackness in commercials and billboards. In addition to whatever project they completed, students had to submit an artist statement. In three double-spaced pages students were asked to meditate on questions about their process: How was your project inspired by this course? What did you learn from creating this piece? How did you create and implement the various phases? What is the importance of your work outside the classroom? The artist statement allowed both the student and me a glimpse of their thought process and offered me a way to assess their work. This assignment worked so well that I have also used it in my drama course, Blackness and Performativity.

While I taught a college-level course at a predominantly white institution, stand-up and sketch comedy writ large are powerful tools for engaging students, shaping their critical-creative voices, and discussing difficult topics. Using stand-up and sketch comedy in the classroom as teaching tools not only encouraged my students' intellectual development but also afforded me the chance to present a fuller version of myself in an academic space and, in the process, provided the opportunity to connect with my students as people.

Note

1. *Callbacks*: when a comedian refers to a joke made earlier in the performance. *Act outs*: instead of recalling an event, a comedian will act it out for viewers to experience. *Crowd work*: a variety of methods by which the comedian directly engages with the audience to build a rapport that will further enhance the performance. This can include asking a specific audience member a question, cracking jokes about an audience member, and other methods of engaging the audience.

Works Cited

"The Chris Rock Show—Confederate Flag." *YouTube*, uploaded by Alberto Fo Sho, 10 June 2012, www.youtube.com/watch?v=SZ8_49BRSiw.

"Chris Rock—Tupac Shakur Boulevard." *YouTube*, uploaded by Kali Marley, 20 Apr. 2008, www.youtube.com/watch?v=8DzkSgvt6UE.

Fredrickson, George M. *Racism: A Short History*, Princeton UP, 2015.

"Frontline: Clayton Bigsby." *YouTube*, uploaded by Comedy Central, 11 Nov. 2019, www.youtube.com/watch?v=BLNDqxrUUwQ.

"The Racial Draft." *YouTube*, uploaded by Comedy Central, 30 Dec. 2017, www.youtube.com/watch?v=2z3wUD3AZg4.

"Racial Pixie." *YouTube*, uploaded by The JayRey Show, 30 Mar. 2020, www.youtube.com/watch?v=rG1z5NF-Mjo.

"Racist Locksmith." *YouTube*, uploaded by redspirit8, 25 Dec. 2013, www.youtube.com/watch?v=gsFjewV4QZc&t=12s.

"The Richard Pryor Show—To Kill a Mockingbird." *YouTube*, uploaded by SoftLipps, 13 Mar. 2011, www.youtube.com/watch?v=bE1f4awlxVc&t=2s.

Lisa Smith

Using Comics to Teach Analytical Writing

The world of modern-day comics is remarkably dynamic, textured, detailed, and popular. In it we encounter infinite earths and limitless timelines, rebooted characters who return with a different gender or racial identity, superheroes and villains who routinely return from the dead, competing origin stories, and a robust history of crossover story lines. The popularity of the Marvel superhero movies, comic arts conventions such as Comic-Con International, and the expanding and diverse readership of printed and digital comics testify to the growth of the genre in popular culture. Even in university settings, as Hillary Chute notes in her recent book *Why Comics?*, comic texts have become respected and appreciated (4–5).

As a form of comedic narrative, comics have distinct advantages due to their unique utilization of images and text. Elements such as panel size and placement, color variation, foregrounding and backgrounding of images, and differing angles and perspectives work together to create what Robert S. Petersen calls "visual connections between elements," which enable readers to receive the images "with almost no need for explanation" (xix, xvii). These compositional components allow writers and illustrators to "more economically tell the joke" as they lead readers to see the words and pictures in the order and with the emphases that they desire (xix).

Despite their popularity and advantages as a comedic genre, in both secondary and postsecondary classrooms, comics still encounter barriers to full curricular integration, especially in writing courses and among teachers who are intimidated by the intricacies of the genre. While instructors may be willing occasionally to utilize comics in their literature classes, they seldom consider using comic texts to teach writing, perhaps put off by student unfamiliarity with the genre or the complexity of the comics universe. However, comic texts offer a unique, effective, and enjoyable way to help student writers learn analytical writing, even if the instructor is not a comics expert and the students are inexperienced comics readers. In fact, the medium's unique blending of text and image can make comics more fun and profitable for students to analyze than novels, short stories, or even films. How, then, can instructors teach their students to write analytically by connecting them with this "juxtaposed sequential visual" form of art (McCloud 8)?

This essay details how I use volume 1 of the comic book series *Hawkeye*, titled *My Life as a Weapon,* by Matt Fraction, David Aja, and Javier Pulido, to teach analytical writing in my first-year undergraduate writing course. I identify key elements of the writing assignment, highlight resources that help students master the comic book form as a means of engaging with the paper assignment, discuss the content covered in each class in the unit, and share my evaluation of the experience. The writing assignment, which focuses on analysis and the use of outside sources, is included in the appendix to this essay. I believe this teaching approach can be applied to many comic texts and to many types of writing courses.

Background and Assignment

My writing class at Pepperdine University, a private liberal arts college in Malibu, California, runs one semester and typically has eighteen traditional first-year students who can vary widely in their writing experience and preparation. The course includes four writing assignments: an argument analysis paper, an argument paper, an analytical review paper, and a concluding research paper that varies in approach. The analytical review paper is the third paper in the term and is the assignment that features a comic book.

My goal for the review paper is for students to further develop their analytical writing skills, meaning their ability to separate and identify different elements of a whole, and then to examine and evaluate the effectiveness of those elements. As writing instructors know, teaching students to analyze effectively and deeply is important as a means of preparing them for their future educational and professional careers. However, I have found that students often struggle to do actual analysis—they tend to drift into simple description, on the one hand, or unsupported personal opinion, on the other.

For an analytical writing assignment, a comic book offers advantages that other media lack. Movies are so familiar to students that they often have trouble transitioning from viewer to critic, short stories can cause complaints of an inadequate amount of material to analyze, and novels require a significant amount of class time to discuss and can be overused in high school English classes. Comics, however, take students out of their comfort zones, requiring them to work with a fresh medium that has its own structure, narrative style, and literary and visual devices. While this can be challenging for students, it can also be engaging and actually make it easier for students to avoid simple description or opinion and engage instead in thought-provoking analysis. In fact, a recent study of community college students published in the *Journal of Graphic Novels and Comics* reports that "comics engage critical thinking at similar or greater levels as compared with critical thinking engagement in traditional (no images) books" (Krusemark 71).

My analytical review paper assignment asks students to determine the effectiveness of the comic by separating and analyzing the varying features of the text in order to decide whether or not they would recommend the book. Students are required to use at least three outside sources in their papers and to turn in an ungraded outline and a graded rough draft before submitting the final version of the paper.

One of the most crucial features of the assignment is the choice of which comic to analyze. First, the comic should be freestanding in terms of story line, meaning that little to no knowledge of a backstory is necessary. The comic should also be complex enough to provide material for analysis and should be of a manageable length—one volume containing approximately six individual issues usually works well. And, of course, a comic that is appealing both visually and from a narrative perspective is helpful in keeping students' attention.

Volume 1 of *Hawkeye* works well for this assignment for several reasons. Published by Marvel in 2013, this freestanding volume of six issues gives a peek into the life of Avenger Clint Barton, or Hawkeye, when he's not being an Avenger. It is a critics' favorite and is fast-paced and action-packed to keep reader interest. The nonlinear plotline, creative variety of panel shapes and sizes, intricate drawing and coloring, and unique story line of a hero on his day off all give students plenty to analyze without requiring knowledge of a backstory. I utilize the first five issues of volume 1 and find it is a perfect comic for students to examine regardless of their comics background.

Preparation and Resources

Even though I was a complete comic book novice when I first envisioned this assignment, I found that basic preparation was enough to enable me to guide students through the assignment. I read two foundational texts on the principles and practices of comics: *The Power of Comics: History, Form, and Culture*, by Randy Duncan, Matthew J. Smith, and Paul Levitz, and *Understanding Comics: The Invisible Art*, by Scott McCloud. I also viewed several detailed online reviews of *Hawkeye*. Like me, the majority of my students were not familiar with the format of a comic book, the theory and practice of comics, or even the intricacies of the DC or Marvel Universe, so by moderating expectations, offering helpful resources, and teaching background material on comic texts during class, I was able to adequately prepare students for the assignment.

To begin, setting proper expectations is key to reducing potential student anxiety caused by venturing into an unfamiliar genre like comics. It is helpful to explain to students that they are approaching the comic as informed readers, not as comics experts. Just as they have analyzed films and novels in other courses based on the preparation provided in class, so too can they feel comfortable examining the comic as informed readers whose judgments are valid even without extensive specialized training.

Students do need adequate resources for this assignment, however, especially if a research component is included. I typically put on print course reserve the two texts that helped me the most: *The Power of Comics* and *Understanding Comics*. A reference librarian adds links to our class website that take students to electronic books and databases on comics that are helpful for the research portion of the assignment. I offer links to two online reviews of *Hawkeye* on the class website since online reviews of comics tend to be more detailed than print reviews (Sava; Whitbrook). Lastly, I post several sample papers from earlier classes, which review works other than *Hawkeye*, to help students visualize what a strong analytical review paper looks like.

Class time is the most important part of student preparation for this assignment, and I use four ninety-minute classes to give students some background on comics and to allow them to brainstorm ideas for their papers. In the first class, I discuss the important features of an analytical review paper, emphasizing that students will need to offer their own analyses of the effectiveness and value of *Hawkeye* and support each point with material from the comic, ultimately recommending the book or not. I usually utilize popular movies during this class session to discuss how to identify and analyze different cinematic elements, such as plot, characters, setting, soundtrack, dialogue, theme, cinematography, and so on. This discussion shows students the process of analysis that they will use for *Hawkeye*.

In the second class, I provide students with basic background on comics and features of comics that are useful for evaluation, organized into three categories to make them more accessible—story elements, composition, and layout.[1] In our examination of story elements, we focus on how the narrative progresses, evaluating components such as plot, character, and setting. This category is the most familiar to students from their previous experiences with literary analysis. In terms of composition, we discuss how the individual panels are composed, noting elements such as panel size, color, background detail, angle, and perspective. Our analysis of layout focuses on how the panels work together in terms of sequence, time and space, transitions, and gutters, among other elements.

The third class is a highly interactive session in which we work through the comic book together, one issue at a time. I allow students time to look through each issue themselves and record what they notice about the text based on the features we identified in the previous class session. We then discuss each issue as a class, which ensures that students understand the story line and how the different features work together. My goal is for students to come away from this discussion with ideas about the comic that will get them started on their own papers.

The fourth class is a writing workshop in which students develop outlines for their papers so that I can give feedback on their content before they start writing. These outlines show their thesis statements and main ideas—specifically, the features of *Hawkeye* they will evaluate, the main points they will make about those features, and the material they will use for support.

Results and Evaluation

Overall, the results of the comic book assignment are always very positive. Most students recommend *Hawkeye* in their papers and analyze three features of the book. Grades on the review paper are often higher than grades on the previous two papers. I usually solicit student feedback on the assignment using an in-class writing assignment.

Several of my pedagogical goals are realized through the assignment. First, students enjoy writing the paper, usually because they find the comic engaging. The interplay of text and images appeals to most students, and some even note in their feedback their weariness of reading novels and their excitement for learning about a new genre. Students often comment that they plan to read more comics in the future.

Second, the comic pushes students out of their comfort zones and forces them to concentrate in order to analyze the text. They usually realize quite quickly that they will need to read the comic more than once in order to write a successful paper. One student noted in her feedback, "I've never read comic books since elementary school, and I don't know anything about heroes. So, this is the most difficult paper I've written so far."

The length of the comic adds more to the assignment than one might expect. Each semester, some students note that they feel they can engage with the work as a whole because it has more to analyze than a short story but is not as unwieldy as a novel. Some even comment that the comic is easier to write about than a feature-length film.

Lastly, and not surprisingly, using a less traditional medium like a comic book appeals to students who can sometimes feel like outsiders in a writing class—comic book fans themselves, visual learners, and those who struggle with reading large amounts of text. In one of my classes, a student who had never spoken once in class but who loved comics became my "comic book expert" and shared often about the genre. His analytical review paper demonstrated marked improvement when compared with his work earlier in the semester. The paper of another self-professed comics lover reflected similar improvement. Another student gratefully noted, "I am not the best at reading books and writing essays on them, which is why I liked the comic book because it was something new that constantly kept me in it."

Perhaps because of the use of images and iconic story lines and characters, comics also appeal to many international students. One noted that "writing the review of a comic book was a new experience that I will cherish for a long time." Of course, those students who are artistically inclined enjoy the opportunity to bring their expertise to the assignment as well, as many students respond very positively to the artwork in the text and enjoy including it in their analyses.

Adding a comics assignment to a writing class can be a rewarding experience for both the instructor and the students because it offers a unique reading experience that forces student writers to interact with a fresh, stimulating, and complex genre. As one student who enjoyed the "creative nature" of the assignment noted, "It felt like an analysis of an art project alongside a work of literature."

Note

1. The features of comics that I share with students are based on the material in Duncan et al. (xi–xiv, 103–62).

Works Cited

Chute, Hillary. *Why Comics? From Underground to Everywhere.* HarperCollins Publishers, 2017.
Duncan, Randy, et al. *The Power of Comics: History, Form, and Culture.* 2nd ed., Bloomsbury, 2016.
Fraction, Matt, et al. *My Life as a Weapon.* Marvel Worldwide, 2013. Vol. 1 of *Hawkeye.*
Krusemark, Renee. "Comic Books in the American College Classroom: A Study of Student Critical Thinking." *Journal of Graphic Novels and Comics,* vol. 8, no. 1, 2017, pp. 59–78, https://doi.org/10.1080/21504857.2016.1233895.
McCloud, Scott. *Understanding Comics: The Invisible Art.* HarperCollins Publishers, 1993.
Petersen, Robert S. *Comics, Manga, and Graphic Novels: A History of Graphic Narratives.* Praeger Publishers, 2010.
Sava, Oliver. "How Did *Hawkeye* Become Marvel's Best Comic?" *The A. V. Club,* G/O Media, 7 Dec. 2012, aux.avclub.com/how-did-hawkeye-become-marvel-s-best-comic-1798235313.
Whitbrook, James. "Six Reasons Why Matt Fraction and David Aja's *Hawkeye* Is One of Marvel's Greatest Comics." *Gizmodo,* G/O Media, 21 July 2015, io9.gizmodo.com/6-reasons-why-matt-fractions-hawkeye-is-one-of-marvels-1719279859.

Appendix: Analytical Review Paper

Writing Prompt

Write a three- to four-page analysis of issues 1–5 of *My Life as a Weapon.* You may address both the positive and negative aspects of the text, but ultimately you must make a recommendation for whether or not your audience should read the book.

Outside Sources

Cite at least three outside sources in your paper: at least one source must be either a book or a periodical; cite from *My Life as a Weapon* and include it in your list of works cited but do not count it as one of your three outside sources.

Documentation of Sources

Use MLA9 parenthetical documentation and include a list of works cited, which should include your three or more outside sources and the comic book.

Suggestions

Do not summarize the comic; I have read it, and I am the audience for your paper. Be specific, not general. Support your points by referencing the comic book.

Aaron Duplantier

Teaching Long-Form Analytical Writing Using *YouTube*

In college composition, the freedom to design coursework at many institutions means that instructors have some agency regarding the central text of study. The problem, then, is considering what sort of text appeals to today's traditionally aged student. To that end, teachers of composition have taken a variety of tactics to garner this generation's buy-in. Humor, or lightheartedness in general, is a benign means to generate a student's buy-in, but what is actually funny can be elusive from the teacher's perspective. My approach has been to turn to new media and *YouTube* in this specific case. *YouTube* is an ever-evolving black hole of content that provides access to edgy humor and captivating, provocative content creators. The assignment I describe here is an analytical paper based on *YouTube* creators that teaches or reinforces research integration, scholarly database navigation, and some basic analytical writing skills that students can potentially apply outside a general education humanities course or a writing class. I currently teach this at a university, but the assignment can also be used in an advanced or intermediate high school writing or English course. This is a technology-heavy assignment and is ideally presented in a physical setting where students have ready access to the Internet and where the teacher has access to a projector and Internet in the classroom.

Students in the United States are generally introduced to the concept of producing written textual analysis on the secondary level alongside their required reading, mostly works belonging to the Western canon. The consequent problem is that *textual analysis* becomes synonymous with *literature* in many students' minds. I typically assign this paper on the freshman level, and for many students it is the first time they are being asked to analyze a text outside an English literature assignment. From a pedagogical perspective, it is imperative that students progressing up the academic ladder understand that textual analysis is not just restricted to Shakespeare or Emily Dickinson because, more than likely, those same skills will be expected in STEM and other academic disciplines outside the humanities with no introduction by the instructor as to how to generate them. Conveying textual analysis through *YouTube* has worked well for me because the site's content tends to be lighthearted and easy to consume: videos on the platform are usually no longer than five to ten minutes in length due to Google ad revenue demands, so this project is not an attention monopoly on students. *YouTube* is also a nice mix of alphabetic, written language and spoken word, which challenges students to come to grips with a few different communication modes with the text at hand, not dissimilar to the electronic texts they engage with voluntarily every day. Notwithstanding is *YouTube*'s graphic user interface, which can often function as its own sort of interpretative language. I have also tied this assignment in the last two years specifically to librarian visits to my face-to-face class, using it as a means of reinforcing the notion of peer review for my students. This assignment can be an excellent tool for meaningful research because when *YouTube* creators get serious, they dig indelibly into real-world issues that have been the focus of scholarly writers and researchers for some time, dealing with representations of race, mental health, gender, sexuality, and so on. As the platform became more popular in the mid-2000s, one of the most interesting burgeoning genres on *YouTube* was the coming-out video, which made marginal, queer identity more visible to a wider audience. Some of the most memorable of these videos were those of US soldiers coming out to the *YouTube* audience in defiance of the military's "don't ask, don't tell" policy. And this is just one example of the way *YouTube* can introduce prescient issues into class discussions.

Choice, too, becomes an important lesson for this assignment. As students advance within their chosen disciplines, they will be offered more opportunities to choose what research topics they pursue. Not only how they choose but also what they choose to study will convey their intellectual competence. Introductory courses often do not provide this opportunity to choose because it can be difficult for instructors to negotiate students' individual decision-making. And this is understandable, especially for those of us who teach four or more sections of a first-year writing course each semester, sometimes with over a hundred students in total. A solution to this problem might be to offer students a set of five research topics from which to choose instead of giving them the freedom to pick whatever topic they want. *YouTube* is full of diverse content and unique personalities. By restricting the types of content students can select, I try to give students just enough information so they can choose a successful *YouTube* creator for this project. In the assignment, students focus on one *YouTube* creator's body of videos, which I refer to in class as a "*YouTube* personality." And picking one creator from the thousands of creators on the platform provides students with enough freedom to give them a taste of what's to come in their future research experiences. It is possible that a student may select a *YouTube* creator who is not well suited to the assignment, but this has become rarer the more I have taught this assignment, and I try to guide students in the selection process.

Much of the textual analysis students generate for this assignment comes from isolating larger themes of a creator's work and digging deeply into those. Or, alternatively, writing about the various strategies these creators use in crafting their messages, style, and so on. For example, one student, Kiersten, selected Hank Green as her *YouTube* personality for this assignment. Hank and John Green are two very popular *YouTube* personalities who are known as the "vlogbrothers" (www.youtube.com/vlogbrothers). Though originally recognized for his *YouTube* content, John Green achieved mainstream success as the author of the young adult novels *The Fault in Our Stars* and *Paper Towns*, among others. While John's career has become more centered on his publishing and film adaptations, his brother Hank, vivacious and filled with quips, still vlogs consistently and is focused on educational content. Kiersten took as the basis of one of her points of analysis how and why Hank Green makes educational content distinctly compelling in his videos. She tied in a scholarly article written by Judy Willis and published in the journal *Educational Leadership*, which argues that education ought to be fun and entertaining because the release of dopamine makes intellectual memories last longer. Kiersten established this idea with a quotation from Willis's article. From there, Kiersten elaborated by stating, "When Hank Green presents information in a fun and compelling way, he is able to make students more compelled to learn and therefore more capable." This method of analysis is no different than what an instructor might find in conventional undergraduate literary analysis. What changed, though, is that Kiersten had to apply the traditional model of analysis, direct quotation, and elaboration that many students use in a literary context to a *YouTube* creator's video. I think it is important to note, and you can probably tell by the sample student quotation above, that the wheel is not reinvented with this assignment. The central text is just different. In the drafting phase, I tend to push for a fairly rudimentary organization for this paper, with each unique analytical idea constituting its own paragraph, since the paper falls earlier in the semester.

One of the great things about using *YouTube* as a platform for analysis is the copious evidence it provides students to draw from in order to prove their points. For example, one student, Julia, wrote about the high-energy, hip *YouTube* personality Emma Chamberlain and Chamberlain's decision to leave high school and pursue her *YouTube* career full-time. Traditional institution-based education and its relevance are often bandied about by new-media stars. Being an *Instagram* model or a *YouTube* creator or whatever the case may be is a full-time gig. Quitting school was apparently an emotionally taxing decision for Chamberlain, one she dealt with openly on her *YouTube* channel. In this assignment, Julia used one of Chamberlain's videos, "Why I Left School," to try to understand why Chamberlain had made that decision. Julia provided a direct quotation from Chamberlain: "You have to show up to school Monday through Friday and sit in a classroom for eight hours because that is what you're supposed to do. That's what society says you're 'supposed' to do" (Chamberlain 08:49–08:53). Julia unpacked this quotation by stating that the traditional educational path "may not be the right fit for some," including people like Chamberlain. Julia tied this idea to a scholarly quotation that claims that public schooling in the United States does not have the proper mechanisms to support stress-related events in students, which Chamberlain apparently suffered from. (The article from which the quotation was taken was published in a peer-reviewed journal titled *Children and Schools*.) The universality of Chamberlain's message, and how Julia proved that traditional schooling is not a good fit for some, is further emphasized by Julia's use of user comments.

YouTube user comments are a rich source of evidence that can be used to support analytical ideas. While user comments on *YouTube* can be toxic, sifting through them often reveals some oddly affirming and significant messages. Not everyone is a troll. This is another important lesson of this assignment, though, granted, it is one tied to *YouTube* and new media rather than conventional academic skills. Julia saw comments from *YouTube* users who related to Emma's struggles with school and quoted the user comments to support her argument. Julia used Chamberlain's video to give the reason why Chamberlain left school, provided a possible external reason using a scholarly source, then emphasized the value of Chamberlain's message with user comments that connected to the video's content. This is a solid approach to using a variety of the evidence on *YouTube* for the sake of textual analysis.

Depending on your needs as a teacher and what you'd like to do with this assignment, your students' analyses and their learning outcomes can take lots of different trajectories. While they will learn a thing or two about online user commenting by simply being asked to read those comments closely, the question is what relevance that will have to your individual class. One of the other things my students write about for this assignment is *YouTube* itself. For example, some of my students have written quite a bit about how *YouTube* handles the "Recommended Videos" section in relation to their *YouTube* personality, about Google Analytics, or about other insular aspects of the platform that may seem more relevant to a media studies class. For instance, one of my students, Jonas, wrote about the *YouTube* channel H3H3 productions, hosted by Ethan and Hila Klein (www.youtube.com/h3h3Productions). These are two exceptionally well-known *YouTube* creators who produce comedic riffs on popular genres commonly featured on *YouTube*. Jonas's analysis pinpointed how Klein and Klein's use of the so-called reaction video, which features creators simply reacting to things, has aided in their popularity. Jonas cited specific evidence from their body of reaction content, writing that Klein and Klein's use of "hazmat suits" as funny costumes, their specific vocal tics, and their "reaching out to the people they were reacting to" have made them memorable. Essentially, Jonas's analytical output was a comparison and contrast based on an internally generated cultural question belonging to *YouTube*. And that is something I find invigorating about using *YouTube* as a learning tool, all of the many cultures, genres, and spaces that exist within the platform. This could manifest itself chaotically in execution, which is why this assignment needs some careful front-end mediation, but it is one my students take joy in.

It is important in the prewriting stage that students choose a *YouTube* personality who has reasonable analytical potential. Successful means for this, insofar as I have experienced it, are based on putting restrictions on the kind of content students can select. Since I call it a "*YouTube* personality," a corporate *YouTube* channel like Vevo or Universal Music or Disney is out of the question, even if the content is interesting or analytically rich. Since students focus on a singular amateur creator, it's useful to steer students to creators who are going to offer solid returns to their search queries on library databases and elsewhere. So, a *YouTube* creator who only produces prank videos is not going to be very effective for this project. For this assignment, a *YouTube* creator's comedic content should be more satirical in nature. In other words, fluffy, empty comedy should be avoided. Creators who have worked well for this assignment include Casey Neistat, Jake Paul, Liza Koshy, Lilly Singh, and James Charles. The base standard that I set for students' analyses, since I generally teach this assignment in an introductory writing class to mostly freshmen, is that students bring something to the surface that is not already there. This helps students understand what the project calls for.

The day I present this assignment in my face-to-face classroom (I also teach this assignment in my online courses), I select a *YouTube* personality to demonstrate how the analysis is meant to be executed, using the projector and symposium liberally, then walk students through as many of the features of the platform that students have at their disposal and can use in their analyses. The last couple of years, I've been using as an example a *YouTube* creator who posts under the username "CandidMommy" and who produces vlogging videos geared toward mothers (www.youtube.com/CandidMommy). In the past, I toyed with the idea of picking young, stylish creators like Emma Chamberlain who were more on my students' level, but then I realized that doing so drew attention to the age gap between me and my students and might have been perceived as a weak attempt to try to connect with my students culturally. This is partly how I grew fond of what I call the "out of left field approach." CandidMommy is a vlog creator that none of my fresh-out-of-high-school students would ever imagine picking for this assignment, so as we watch a short video by CandidMommy called "What I Ate Wednesday | 3 Solid Meals," students all look at me, heads cocked in bemusement, mildly annoyed at what I've forced them to experience. The video is simply a mother walking us methodically through three meals she prepared on a given Wednesday. But the jolt of my choice of example is enough to make students all carefully consider my following tutorial. I show them how to use user comments to back up their analyses, how to isolate pertinent dialogue and content from the video, how to find metadata and Google Analytics, and how to consider the depth of something that may seem banal. It is a strategy, originating from this assignment, that I have used in many other course assignments and lectures—a distinct moment of surprise, something unexpected that encourages students' attention.

The assignment, as I teach it in my first-year writing course, takes place over the course of three weeks based on a meeting schedule of two days per week. The first day of the first week is my introduction of the assignment, followed by a day in which students dwell on the prewriting selection of a *YouTube* personality, which we discuss as a class. When students present their choices, it proves a good time to emphasize creators with high analytical potential for the writing assignment, those who aren't just producing *YouTube* content about pranks, reactions, or other kinds of purely surface-level stuff. Prior to the day I introduce this assignment, I have students watch for homework a video called "How to Trick People into Thinking You're Good Looking." The video, by Jenna Marbles, was uploaded on 9 July 2010 and had roughly seventy million views as of June 2020. Jenna is an old-school *YouTube* personality. Her ribald, edgy humor and perspective as a woman capture the unique viewpoints that can surface to the top of the *YouTube* hierarchy. In the video, Jenna holds no punches in framing the place of women in our society as subjugated. She describes her makeup routine before going to work, calling herself a "street walker" and referring to herself in other disparaging terms at various points, using a sarcastic monotone voice to communicate her lack of excitement in the process of beauty preparation ("How to Trick People" 01:03–01:26). The video jump-cuts between various phases: Jenna first appearing without makeup, then straightening her hair and applying eyeliner, then crying over her master's degree from Boston College, then making fun of her carefully curated *Facebook* photos. When we discuss the video in class, I try to get students to distinguish the hyperbole of the humor from the underlying message. Jenna is raucously funny at times, but she's also saying something. And that's why it's useful. And making those kinds of distinctions is why I find *YouTube* a powerful text for learning and media literacy.

Works Cited
"How to Trick People into Thinking You're Good Looking." *YouTube*, uploaded by JennaMarbles, 9 July 2010, www.youtube.com/watch?v=OYpwAtnywTk.
"What I Ate Wednesday | 3 Solid Meals." *YouTube*, uploaded by CandidMommy, 31 Aug. 2016, www.youtube.com/watch?v=mjgVmzdlm9w&t=1s.
"Why I Left School." *YouTube*, uploaded by emma chamberlain, 26 Oct. 2017, www.youtube.com/watch?v=lllgEOoka8Q&t=585s.

Eric Kennedy and Jade Lennon

Absurdist Television in the Writing Classroom

This essay presents evidence of a course that was successful in combining the standard college composition course with the viewing and analysis of television comedies. The course, taught at Louisiana State University in spring 2018 and titled Absurdist Comedies and Cultural Commentary, examined current cultural issues as they are represented in three contemporary absurdist comedies—*South Park*, *Rick and Morty*, and *Crazy Ex-Girlfriend*—with an aim at analyzing and constructing arguments through textual analysis and academic research.

Offered as a special emphasis of Louisiana State University's writing program, the course was designed to meet the university's general education standard in the area of English composition, which consisted of the goals of practice in argumentative writing and research-based inquiry, through engagement with materials that may be seen as misplaced or underutilized in the college writing classroom. In this essay, I, Eric, detail how the course was created. The main focus here is to offer potential comedy and writing instructors an idea of how to form an effective composition course around the viewing of television shows as well as to demonstrate how a focus on absurdist comedy opens new avenues for students to explore and experiment within these courses. The major concern addressed in this section is how to make such a course fit in with already present university composition course programing. The biggest hurdle in this is how to make sure the administration understands the value of such a course as being significantly more than just an excuse to watch TV.

Intertwined with these details of the course design is a student's perspective, given through brief but genuine reflections from an exemplary student in the Absurdist Comedies course, Jade Lennon. A 2020 graduate of Louisiana State University who has since attended New York University's film studies graduate program, Jade reflects on the work done in the class as a sophomore and discusses how the close examinations of absurdist television positively affected her critical analysis and composition skills. Where my discussion of the course focuses on the conceptualization of the course, Jade's interpolations discuss her takeaways on the course in practice. The reflective nature of these interpolations is aimed at offering an evidentiary experience of the success of such a course and at providing instructors with insight into how the course and its material is perceived by the students meant to benefit from it.

In her anecdotes related to a composition course "that situates feminist and queer theory as a lens through which to view, analyze, and discuss contemporary television," Alexandra Gold relates multiple responses to her use of popular media within the classroom: one acquaintance remarks that he "wouldn't pay for that," and another states that "she couldn't imagine 'wasting her parents' money' pursuing such topics" (156). These types of reactions to even standard courses within the humanities have become fairly common within the ever-encroaching neoliberal restructuring of the university system. Courses centered on forms of popular media and technology, particularly within the humanities, are often met with skepticism from administrations that question the usefulness of liberal arts within the data-driven structure of contemporary education. As Cynthia Selfe has noted, "[M]any teachers of English composition feel [technology] antithetical to their primary concerns and many believe it should not be allowed to take up valuable scholarly time or the attention that could be best put to use in teaching or the study of literacy" (412). While the technological advances and growing presence of media in the everyday lives of students, instructors, and administrators alike has opened the pathway for more innovative course designs, the inclusion of popular forms of media in college classrooms, particularly those within the general education curriculum, still commonly finds resistance within the university.

My proposal for Absurdist Comedies and Cultural Commentary, presented in the fall of 2016, was met with similar skepticisms, including questions about the value of the shows I had proposed as part of the course, which are seen by some as lowbrow programs, and about the amount of TV that students would watch. These responses were not unexpected, nor were they particularly unreasonable. The general education writing course, after all, is meant to prepare a wide array of students from across the curriculum with skills applicable to a variety of coursework. With that initiative in mind, my argument for the course was that students would learn to engage actively with a passive medium. Students would begin to see how intricately the same topics that they often choose for their general education writing course papers (gun control, medical obesity, abortion, race, and gender inequality being some common examples) are dealt with through modes of pop culture and how they can then take what they observe and learn through these mediums to develop and effectively express their own thoughts through discussion and writing.

This position on the usefulness of television and comic texts in the college writing classroom is perhaps best emphasized by John Bryant, who writes that "in rooting out the assumption and priorities within a comedy, students are only a few steps away from examining more carefully the logic and assumptions behind what they may perceive to be absurdities" and that "comic texts are such fruitful resources for the study of argument because they depend upon the often joyful subversion of accepted 'truths'" (132). Absurdist comic texts are particularly founded in this subversion of accepted truths, and *South Park*, *Rick and Morty*, and the first season of *Crazy Ex-Girlfriend* were selected because these shows emphasize their engagement with cultural "truths" deliberately and directly, often without metaphor or suggestiveness, in order to dissect the viewer's understanding of truth and challenge the acceptance of meaning as inherent.

Jade: I signed up for this course because I needed it for a general education requirement and because, out of the many argumentative composition courses offered, it looked the least boring. At first I didn't think I would put much effort into the class. Instead, I thought I would just do the minimum required to get by. However, because the course material included a wide array of topics to discuss, I had the liberty to write about subjects and issues I actually cared about. Because I wrote about topics that were important to me, I made an active effort to present a strong, persuasive argument. What also led me to want to make a strong argument was that the shows we had to watch were fairly controversial, which allowed me to discuss how a topic was dealt with in a particular show from a critical perspective.

In getting students to challenge commonly held cultural beliefs, I introduced the course with a lecture on existentialism and the absurd through a crash course in the philosophy of Albert Camus that ended with a sound bite from *Rick and Morty* that became the class motto: "Nobody exists on purpose. Nobody belongs anywhere. Everybody's gonna die. Come watch TV" ("Rixty Minutes" 00:18:09–00:18:15).

This popular quotation from *Rick and Morty*, an animated adult series about a man and his grandson's chaotic adventures across the multiverse, served as a productive avenue through which students could understand the absurd and its place in popular culture and in their development as writers. Far too often, general education composition students are concerned with what they see as the right way of doing things—a notion reinforced by secondary school concerns of teaching to the test and the five-paragraph essay model. However, with a slightly reworked and simplified discussion of the absurd through Camus's insistence "to live without appeal" (55), I explain that what Camus calls for is the recognition of meaninglessness as it is tied to the human experience and that our ability and willingness to acknowledge a lack of inherent meaning allows us the freedom to make meaning through active reasoning. Thus, Camus's philosophy becomes a touchstone for student writers to see writing and argumentative analysis as a creative act less concerned with structural tent poles and more concerned with expressive reasoning supported through stylistic clarity that emphasizes their personal writerly voice. In other words, presenting the writing process as one of meaning making frees even the most writing-averse students from the rigid confines of format-driven report-style essay writing and encourages them to explore their knowledge bases and ways of knowing.

Jade: The fact that the shows we covered in class were absurdist made it more challenging to form a concrete argument because it required creating something logical from a nonsensical source. When you try to make sense out of nonsense, it's extremely necessary to be clear and detailed in your writing in order to show how you arrived at your conclusion based on nonsense. Also, you have to explain why the nonsense isn't just nonsense and why it matters.

The choice of texts to work from is important in accomplishing this, and the Absurdist Comedies and Cultural Commentary course was designed with a three-unit scaffold structure, with each unit focused on one of the chosen television texts. My role as instructor was to guide students through a development of comprehension and interpretation skills that "involve the *construction* of meaning out of textual cues" (Bordwell 3). Each episode was paired with a critical reading from sources across the critical spectrum, including blogs, pop culture websites, and scholarly journals and books. The readings ranged from analysis of the shows themselves to those that established more abstract connections with the thematic and cultural content of a particular episode. A large part of the course required students to find their own sources to match to episodes of their choice, which they would then guide the class through as a multimedia presentation.

Jade: To clarify my observations, it's best to describe them in the context of one of our assignments. For the first paper we were tasked with making an argument about any episode of *South Park*. I chose to write about an episode that focused on immigration, which was an issue I cared deeply about. Since immigration was so important to me, I watched this episode with a very critical lens, which made me think more about how the matter was presented and why I did not agree. Knowing that the show prides itself on being nonsense that shouldn't be taken seriously, I had to explain why it mattered that the subject of immigration was not handled well. I also had to be very detailed when explaining the specific points of the episode's plot that, in my opinion, presented the issue poorly in order to clearly show why I disagreed with it.

In the first unit, students were introduced to the basics of textual and visual analysis through *South Park*. I demonstrated *South Park*'s penchant for stating its thesis outwardly in each episode (seen most clearly in earlier seasons of the series in which a character would make a speech expressly stating what they learned in that episode). The realization that a television show had a thesis, much less that a character in the show would state it outwardly, was a novel and surprising concept for students. Once they understood the function of this, they were able to identify a thesis in each of the episodes we watched throughout the semester, applying a search for thesis statements in the more overt delivery of the series we would watch the remainder of the semester.

The second unit, on *Rick and Morty*, introduced more complex structures of analysis and writing processes. Here I emphasized the show's use of A and B plotlines—the primary and secondary narratives of each episode. I described how these plotlines shared thematic purposes, and students began to identify the rhetorical purposes of each plotline as the thematic argument of each episode, effectively defining a thesis using these analytical practices. *Rick and Morty*'s emphasis on nihilism and the absurd allowed for more complex and diverse discussions of each episode's engagement with cultural topics.

For these first two units, students wrote analytical essays on one episode of the respective series in which they evaluated the episode's cultural argument and discussed their individual response to that argument. The interweaving of measured analytical thought and personal reflection proved effective in allowing students to develop critical thinking skills and to experiment with writerly voice in their writing.

In the final unit, students viewed the entirety of season 1 of *Crazy Ex-Girlfriend*, a musical comedy about a woman who upends her life to pursue an ex-boyfriend. A self-aware metatext, the show is riddled with allusions and references to a plethora of pop culture artifacts, using them not just as homage but also as a commentary on the way in which these artifacts influence our construction of reality and meaning. This play with pop culture offers an often stark critique of a wide range of sociocultural topics, such as mental health, toxic masculinity, romantic relationships, representations of Jewish mothers, and even costuming in romantic comedies. Students were able to analyze the argumentative commentary apparent in these episodes through the application of skills developed in the previous units, bringing to their viewings an understanding of teleplay structures and argumentative reasoning.

The unit and the course were capped off with a lengthier argumentative research essay in which students were given the following prompt:

> We have spent the semester developing analytical skills that help distinguish how an argument is constructed both in television shows and in popular and scholarly writing. We have also worked toward building our own arguments out of those analyses, expressing opinions and taking a stance on specific topics. Your final essay will combine these skills to examine a topic through the medium of television using the absurdist comedies we have watched—*South Park*, *Rick and Morty*, and *Crazy Ex-Girlfriend*—in order to engage in a larger conversation about a topic of your choosing and the various modes of representation of that topic that you find in your viewings and other research.

Through a semester of deconstructing absurdist texts that may otherwise be understood as nonsense, students were ultimately asked to, and proved able to, reconstruct and make meaning out of that nonsense in order to express something tangible and reasoned. Effectively, students began to approach their writing as a way of making and communicating meaning by actively engaging with not just critical texts but also texts commonly seen as outside the purview of the university. When surveyed at the end of the course, students were overwhelmingly positive about the skills they had learned and the developments they had made as writers and thinkers over the semester.

Jade: Because the source was absurd, there were many ways it could be interpreted, so it was important to address possible arguments that could discredit my points. I had to be clear and detailed in explaining how I had arrived at my conclusion from something absurd because if I wasn't careful the argument could seem crazy. For instance, if I were writing about the dangers of climate change, I could assume my audience was already familiar with the discourse around it and agree that it was bad, so I wouldn't feel the need to be super clear in order to sound logical. Obviously, these skills are vital to effective argumentative writing, so teaching them in an introductory class in a way that is accessible and engaging, as they were in this course, is very beneficial for students. Prior to this course, the only other class I had that taught argumentative writing was in high school, and we had to write about transcendentalism, which was neither engaging nor very accessible as an introduction to argumentative writing.

By building on skills they had learned in previous composition courses, students effectively linked their understanding of critical contexts to what would otherwise be their passive engagement with either the media in question (i.e., passive television viewing) or with a topic they are uninterested in. This is not to say, of course, that direct engagement with sociocultural issues, as in a standard general education writing course, or with topics such as transcendentalism, in the example that Jade gives above, cannot be effective approaches to building the framework of academic excellence. However, by working with current cultural artifacts, students like Jade found it easier to engage with materials, even when those materials included a scholarly essay on nihilism that accompanied our introduction to *Rick and Morty*. This makes the engagement with current cultural issues for which writing program courses tend to strive no less effective, as Mimi White has argued:

> Certain cultural practices may express issues and ideas from a prior social formation, whereas other artifacts embody progressive elements that look forward to future forms of social and material practice. In this

context, cultural artifacts and texts have the potential to criticize and challenge the status quo by carrying ideological positions that are out of phase with the current, dominant mode of ideological production. (125)

By working within the context that White describes, absurdist comedies offer students a critical space in which to challenge social concerns in a multitemporal (past, present, future) context and allow them to consider the ways in which meaning has, is, and will be constructed.

Works Cited

Bordwell, David. *Making Meaning: Inference and Rhetoric in the Interpretation of Cinema*. Harvard UP, 1989.

Bryant, John. "Comedy and Argument: A Humanistic Approach to Composition." *The Journal of General Education*, vol. 36, no. 2, 1984, pp. 126–40.

Camus, Albert. *The Myth of Sisyphus*. Translated by Justin O'Brien, Vintage Books, 1955.

Gold, Alexandra. "Not Our Regularly Scheduled Programming: Integrating Feminist Theory, Popular Culture, and Writing Pedagogy." *Feminist Teacher: A Journal of the Practices, Theories, and Scholarship of Feminist Teaching*, vol. 26, nos. 2–3, Jan. 2016, pp. 156–78.

"Rixty Minutes." *Rick and Morty*, directed by Bryan Newton, season 1, episode 8, Warner Brothers, 17 Mar. 2014.

Selfe, Cynthia L. "Technology and Literacy: A Story about the Perils of Not Paying Attention." *College Composition and Communication*, vol. 50, no. 3, 1999, pp. 411–36.

White, Mimi. "Ideological Analysis and Television." *Channels of Discourse, Reassembled: Television and Contemporary Criticism*, edited by Robert C. Allen, 2nd ed., U of North Carolina P, 1992, pp. 121–51.

Jeffrey M. Cordell

Mrs. Maisel, Amy Sherman-Palladino, and a Pretty, Perfect Pilot

Lucky to grow up in a time of funny women writing must-see television shows, I truly enjoy watching so many of the top-tier female-centered sitcoms available on the Internet today. Women comedy writers shaped my idea of what "funny" can be. They also point the way to social changes by inviting us first to laugh at the inequities of the status quo. Comedy is, after all, a collective social corrective. Having clocked Treva Silverman's writing credits on *The Mary Tyler Moore Show* and Linda Bloodworth-Thomason's scripts for *Designing Women*, I memorized the name Diane English while watching *Murphy Brown*. In the twenty-first century, I've gleefully joined the fandoms for modern female comic revolutionaries who can run their own shows like Tina Fey, Amy Poehler, and Jenji Kohan. Now I've added Amy Sherman-Palladino to this list of artist-heroes because I am addicted to her Amazon series *The Marvelous Mrs. Maisel*. She hooked me with the first episode.

The pilot aired on 17 March 2017 ("Pilot"). At the time of this writing, the episode is available for purchase on *Amazon* and is free for *Amazon Prime* subscribers. The pilot was written and directed by Sherman-Palladino. One of the reasons this television episode works well as a classroom text is because, with Sherman-Palladino in the role of writer and director, authorship is clearer than it is in many other instances. With a team of writers plus a director, or even with one executive producer and one director, the conversation can become distracted or sidetracked by desires to attribute the work correctly. In addition, Sherman-Palladino made history with *Mrs. Maisel*'s pilot. In 2018 she became the first woman to win Primetime Emmys for both Outstanding Directing and Outstanding Writing. Therefore, the pilot episode's authorship is both singular and highly decorated.

However, the script for the pilot episode—and of most television shows, to be honest—is not something easily acquired and read on paper. The published pilot is neither affordable to purchase in a paper version from online vendors, nor is it easy to acquire on the Internet without memberships or possible copyright infringement. This is understandable and unremarkable. The pilot was intended to be roughly an hour long, and viewing it online is easy and affordable. The paper script was only meant to be used by staff members, actors, designers, and crew members in the making of the fully realized television experience. Plus, television scripts are not seen as a commodity worthy of distribution in US entertainment culture—except to die-hard fans who may spring for a signed copy as a collectible artifact.

The Pedagogical Idea: Writing while Watching

This pair of circumstances—Sherman-Palladino's award-winning status as writer and director and the absence of a readily available print version of the script—makes for an exciting and flexible classroom experience suited to a variety of disciplines and courses.

The pedagogical idea of writing while watching is based on revelatory learning experiences I had as a high school and college student in classes such as Writing and Society and Scriptwriting. I have used this technique as a writing mentor when scripts were perfect for a student's trajectory but unavailable. In Writing and Society, we were asked to note and transcribe as much of what we were seeing as possible in the course of multiple viewings of a video. The goal was to enhance the ways in which we were experiencing the media and its messages. Then we practiced analytical thinking, using our own recorded versions of the video text as evidence. In Scriptwriting, an upper-level college course, we watched and transcribed several episodes of the sitcom *Mad About You*. We used our hard-fought scribblings to produce spec scripts, as if we were auditioning for gigs as series writers.

These formative video-capturing exercises, out-of-class reviews, and classroom discussions permanently heightened my awareness of the scriptwriter's craft prior to interpretation. These notes and scripts also proved to me that writing comedy is real work, much tougher than writing drama. I learned that one maddening aspect of comedy is its mutability as it moves from author to interpreter. How does an artist nail down comedy's details, rhythms, viewpoints, and timings with any degree of certainty?

That last question is central to Mrs. Maisel's journey in her "marvelous," eponymous show. And, given her award shelf, Sherman-Palladino seems to have found all the answers. How do we open up our own comedy notebooks and investigate? Here is a five-step outline to consider:

1. Students view the pilot from start to finish several times.
2. Individually or in teams, students select a specific scene or a pair of related scenes for closer study. I recommend scene lengths of forty-five to ninety seconds. Students establish a hypothesis about how the scene works and what the scene contributes to the structure and meaning of the episode as a whole.
3. Students write their own script of what they are seeing, hearing, and experiencing. Students should account for as much as possible, including dialogue and stage directions. To what degree students should follow any particular format is best left to the instructor and disciplinary preferences. First and foremost, this is not a formatting drill but a chance to resurface the foundational written work of a woman-centered comedy series pilot. I recommend that this stenographic work be done during a specific viewing session, with the ability to stop and start as many times as is needed. Closed captioning and audio descriptions can be helpful but often contain inaccuracies or underlying assumptions that are no more accurate than a viewer's own perspectives on the relationship of the visuals to the spoken words.
4. Upon completion of the script work, students write reflections on what the process caused them to see or hear differently, perhaps more deeply, than when they first viewed the pilot episode in its entirety. Where were they most certain or uncertain about Sherman-Palladino's authorial intentions? Why? At what points did the pilot reveal itself to be risible in the world of the show? In the world of the viewer? In both? What determines the smiling-to-LOLing spectrum of this particular television show?

5. The scripts are submitted and shared with the entire class. Comparisons among scripts for the same scenes can be a particularly vibrant starting point for discussion. Reflection papers are submitted to the instructor after students use them to support class discussion and debate.

Such work turns a brighter spotlight on the work of a woman writing a historically significant, popular comedic text for performance on recorded media. Further, it allows students to more closely engage with one of the most brilliant facets of the pilot script and the series in general. Mrs. Miriam "Midge" Maisel is established as a devoted student of comedy who writes, analyzes, and practices with comic material until she learns how it works. Then she makes it her own. Of course, she often chooses to jettison that careful work at life-changing moments of stream-of-consciousness stand-up. Over time, the structured work adds greater depth and security to the unplanned rants. Her most calculated moves and her riskiest choices are both bites taken from the sweetly poisoned fruit of the tree of knowledge. However, what becomes clear during the moments of Midge's triumphs as a female comedian is that her entire trajectory—both thoughtful and reckless—is being carefully orchestrated by another comically gifted woman writer who is not leaving anything to chance: Sherman-Palladino. Diving into the pilot allows comedy audiences to become comedy readers of their own notes, thereby locating Sherman-Palladino and her work within their own language, experience, and sense of humor. This carries the potential for powerful viewing and revisioning. We each become Mrs. Maisel, the student of the form, and Sherman-Palladino, the master of the genre.

Three Examples

I have selected three short scenes to help illustrate this idea's potential for teaching. The excerpts below are the words I've chosen to best represent my viewing experiences with the pilot episode of *The Marvelous Mrs. Maisel*.

The pilot begins on the day that Miriam became Mrs. Maisel, and so shall I. After viewing the pilot in full, with its amazing soundtrack and incredible variations in volume between silent and raucous scenes, I am floored that the first vocal utterance heard in this woman's comedy is "Shhh." This is something I only became aware of after I had transcribed the scene. Midge is not a woman who will heed a shushing or stay quiet if there is comic comment to be made. And we are being told to "Shhh," we shall quickly learn, because a woman is about to speak at her own wedding and we should pay attention. That is, after all, highly unconventional. The "Shhh" works as suppression and liberation.

Here is one way to transcribe the rest of the scene:

Black screen. We hear the chatter of guests at a party. Then the rings of silverware tapping on a glass. Then: "Shhh."
WOMAN'S VOICE *(commandingly but pleasantly rhetorical)*: Who gives a toast at her own wedding?
INT. Reception hall. Evening.
We see the WOMAN from the waist up, standing at a microphone in wedding dress and veil, with her reception in the background—complete with a band in pink tuxedo jackets.
WOMAN. I mean, who does that? Who stands in the middle of a ballroom after three glasses of champagne on a completely empty stomach—and I mean *completely* empty because fitting into this dress required no solid food for three straight weeks. Who does that?
(Beat—the WOMAN's hands flick out, palms up on either side of her bustline as she self-referentially smirks.)
WOMAN. I do.
(The room melts into warm laughter and applause for the WOMAN—as they know her well—and the camera zooms out to capture the entire extravagant, winter-white affair, including a five-tier wedding cake.)   ("Pilot" 00:00–00:35)

This woman, who does things that others dare not do, remains nameless throughout the opening sequence. And the sequence begins in darkness, then turns a spotlight on a woman at a microphone, then opens wider to capture the audience when their response is required. With these last two words, "I do," Miriam marries herself in a celebration of comic ego. And the crowd loves it. The pilot will end with this same woman performing her first real stand-up routine at The Gaslight on the night her cheating husband, Joel, walks out on her. She will be drunk and disheveled, having exposed her naked body to a room full of strangers. This is a powerful reversal of the initial static situation. Moreover, Sherman-Palladino's first thirty seconds of the pilot adroitly establish that this will be a story about the difficulties a woman will face when she inserts stand-up comedy into her married life. No matter what the men may do or what the crowd may think, the seeds of disharmony were there from the very beginning.

The next sample excerpt from the pilot takes place after Joel and Midge go to The Gaslight. Joel seems eager to polish his comedy routine. Midge barters her brisket for a better time slot, which Joel uses to perform Bob Newhart's bit about Abe Lincoln receiving advice from an image consultant prior to the Gettysburg Address. A worker at The Gaslight, Susie Myerson, appears amusingly baffled by the forceful Miriam yet completely disappointed that Miriam is with a plagiarizing schmuck like Joel.

INT. Taxi. Night.
JOEL is sleeping on MIDGE's shoulder. MIDGE is referencing her pink notebook and notes from his set tonight.
MIDGE. You got three more laughs tonight than you did last time, and a couple of extra, like, laughlets. *(Worried, mostly to herself, preoccupied about SUSIE's body language.)* . . . I don't know what she was shaking her head for . . .
JOEL *(sleepy, disconnected)*: Mmm?
MIDGE. Nothing. You were great.
JOEL *(eyes closed, smiling, slurry)*: I was great.
MIDGE. You know, you don't really say "hello" to the audience. Maybe you should write a beginning—something that says who you are or something. Whaddaya think?
JOEL does not respond, still in a haze. MIDGE kisses him on the forehead like a little boy.
MIDGE *(quietly drafting out loud, riffing, flipping around in her pink notebook)*: Good evening. What a nice . . . *(That's not it. Take two, louder and more confident.)* Good evening, ladies and gentlemen. Thank you for the nice—nice—"Nice" is a bad, bad word. *(Big breath in, like she's about to dive under. Take three, really ready to swing with her pen poised.)* All that applause for me? What am I, putting out after? *(A thoughtful pause in which a weary amount of experience becomes a moment of verbal revelation.)* One standing ovation, everyone goes home pregnant.
(She's said it almost too fast, but as she lets herself hear it, she knows: it works. She smiles to herself and writes down the line.) ("Pilot" 14:53–15:45)

Noteworthy here is the powerful shift from Midge making notes and giving feedback about Joel's comedy routine to an original piece of introductory comedy that she is best able to deliver. Sherman-Palladino also keeps the literal tools of comic writing—the pencil and book—at the visual center of the scene. In terms of action, we watch an innately funny woman thinking and taking notes, while a man sleeps through her helpful post-show analysis. Midge is restless, while Joel relaxes in his privileged, albeit false, sense of security. Finally, it is potent to end the scene with the word "pregnant," for here is another moment where Midge finds a self-aware joke living within the standard language of marriage and family life. A few minutes later, we will learn that the couple already has two children.

The third sample scene establishes more of Midge's routines and relationships. I deeply enjoy the ancient stichomythic quality of this dialogue, its mixing of cocktails and math, and its comic portrait of two women measuring themselves and others. And none of it is a joke. For the record, even after multiple viewings and labeling it as one of my favorite exchanges, the writing did not make me laugh out loud until I made the effort to capture it on the page.

INT. Living room of the Maisel apartment. Dusk.
Close-up on a black-and-white television set broadcasting a beer commercial. We hear the jingle "For fun it's the premium one . . ."
The petite IMOGENE sits in a curved, modern sectional sofa. She drinks a daiquiri and keeps her ankles crossed. There's a notebook in her lap. MIDGE, wearing black tights and leotard, holds a measuring tape. Her left foot is perched on an ottoman. MIDGE calls out measurements for IMOGENE to record. Their speech often overlaps.
IMOGENE. . . . so she's going on and on about this miracle treatment she had done in New Mexico. It involved goat's milk and avocadoes.
MIDGE. Right ankle: 8, left ankle: 8.
IMOGENE. They smear it on your face, wrap a hot towel around your head, and stick two straws up your nose.
MIDGE. Right calf: 11, left calf: 11.
IMOGENE. So you can breathe, you know, through the straws. *Then* they put you on a boat and they row you out to sea—
MIDGE. Right thigh: 18
IMOGENE. And they drop the anchor, and you sit there for *four* hours.
MIDGE. Left thigh: 18 and a half.
IMOGENE. Then they row you back in—
MIDGE. Hips: 34.
IMOGENE. And they scrape you down—
MIDGE. Waist: 25.
IMOGENE. —slap you in the face with old banana skins—
MIDGE. Bust: 32.
IMOGENE. —charge you seventy-five dollars and send you home. She thinks she looks twenty. I think she looks the same.
MIDGE *(on IMOGENE's wavelength about this)*: Mmm.
IMOGENE. God, you are so proportional! How long have you been measuring yourself like this? *(Flips back through the record book in her lap.)*
MIDGE. Every day for ten years.

IMOGENE. Even when you were pregnant?
MIDGE. Mmm.
IMOGENE. There's not enough daiquiris in the world. *(Raises her glass and sips with a mix of astonishment and admiration.)*
In the rare silence, we hear two things: JOEL returning home from work through the front door and Ed Sullivan announcing his next guest, Bob Newhart.
("Pilot" 20:36–21:24)

Again, the act of recording is central to the scene. Tellingly, it keeps interrupting Imogene's bizarre story of another woman's vain quest for a youthful face. The scene also focuses on a woman's body—it is a clock, it can carry a child to term, it may be recorded by part names and inches. The speeches and the visuals allow viewers to fully commodify Midge's body and her personal relationships—friends, husband, parents, and children. Her career in comedy will also baldly and unapologetically turn these things into commodities. This body consciousness reaches its zenith when Midge exposes her breasts and entire upper torso at The Gaslight in frustration at being cast aside for another woman. She ends up being carted off to jail for public indecency. The TV audience is howling, but I distinctly remember not laughing during my first viewing. This comedy business has serious consequences.

Speaking of consequences, about fifty-four minutes from Sherman-Palladino's pilot remain to be mined by you and your students. My goal here was to warm up the audience and test the microphone, as it were. Who exits an essay like this? I do. (Thanks, Midge. Thanks, Amy.)

Work Cited

"Pilot." *The Marvelous Mrs. Maisel*, created by Amy Sherman-Palladino, season 1, episode 1, Amazon Studios, 17 Mar. 2017. *Amazon Prime Video*, www.amazon.com/Pilot/dp/B0875K26X2.

Shelly A. Galliah

Learning through Failure: Workplace Comedy in the Professional and Technical Communication Classroom

In one infamous scene from Mike Judge's classic film *Office Space*, a bored, downtrodden Peter Gibbons (Ron Livingston) is puttering away at his cubicle when his boss, Bill Lumbergh (Gary Cole), saunters by to remind Peter that he omitted the cover sheet on his most recent TPS (test procedure specification) report (*"Office Space"*). Even though Peter acknowledges his error and the new process, Lumbergh loiters, repeats his message, offers to send another memo, and talks down to his employee. After Lumbergh departs, several middle managers and coworkers annoyingly interrupt Peter, recapping the new protocol and the memo announcing it. Throughout these "friendly reminders," which cause Peter to grow increasingly irate, the audience sees all the personnel to whom he must report as well as the tedious paperwork and repetitive directives that often make his job wearisome, if not intolerable.

This scene is well suited to the professional and technical communication classroom for several reasons. Most obviously, students familiar with IEEE (Institute of Electrical and Electronics Engineers) documentation find this exchange amusing because TPS reports, used for quality assurance ("IEEE 829 Documentation"), exemplify mandatory but mundane paperwork. Shown early in the semester, this clip also inspires students to discuss how the conversations between Peter and his coworkers reveal fundamental professional communication flaws—inappropriate tone when addressing subordinates and coworkers, abundant memos ignored by employees, dysfunctional interoffice messaging—as well as the drawbacks of crowded cubicle culture. For these and other lessons, *Office Space* reveals the pedagogical potential of one popular culture genre: the workplace comedy.

Admittedly, there are several debatable functions of popular culture—affirming social values, conveying information, enlightening audiences, providing therapy, functioning as a safety valve, or simply offering pleasure (Takacs 41–61). Comic popular culture, such as *Office Space*, functions in several of these roles while demonstrating and enlivening professional and technical communication content and, more importantly, increasing student engagement. Let me explain why comedy is necessary. For many of my students, Professional and Technical Communication is only their second writing-intensive course since first-year composition, which they completed two or more years earlier, so their writing skills might be rusty. My university is also a technological school with an engineering-heavy focus, so there is also occasional resistance from those who view Professional and Technical Communication as yet another humanistic hurdle on the long path to their degrees. Lastly, professional and technical communication content, though important, is often quite dull. Therefore, developing strategies to improve students' written and verbal communication while maintaining their attention and cooperation is crucial. And one of these strategies is to encourage learning through humorous communication mishaps. Workplace comedy in particular enables these errors to be exaggerated, writ large for students to understand.

Failure is an also appropriate instructional strategy because it is a key concept in the lexicons of students who attend technological universities: for instance, many students will have taken engineering courses that address disasters in design. In *Success through Failure: The Paradox of Design*, Henry Petroski, a respected engineer, presents a series of examples of engineering marvels that have not been constructed from previous successful plans but from new designs that anticipated and averted spectacular failures. He iterates that it is part of the engineering mindset to study malfunctions to not only determine what went wrong but also avoid previous errors in designs and artifacts. Furthermore, many failures (such as the *Challenger* disaster, which many students at my university regularly examine) often begin with lapses in documentation or problems in workplace communication.

Workplace comedy, then, helps solidify course content while making communication failures more accessible. In my class, the initial assignment asks students to construct employment documents, but the second is a short report analyzing questionable technical and professional communication. (One of the other goals of the second assignment is to familiarize students with the features of *Microsoft Word*—templates, headings, layout, and so on—which they will need for their longer white papers.) Comic segments shown in class serve as a bridge between these two course components and scaffold the informal report assignment.

Previously, I used clips from *Office Space*, satirical comedy programs, *Seinfeld*, and Monty Python (especially *Meetings, Bloody Meetings*) to demonstrate ineffective communication, ineffective workplace relationships, and inappropriate audiences and purposes. Truthfully, I regularly avoided using *The Office* (2005–13) because of my (misguided) opinion that it is too obvious a choice and often inappropriate in content, but because several students have suggested its suitability, I have since integrated this program into the classroom.

The Office: A Workplace Comedy with Enjoyable and Educational Failures

From my own and my students' investigations, I have learned that the workplace comedy *The Office* is especially suitable for the professional and technical communication classroom. Whether one considers it a mockumentary or a comedy verité (what Trish Dunleavy refers to as a hybrid genre fusing the reality TV subgenre—the docusoap—and the situation comedy), the characters, setting, and scenarios of *The Office* are far more realistic (and often uncomfortably familiar) than those in typical situation comedies. The program's debts to reality programming—certain camera aesthetics, individuals who (often clumsily) acknowledge they are being filmed, self-conscious comic performances—are blended with flawed, average characters and serial narratives, such as Jim and Pam's relationship, Michael's lack of emotional intelligence, and power-hungry Dwight's devious machinations. Soper explains that much of the program's appeal derives from how "we laugh or cringe as we observe people much like ourselves unwittingly revealing their foolishness through talking head interviews, banal everyday situations, and seemingly unscripted exchanges with office mates" (83). The absence of a laugh track and the presence of awkward silences further allow the program's deadpan humor, absurdity, and realism to stand out.

Illustrating a typical white-collar American office, that of the Scranton, Pennsylvania, branch of the paper company Dunder Mifflin, *The Office* has a large cast that represents occupational roles students might encounter in their future employment: both competent and inept managers and middle managers, administrative assistants, accountants, salespeople, warehouse workers, and various representatives of customer service, human resources, quality assurance, supply relations, and so on. Many of the most memorable characters from *The Office* are failed professionals who lack the self-awareness to step outside themselves and critically reflect on their shortcomings, many the result of inadequate or inappropriate communication. The most prominent of these failed professionals is the manager, Michael, who often puts his needs ahead of those of his employees while regularly not conforming to his company's plans or protocol. The employees, though they usually comply with Michael's wishes and bizarre choices, often seem both bored and broken by the uninspired and tedious routines of their jobs.

Along with its credible workplace and characters, the subject matter of *The Office* is relevant for discussing document planning, workplace communication, manager-employee relations, inclusive messaging, and cross-cultural communication challenges. Many episodes offer object lessons relevant to a professional and technical communication course. Season 2, for instance, contains these gems: "Performance Review" (episode 8), which highlights Michael's inappropriate interoffice messaging; "Dwight's Speech" (episode 17), which demonstrates Michael's failure to consider context and audience; "Drug Testing" (episode 20), which contends with dishonesty and unethical workplace relationships; and "Conflict Resolution" (episode 21), which addresses problems with violating privacy and maintaining employee morale. Still, other episodes must be carefully contextualized (and introduced with huge spoiler alerts) to avoid offending the class. Especially tricky are those episodes that expose Michael's insensitivity to women's issues, diversity, and the LGBTQ community: "Diversity Day" (season 1, episode 2), "Gay Witch Hunt" (season 3, episode 1), "Sexual Harassment" (season 2, episode 2), "Boys and Girls" (season 2, episode 15), and "Women's Appreciation" (season 3, episode 19). Although students are encouraged to analyze more risqué episodes, they know these episodes might not be viewed in class.

Overall, the program's realistic (but exaggerated) scenarios and characters' poor decisions lure students in. Laughter illuminates key course concepts while allowing them to practice the cognitive skills required for their own projects. Despite *The Office* having ended when many of my students were still in grade school, their first-year *Netflix* binges have more than familiarized them with it.

Integrating *The Office* while Scaffolding an Assignment

In my course, I use select episodes from *The Office* when introducing and contextualizing the second assignment, an informal report in which students analyze a case study for its professional and technical communication difficulties. *The Office* helps steer students toward comedy and away from reworking real examples previously analyzed in their engineering classes, which might result in problematic dual submission. It is not necessary that they focus on *The Office*, but they must examine a popular culture representation of some workplace. Here is the brief version of the assignment's instructions:

> This assignment assesses your ability to examine a chosen case study for the effectiveness of its professional and technical communication, such as the consideration of audience, and the clarity, usability, ethics, and professionalism of messages. For your analysis, please choose a representation of a communication problem from a television program or film that depicts a fictional workplace. Your analysis must be substantiated with appropriate evidence from your case study and from two or more of these relevant sections from Mike Markel's textbook: "Intro to Technical Communication" (1–16), "Understanding Ethical and Legal Considerations" (17–40), "Analyzing Your Audience and Purpose" (82–123), and "Writing Definitions, Descriptions, and Instructions" (533–75).
>
> To get practice using the report genre, you will convey your analysis through a brief informal report consisting of the following four sections (and as many subsections as required): summary and context of case study, analysis of case study, recommendations, and pedagogical implications.
>
> The following are the goals of your assignment: to apply standards of effective professional and technical communication, to analyze a case study for professional or technical communication failures, to construct a brief but substantive informal report, and to synthesize the case study with course materials.

For the students, the course materials and class activities are organized so that the final assignment is scaffolded in four stages: analyzing a segment in groups (face-to-face, ideally, or online), reviewing strong examples of students' reports, composing an assignment benchmark (i.e., explaining and selling their idea in a discussion forum), and submitting their final reports. Students are also permitted to revise this assignment by the end of the term.

Scaffolding is one of the practices associated with Lev Vygotsky's theory of the zone of proximal development, defined by Vygotsky as "the distance between the actual developmental level as determined by independent problem solving and the level of potential development as determined through problem solving under adult guidance, or in collaboration with capable peers" (103). According to Vygotsky, when students are in this zone, appropriate assistance from more knowledgeable others, guidance from tutors, and supportive activities from educators all enhance the learning process. In my class activity, which preps students for the report, the more knowledgeable other might be that student who has watched every episode of *The Office* and who understands its characters, themes, and plotlines or that peer most familiar with the textbook's materials. Social interactions between students and tutors allow the former to develop and model behaviors and skills in an environment in which mistakes are permissible. In the classroom, scaffolding includes modeling a skill, providing an outline, offering hints or cues, or transforming material or activities (Wood et al.). Scaffolding permits students to practice skills on low-stakes assessments, which ideally should occur at regularly spaced intervals both inside and outside the classroom (Lang 133). In keeping with James Lang's advice that instructors should provide an "organizing framework with hierarchies and key concepts" (103) that allows students to build connections and fill in content, thereby enforcing independent learning, my in-class activity is driven by a series of precise questions, whereas the discussion has detailed prompts. Therefore, students intermittently practice deconstructing comic episodes and supporting their argument with evidence. In the first low-stakes group activity, they rehearse the thinking, analyzing, and writing required for their second assignment, the high-stakes assessment. Reviewing examples of student assignments further acquaints them with assignment standards and the report format.

Here I focus on the first scaffolded in-class lesson involving a segment from an *Office* episode titled "Stress Relief," which former students have previously investigated. One of the most widely watched two-part installments of *The Office*, "Stress Relief" aired immediately after Super Bowl XLIII on 1 February 2009. This over-the-top episode was intentionally constructed to attract viewers unfamiliar with the show, so its notoriety and exaggeration make it accessible to both fans and nonfans. The instructions advise students to pay close attention to the events and communication catastrophes in the fire drill scene, the episode's five-minute cold open, which we also viewed in class ("Fire Drill").

The episode begins with a disgruntled Dwight (Rainn Wilson) muttering that everyone ignored his fire safety talk last week but that it was "[his] own fault for using PowerPoint. PowerPoint is boring" ("Fire Drill" 0:33). The scene then cuts to him hammering and wedging the office doors shut and applying a blowtorch to their metal plates before lighting a cigarette and throwing it into a trash basket doused in lighter fuel. A straight-faced Dwight then stares into the camera, announcing, "Today, smoking is going to save lives" before returning to his seat and awaiting the ensuing chaos. Soon, Pam yells "Fire!" (1:23), Michael panics while ironically yelling at everyone to stay "fu—ing" calm (1:38), and employees stampede through the office, revealing their total lack of safety preparedness. The shaky camera struggles to keep up with the staff's erratic movements. Oscar tries to escape through the ceiling tiles; Michael heaves a chair at a window; others transform the photocopier into a battering ram. During this bedlam, a macabrely calm Dwight repeatedly urges his coworkers to recall appropriate procedures (2:27, 2:38, 2:44, 2:59) before finally yelling out, "Use the surge of fear and adrenaline to sharpen our decision-making!" (3:19). Finally, Dwight stands on the desk and announces that the fire is merely a training exercise while Stanley is suffering from a heart attack. Not surprisingly, no one knows CPR.

The opening scene of this episode grabs students' attention while affording them an opportunity to work toward the learning objectives of the second assignment. After viewing this episode, groups respond to the following prompts, which all cohere with the analysis level of Bloom's taxonomy. Thus, students get to practice the cognitive tasks necessary for the final assignment.

> Explain how Dwight's *PowerPoint* on fire safety and his live drill violate Markel's standards of excellence in professional and technical communication (7–8).
> Analyze Dwight's failures in choosing the most effective communication medium for subject, purpose, and audience. Use evidence from Markel's chapter "Analyzing Your Audience and Purpose" (82–123) to justify your claims.

Illustrate how the staff members avoided their ethical responsibilities to their fellow employees, to their workplace, and to the environment. Incorporate advice and evidence from Markel's chapter "Understanding Ethical and Legal Considerations" (17–40) into your analysis.

Deconstruct the various instructional flaws shown in the segment. Support your argument by citing Markel's advice for writing instructions and manuals from "Writing Definitions, Descriptions, and Instructions" (533–75).

Write a brief memo to Dwight, explaining the problems in the incident, analyzing his behavior and making suggestions for improvement. Use any content from Markel's textbook to support your argument.

Depending on the length of the class and the level of student engagement, groups are tasked with responding to one or two of the above prompts; overlap between prompts allows one group to compensate for gaps in other groups' responses. The goal is for students to practice the process of supporting their argument with evidence from the program and synthesizing this evidence with material from the textbook.

The subsequent class session focuses on assessing successful student examples of reports from the perspectives of content, organization, and use of the informal report genre. First, students read a report on the fire drill scene and, in small group and large class discussions, compare its analysis with that of their group. Other strong examples of recent student reports have examined problems depicted in the workplace comedies *Parks and Recreation*, *Silicon Valley*, and *Outsourced*. For instance, one student investigated several episodes of *Parks and Recreation*, focusing on the pit: a dangerous and garbage-strewn empty lot that Leslie Knope tries to recuperate and transform over the duration of the show. The student divided her report into the following sections: "Failed Safety Precautions," "Unethical Environmental Documentation and Practices," "Unclear Professional Communication," and "Problematic Cross-Cultural Messaging." This and other strong examples of student reports are available on the *Canvas* course website. After perusing these reports, students submit a summary of their chosen case study in an online discussion forum. Using the terminology they have been practicing, and relying on other student reports as models, they outline their report structure, indicating at least three professional and technical communication problems that they have so far examined.

Putting Humor to (Good) Work

By partaking in the in-class activity, exploring examples of reports, and participating in the online discussion, students practice thinking critically about comedy, applying relevant textbook materials, synthesizing information, and accepting and offering peer feedback. They also create content from which others may learn. That is, in the final section of their report, which is meant to address pedagogical implications, they move to the evaluation level of Bloom's taxonomy (Armstrong) when they argue for integrating their case study into the course and to devising when they make a course plan that pairs their chosen segment with certain readings. If students provide permission, their proposals and their reports become integrated into the course curriculum.

Students' involvement in this scaffolded assignment and their progression through these more complex cognitive tasks would not be possible without the settings, scenarios, characters, and valuable lessons provided by workplace comedy, which entertains students, maintaining their attention and enabling them to put humor to work.

Works Cited

Armstrong, Patricia. "Bloom's Taxonomy." *Vanderbilt University Center for Teaching*, Vanderbilt U, 2022, cft.vanderbilt.edu/guides-sub-pages/blooms-taxonomy/.

Dunleavy, Trish. "Hybridity in TV Sitcom: The Case of Comedy Verité." *Flow*, 11 Dec. 2008, www.flowjournal.org/2008/12/hybridity-in-tv-sitcom-the-case-of-comedy-verite.

"Fire Drill." *YouTube*, uploaded by The Office, 14 Aug. 2017, www.youtube.com/watch?v=gO8N3L_aERg.

"IEEE 829 Documentation." *Coley Consulting*, 2001–19, www.coleyconsulting.co.uk/IEEE829.htm.

Lang, James. *Small Teaching: Everyday Lessons from the Science of Learning*. Jossey-Bass, 2016.

Markel, Mike. *Technical Communication*. 11th ed., Bedford / St. Martin's, 2015.

"*Office Space* (1/5) Movie Clip—Did You Get the Memo? (1999) HD." *YouTube*, uploaded by Movieclips, 11 Aug. 2015, www.youtube.com/watch?time_continue=1&v=jsLUidiYm0w&feature=emb_logo.

Petroski, Henry. *Success through Failure: The Paradox of Design*. Princeton UP, 2006.

Soper, Kerry. "The Pathetic Carnival in the Cubicles: *The Office* as Meditation on the Misuses and Collapse of Traditional Comedy." *Studies in American Humor*, no. 19, 2009, pp. 83–103. *JSTOR*, www.jstor.org/stable/10.2307/42573564.

"Stress Relief." *The Office*, created by Greg Daniels and Ricky Gervais, season 5, episode 13, Deedle-Dee Productions / Universal Media Studios, 1 Feb. 2009.

Takacs, Stacy. *Interrogating Popular Culture: Key Questions*. Routledge, 2015.

Vygotsky, Lev S. *Mind in Society: The Development of Higher Psychological Processes*. Harvard UP, 1978.

Wood, D., et al. "The Role of Tutoring in Problem Solving." *Journal of Child Psychology and Child Psychiatry*, vol. 17, 1996, pp. 89–100, https://doi.org/10.1111/j.1469-7610.1976.tb00381.x.

Anja Müller-Wood

A Formalist Approach to the Comic

The comic is a notoriously elusive concept. Its inaccessibility is equally apparent in contemporary sitcoms and Renaissance comedies, although one important reason for its seemingly intrinsic elusiveness stands out the further back in history one goes. Topical jokes and puns get lost over time, and the most beloved of Shakespeare's comedies contain material that is obscure (and possibly doomed to remain so) to today's audiences. Given that spectators might be baffled even by present-day entertainments (and unable to explain what exactly makes them comic), a text's language is an imperfect gauge of its comic quality, which seems to lie elsewhere—namely, as I argue, on the level of structure and form.

Consider a well-known instance from Shakespeare's *As You Like It*: the climactic encounter between the comedy's lovers, Orlando and Rosalind, in act 3, scene 2. The two discuss the nature of love in general and Orlando's unrequited infatuation with Rosalind in particular—while he is blissfully unaware that the young shepherd Ganymede sitting beside him is in fact Rosalind in disguise. As Ganymede, Rosalind claims to be able to cure Orlando of his lovesickness, "if you would but call me Rosalind and come every day to my cote and woo me" (3.3.414–15).

Although the scene is central to the play's romantic entanglement, little in it is comic per se: especially for twenty-first-century students, Rosalind's hyperbolic disquisition on the symptoms of lovesickness—the "careless desolation" of ungartered hose and unbanded bonnet (Shakespeare 3.2.371)—and its cure with the aid of a frenzied exhibition of stereotypical feminine behavior (a "living humour of madness" [3.2.407]) is likely to come across as enigmatic if not twee. Yet although it serves as a reminder of the brief shelf life of many jokes, the parodic encounter between Shakespeare's lovers also points toward a more accessible and enduring source of the comic. For what is comic here is the situation itself: spectators are witnessing a practical joke on the part of Rosalind, who mercilessly takes advantage of Orlando's ignorance of the true identity of his confessor. The audience knows not only that Rosalind herself has a crush on the "love-shaked" Orlando but also that she is willing to mock him, first, by savaging the pedestrian poems he had scattered throughout the Forest of Arden and, second, by announcing, prior to their meeting, that she will "treat [Orlando] as a saucy lackey, and under that habit play the knave with him" (3.2.357, 290–92). Let in on Rosalind's prank, spectators are made her accomplices, vicariously experiencing her triumph through their own pleasure.

The comic, then, might manifest itself in especially tangible ways on a nonlinguistic level, for example in an instance of low comedy such as Rosalind's practical joke (Ellis 33). When teaching drama, it is therefore more productive (at least initially) to resist the inclination to explain what is comic about a particular scene in a play or how this connects to the play's historical context and concentrate instead on the question of how the comic works. This requires a focus on form, although the formalism I propose to adhere to differs from other branches of formalist scholarship (Frye; Booker), which—in identifying the enduring basic patterns, characters, and motifs of literature—approach texts as relatively static entities with essential features. Instead, I suggest that a discussion of literary form needs to include the "transactions" taking place between text and recipient (Weitz 65) in the light of their communicative goals. In the case of comic texts, the goal is "to move . . . [recipients] to laughter" (Charney 9), and the interest should be to investigate the strategies by which this effect is achieved (Farley-Hills 3). The aim is not to create a taxonomy of such strategies but to identify and explore what can be considered the fundamental mechanism on which many comic constellations rely. The key to understanding the comic, I argue, is examining the way playwrights manage information—that is, to investigate how they orchestrate the audience's knowledge about the plot. This is true whether plays are read or are watched onstage, although in the following I only use the terms *spectators* and *audiences* when talking about the recipients of plays.

These interconnected claims are informed by the observation that in drama information circulates through two different circuits of communication, the one connecting the characters onstage, the other mediating between stage and spectators. To draw an analogy with a distinction made in classical narratology (Pfister 27), plays have a story level and a discourse level, and, as in narrative texts, the "what" and the "how" of representation of drama affect each other in complex and sometimes conflicting ways. The full scope of their interaction is only apparent thanks to the spectators' "wide-angle perspective upon events" (Weitz 73), from which characters' speech and actions might take on a different, even contrary, meaning. The most potent constellation in the theater is a situation of "discrepant awareness" between characters and audience (Evans ix): an informational advantage on the part of spectators that for Bertrand Evans constitutes a fundamental principle of "dramatic method" (viii). Accordingly, the key strategy for dramatists is to create misunderstandings among characters (e.g., through all kinds of disguise, real or metaphorical), thereby setting up a clash of divergent frames of reference that result in dramatic or situational irony, such as that illustrated by the example above (Weitz 73). Asides or addresses *ad spectatores* serve as markers to identify this conflict and guarantee that audiences know what is going on.

The scene from *As You Like It* is a perfect example of discrepant awareness and shows that even in a "structurally simple" (Evans 95) comedy such as this the strategy can be used to great effect. The play can be considered structurally simple because there is only one group of disguisers (Rosalind and the associates in her voluntary exile in the Forest of Arden) whose schemes are not interrupted by alternative ploys; as a result, spectators find themselves in a relationship of absolute and unquestioned complicity with Rosalind. This example thus supports an established but not uncontested explanation of humor, namely that it is brought about whenever an observer experiences a sense of superiority vis-à-vis a perceived situation, event, or person. Renaissance playwrights—with Shakespeare probably foremost amongst them (Evans viii)—were intuitively drawn to this constellation. An early theoretical discussion of it is Thomas Hobbes's *The Elements of Law*, in which Hobbes maintains that "the passion of laughter" that is for him the symptom of humor "is nothing else but a sudden glory arising from sudden conception of some eminency in ourselves, by comparison with the infirmities of others, or with our own formerly" (54–55). The need to ascribe liberating or transgressive qualities to humor (Storey 422), which characterizes the more recent academic debate around it, might be seen as a rejection of the negative connotations of moral superiority ostensibly entailed in Hobbes's view. Yet contemporary scholars uneasy about the superiority hypothesis not only appear to ignore how popular this strategy has been in the history of theater but also overlook that Hobbes's hypothesis draws attention to another, more neutral notion of (temporal) distance when he observes that people laugh not only about the infirmities of others but also about their own in the past ("our own formerly"). Distance has been identified as a crucial element of the comic (Weitz 71), as it prevents empathetic engagement with characters and makes laughter about them possible. Far from inducing analytical coldheartedness, however, this detachment "exposes a correlative engagement with events as they become imminent structure" (Cartwright 12).

The scene in question underlines that reminding the audience of their inevitable cognitive superiority is a productive means to orchestrate spectators' expectations. Rosalind's prank allows Shakespeare both to slow down the plot and to establish an immediate erotic frisson between two characters who up to that point have hardly spoken to each other. And although Rosalind maintains the monopoly on manipulation throughout, the encounter nevertheless provides the basis for a moment of tension that spectators potentially find rewarding. When, at the beginning of their dialogue, Shakespeare has Orlando comment on the "finer accent" that makes Rosalind stand out among the rustics in the Forest of Arden (3.2.332), he threatens to reveal her identity but defuses the situation through a lengthy explanation on her part that culminates in a triumphant metatheatrical gag, made for the benefit of the audience alone: "I thank God I am not a woman, to be touched with so many giddy offences as he hath generally taxed their whole sex withal" (3.2.339–41). Precisely because structurally it is such a straightforward play, *As You Like It* draws attention to discrepant awareness as a fundamental principle of comic dramaturgy—an elementary building block that can be submitted to variation, recontextualization, and refinement in ever new dramatic contexts. This technique is not even bound to a specific genre, and "any matter . . . , real or imaginary, may be handled in comic fashion, and the comic quality may be sought in the most extreme forms of black, absurd, or surrealist writing" (McFadden 5).

A dramatic example from another genre—which also evinces a somewhat more elaborate comic structure than that of Shakespeare's comedy—may help test this hypothesis. In *The Revenger's Tragedy*, Thomas Middleton makes the death of a character the source of the comic, in keeping with the principle that if the plotting is right, spectators are likely to laugh even about a character's violent demise. The comic qualities of Middleton's gory Jacobean tragedy have been commented on before (e.g., Brooke); as in *As You Like It*, the roots of the play's "comic extravagance" (Neill 398) lie in the way Middleton manages information, not in the content of this information. This distinction becomes apparent in one of the tragedy's subplots, which deals with the sibling rivalry between a Duke's sons from two marriages whose conflicting ambitions and desires are played off against each other to great dramatic effect. The Duke's sons from his second marriage plan to rescue their younger brother from imprisonment by having their older half brother Lussurioso (heir apparent of the Duke's fortune), at that point also in prison, executed. The Duke, however, whom they falsely believe to have convinced that his firstborn deserves to die, has in the meantime ordered Lussurioso's release, so that when the brothers present the prison officers with the Duke's "command of present death" (Middleton 3.2.2), there is only one son left to be killed: their younger brother.

Spectators are likely to anticipate the breakdown of the brothers' plan and all this entails not least because they have learnt before that the Duke has "spied through" their plot (Middleton 2.3.104), and Middleton's arrangement of the subsequent sequence further exploits this cognitive advantage: in a quick succession of short alternating scenes, spectators are presented with the brothers' self-satisfied delight about their plan (3.1), the release of Lussurioso from prison (3.2), the brothers' delivery of the Duke's warrant (in the form of his signet ring) for their half brother's immediate execution (3.3), and finally the moment when the disbelieving youngest brother is taken to the block (3.4). Whatever the responses of real spectators witnessing the back-and-forth between these different perspectives might be, the careful contrapuntal orchestration of these perspectives seems to engineer a sense of glee not only about the brothers' unjustified optimism but also about the "jesting defiance" with which their younger brother finally seems to accept his fate (Brooke 20): "Well – / My fault was sweet sport, which the world approves; / I die for that which every woman loves" (Middleton 3.5.79–82). If this pat conclusion offers the audience a license to laugh, it also paves the way to an even more vehement moment of schadenfreude when the younger brother's siblings learn of his death. When presented with his "yet bleeding head" (3.6.34), they still (wrongly) take it to be that of Lussurioso, for whom they feign to grieve (their pretence signaled to spectators in asides) until their hated half brother suddenly appears on the scene. Their shock of recognition—which comes as no surprise to the audience—is marked by their sheepish "O!" (3.6.45), a woefully incongruous response to the disastrous result of their plotting and therefore likely to reinforce the audience's inclination to laugh.

This farcical sequence is no marginal instance of comic relief but productively connected with the play's main action: the bloody vendetta of its protagonist, Vindice, which consists of a string of deadly pranks expiring in a moment of anticlimax similar to that of the subplot just discussed. In true prankster fashion (Auden 49), the as yet undiscovered revenger triumphantly discloses his identity to the survivors of his killing spree at the end of the play, but instead of being rewarded with astonishment and awe he is brought to justice. Thus, the comic in Middleton's play is in a very fundamental sense tied to the "tragic inevitability" that propels both plots (Snyder 5), providing support for Susan Snyder's observation that the comic "shapes" the genre of tragedy by providing "the ground from which, or against which, tragedy develops" (4, 5).

However, comic potential lies not only in the omniscience of spectators, and my final example illustrates the effect when spectator privilege is spectacularly debunked by a surprise plot twist. Ben Jonson's *Epicoene*, too, is a comedy based on the manipulative potential of discrepant awareness, the machinations of its protagonist, Dauphine—whose goal is to secure his uncle Morose's fortune by first tricking the pathologically noise-sensitive man into a disastrous marriage and then rescuing him from it—recalling those of Shakespeare's Rosalind. The audience is let in on this plan, which Dauphine pursues with great determination and the help of several cronies, making sure that his uncle's presumably silent bride (the eponymous Epicoene) not only proves to be an insufferably garrulous woman but also is revealed not to have been a virgin at their marriage. Unaware of the fact that his misfortune had been manufactured by Dauphine, Morose signs over his fortune to his nephew, who promises to free him from his wife.

That pledge, however, entails Dauphine's final trump card, of which even the audience is unaware. Having secured his inheritance, he discloses that the shrew from whom he has just rescued his uncle is in fact a boy in disguise. Pulling off Epicoene's wig, he rebuts Morose as well as the friends who had believed themselves to be Dauphine's accomplices, all of whom are onstage at this moment; above all, however, this triumphant reveal is a snub to the spectators, who are thereby disabused of whatever delusions of informative privilege regarding Dauphine's machinations they might have harbored. In that, however, his spectacular revelation uncovers the practical joke at the expense of the audience that lies at the heart of the play, with which Jonson himself reminds spectators that in the final analysis even their omniscience is a product of the plot, created by the ultimate mastermind behind whatever happens onstage: the playwright (Levin 130).

In this essay I have argued for a formalist approach to the comic—that is, one that concerns itself with the question of how comic effects are created rather than what they mean, and I have suggested that this is achieved by investigating how playwrights manage audience knowledge. Apart from presenting a perspective that is, more than others, able to shed light on what might make theatrical audiences laugh, this shift in attention entails further pedagogical benefits, notably fostering students' general awareness of the complexity of literary communication and the limits of genre categories. The recognition, finally, that the comic is not the defining quality of a finite set of textual objects (comedies) but an aesthetic mode defined by particular informative structures might draw attention to the question of which kinds of comic effects are likely to endure cultural and linguistic change. Considering the examples discussed in this essay, effects that are likely to endure are those which let audiences enjoy the benefits from the privileged position granted to them by the playwright, regardless of whether they understand all the words the playwright puts in the characters' mouths.

Works Cited

Auden, W. H. "The Joker in the Pack." *Shakespeare's Tragedies*, edited by Harold Bloom, Chelsea House, 2000, pp. 47–50.

Booker, Christopher. *The Seven Basic Plots: Why We Tell Stories*. Bloomsbury, 2004.

Brooke, Nicholas. *Horrid Laughter in Jacobean Tragedy*. Harper and Row, 1979.

Cartwright, Kent. *Shakespearean Tragedy and Its Double: The Rhythms of Audience Response*. Pennsylvania State UP, 1991.

Charney, Maurice. *Comedy High and Low*. 1987. Peter Lang, 1991.

Ellis, David. *Shakespeare's Practical Jokes: An Introduction to the Comic in His Work*. Associated University Presses, 2007.

Evans, Bertrand. *Shakespeare's Comedies*. Oxford UP, 1967.
Farley-Hills, David. *The Comic in Renaissance Comedy*. Macmillan, 1981.
Frye, Northrop. *Anatomy of Criticism*. 1957. Princeton UP, 2000.
Hobbes, Thomas. *The Elements of Law: Human Nature and De Corpore Politico*. 1640. Oxford UP, 1994.
Jonson, Ben. *Epicoene; or, The Silent Woman*. 1609. The Alchemist *and Other Plays*, by Jonson, edited by Gordon Campbell, reissue ed., Oxford UP, 2008, pp. 119–210.
Levin, Kate D. "Unmasquing *Epicoene*: Jonson's Dramaturgy for the Commercial Theater and Court." *New Perspectives on Ben Jonson*, edited by James Hirsh, Associated University Presses, 1997, pp. 128–53.
McFadden, George. *Discovering the Comic*. 1982. De Gruyter, 2014.
Middleton, Thomas. *The Revenger's Tragedy*. 1606. *Thomas Middleton: The Collected Works*, edited by Gary Taylor and John Lavagnino, Clarendon Press, 2010, pp. 543–93.
Neill, Michael. "Bastardy, Counterfeiting, and Misogyny in *The Revenger's Tragedy*." *SEL: Studies in English Literature, 1500–1900*, vol. 36, no. 2, 1996, pp. 397–416.
Pfister, Manfred. "Zur Theorie der Sympathielenkung im Drama." *Sympathielenkung in den Dramen Shakespeares: Studien zur publikumsbezogenen Dramaturgie*, edited by Werner Habicht and Ina Schabert, Fink, 1974, pp. 20–34.
Shakespeare, William. *As You Like It*. 1599. Thomson Learning, 2005.
Snyder, Susan. *The Comic Matrix of Shakespeare's Tragedies:* Romeo and Juliet, Hamlet, Othello, *and* King Lear. Princeton UP, 1979.
Storey, Robert. "Comedy, Its Theorists, and the Evolutionary Perspective." *Criticism*, vol. 38, no. 3, 1996, pp. 407–41.
Weitz, Eric. *The Cambridge Introduction to Comedy*. Cambridge UP, 2009.

Richard Obenauf

Mankind, the First English Comedy: A Long-Overlooked Teaching Option

The first English comic play is the anonymous late medieval morality play *Mankind*, likely written and performed by monks in East Anglia as part of the Shrovetide festivities of 1471. Written about five years before the arrival of the printing press in England, it contains brief but lewd attacks on corruption within the medieval church that subsequent generations sought to curtail in the Protestant Reformation. Despite these daring criticisms, the central teachings of *Mankind* are characteristically medieval and include the duty of all of humankind to submit to authority, whether spiritual or temporal; to avoid temptation of all kinds; and to repent after falling into sin, and sometimes preemptively as well. The play comically dramatizes the battles between good and evil, between body and soul, between worldly vices and eternal bliss. These themes are deftly built into a dramatic strategy that hilariously encourages the audience to fall into sin. I find that this clever dramatic device can be put to good use in the classroom because it so ingeniously illustrates the play's mischievous warnings against succumbing to peer pressure.

This short play of around nine hundred lines opens with a sermon in which Mercy, the play's spiritual advisor, counsels the audience to avoid temptation and to persevere in good works (*Mankind*, lines 1–44). Allegorical representations of vice named Mischief, Nowadays, New-Guise, and Nought badger Mercy and mock his solemnity (45–185). After they exit, Mankind, who represents all of humankind, articulates that he is made of a body and a soul, cursing his flesh as a "stinking dunghill" that corrupts his soul (186–216). Mercy implores him to resist temptations of the flesh and other worldly vices (217–44). Mankind works in his field and defies the vice characters' initial attempts to lead him astray (245–330). The action then shifts to the audience, which is tricked into singing an obscene Christmas carol and then into paying to see the spectacular devil Titivillus (331–528). This device is mirrored in subsequent scenes as Mankind is corrupted by Titivillus and the vice figures (529–661). In a parody of courtroom drama, Mankind swears his loyalty to Mischief and the other vices in a mock trial (662–733). Mankind descends into crime and sin until he is about to hang himself in despair that he is no longer worthy of receiving mercy, at which point Mercy beseeches him to beg for forgiveness, which he does (734–900). In his final sermon, Mercy instructs the audience to forsake worldly pleasures and to beg for mercy so that they, too, may achieve the eternal bliss of Christian salvation (901–14).

A window into rural medieval life that has been concealed from undergraduates because of its obscenity, *Mankind* contains material considered "unprintable" (Adams 311) a century ago, yet this material was staged by monks in the fifteenth century. Students are excited to read something that has been considered objectionable even in scholarly settings, and there are other good reasons for teaching it. The play is roughly contemporaneous with the more frequently taught morality play *Everyman* and is similar to it in length and theme. However, *Everyman* is a sober portrayal of the arrival of death that lacks not only the vice figures and the slapstick comedy they stir up in other morality plays but also the warnings against worldly temptation that make *Mankind* so effective and that surface in later receptions of the genre. While other comic morality plays were likely staged in the late Middle Ages, no manuscripts survive of anything quite like *Mankind*. Students should not be given the impression that this play is representative of medieval literature, so I suggest assigning *Mankind* as a substitute for *Everyman* only if your syllabus contains other examples of serious medieval literature, or assigning it alongside *Everyman* to provide additional context for later works that build on the genre, such as Christopher Marlowe's *Doctor Faustus*.

I recommend spending a few minutes giving a brief lecture on *Mankind* and its context before students read it. Given the play's obscene and violent material, as well as its theological content, a brief preemptive statement about how you expect the class to discuss *Mankind* can help you steer clear of emotionally charged debates over religion. For example, I note that it was likely staged on Saturday, 23 February 1471, as part of the pre-Lenten festivities and that its raucous humor was encouraged by the carnivalesque atmosphere. I compare Shrovetide to Saturnalia, Mardi Gras, spring break, and Halloween, but I also preview that both in its form and in its content the play warns against overindulgence—even when (or perhaps especially when) worldly pleasures seem to be most alluring. From this vantage, I tell my classes, we will read the play, a rich and entertaining example of medieval culture, not to quibble with its theology or its worldview, but as anthropologists and historians and literary scholars whose interests center on the beliefs and customs of its first audience. Making this clear from the beginning also has the advantage of putting religious skeptics and those of other faith traditions at ease. I confess my sincere belief that the English Middle Ages are as distant from and as foreign to us as anything I have read from any other culture—and that although the strict hierarchy of the medieval world casts a long shadow into the present, we moderns struggle to comprehend the rigidity of the worldview contained in this play. I have found that justifying my reasons for assigning this play helps students have a positive experience reading and discussing it.

I state at the beginning of discussion that the play illustrates material that may be upsetting to some students, including obscenity, depictions of blasphemy, and references to rape and murder; students who wish to sit silently or excuse themselves are allowed to do so. Although students often begin our discussion confused about whether this comic play is serious or satiric, they need little guidance to establish that it is, in fact, both. Students identify that Mercy's sermons as well as Mankind's earnest speeches point to the playwright's sincerity in his overall message. It is useful to spend a few minutes asking students to summarize the play's main teachings, in particular because the medieval Christian worldview is unfamiliar to most modern readers. For example, students do not tend to think of their bodies as a "stinking dunghill" (*Mankind*, line 204) or of adults as striving to be meek and childlike (819–22). Nor do they generally believe that true happiness is never to be found in this life (1–44). Mercy's insistence that both repentance and good works are necessary for salvation is a typical medieval Catholic view, yet many Christians in my classes are unfamiliar with these tenets. I try to direct the discussion toward the many contrasts at war in the play, most importantly between good and evil and between soul and body. Both in its words and in its action, *Mankind* illustrates that, for late medieval Christians, it was difficult to resist temptation because of its ubiquity, because of one's sinful body, and because of devils who lay unforeseen obstacles on the path to righteousness.

From there, students soon discover that the vice figures and the devil Titivillus speak the most outrageous blasphemies and obscenities in this play—and that such material tends to serve the play's moral message. As is common in comedy and in satire, the playwright capitalizes on devices to license material that might not normally be tolerated. The following mitigating factors merit attention in any discussion of this play: First, it is worth reiterating that the play was staged during pre-Lenten festivities, when medieval English society invited boisterous mockery and scatological comedy. Second, offensive material is voiced only by allegorical representations of sin (perhaps mitigating the actors' sin in performing the material), rarely by Mankind (whose descent from purity is enacted through the play), and never by Mercy (who remains free of sin). Because this play teaches sound doctrine and was first performed at Shrovetide, the playwright apparently had some leeway to offer some passing attacks on corruption within the church, such as a corrupt "Pope Pocket" ("wallet") who is not merely married but willing to sell indulgences to those who perform oral sex on his wife (*Mankind*, lines 131–46). Aside from these isolated attacks, the earthy comedy in *Mankind* warns against the pursuit of worldly pleasures, at times trapping the audience into sinning while they virtuously attend a putatively moral play.

To demonstrate how deftly the playwright has woven the play's thematic and dogmatic material into its structure—like the invitation from Nowadays to join him in the worthy activity of singing a "merry cheer" (*Mankind*, line 334)—I invoke my duty as the teacher to quote the text and ask students to join me in a call-and-response of the obscene Christmas carol, using the melody of "Deck the Halls." Suddenly, like the play's first audience, students become ensnared in the very vices that Mercy advises both Mankind and the audience to avoid when they sing, "It is written with a coal / He who shitteth with his hole / Unless he wipe his arse clean / On his britches it will be seen" (335–41; repetitions omitted). By the time they repeat the "Holy, holy, holy" (343)—with a lewd emphasis on "hole"—classes erupt into laughter that serves an important pedagogical objective. Once things calm down, we look at other ways in which the playwright trapped members of the original audience in the very sin they were being warned to avoid, such as when they are tricked into betraying their morals and perhaps their souls when the actors halt the show to take up a collection before they will bring out the spectacular devil Titivillus.

I also recommend using *Mankind* as an opportunity to discuss allegory. After noting other examples of allegory, such as George Orwell's *Animal Farm*, we see how the allegory in *Mankind* operates not only on a literal level but also on secondary and tertiary levels of meaning. Each semester we end up focusing on different aspects of allegory that interest the class, but I always try to make sure we look at two in particular. First, I direct students to the parody trial (*Mankind*, lines 662–733), which begins with Mankind wearing a long flowing coat that becomes increasingly foppish until it is described as a jacket of fencing (719), a coat of chain mail that provides no defense at all against the elements. Students easily grasp the physical comedy and its satire against the vanity of fashion, but they usually need to be told that clothes often represent a character's spiritual condition in medieval literature in order to see that Mankind begins the scene (and the play) with sufficient warmth and protection from the elements and from sin, but the longer he associates with the vice figures and falls victim to their worldly pleasures, the less protection he has against them.

Second, because students need to understand that the play signals more than just its surface teachings about salvation, such as the worldly obedience enforced through the threat of eternal damnation, I like to showcase the passing reference to Mercy's example of the horse who obeys the master when hungry but bucks him in the mud when overfed (*Mankind*, lines 241–44). On a secondary level, students might understand the suggestion here to be that God can spiritually feed those who are hungry but not those who have overindulged in worldly pleasures. And on a third level, Mercy's warning further implies that people who succumb to temptation also run the risk of bucking their soul and their master into the mud, soiling everyone around them and leading to chaos in society. Through this example, students can better appreciate the play's lesson that obedience and subservience were spiritual as well as temporal imperatives in late medieval England.

Students often struggle to comprehend the rigidity of the social hierarchy in the English Middle Ages, in part because even those who believe in traditional forms of authority and power structures nevertheless believe in a theory of the individual that did not arise until well after this play's first performance. Many aspects of the play (and indeed of a great deal of medieval and early modern literature) that strike modern readers as bizarre or backward (especially the play's misogynistic humor) make sense in light of the Great Chain of Being, so it can be worth spending a few minutes describing that medieval conception of society as an infinitely long chain or infinitely tall ladder in which no two things in society or in the universe occupy the same link or rung, and in which everyone and everything has a specific purpose to fulfill. Mercy's opening sermon clarifies that all humans are subordinate to God (*Mankind*, lines 1–44); in his speech just before Mankind's entrance (162–85), Mercy condemns the vice figures as being worse than beasts because animals, he explains, act according to their place in the hierarchy. The playwright signals repeatedly that failure to conform to this hierarchy is sinful. The play's central teachings of avoiding falling into temptation and constantly begging for mercy may thus be read as both religious and social advice. The playwright's concern with judgment is appropriate for a play centered on preparing medieval Christians for Judgment Day, but he also suggests that all actions were closely monitored in his society to ensure social order.

    A background in medieval literature is useful but not necessary for teaching this play, which merits a place in a variety of courses. Surveys of drama, of comedy, of Renaissance drama, and of English literature more broadly would be more engaging for including *Mankind*. I teach this play in an introductory survey in my university's Honors College, where first-year students read it after a sequence of two medieval romances in translation. We then read Marlowe's *Doctor Faustus* (A-text, 1604), and, later in the semester, we watch the Mozart–Da Ponte opera *Don Giovanni*, which is derived from a parallel tradition yet contains many familiar elements of the genre of the morality play. I also teach this play in an upper-division seminar on satire, where the social and religious concerns expressed in *Mankind* allow the play to serve as context for Erasmus's *In Praise of Folly* and Thomas More's *Utopia*. In both of these courses, I emphasize the significance of the printing press in the Reformation, since *Mankind*—which survives in just one damaged manuscript—was written about five years before the printing press came to England; some of the ideas expressed in the play gained traction almost immediately after the press enabled reformers to widely circulate criticisms of the church.

    It is no longer difficult to obtain a copy of *Mankind* for your students to read, and you may already have a text in your course materials. *The Broadview Anthology of British Literature* (Black et al. 644–63) and *The Broadview Anthology of Tudor Drama* (Stewart et al. 1–24) both include annotated editions of the play, while *The Longman Anthology of*

British Literature presents a modern acting edition of *Mankind* by Peter Meredith that modernizes the spellings but preserves the original vocabulary and provides useful notes (Damrosch and Dettmar 587–612). Stand-alone alternatives include G. A. Lester's volume in the Methuen series New Mermaids, *Three Late Medieval Morality Plays:* Mankind, Everyman, *and* Mundus et Infans, which updates the spellings and supplies superb footnotes. Another obvious choice is Everyman *and* Mankind, edited by Douglas Bruster and Eric Rasmussen, part of the Arden Early Modern Drama series; this very accessible version updates spellings and provides thorough commentaries and introductions. The TEAMS Middle English Texts series edition of *Mankind*, edited by Kathleen M. Ashley and Gerald NeCastro, retains the medieval spellings and would be most appropriate for use in graduate seminars or with advanced undergraduates; Ashley's introduction is essential reading for anyone teaching this work at the graduate level.

I enthusiastically endorse pairing *Mankind* and *Doctor Faustus* because these two works, taken together, so neatly highlight many shifts and continuities from the Middle Ages into the Renaissance. *Mankind* also helps illuminate some of the scenes of comic relief in *Doctor Faustus* that mirror the play's main action and likewise serve to reinforce the play's moral and dramatic content. Marlowe's Seven Deadly Sins are stock figures reminiscent of the worldly vices in *Mankind*; the Old Man who urges Faustus to repent at the end is also seen by students who have read *Mankind* as a stock figure, this time a manifestation of the Mercy figure. And although the tragic ending of *Doctor Faustus* is rather different from the repentance and salvation found in earlier morality plays, the final chorus ultimately teaches the same lesson of humility at the heart of *Mankind*, a surprising continuity between the Middle Ages and the Renaissance.

Mankind is an excellent text for students to use in assignments in which they compare and contrast it with another work, whether connected by period, genre, or thematic content or distinct from the form and content of the play. *Mankind* contains many points of contact for subsequent seminar discussions of other works. For example, Mankind is composed of a body and a soul but not a mind, a point that is neither obvious nor significant until students read works from the Renaissance and Enlightenment. The work's themes of honor, loyalty, duty, and subservience are common in other medieval texts; themes of moderation are common in moral literature from ancient satire through modern essays, even though Horace and Samuel Johnson treat the subject differently than does the *Mankind* playwright; something as simple as the difference between humans and animals is useful to echo in discussions of works that take different views (recall that in *Mankind* animals instinctively adhere to their place in the Great Chain of Being, whereas humans struggle to control themselves so as not to disrupt the hierarchy). When students in my classes read the *Narrative of the Life of Frederick Douglass* later in the semester, they often come to a deeper understanding of the relentless pressure of the English Middle Ages and of the antebellum South: for the *Mankind* playwright, the Shrovetide festivities licensed activities, obscenities, and criticisms that might not normally be permissible even as the entertainment reinforced the existing order, while Douglass's famous comments about the excesses permitted during the week between Christmas and New Year's in chapter 10 of his narrative (44–45) suggest a similar climate in which activities not normally allowed were actively encouraged so as to prevent uprisings the rest of the year. Each time I teach *Mankind* I discover additional connections to other works, and I expect that other instructors will have a similar experience when they add this long-neglected comic play to their courses.

Works Cited

Adams, Joseph Quincy, editor. *Chief Pre-Shakespearean Dramas: A Selection of Plays Illustrating the History of the English Drama from Its Origin Down to Shakespeare*. Houghton Mifflin, 1924.
Ashley, Kathleen M. Introduction. *Mankind*, edited by Ashley and Gerald NeCastro, TEAMS Middle English Texts, 2010, pp. 1–12.
Ashley, Kathleen M., and Gerald NeCastro, editors. *Mankind*. TEAMS Middle English Texts, 2010, d.lib.rochester.edu/teams/text/ashley-and-necastro-mankind.
Black, Joseph, et al., editors. *The Broadview Anthology of British Literature*. Vol. 1, Broadview Press, 2006.
Bruster, Douglas, and Eric Rasmussen, editors. Everyman *and* Mankind. 2009. Bloomsbury, 2015.
Damrosch, David, and Kevin J. H. Dettmar, editors. *The Longman Anthology of British Literature*. Vol. 1A, 4th ed., Longman, 2010.
Douglass, Frederick. *Narrative of the Life of Frederick Douglass*. 1845. Edited by Philip Smith, Dover Publications, 1995.
Erasmus, Desiderius. *In Praise of Folly*. 1509. Translated by John Wilson, 1668. Edited by T. N. R. Rogers, Dover Publications, 2003.
Lester, G. A., editor. *Three Late Medieval Morality Plays:* Mankind, Everyman, *and* Mundus et Infans. Methuen Drama, 1981.
Mankind. Circa 1470–71. *Medieval Drama*, edited by David Bevington, Houghton Mifflin, 1975, pp. 903–38.
Marlowe, Christopher. *Dr. Faustus*. 1604. Edited by Thomas Crofts, Dover Publications, 1994.

More, Thomas. *Utopia*. 1516. Edited by Ronald Herder, Dover Publications, 1997.
Mozart, Wolfgang Amadeus, and Lorenzo Da Ponte. *Don Giovanni*. 1787. Edited and translated by Ellen H. Bleiler, Dover Publications, 1985.
Stewart, Alan, et al., editors. *The Broadview Anthology of Tudor Drama*. Broadview Press, 2021.

Andy Felt

Using Comic Insults as an Approach to Shakespeare

I teach at a small private liberal arts college, and when I was first starting out a little over ten years ago I taught a lot of beginning-level acting classes. In a small department at a small college, our class sizes are refreshingly (you guessed it) small, and most of the time my introductory classes are made up of five or six new theater majors and nine to ten nonmajors from a variety of academic programs. One of my areas of interest is in producing Shakespeare, and I quickly realized that my theater majors and minors needed audition monologues in blank verse. Embedding a soliloquy project in the introductory acting class, Acting I, would provide multiple benefits for both the individual theater students and the department. I was also drawn to the idea of having nonmajors complete a project in Acting I that would feel like it contained some real academic rigor. Once I implemented it, the Shakespearean monologue project clearly served an important purpose in the course, but it also revealed the need for me to find a way to make students more comfortable with Shakespeare's language before diving into the assignment. I have found success in using a Shakespearean insult exercise to do just that. In this essay I briefly discuss my reasons for adding a Shakespeare monologue to an introductory acting course before explaining how I use the insult exercise as well as some of the benefits I have discovered from starting off the soliloquy unit with it.

For incoming theater majors and minors, the benefits of including a Shakespeare monologue in the Acting I curriculum were immediately clear. Assigning a good Shakespearean monologue to each of my theater majors in their first year ensures that they will at the very least have one decent blank verse piece to use for auditions both for our program and for regional summer stock companies. Also, I wouldn't have to keep listening to the same *Romeo and Juliet* or *Hamlet* monologues over and over again in auditions. Most of my students initially don't know any Shakespeare plays beyond those they have encountered in high school, and they inevitably prepare the most famous speeches for their auditions. I have heard "To be or not to be" and "Oh Romeo, Romeo" countless times in auditions. "If we shadows have offended" is probably the third most popular, in case you were wondering.

The second benefit of including a Shakespeare monologue was that I would be able to introduce students to Shakespeare's work in a less threatening environment than a rehearsal. Most young actors who are sitting down to table work on their first Shakespeare play are incredibly reticent to speak up and ask important questions about their characters, the intricacies of the multiple story lines, or all the expressive poetry found within the text itself. I believe they are uncomfortable with revealing how little they know about Shakespeare's writing in front of the entire company. This is especially true if there are actors in the cast who have been in multiple classical productions and are more comfortable with speaking up at the table. By introducing freshman theater majors to this work in a classroom setting where most students are on the same footing, I can better prepare them to jump right into working with Shakespearean text when they are cast in a production.

A third benefit of including a monologue from Shakespeare's work is that, in order to fully understand the motivations of the character in the moment of the soliloquy, students have to carefully read the entire play. Having students engage with a classical text introduces them to the important work of developing their own methodology for approaching canonical plays, something that will undoubtedly prove useful throughout their four years in an academic theater program and throughout their careers. I knew that including a Shakespearean monologue in Acting I would be a great idea for those students who were interested in theater, but what about the other students who were just looking for a fun way to fulfill a general education requirement? I suspected that many of the students in my beginning-level acting class, and particularly the nonmajors, would be resistant to the assignment.

The first time I included the Shakespeare monologue assignment in Acting I, I was teaching a class made up of all first-year students as a part of an interdisciplinary collaboration with a professor in our communications department. We decided to focus on Shakespeare and politics as a way of combining content across our two classes. Those students in the class who were not theater majors were unsurprisingly resistant to the idea of having to read an entire Shakespeare play and memorize a three-to-six-minute-long chunk of blank verse. Some commenced with overly vocal protestations of how unfair the assignment was for an introductory class. Of course, they all eventually connected with their plays and characters and did a great job performing their respective pieces. The real payoff came toward the end of the semester, after students had returned from the Thanksgiving break. Three of them told similar stories about sharing their soliloquies with family members. My favorite was from a student who said that when an uncle asked him what classes he was taking at that "fancy college" and the student answered him, his uncle began making fun of him for taking an acting class. The general idea he was trying to get across to his nephew was that such a class was pointless and a waste of time and money. The uncle said, "What are you actually learning in that class?" The student responded by performing his soliloquy. As chance or perhaps fate would have it, I had assigned this particular student the "Saint Crispin's Day" speech from *King Henry V*, and he was quite good at performing it. While it might not be possible to reenact a scene study or a good idea to share the warm-up techniques and improvisational games from the course, fully performing a Shakespearean soliloquy with intention and commitment is a concrete demonstration of an acquired skill from a beginning-level acting class. Unfair or not, the fact that it is Shakespeare and not David Mamet or Neil Simon also lends the demonstration an air of culture and refinement to the course content (perceptions I have fought against as a modern Shakespearean director, but that's a paper for another time). I started including the assignment in all my Acting I sections, and I encouraged my colleagues to include the assignment in their sections as well.

As I began assessing the assignment, I quickly realized that my method of introducing the students to their monologues left a lot to be desired. I was pretty much just handing them a copy of their monologue, giving them a crash course on iambic pentameter, and then instructing them to carefully read the play their piece was from over the weekend. They would typically come back the next week still incredibly apprehensive about performing Shakespeare and nervous about the amount of text they didn't understand. Over the ensuing couple of weeks, I was spending a lot of energy trying to get students excited about and engaged with the material. We were also spending a significant amount of class time deciphering the text when it would have been far more efficient for students to do most of that basic comprehension work on their own. In trying to address the lack of an introduction to the work, I decided to start the Shakespeare section of the class with a classical vocal warm-up exercise. In my years as a Shakespearean actor I had often encountered an old vocal warm-up that is rumored to have come from the Royal Shakespeare Company. The text of the warm-up typically runs something like this:

> What a to-do, to die today at a minute or two to two
> A thing distinctly hard to say, but harder still to do
> For they'll beat a tattoo at twenty to two
> A rat-a-ta-ta-ta-ta-ta-tattoo
> And the dragon will come when he hears the drum
> At a minute or two to two today
> At a minute or two to two.

This serves as a decent diction warm-up, and it has some good rhythmic elements that help get an actor's voice and mouth ready to speak Shakespeare's text. Students had fun with it, and I would encourage them to try it with different characterizations—as a pirate, an ancient Roman senator, or a tyrannical king, for instance—with varying degrees of success. However, I was still looking for something that would get them excited about working with classical text. I found the Shakespeare insult exercise while looking through some of my old notebooks from graduate school. I had the opportunity to spend a term in London while in the MFA program in directing at Ohio University and was lucky enough to study Shakespearean acting with Brigid Panet, an associate teacher at the Royal Academy of Dramatic Art. In one of our classes a fellow student brought in a sheet listing Shakespearean insults, and we used it as a warm-up for a few of our classes. I don't remember receiving a lot of input from the instructor on how to use the exercise in a classroom, and my notes from that particular class are embarrassingly sparse. However, there was something bawdy and mischievous about the exercise, so I decided to give it a try in my Acting I course.

The basic idea of the sheet is simple. There are three columns of words that are used as insults specifically in the works of Shakespeare or that were more generally known as insults in the Elizabethan era. Students need only say the word "Thou" and then read one word from each of the three columns to create a Shakespearean insult. A quick Internet search of the phrase "Shakespeare insult sheet" will generate a slew of documents.[1] I find the ones that use hyphenated phrases in the middle column most effective because rhythmically the insults that these sheets produce feel the most like Shakespearean prose to me. Typically, I have students face each other across a large room (or the stage of a theater if possible) so that they are also working on vocal projection. Then they pick someone on the other side of the room and let their insult fly. It is important that the group of students are completely at ease and comfortable with one another before attempting the assignment in this setup. If students are still a little uneasy being silly with one another, this exercise can quickly lead to an awkward and uncomfortable atmosphere in the room. Usually this exercise falls right in the middle of the semester for my classes, so I have had plenty of time to get students comfortable with one another. If for some reason I think the class isn't quite ready to hurl insults at one another from across the room, I have students stand in one long line and throw their insults at me. This ensures that no student will have their feelings hurt.

One of the benefits I see right away is that most of the time students become very relaxed because of the comedic nature of the exercise. It's hard to stay uptight and nervous while forcefully saying "Thou gleeking, swag-bellied, flap-dragon!" at the top of your voice. The exercise creates moments of silliness that are built around Shakespearean words and phrases. Another benefit is that students jump right in with speaking Shakespeare out loud without feeing overly self-conscious about mispronouncing words or not being able to understand the meanings. Even if students have no idea what the words they are saying actually mean, they still begin to enjoy the way the syllables combine in their mouths. There is also some nice reinforcement I can do with demonstrating the concept of coloring your words with specific meaning regardless of the literal meanings of the words you are using. I like to use the phrase "Have a nice day" to demonstrate this. Using tone and inflection I demonstrate to the class how you can say that phrase and have it mean exactly what the literal meanings of the words imply, but when said with contempt or anger those words convey the exact opposite. Here, too, with the Shakespearean insult sheet I can reinforce that it doesn't necessarily matter what the words mean. If the intention behind the phrase is to insult or demean, then the words could be absolute gibberish and still get the same point across.

I also encourage students to not worry about getting the pronunciations correct. In fact, I encourage them to make a strong choice based on what feels right or sounds better and just go with it. If I have international students or students for whom English is a second language, I also use this moment in the activity to demonstrate that Shakespeare's language is difficult even for seasoned English speakers. Non-native speakers of English are sometimes nervous about the Shakespeare monologue assignment, and it doesn't hurt to check in with them often to make sure they aren't overwhelmed. One way I have found to set all my students more at ease with Shakespeare's text is to freely admit my own uncertainty about a word's pronunciation in the moment. This happens occasionally with phrases on the insults sheet, and I take the opportunity to point students to resources that can help them with pronunciations of words they might not know. (I particularly like Definitions.net.)

Once students start to relax and have fun, I then assign them some homework. I ask them to try to come up with two or three of the best possible insults using the sheet and to practice them before our next class. I let them know that I will be awarding kudos for the following categories: the grossest insult, the funniest insult, and the overall most insulting insult. This assignment requires students to do a little research in order to find out the meaning behind the phrases. I make sure to warn them not to take anything for granted. For example, the insult "horn-beast" might sound straightforward until you learn something about the Elizabethan imagery associated with cuckolding. I use this as an opportunity to introduce students to resources for understanding Shakespeare outside of *SparkNotes* and *Wikipedia*. In my opinion, the most valuable resource is *Open Source Shakespeare*, a website containing Shakespeare's complete works and incredibly handy features. For the insults assignment I point students to the website's text-search function, which allows them to see every place that Shakespeare has used a particular word. The task I set for students is to look up exactly where Shakespeare has used the insult they want to know more about so that they can gain a contextual understanding of how he employed the term. I let them know that the best way for them to understand precisely what the insult is saying is to analyze the dramatic moment in which Shakespeare uses it. I also encourage them to think about the many different ways they can insult someone and to vary their prepared insults by considering their use of pitch, tone, sarcasm, anger, haughtiness, pretention, and so on. The next class session we start with their best insults, and I award prizes. By this point students are typically having fun and are much more open to receiving their soliloquies and being introduced to iambic pentameter.

I have come to see the Shakespeare insults exercise as an icebreaker of sorts in my beginning-level acting classes. I love being able to "introduce methods of researching classic text for comprehension" without ever calling it that. The assignment also seems silly and fun while allowing me to reinforce multiple beginning-level acting principles. Most importantly, the insults exercise is an active exercise that relaxes and fully engages students with myriad backgrounds and skill levels. It uses juvenile comedy to introduce students to Shakespearean performance. While it might seem like the exercise insults the great bard's memory or demeans the beautiful and erudite poetry of his plays, I contend that it is entirely appropriate when one considers Shakespeare's place in his own time. When we engage with his plays, we do so with the full weight of more than four hundred years of Shakespeare's being held up as the pinnacle of English playwrighting. Yet Shakespeare wasn't writing his plays specifically for the Elizabethan literati, or for the university wits, or even for the rich nobles who supported him. A popular theatrical writer and producer who I contend has less in common with Federico Fellini and Ingmar Bergman than with Stephen Spielberg and James Cameron, Shakespeare was writing for everyone. His writing is full of comedy that comes in many flavors, from juvenile to sophomoric to slapstick to even gross-out. In fact, the more I use the exercise, the more I become convinced that if one even suspects the joke or reference might be sexual in nature, odds are that it is. It is also probably far more offensive than one could have ever imagined.

Note

1. See, for instance, www.nosweatshakespeare.com/resources/shakespeare-insults/ or iwastesomuchtime.com/77816.

Ameer Sohrawardy

Performing Equivocating Sententiousness in Shakespeare's *Othello*

Shakespeare's *Othello* may seem like an unusual choice for a unit on comedy. The play has been entrenched in the tragedy subgenre for as long as it has been considered canonical. This essay suggests, however, that an undeniable interdependence exists between comedy and the more serious matters of race and specious opportunism around which discussions of the play usually galvanize. I suggest a lesson plan for recognizing this interdependence and for recuperating oft missed opportunities for teaching comedy with Shakespeare's noncomedic works.

Two moments of witty sententiousness provide entry points for teaching *Othello* as a text dependent on comedy for delivering its tragic conclusion. They both occur in act 1, scene 3. Brabantio and Othello appear before the Venetian duke and council. The council has summoned Othello because Venice needs the Moor's military expertise to defend Cyprus against the approaching Turkish naval fleet. Brabantio appeals to the authority of the Venetian state to punish the man who has supplanted him as Desdemona's chief patriarchal authority. Not knowing that Desdemona's new husband is Othello, the Duke of Venice offers Brabantio "the bloody book of law / . . . though our proper son / stood in your action" (1.3.67–70). After realizing that the "particular" (1.3.55) man that

Brabantio wants imprisoned is the very General on whom the general welfare of Cyprus and Venice depends, the Duke slyly reverses his position. He not only sanctions Othello and Desdemona's union but also accepts Othello's exotic narration (of how the Moor won Desdemona through her "greedy ear") as a tale that "would win my [the Duke's] daughter too" (1.3.173).

Brabantio is irate at the obvious, military-minded opportunism of the entire proceedings. Sensing this, the Duke tries to placate him with the sort of rhyming sententiousness found in some of the funniest scenes in Shakespeare's comedies. The Duke tells Brabantio:

> Let me speak like yourself and lay a sentence
> Which, as a grise or step, may help these lovers
> Into your favor:
> When remedies are past, the griefs are ended
> By seeing the worst, which late on hopes depended
> To mourn a mischief that is past and gone
> Is the next way to draw new mischief on.
> What cannot be preserved when fortune takes
> Patience her injury a mockery makes.
> The robb'd that smiles steals something from the thief;
> He robs himself that spends a bootless grief. (1.3.204–10)

The instructor may point out that the Duke has done the exact opposite of what he had promised Brabantio just moments earlier. And, so, if the instructor performs the Duke's dialogue before the class with the sincerity of an oily apologist, the audience should chuckle softly. I would suggest letting the Duke's counsel to Brabantio sound like exactly what it is—mollifying assurances designed to cajole acceptance from a listener who sees right through the equivocation.[1]

Brabantio's sarcastic retort to the Duke is the second instance of witty sententiousness in this scene. Desdemona's father not only recognizes the speciousness of the Duke's logic but also challenges the Duke, in equally trite, rhyming lines, to commit his own logic to its bitter conclusion. Brabantio seethes:

> So let the Turk of Cyprus us beguile
> We lose it not, so long as we can smile
> He bears the sentence well that nothing bears
> But the free comfort which from thence he hears
> But he bears both the sentence and the sorrow

> That, to pay grief, must of poor patience borrow.
> These sentences, to sugar, or to gall,
> Being strong on both sides, are equivocal. (1.3.210–17)

Filmed versions of this speech, like the Duke's before it, overlook the import of Brabantio's complaint; the scene has obvious potential to be staged to caustically humorous effect. In no filmed versions of the play does the actor playing Brabantio deliver his response to the Duke's equivocation with the mixture of aggrievement, rage, and passive-aggressive vitriol called for by the lines.[2] As I argue, the exchange between Brabantio and the Duke is crucial to understanding why Othello dies by suicide in act 5.

To lay the foundation for performing this interpretive analysis, I have students complete a simple exercise in close reading. After having them note Brabantio's tone of voice when he complains to the Duke, I have students rewrite Brabantio's above-quoted sentences in their own words. Adhering to subject-verb-object syntactical order, students render the following sentence most often: "And so let the Turk beguile us of Cyprus. We do not lose Cyprus, so long as we can smile." We use these transcriptions to begin a fruitful discussion of the ways in which Brabantio effaces the Duke's privileging of the General's affairs over Brabantio's "particular grief" (1.3.55). We notice, with some amusement, Brabantio's denuding of the Duke's specious logic: if the Duke were to follow his own advice and accept the loss of Cyprus as past remedy and grief, and so worthy of nothing more than a smile, then Othello wouldn't be receiving the exceptional treatment that he is. These interpretations are insightful and satisfy most of the class. But later, when we discuss the play's conclusion, these satisfied students are either puzzled by Othello's decision to kill himself or else offer reasons for it that are unmoored from this earlier exchange between the Duke and Brabantio.

But not all students render Brabantio's line the way it is rendered above. A few of them rewrite the lines as "So let Othello beguile us Venetians. We do not lose Venice [some substitute "Desdemona" in place of "Venice"] so long as we can smile." It is these students whom I call on when class discussions turn to Othello's fifth-act suicide. I ask these students to explain their decision to make Othello, and not "the Turk," the subject preceding the verb "beguile." They proffer that Brabantio is still thinking about his loss (of Desdemona to Othello) even as he is critiquing the Duke's politic speciousness. Some students even note that they became convinced of this line interpretation after watching the in-class performance of an embittered Brabantio. I ask the class to reflect on whether this interpretation of Brabantio's lines is convincing to them, even though it has only been proffered by a few students. Many are not swayed.

And, so, I ask those in the minority, particularly those moved by the in-class Brabantio performance, to defend their line interpretation. I do so by asking one of them to play the role of Othello during the exchange between Brabantio and the Duke. When this exercise is successful, then at the moment when the Duke offers his equivocal advice, Othello exults in the "free comfort" about which Brabantio had earlier complained. Sometimes a student playing the role of Othello pumps their fist. At other times, the reaction may be a big smile. When I play the role of Othello alongside two students, I turn away from Brabantio and the Duke and face the audience. I allow students to see a look of visible gratification on my (i.e., Othello's) face at the moment of the Duke's equivocation. Irrespective of who plays Othello, the Moor's reaction to the sententiousness in Brabantio and the Duke's exchange invariably provokes audience laughter. Such laughter is evidence that audiences recognize Othello's profit from the Duke's equivocation.

On our first pass at interpreting the Moor's suicide, students often make perceptive observations about Othello's mindset; they often do so without seeing any need to refer back to act 1. Othello's final speech of the play begins with the following line: "I have done the state some service, and they know't. / No more of that. I pray you, in your letters, / when you shall these unlucky deeds relate, / speak of me as I am; nothing extenuate" (5.2.348–51). Just before he plunges the dagger into his own chest, Othello once again instructs his biographers to "[s]et you down this, / and say besides, that in Aleppo once / where a malignant and a turban'd Turk / beat a Venetian and traduced the state, / I took by the throat the circumcised dog, / and smote him, thus" (5.2.360–65). In the instant that Othello speaks the word "thus," he stabs himself fatally. Students observe that if Desdemona has been granted to Othello by Venice for his military prowess, then Othello's lines express confusion about whether his punishment for murdering his wife should be a private, particular matter or a general, public one. When the words "smote him" are pronounced, Othello is invoking the "turban'd Turk" of Aleppo that he has vanquished in his public service to Venice. Yet, when the "thus" is spoken, the vanquishing blade pierces Othello's own person. Othello's putatively schizophrenic breakdown occurs somewhere between the "smote him" and the "thus"—between his military privileging and the sententious exceptionalism that has procured him that privilege.

This is a tenable explanation for Othello's suicide; but some students nevertheless remain unsatisfied with it. Interestingly, some of these unsatisfied students are also among the small coterie of interpreters who had proffered the transcription "So let Othello beguile us Venetians. We do not lose Venice [or, alternatively, "Desdemona"] so long as we can smile." Without identifying these students as part of this smaller interpretive community, I pay attention to them while asking the entire class to reflect on two moments of frustration that Othello encounters just before his suicide. Both of them occur after Cyprus is out of danger.

Othello receives a missive from Venice's patricians informing him that he has been relieved of his post and that Michael Cassio has been selected to fill his position. News of Othello's replacement is corroborated by the play's other characters, although we don't hear the sentences of that missive related by anyone besides Iago. He relates them to Roderigo in the following exchange:

RODERIGO. Is that true? Why, then Othello and Desdemona return again to Venice?
IAGO. Oh, no, he goes into Mauritania and taketh away with him the fair Desdemona. (4.2.242–43)

Students reflect on the fact that this substitution represents two affronts to the Moor. Othello already suspects that Cassio has replaced him in the bedroom. To receive news that he has been replaced in the boardroom by that same Cassio is like salt applied to an open wound. The very Venetian patricians who once simultaneously approved his marriage to Desdemona and his command in Cyprus now countermand their own proclamations. Students note that these Venetian patricians efface their own hypocrisy and opportunism when they remove Othello from his post as soon as the Turk becomes a nonthreat.

I also ask students what they think of Iago's report about Othello's reassignment to "Mauritania," and, as I pronounce the place-name aloud, students hear the traces of the word *Moor*. Some students believe that it is further evidence of the duplicity of the Venetian patricians. Others suggest that perhaps Iago is fabricating a sentence that doesn't appear in the letter in order to urge the racist Roderigo to stay the course in their ploy against Othello. Irrespective of whether they believe the Mauritania instructions are real or fabricated, from Venice or from the mind of Iago, students agree that Othello probably feels betrayed by the very Venetians who once privileged him.

After this discussion, I challenge students to detect patterns linking Othello's final lines to the earlier exchange between Brabantio and the Duke. I pay particular attention to the responses of those students who substituted "Othello" in place of "the Turk of Cyprus" in the Brabantio line transcription assignment. Invariably, several members of this smaller interpretive community opine that Othello's sense of frustration at his treatment by Venice's patriarchs may have carried over into his final, self-canceling actions. At this point in class discussions, I ask students directly why they chose to keep "Turk of Cyprus" together as one subject unit, to put "us" in the primary object position and "it" in the secondary object position rather than put "us" in the primary object position and "of Cyprus" in the secondary object position (e.g., "Let the Turk beguile us of Cyprus").

Having considered Othello's "Turk" reference in his final speech, this second group of students speculate that perhaps the Moor's idea of himself as a Turk has been affected by Brabantio more profoundly than Othello initially perceived (or is now willing to admit). Perhaps laughing off the association in act 1 has made Othello realize it more keenly and feel it more bitterly in act 5, we muse.

At this point, I challenge students and myself to understand overlaps between the different camps of interpretation into which our *Othello* discussions have organized. This is an excellent opportunity for students to reflect back on the interpretive choices that they've made and to write about how they've linked those choices together (or faltered in doing so). Without announcing the filters that I'm using to select certain student-interpreters, I read aloud the reflections of students who overlap in two groups—those who rewrote "So let the Turk of Cyprus us beguile..." as "So let Othello beguile us Venetians. We do not lose Venice [or "Desdemona"] so long as we can smile" and those who noted Othello's bitter realization in act 5. Invariably, students who belong to this overlapping group note that if Othello understands Brabantio's lines to mean "The man that Venetians have been assuming is the 'Moor of Venice' is, in fact, the 'Turk of Cyprus,' and this Turk has already beguiled Venice generally and Desdemona particularly into trusting him," then Othello's final actions suggest that the Moor may have come to internalize this particular intention of Brabantio as his own. I ask the class to evaluate this provocative suggestion. Even those in my class who wrote about their struggles to detect any connection between acts 1 and 5, and those who did not find the humor in our act 1 dramatizations, now opine that the despondent Othello of act 5 reminds them of the aggrieved Brabantio of act 1.

They wonder if Othello may not have recognized a transformation in his own status—from an insider to a sententious joke to the butt of that joke. A few student-actors who had played Othello earlier even opine that the ignored protestations of the once privileged Brabantio probably echo portentously in the now deprivileged Moor's ears.

If our discussions are successful, students observe that Othello isn't just a victim to the antinomies of public and private influence in Venice. Othello seems lost between the two interpretations of Brabantio's lines proffered by students in their transcription exercises. He isn't sure whether he is the defender of Venice against the Turk or if he actually *is* the "Turk of Cyprus."

We return to examine Othello's final speech, this time more attentive to how the Moor's sensitivity to sententiousness might be guiding his actions. A few students immediately note that Othello sentences himself to suicide. Othello dictates, sentence by sentence, the terminal story that shall constitute the "letter of his life," and he punctuates that story with the culminating dictation—"thus" (5.2.365). Other students expound on this observation by noting the self-abnegating sententiousness with which Othello conflates the roles of judge and accused. He kills himself as both the "Turk of Cyprus" and the defender against the Turk, in a manner reminiscent of how the Duke's act 1 sententious declaration had both defended and damned. Occasionally, a very perspicacious student will explain the Moor's decision to kill himself as an "acceptance" of the challenge that Brabantio issued to the Venetian patriarchy, but which the patriarchy dared not accept: to follow the logic of the "[w]e lose it not, so long as we can smile" advice to its inevitably tragic conclusion.

In tracking the play's use of sententious humor from its first act to its fifth, we arrive at a troublingly fraught question: Could a mind capable of detecting indignity, yet remaining silent about it when that indignity serves its particular interests, also be inclined to subconsciously or unconsciously reproduce such indignity against itself rather than admit its earlier culpability?

Othello invites the smaller interpretive communities that I've described to become insiders to its particular brand of humor. With judiciously planned assignments that filter for such interpretive communities within their own classroom, the instructor of Shakespeare may open channels for the play's communications. If actors mine Brabantio's lines and reactions for their comedic potential, then the patriarch's bitterness resonates right until Othello's final actions (and perhaps even through those actions). Teaching the comedy in *Othello* thus enables a number of rich and important interpretations that would otherwise be opaque to students and teachers.

Notes

1. Unfortunately, clips from filmed versions of *Othello* do not aid the instructor in pointing out the comedic potential latent in the scene. However, in acting out their version of the Duke, the instructor may draw inspiration from some of the better screen performances of cagey, silver-tongued patriarchs such as Theseus in act 4, scene 1, of *A Midsummer Night's Dream* or the Duke in *All's Well That End's Well*'s third act.

2. Brian Protheroe's Brabantio, from the 2015 Royal Shakespeare Company production, comes closest (*Othello* [Khan]). Protheroe lingers on the word "smile" and momentarily stretches a forced, feigned smile across his face with his fingers. The 1981 BBC version starring Anthony Hopkins and Bob Hoskins also features a convincing Brabantio (*Othello* [Miller]). Although no film version of the play that I have been able to find stages Othello as an active listener to Brabantio's lines, Othello is often positioned at the periphery of the stage, outside the camera's frame, with Brabantio and the Duke standing face-to-face.

Works Cited

Othello. Directed by Iqbal Khan, Royal Shakespeare Company / Opus Arte, 2015.
Othello. Directed by Jonathan Miller, British Broadcasting Company, 1981.
Shakespeare, William. *Othello*. *The Norton Shakespeare*, edited by Stephen Greenblatt et al., vol. 2, W. W. Norton, 2008, pp. 385–457.

Tiffany Potter

The Changing of the Joke: Restoration Libertine Sex Comedies

Students have long found the sex comedies of the English Restoration to be funny on first read, distinct from many earlier plays whose comedy can be opaque to students. But the experience of teaching Restoration comedy has changed significantly in the last decade as students have become more actively attuned to the coercive dynamics and classist and gendered structures that underpin sex comedy as a genre: an imagined version of an aristocratic life that celebrates privilege and its pleasures regardless of the sufferings of those exploited in the performance of libertine identity. Many teachers have removed the comedies of playwrights like William Wycherley, Sir George Etherege, and Aphra Behn from their courses because their content is potentially disturbing to students. But to cut such plays is to commit two wrongs: to deny students brilliant comedies that give us insight into their historical moments and, worse, to silence the contemporary voices who turned those privileged assumptions to very different cultural work: as this essay points out, 350 years ago, Behn interrogated exactly the same things that modern readers find troubling about historical sex comedy. And that leads to the following question: How do we teach comedy that many students can no longer find funny?

This essay describes a module that pairs two of the most famous sex comedies in literary history, William Wycherley's *The Country Wife* and Aphra Behn's *The Rover*, in a way that invites students to investigate the cultural frameworks of Restoration comedy. When these two texts are taught together, students can see a critical moment of historical debate and disruption being staged in two plays that are utterly hilarious in some parts and deeply troubling in others: pairing these two comedies illuminates how the same form of comedy can both endorse and interrogate identical codes and conventions, allowing students to recognize the assumptions that underlie stagings of Restoration libertinism. Wycherley's play is a revel, a celebration of the power of one brilliant man to pleasure the world. After establishing the conventional Restoration perspective on sex comedy by considering the ribaldry and wit of *Country Wife* (including the dark threads of the fate of young Margery Pinchwife and Horner's control over the women who—quite joyfully—consent to sleep with him), the module moves to Behn's play, which applies a more critical lens to the genre. *The Rover* is in theory a standard libertine comedy about Willmore, a Horner-esque English aristocrat romping about Naples during an interregnum Carnival, but the play's attention instead is from the beginning on three women: Florinda, seeking a love match; Hellena, planned for the convent and looking for any "handsome proper fellow of my humour above ground, though I ask first" (Behn 1.1.44–45); and Angellica Bianca, the most powerful courtesan in Naples, who trades status for love and becomes a near tragic heroine. Like Wycherley's Horner, Willmore is the sexy man immediately desired by all women, but Behn's version stages the ugly side of seduction comedy in a form that has been read for centuries as a rollicking masquerade party yet makes shockingly clear the coercive dynamic faced by Restoration women in the sexual economy, from prostitution to the marriage market. As students note, however, Behn's play pushes beyond the realms of consensual exchange in agreed-upon contexts to a world where Florinda is assaulted nearly every time she leaves the confinement of her home. Reading these two plays together allows students to come to terms with the staging of the comedy of desire in this patriarchal and politicized historical moment and with the challenge of analyzing these plays now, when coercion isn't funny but wit, foolery, and flirtatious games still are.

This module teaches the plays as comedy, as culture, and as a case study in sex as a tool of culture. To start, I explain that humor is not static and that "what is funny" is an evolving notion. In particular, what people found funny during the Restoration and eighteenth century is considerably cruder than what students might expect from period descriptors like "the age of reason." Satire was sharp and frequently cruel, as can be demonstrated quickly with excerpts from the poet laureate John Dryden's evisceration of his dramatic rival, Thomas Shadwell, in "MacFlecknoe." And as Simon Dickie documents right from the opening sentence of *Cruelty and Laughter: Forgotten Comic Literature and the Unsentimental Eighteenth Century*, "Eighteenth-century Britons—or a high proportion of them—openly delighted in the miseries of others" (1): books of jests, plays, essays, and fiction were full of widely repeated jokes made at the expense of those who were poor or those with disabilities or disfigurements, with a frequent delight in tales of women beaten, tricked, and otherwise abused. On the stage, audiences also enjoyed comedy of wit and manners, populated by clever, upper-class men and women tricking one another out of inheritances, property, money, sex, and spouses. The pleasure in these plays is partly in the audience's sense of being in on the joke, even as they might be scandalized by such behavior in their real lives; audience acceptance of the humor also counts on the aspirational pleasures of spying on privileged lives, universal from the Horners and Fidgets to the Kardashians. These two elements—comedy at the expense of the less powerful and the pleasure of in-group privilege—combined with their articulation in a quotable language of wit, drive much of the Restoration comic experience.

So, where twenty-first-century readers might well shudder, Restoration audiences were gleefully entertained. That gap is a fascinating entry to teaching. From the start, I make clear that the light and dark will necessitate reading these two plays as a pair. First we read *Country Wife* as much as possible through the eyes of Restoration audiences, valuing the wit and the very emphatically not-Puritan view of the imagined possibilities of privilege. We are always conscious that we will also be examining the dark underbelly of these same values of privilege, the same nodding to the assumed values of Charles II, and the same opacity of the rules of courtship, seduction, and coercion in *The Rover*. Knowing that they will be revisiting these ideas through another lens to some degree frees students to engage the plays as they were written, to see the cultural projects these plays served in their own day. Making the strategy behind the course design explicit allows students to appreciate the art on its own terms without feeling as if they are abandoning their personal values in doing so.

I devote five hours of class time to each play, devoting one class session of sixty to ninety minutes on *Country Wife* to draw students' attention to two scenes that form a particularly strong connecting thread with *Rover*: the hilarious "china scene," in which Horner and Lady Fidget have enthusiastic sex while her oblivious husband giggles nearby at Horner's supposed status as a eunuch (Wycherley 4.3), and the "tea table scene," in which the play's ladies use witty code to dissect female desire, how a woman can pursue sex, with whom, and what that means for the wife-as-property marriage convention (2.1.343–436). A parallel scene at the end of act 1, in which male characters banter about manliness, is discussed in the next class in conjunction with the Pinchwife plot.

These plays can be taught many ways: an instructor might choose to focus on issues of language, gender, political affiliation, or nationalism. The classes on these three scenes address how status is established and attacked. Characters in both plays seek not only pleasure but also power and control. Horner willingly surrenders his reputation to perform his brilliance to an audience of two: the Quack and himself. In Horner's realm, status comes from wit and knowledge rather than from rank (as cuckolded Sir Jaspar might never figure out) or virtue (which ultimately excludes the moral but boring Alithea and Harcourt). Still, Pinchwife's abuse of his wife suggests that games of dominance have their limits, though his only penalty is to be treated as unfashionable before returning to the presumed purgatory of the country. Serving primarily as a way for Horner to demonstrate his triumph over Pinchwife, Margery's suffering is blunted by her status as "country"—unwitty and unwitting—and the play's end focuses on her moment of pleasure in cuckolding her husband rather than on her lifetime of misery to come.

After this setup, students close-read the tea table scene in groups of three, with one student in each group focusing on one of the scene's three characters. They read the scene aloud and then spend ten minutes discussing the following questions:

> What social norms are debated in the scene? (Students often note gendered desire, adultery, tension between virtue and reputation, and the degree to which men can be objectified in sexual exchange, particularly by rank.)
> How is the discussion coded? (impersonal pronouns, abstractions, performance)

> What happens when the coding breaks down? (sharp response of peer group regulation: "Be continent in your discourse, or I shall hate you" [Wycherley 2.1.422])

Students often reach the ahistorical but useful conclusion that the women in Wycherley's play are negotiating the idea of consent. Pressed further, they recognize the scene's assertion of private practices among women where knowledge that is technically unspeakable is still disseminated; these characters understand the conservative codes of upper-class marriage but also that such requirements of disempowerment are malleable, as long as the subversion and its conversations are private (affecting only virtue) rather than public (affecting reputation).

The china scene, arguably literary history's most famous scene of intersecting implications of knowledge, sex, power, and privilege, puts theory into action. We read it aloud with assigned parts, and I tell students, "If you think it might be a dirty joke, the audience probably did too, so you can keep that context in mind as you are reading and imagining performances." There are staged versions available on *YouTube*, but none are so funny as the ones that students suggest when asked to imagine how one could stage the scene: Horner and Lady Fidget in silhouette (inviting pieces of china like the vase that appears later in the scene to comic use); sound effects heard by every character except the aged Sir Jaspar; and even *Avenue Q* style puppetry, where actors playing Horner and Lady Fidget say the lines quite seriously while manipulating smutty Muppet-like puppets. The potentially valuable exercise of spending class time to prepare stagings (followed with written critical rationales) does not work with the timelines of my institution, but a short breakout session to create a thirty-second elevator pitch for staging is highly engaging and facilitates a strong sense of the comic and cultural implications of the scene.

One universal in the suggested stagings is that these scenes are about pleasure, subverting norms that would restrain female desire in a way that is public and performative for those in the know and hidden from the understanding, though not the vision, of the out-group. The china scene represents pleasure situated in the perception of power: the audience revels in in-group knowledge of manipulations, and all the players in the scene (unlike Margery Pinchwife later) are self-aware as they manipulate the system that would render them desexualized objects of marriage-market exchange. The play's inclusion of the audience in in/out dynamics co-opts them into the celebratory mood, and many students are sufficiently swept away to overlook Margery's sufferings. But Wycherley does pause the revel long enough for a glimpse at the cost to those unable to play the game that drives the plot. Educated in the country, excluded from the tea table scene, Margery has the wrong kind of knowledge: as a married woman, she knows about sex, but she does not understand the systems of the fashionable community known as the Town. Horner seduces the world, and Pinchwife is driven from the community of men he has tried to rejoin in act 1. At the end of the class on these two scenes, the play's focus on power, rank, and politics among libertine men emerges from the discussion of the sex scenes: sex is just a way for the libertine to demonstrate power, and even knowing women play the game at their peril.

Country Wife mostly declines to think about the gendering of sexual gamesmanship, as long as everyone is consenting. In contrast, the shadow that passes briefly over Wycherley settles darkly in Behn's *Rover*, staged the next year, which also uses sex comedy as a device to comment on culture, but viewed through a female comic lens. At its start, *The Rover* could still be in the world of *Country Wife*, with Hellena wittily resisting her brother's attempt to dispose of her in a convent. Uninfected by romance, she dreams not of a love match but of a chance to experience the world, to have forbidden knowledge. She dreams, one might say, of a Horner and the risky freedoms of the women in his world. Our discussion of Behn's take on seduction comedy starts with the ways in which, right from the play's opening lines, Hellena and Florinda articulate the cultural narratives that are being used to define their choices. They consciously choose how they will act, believing—as the audience does from earlier takes on the genre—that these expectations are firm but can be manipulated. Making clear that these characters are absolutely aware of the conduct norms for English women (for whom Behn's Spanish ladies in Naples stand in) sets students up for a critical engagement with the ways in which Behn twists both conservative culture and its Wycherley-esque comic subversions.

That twist is anchored in the character of the courtesan Angellica Bianca, fought over by powerful men willing to spend fortunes for her company. She has all the knowledge that Hellena seeks and more, but she trades her power for love with the rover Willmore. She is beautiful, rich, and smart, but her choice leads to her end as a near tragic heroine (her two blank verse speeches to Willmore in act 5 are nearly indistinguishable from Cleopatra's late speeches in Dryden's contemporary heroic tragedy *All for Love* [1677]). As is true of Margery Pinchwife's story, the play's comic end is dependent on those jest-book views of comedy: the ignorant (adulterous) country girl or the dreamy prostitute can't really be taken seriously. When Angellica is restored to her standing as Don Antonio's mistress, her plot is ostensibly resolved with no harm done, but, like Margery, she will never be the same. Comparing the arc of these two characters—one who knows too little and one who knows too much—invites a smart discussion of the sacrificial characters often needed for comedy and helps students break away from readings that focus on love triangles in order to see something deeper in Behn's examination of status, sex, and comedy.

But it is Florinda's plot that makes this play increasingly difficult for students to find funny. Supposed to be the virtuous beloved, the female half of the bland second couple that helps populate conventional comedies of manners, Florinda instead literally embodies the danger of aspirations of autonomy in love. Looking at Florinda's plot can be a tough day, but it is also an important pedagogical opportunity. Since students know from *Country Wife* and from act 1 of *The Rover* what is supposed to be funny about sex comedy (wit, pleasure, power, subversion, in-groups), they are able to identify the ways in which Behn is turning the conventions: in the same moment that she casts a light on the violent and ugly underbelly of the sexual power plays that *Country Wife* finds funny, she exploits them for profit, staging Florinda's victimization so many times that the joke wears thin long before a wedding.

Decades ago Susan Staves initiated a conversation about "the comedy of attempted rape" in the eighteenth century, noting the startling proportion of eighteenth-century texts that have at least one attempted rape scene. Significant scholarship of the 1990s in particular presented feminist critiques of the ways that comedies of manners danced around the continuum from courtship to coercion, what Toni Bowers has identified as the false dichotomy of "force or fraud." For an upper-level course, I assign the introduction to Bowers's *Force or Fraud* (1–28), which provides a concise historical framework and a set of definitions of terms like *courtship*, *seduction*, and *rape* that are grounded in the legal and popular discourses of the eighteenth century. In this context, Bowers explains, "The distinction between 'force' and 'fraud' crucially came to require a determination of whether the respondent, paradigmatically female, colluded in or resisted her own fall, and it posited collusion and resistance as necessarily exclusive acts" (8). Bowers interrogates this constructed opposition, examining the feminist implication of a female figure who manages social demand in a way that enables both desire and social stability ("compromised and complicit yet still virtuous" [38]) as well as how the eighteenth-century binary of rape and seduction renders invisible the coercive aspects of seduction narratives. In advanced seminars, I assign two additional readings that occupy opposing positions on sexual violence in Restoration drama so that students can examine a range of thinking on the literary-critical implications of the sex comedy plot. Jean Marsden's essay "Rape, Voyeurism, and the Restoration Stage" hypothesizes a link between a proliferation of rape plots onstage and the emergence of women actors in female roles (185). Derek Hughes's "Rape on the Restoration Stage" rejects Marsden's readings, separating out "forcible rape" from "bedroom tricks" (227) to argue that many rape plots act primarily in service of political points related to the exclusion crisis, foregrounding the complex political metaphors that are also addressed in Bowers's analysis.

Having this kind of scholarly dialogue to hand, students are equipped to discuss the implications of *The Rover*'s serial rape attempts and Behn's groundbreaking challenge to Restoration comedy's convention of rape as plot device. Florinda suffers four sexual assaults, and Behn makes each one a version of the comedy of attempted rape. In backstory explained in the opening scene, audiences learn that Florinda was "preserved from all insolences" (1.1.61) during the siege of Pamplona by Belvile (a white-knight story). In act 3, scene 5 (1–80) she is mistaken for a sexually willing woman by a stumbling-drunk Wilmore, who enters the scene looking for a place to pass out (a physical comedy version of attempted rape). In act 4, hiding from her brother and mistaken for a woman of low rank (and thus high vulnerability) by Willmore, Florinda seeks refuge in an open door; there she is explicitly threatened with violent rape by Blunt, one of Belvile's circle, angry with another woman and seeking to be "revenged on one whore for the sins of another" (4.5.64). Florinda is immediately further threatened by a group of men who enter Blunt's room masked and turn out to be Belvile, her brother, and their friends (attempted rape as comedy of mistaken identity).

First, we identify the traditional comic modes noted above using the other elements of the scenes: I ask students to find scenes that depend on similar tropes of comedy in other texts we have read or in familiar narratives. Students see the white-knight rescue-to-love trope in centuries of popular culture, including the *Twilight* series; the drunken, foolish lover in Sir Andrew and Maria in *Twelfth Night* and in modern iterations like Johnny Depp's character in *The Pirates of the Caribbean* films; the humiliated man redirecting his rage in Pinchwife (also not funny, though we're supposed to enjoy his mocking); and the sex comedy of deceptive or mistaken identity in Wycherley's china scene and in Shakespeare's *Twelfth Night*. Students can still feel appalled at Florinda's status as prey, saddened at Angellica's loss of self, or exhilarated by Hellena's triumphs, but this exercise guides them to recognize how Behn shines new light on old stories, challenging audiences to recognize the social and physical risk, intrinsic to conventional courtship narratives and comic traditions, that has to be willfully ignored in Restoration comedy. Given tools to recognize comic convention and its destabilization, as well as the historical framing and scholarly vocabulary necessary to consider the sometimes deeply disconcerting elements of Restoration sex comedies, students have the keys to reading Restoration comedy and the cultural moment that it examines.

Works Cited

Behn, Aphra. *The Rover; or, The Banish'd Cavaliers*. 1677. Edited by Anne Russell. *The Broadview Anthology of Restoration and Early Eighteenth-Century Drama: Concise Edition*, edited by J. Douglas Canfield, Broadview Press, 2001, pp. 219–74.

Bowers, Toni. *Force or Fraud: British Seduction Stories and the Problem of Resistance, 1660–1760*. Oxford UP, 2011.

Dickie, Simon. *Cruelty and Laughter: Forgotten Comic Literature and the Unsentimental Eighteenth Century*. U of Chicago P, 2011.

Hughes, Derek. "Rape on the Restoration Stage." *The Eighteenth Century: Theory and Interpretation*, vol. 46, no. 3, 2005, pp. 225–36.

Marsden, Jean. "Rape, Voyeurism, and the Restoration Stage." *Broken Boundaries: Women and Feminism in Restoration Drama*, edited by Katherine M. Quinsey, UP of Kentucky, 1996, pp. 185–200.

Staves, Susan. "Fielding and the Comedy of Attempted Rape." *History, Gender and Eighteenth-Century Literature*, edited by Beth Fowkes Tobin, U of Georgia P, 1994, pp. 86–112.

Wycherley, William. *The Country Wife*. 1675. Edited by Peggy Thompson. *The Broadview Anthology of Restoration and Early Eighteenth-Century Drama: Concise Edition*, edited by J. Douglas Canfield, Broadview Press, 2001, pp. 92–154.

Janice McIntire-Strasburg

Modern Chivalry and Satire: Why Teach a Post–Revolutionary War Novel?

Among the many thoughts and ideas lost by glossing over the earliest American writers is humor. Precisely because humor is often timely, many of the jokes and much of the irony and satire are lost to student readers. Elements of Early American humor often need explanation. Though this sometimes detracts from its laughter quotient, with such explanations modern students can see and appreciate how such humor demonstrates issues within the time period. Hugh Henry Brackenridge is one example of an eighteenth-century author who uses humor to comment on contemporary issues. Brackenridge began publishing the text that became *Modern Chivalry* in 1792, just after the Revolutionary War. It began as a gentlemanly pursuit designed to entertain his friends and family and is a satire in the style of Miguel de Cervantes's earlier picaresque novel, *Don Quixote*. It was published in sections and later collected into a novel form, the final edition of which was published in 1819, and was relatively popular in its time; however, the novel is now seldom read. My own university library buries it in the law library. In 2002 I created a web text, hosted on the University of Virginia's American studies website, primarily so that I had a text to teach from.[1] Ed White reproduced a copy of the 1937 Newlin edition in 2009, and, most recently (2017), a Kindle version of the text

275

is available.[2] This seems to indicate an interest in using the early satire on the historical and political ramifications of the new republic, but today the text often needs supplemental materials and translation of its historical and political elements as well as a detailed explanation of what satire is and how it works. This should come as no surprise, since readers often miss the satire in the most modern of texts.

The first step in this process is to make sure that students understand the purposes of humor and how it can be reinterpreted and reunderstood in later ages. Humor does not shy away from hard truths and controversy. The design of satire is to make a reader think and, ultimately, to make their thought agree with the writer's. Texts as old as *Modern Chivalry* highlight this fact while at the same time allowing readers to clarify their own thinking in the process. Brackenridge's central purpose in *Chivalry*—to demonstrate a testing-out of the political principles of the new republic focused on who is qualified to lead—no longer matches today's societal standards. Brackenridge was a member of the American upper-class elite. Educated in law at Princeton University, as many of the Founding Fathers were, his ideals are theirs. He saw the right to vote and hold office as the privilege of persons of his own class—white, educated, land-owning men. He held similar views about women's place in the private sphere. Thus, the travels of Captain John Farrago, the story's hero; his commentary on the times; his social views; and his beliefs on who should be qualified to lead are those of his class and time. Understanding what those views are and how they were formed presents an opportunity to critique the time and trace the evolutionary nature of society and politics. Students can clearly see this elitism in an episode where the captain's manservant, Teague O'Reagan, tries to run for office. The captain states, "[Teague] is totally ignorant of the great principles of legislation; and more especially, the particular interests of this government." Farrago believes that "though doubtless, in such a government, the lowest citizen may become chief magistrate; yet it is sufficient to possess the right; not absolutely necessary to exercise it" (Brackenridge 38). For the captain, and Brackenridge by extension, common citizens' right to vote and lead is a nominal one that should be left to their betters.

It seems obvious that humor texts such as this one essentially take a social and political temperature of the times. Those who teach comic texts have an obligation to contextualize their satire in order to show students that beliefs are not static and are changed by the succeeding generations. Correctly interpreting the satiric elements does not demand that the reader acquiesce to the position. If readers are offended by how the captain treats Teague O'Reagan, his Irish emigrant companion, they should be — all the while recognizing that in that moment of history people did believe and acquiesce. Reading this text and others like it can demonstrate how far we have come as a society and perhaps also how far we still need to go.

Other episodes in the text present a window into what life was like in late-eighteenth-century America. From the 1790s to 1800, Pennsylvania was the frontier. What we recognize today as a populous and relatively sophisticated state was open country without the benefits of churches, police, and social amenities. Brackenridge presents his readers with con men, crooked politicians, and rigged horse races in many of the episodes that highlight the need for these services and establish his priorities for the new government. On his first day out, the captain encounters a horse race in progress. When urged to enter his own mount, he describes his horse as "a common palfrey, and by no means remarkable for speed or bottom," and the race men consider that he is merely trying to increase the odds on his entry (Brackenridge 30). Brackenridge highlights the uncertain legalities of the frontier, offering a public warning that travelers to the area will encounter dishonesty without local law enforcement. Such information offers a context for his opinions and focus. Students can then evaluate his work based on clear evidence of the situation and trace the cultural shifts across time.

From his position as a well-educated and highly observant man, Brackenridge used satire to critique how a new America implemented its political thought and how that thought was understood by the average citizen. Satire's purpose has always been to shed light on perceived wrongs and attempt to sway public opinion so as to create positive change. There is inherent value in teaching students to be careful readers and in developing an understanding that, while the stereotyped group, gender, or nationality may change, bias continues to exist, and purposes can be misunderstood. Jonathan Swift's eighteenth-century satire "A Modest Proposal" is a good example of misunderstood purpose and how radically wrong satire can go when incorrectly interpreted. Anyone who has taught this perfect classical argument incorporating satire will remember that at least some students will be appalled that Swift advocated eating Irish babies. But Swift's purpose was to demonstrate the plight of the Irish poor under English rule. His point is that if the British government refuses to do any better by the Irish poor, they might just as well eat those children and be done with it. In teaching satire and its limitations, an instructor cannot do better than a reading and interpretation of this piece before ever trying to introduce satire in other authors. Swift's satire shows the limitations of the writer's skill, but it also shows the limitations of the inattentive reader.

Teaching older texts in particular requires the instructor to provide a historical and cultural context. Ideally, students would either take an American history course in tandem with the readings of comic literature or have a knowledge of history to draw from as they read. Since this is not always feasible, an instructor without an extensive background in American history can find many resources on early Pennsylvania history, the Whiskey Rebellion, electioneering in the early republic, restrictions on and treatment of immigrants, and other subjects that play a part in the novel's episodic content. Historical and cultural resources, both national and local, are plentiful on the Internet, and asking students to locate such resources helps bolster students' research skills. Instructors can present several sources to get students started and then turn students loose to find others. Though many of Brackenridge's opinions are outdated and offensive, they can certainly spark excellent discussion of the roots and persistence of prejudice and elitism. Additionally, while American politics has undergone major changes since 1797, closer study of this text in light of current political practices may show students that the current system may not be as different as they believe.

Instructors can also use the novel to teach literary critique through a focus on satire's success or failure as a literary trope. What literary devices, situations, and characterizations does the author employ in order to make the satire work? Where does *Chivalry* fall short of its objectives? How much of the problem stems from the historical moment, and how much from authorial oversight? The novel began its literary life as a private tale shared among family and friends and was subsequently submitted for publication. What are the implications of such an expansion of audience? The rhetorical implications of a larger and possibly less favorably disposed audience force a focus on shifting audience expectations.

Chivalry's introduction works well to demonstrate how Brackenridge visualized this wider audience and its critical reception. In it, he situates the text as a study in composition—a public service to improve schoolboys' writing. He states that he will "consider language only, not in the least regarding the matter of this work, much as musicians when they are about to give the most excellent melody, pay no attention to the words that are set to music" (Brackenridge 25). Other satirists have used this same technique to forestall literary criticism of their work. Mark Twain would later employ this same device. Most of his novels and travel books contain a prefatory notice—often ironic or satirical in itself—the most famous being the one accompanying *Adventures of Huckleberry Finn*.

Satire has the flexibility to borrow its devices from many other genres and styles. How many devices can students identify (perhaps with help)? How might they evaluate the effectiveness of those they recognize? An instructor might also assign a creative project by introducing other devices and asking students to try them out by writing an episode of their own.

As a picaresque novel, *Chivalry* uses its loosely organized series of episodes as a device for tying together any number of possible subjects without losing continuity for its reader. Students can approach the work as an homage to Cervantes by comparing Spanish culture and the culture of post–Revolutionary War America or by contrasting the two novels' purposes, or they can approach Cervantes's novel as a well-established literary model from which Brackenridge worked, using *Chivalry* as a way of understanding the picaresque's possibilities and limitations. Any one of these approaches will lead to a rewarding study of how a comic text works.

Another method of approaching the study of *Chivalry* might involve pairing it with a more familiar and modern example of satire in order to demonstrate satire's pervasiveness as a trope. Eighteenth-century texts are generally longer and more elaborate than contemporary texts, and they use language and diction that appear severely outdated to the modern reader. Contemporary examples of satire from websites like *The Huffington Post* or *The Onion* or other media outlets like *The Daily Show* or *The Colbert Report* use a more modern language and style, but they also show that the same devices and techniques used in older works are still being used for the same purposes today. This can show satire's continued relevance in modern times.

The comic remains one of the most flexible of techniques with respect to its subject matter, stylistic devices, and purposes. It affords an author many possible opportunities to achieve authorial goals, but this flexibility can result in correspondingly great opportunities for misunderstanding and misinterpretation. Comic texts are challenging for both the teacher and the student, but they (and *Chivalry* in particular) also have the ability to transcend their historical and cultural moment when properly situated. *Chivalry*'s treatment of immigrants, women, and the general public can lead to discussions of timeless novels and poems as well as those with a shorter shelf life because they are so tightly bound to a particular cultural moment. Some humor simply cannot transcend its particular moment.

I began this essay with a question: Why teach a post–Revolutionary War novel? In other words, what can subjects and ideas so far removed from the present offer students born nearly two centuries after Brackenridge published his novel? *Chivalry* is valuable because it presents a window into an earlier iteration of American culture and history on a more personal level than history itself usually provides. Satires like *Chivalry* offer the additional benefit of the comic (often slapstick) antics of a fictional character, making the lesson more palatable. In addition, it exposes the limits of culture and philosophy grounded in time and place. It has been said that those who ignore history are doomed to repeat it. Older forms of satire teach how the best and worst of historical thought can instigate change. Reading the past can attune the modern reader to the cycles of progression and regression that eventually evolve into the cultural and political present.

Notes

1. See xroads.virginia.edu/~Hyper2/Chivalry/index.html.

2. The appendix contains information on the availability of the novel, recommendations for which editions are best suited to students, and a selection of texts available for further reading and research. Most pertain particularly to *Modern Chivalry*. I have also included Don and Alleen Nilsen's *Encyclopedia of Twentieth-Century American Humor* because, although its primary focus is twentieth-century humor, it also contains definitions of terms and other information useful to any humor text. While not all-inclusive, these resources are a good place to start for those teaching humor.

Works Cited

Brackenridge, Hugh Henry. *Modern Chivalry*. Edited by Ed White, Hackett, 2009.

Swift, Jonathan. *A Modest Proposal and Other Satirical Works*. Dover, 1996.

Appendix: Resources for Teaching *Modern Chivalry*

Extant Texts Available for Reading

Leary, Lewis, editor. *Modern Chivalry, Containing the Adventures of Captain John Farrago and Teague O'Reagan*. By Hugh Henry Brackenridge, vol. 1, New College and University Press, 1965.
> This edition contains only volume 1 and is out of print but can be printed on order.

White, Ed, editor. *Modern Chivalry*. By Hugh Henry Brackenridge, Hackett, 2002.
> This edition is a reprint of the Claude Newlin edition of 1934 and contains all volumes. A scholarly edition, it contains material deleted in other editions.

Modern Chivalry: The Complete 1819 Edition. By Hugh Henry Brackenridge, Kindle ed., 2017.
> This complete edition was edited after Brackenridge's death by his son, Henry Marie Brackenridge, and is a good choice if you want to use the entire text—it was heavily edited from the serial volumes and is much more readable for students. It is also well priced at ninety-nine cents and can be read on a laptop or other mobile device.

Selected Texts for Further Reading

Battistini, Robert. "Federalist Decline and Despair on the Pennsylvania Frontier: Hugh Henry Brackenridge's *Modern Chivalry*." *The Pennsylvanian Magazine of History and Biography*, vol. 133, no. 2, Apr. 2009, pp. 149–66.

Chaden, Caryn. "Dress and Undress in Brackenridge's *Modern Chivalry*." *Early American Literature*, vol. 26, no. 1, 1991, pp. 55–72.

Engell, John. "Brackenridge, *Modern Chivalry*, and American Humor." *Early American Literature*, vol. 22, no. 1, spring 1987, pp. 43–62.

Gilmore, Michael T. "Eighteenth-Century Oppositional Ideology and Hugh Henry Brackenridge's *Modern Chivalry*." *Early American Literature*, vol. 13, no. 2, fall 1978, pp. 181–92.

Halms, Lynn. "Of Indians and Irishmen: A Note on Brackenridge's Use of Sources for Satire in *Modern Chivalry*." *Early American Literature*, vol. 10, no. 1, spring 1975, pp. 88–92.

Harkey, Joseph H. "The Don Quixote of the Frontier: Brackenridge's *Modern Chivalry*." *Early American Literature*, vol. 8, no. 2, fall 1973, pp. 193–203.

Koenigs, Thomas. "Nothing but Fiction: *Modern Chivalry*, Fictionality, and the Political Public Sphere in the Early Republic." *Early American Literature*, vol. 50, no. 2, 2015, pp. 301–30.

Martin, Wendy. "On the Road with the Philosopher and the Profiteer: A Study of Hugh Henry Brackenridge's *Modern Chivalry*." *Eighteenth-Century Studies*, vol. 4, no. 3, spring 1971, pp. 241–56.

———. "The Rogue and the Rational Man: Hugh Henry Brackenridge's Study of a Con Man in *Modern Chivalry*." *Early American Literature*, vol. 8, no. 2, fall 1973, pp. 179–92.

Nance, William L. "Satiric Elements in Brackenridge's *Modern Chivalry*." *Texas Studies in Literature and Language*, vol. 9, no. 3, autumn 1967, pp. 381–89.

Nilsen, Don L. F., and Alleen Pace Nilsen. *Encyclopedia of Twentieth-Century American Humor*. Greenwood Press, 2000.

Patterson, Mark R. "Representation in Brackenridge's *Modern Chivalry*." *Texas Studies in Literature and Language*, vol. 28, no. 2, summer 1986, pp. 121–39.

Rice, Grantland S. "*Modern Chivalry* and the Resistance to Textual Authority." *American Literature*, vol. 86, no. 2, June 1995, pp. 257–81.

Roades, Mary Teresa. "*Don Quixote* and *Modern Chivalry*." *Hispania*, vol. 32, no. 3, 1949, pp. 320–25. *JSTOR*, www.jstor.org/stable/334305.

Whittle, Amberys R. "*Modern Chivalry*: The Frontier as Crucible." *Early American Literature*, vol. 6, no. 3, winter 1971–72, pp. 263–70.

Aaron R. Hanlon

Comedy versus Satire in Eighteenth-Century Contexts

Critics frequently identify the young twenty-first century as a new golden age of satire. Ian Hilsop, editor of the British satirical magazine *Private Eye*, suggests that "Brexit and Donald Trump" are leading factors in the magazine's record-breaking sales (qtd. in Ballardie). But even in 2011, before Brexit and the Trump presidential campaign, *Private Eye* hit its highest circulation in twenty-five years (Dowell). In the United States, critics likewise point to the boost that mockable political figures—Sarah Palin, Donald Trump—give to televisual satires such as *Saturday Night Live*, *The Colbert Report*, or John Oliver's *Last Week Tonight*, just as shows like Jon Stewart's *The Daily Show* thrived on political satire in the George W. Bush era (Zurawik). Between the abundance of satire shows on television, the popularity of satirical journalism and commentary sites like *The Onion*, and the prominent satire columns of journalists such as Alexandra Petri in *The Washington Post* and Andy Borowitz in *The New Yorker*, the claims that we recently witnessed a golden age of satire are reasonable.

My students tend to notice and comment on the prominence and quality of satire across media today. For them, the defining character of contemporary satire is its comic function. When I ask students to reflect on and explain why someone would choose to present a set of claims, values, and arguments in satirical form, as opposed to making the straightforward case in an earnest disquisition on political corruption, the erosion of a shared sense of the truth, or the problem of misogyny in politics, students frequently respond with reference to the persuasive power of humor. Their responses reflect both a rhetorical theory of comedy—that because it can lower our attitudinal defenses, it can make us vulnerable to changing our minds or taking interest in an otherwise boring subject—and a testimonial understanding of how comedy works: it *has worked* this way *on me*. For these reasons students rightly associate this new golden age of satire with comedy, having come to twenty-first-century satire through television networks such as Comedy Central or by laughing along with the live audiences on *Last Week Tonight*, *The Daily Show*, or *Full Frontal with Samantha Bee*. Meanwhile, the industries and networks that produce television satire and late-night variety shows view comedians as prime candidates for hosting such shows, drawing hosts from the ranks of the stand-up circuit.

It is important to recognize, then, that in this age of satire, students are likely to think of satire and comedy as fluid if not interchangeable generic categories. This proves both an advantage and a challenge for introducing students to that other golden age of satire in the English-language tradition, the long eighteenth century.[1] Today's students' awareness of the satirical function of comedy (or the comedic function of satire) proves helpful in generating interest in various things labeled "satire" in the long eighteenth century, from print sources such as Jonathan Swift's "A Modest Proposal" to visual satires such as William Hogarth's "Marriage A-la-Mode." Students likewise find it pleasantly surprising that a poem like "Satyr on Charles II," by John Wilmot, second Earl of Rochester, incorporates blunt vulgarity in its burlesque rendering of the king, much as the twenty-first-century satirical work of hosts like Stewart, Oliver, and Bee uses exasperated monologues full of uncouth language or graphic sexual humor to throttle audience sensibilities or vent spleen at contemptible public figures.

The challenge of reconciling the two golden ages in the classroom arises from the frequent conflation of satire and comedy. This is a challenge not only for understanding relationships between form and function in satire but also for expanding students' awareness of the noncomedic forms satire took from Restoration to Romanticism. The latter part of the challenge is especially important for our ability to teach long-eighteenth-century satire as a mode also wielded by women, to move away from impressions that satire is primarily the domain of male writers. This problem is alive and well; a recent film with Mindy Kaling, *Late Night*, tackles the lack of gender and racial diversity in writers' rooms and comedy shows. In what follows, then, I describe a pedagogical strategy and an assignment meant to address the challenge of distinguishing between comedy and satire even as these two modes frequently rely on each another.

Conceptual Framing

Reframing eighteenth-century satire as not only inclusive of comedic modes but also more modally diverse than comedy per se yields two particular benefits. First, it helps students recognize a fuller range of satirical modes besides the comedic, including satire driven more by invective, burlesque, or parody than by comedy. Second, by distinguishing between satire's comic function and its other functions, students can develop a more precise understanding of how satire does comedy. Invective and burlesque, for example, might bring students to laughter, thereby having a comic effect; but to the extent that comedy is the framework for reading such texts, one might miss not only the other satirical modes prominent in the period but also the precise mechanisms by which satire achieves its effects.

For this reason I like to provide students with satirical texts that exemplify noncomedic strategies for satirical critique, establishing thereby a conceptual framework for satirical modes that helps students break free of the expectation that if we label something "satire," we must therefore respond to it with laughter (whether full-bodied laughter or the wry chuckle of one who realizes they are in on a joke). I prefer Ashley Marshall's definition of eighteenth-century satire as inclusive of "works that have long been treated as satirical or partly satirical, as well as those that were originally identified as satires by their authors" (xi). To provide students with an exemplary overview of prominent satirical modes in the period, I focus on a rotating collection of texts, each of which foregrounds a different approach to satire.

Swift's satirical syllabus staple, "A Modest Proposal," offers a clear example of noncomedic satirical irony, in large part because of its classical rhetorical structure. The proposer's slow and measured buildup to the horrific thing—which is not what Swift would earnestly propose—followed by a litany of justifications for the horrific thing, followed by a *refutatio* (the section in which the proposer addresses potential counterarguments) in which Swift couches his earnest proposals allows students to break apart the mechanism of Swift's irony and see how the parts work together to produce it. The only alternative proposals the proposer can imagine to the scheme of treating the infants of the poor like livestock for the consumption of the rich are practical proposals for which the historical Swift advocated. For example, when the proposer claims in the *refutatio*, "I can think of no one Objection [to eating infants], that will possibly be raised against this Proposal. . . . Therefore, let no Man talk to me of other Expedients," he goes on to list expedients like urging the Irish to buy goods from Irish as opposed to English producers (Swift 237). Providing students with Swift's pamphlet, "A Proposal for the Universal Use of Irish Manufacture," in which Swift made the argument for Irish consumption of Irish goods, allows students to compare the ironic "modest proposal" of Swift's satire to Swift's actual policy suggestions while at the same time witnessing the proposer's treatment of serious solutions as minor objections to be argued against in favor of the gruesome solution of raising human infants for food. In short, students can formally identify Swift's irony as saying what one does not mean by placing what one does mean in the *refutatio*, the part of the argument ordinarily reserved for addressing arguments against what one thinks should be the case.

Beginning with such a study of "A Modest Proposal" establishes something important: that not all irony is comic irony, or irony for which humor is a guiding rhetorical objective (even though much of today's online and television satire relies on comic irony). Establishing this is essential for distinguishing between ironic modes in eighteenth-century satire. Contrasting "A Modest Proposal" with an example of comic irony, such as Maria Edgeworth's "An Essay on the Noble Science of Self-Justification," can further clarify the distinction between irony and comic irony. Edgeworth's essay is a kind of satirical advice column for women managing household disputes with husbands who presume their wives' innate inferiority of intellect and self-control. Edgeworth writes "chiefly to married ladies" in the mode of the conduct book for instructing women on how to be good wives, but the tongue-in-cheek advice is about conquering husbands through sheer force of difficult personality and rhetorical evasiveness. "Regularly appeal to the decision of reason at the beginning of every contest," writes Edgeworth, "and deny its jurisdiction at the conclusion." Edgeworth's closing entreaty to women, "long may you prosper in the practise of an art peculiar to your sex! . . . long may your husbands rue the hour when they first made you promise '*to obey*'!," works like a punch line to a joke on husbands for thinking their wives incapable of measure and rationality. Edgeworth's gotcha moment has a comic function that Swift's gotcha—rationalizing baby eating—does not.

Beyond comic and noncomic irony, texts like Rochester's "Satyr on Charles II" offer a stark example of the roles of invective and burlesque in eighteenth-century satire. When Rochester writes of the king, "Restless he rolls about from whore to whore / A merry monarch, scandalous and poor" (Wilmot), students can get a sense of how the poem works as a sharp rebuke of the king's misplaced priorities, not as a lighthearted jab aimed at generating laughs at the king's expense. The contemptuous tone of the piece is further highlighted in Rochester's burlesque rendering of the king—his skillful effort in reducing the monarch to base human desire. The graphic image of Charles II in coitus—"Yet his dull, graceless bollocks hang an arse"—is not comic but pathetic, a vitriolic exposure of what Rochester perceived as the king's gravest inadequacies as a head of state, a tendency to put his own passions and desires above national well-being and debase the kingdom in so doing. One might further contrast this type of invective and burlesque in "Satyr on Charles II" with the function of parody in a poem such as Aphra Behn's "The Disappointment," which was initially published in 1680 as part of Rochester's *Poems on Several Occasions* and mistaken for Rochester's. However, "The Disappointment" foregrounds parody of the pastoral tradition—rather than invective or comedy—as a means of satirical commentary.

I offer these brief—and incomplete—discussions of a handful of sample texts to demonstrate how one might work through them with students to develop an example-based taxonomy of satirical modes in the period and thus to show that while comedy is frequently an important component of satire, neither comedy, nor irony, nor comic irony are synonymous with satire in the period. This conceptual framing is important for laying the groundwork for the following exercises and assignment, which are designed to help students further identify and explain both comic and noncomic elements of satire.

Exercise and Assignment

I characterize the following as reverse-engineering exercises because they prompt students to take a text apart to put it back together again and thereby to focus their thinking on how and why textual components work as they do. This reverse engineering begins with a take-home assignment and concludes with collaborative close reading in the classroom.

I typically offer the reverse-engineering assignment toward the end of a course because it builds on the conceptual framework discussed above. Throughout the course I will have encouraged students to develop a vocabulary and taxonomy for different modes or formal components of satire, deferring big-picture questions, such as in what ways satire itself is a genre or a mode, until after students have studied a multitude of satirical texts in detail. Because students have defined and discussed concepts including irony, comic irony, burlesque, invective, hyperbole, understatement, affectation, and others, they have in place the conceptual framework they need to undertake the assignment.

The assignment itself begins with a creative exercise common in the teaching of satire: I ask students to choose a satirical text from the syllabus and write their own imitation of it. I leave the imitative approach open, meaning instead of directing students to imitate any particular formal feature of their chosen text, they can choose which features stand out or which they prefer to identify as representative of the text's satirical approach. In practice this means that while some students will imitate the form of a poem or the central conceit of a prose satire ("A Modest Proposal" is a popular one), other imitations will be based on the tone or topic of the original text. I find that this freedom to choose an axis of imitation spurs students to careful close reading, because in recognizing they have to imitate the text such that I can identify what they have done as an imitation, they have incentive to be particularly observant, particularly sensitive to what their chosen text is doing and how it does it.

Once students have completed their satire imitation, their next step is to annotate it with references to the text on which the imitation is based. In the past I have used a website called *Genius*, which was designed to allow users to interpret and annotate song lyrics (the platform started out as *Rap Genius*) but which also allows users to upload their own text for public annotation; but *Google Docs* or similar software would also work for this assignment.[2] Students' annotations should name and explain the moves they made, at each turn, in imitating their primary text, again using references to the primary text to compare what they have done to what they have picked up on in the primary text. (I usually require a minimum of ten annotations, but this number may vary.) Students first copy and paste their imitation into the annotation platform, then provide annotations. Once students have completed their annotations, the result is a full online text of their imitation with their annotations embedded in each annotated line, such that one could click on the line and see the annotation. If students have done this work diligently, the assignment should reflect a detailed account of close reading in the annotations and an expression of a salient component of satire that each student has identified in the primary text and chosen to imitate and explain. If one wanted to focus this kind of assignment specifically on identifying comic strategies, one could simply direct students to reverse-engineer the comic in their imitations rather than disaggregate the various strategies present in satire.

Once students have completed the assignment—which should then be available on a collaborative text annotation platform of some kind—subsequent classes can be spent collaboratively annotating the imitations and primary texts. Instructors might assign a few of the imitations for the entire class to read in preparation for the classroom session (covering the annotated imitations in clusters over several class sessions), then allow students to work on laptops or other screen devices in groups to add their comments, questions, and observations to the author's annotations. These then become the basis for further class discussion of the primary texts and imitations. The purpose of these collaborative annotation sessions is not to have students evaluate the quality of the imitations but rather to note their observations and questions beyond the author's annotations or to demonstrate and synthesize commonalities and divergences in how students have interpreted the primary texts.

In the end, the combination of the annotated imitations and the further comments and questions generated collaboratively in small groups and in class discussion provide a retrievable record of how students reverse-engineered their primary texts and explained the features and functions of satire. They now have a detailed record of the differences between comedy and irony, burlesque and invective, as well as an account of how these modes often come together to produce multiple effects.

Notes

1. Marshall notes the critical tendency to label the period from circa 1658–1770 as "the great age of satire" and argues that nevertheless critical reception has been too narrowly focused on those texts that "have stood the test of time" (xi).

2. In the past, *Genius* staff members have worked with me to make these assignments private for students who would prefer not to have their work be accessible online.

Works Cited

Ballardie, James. "Are We Living in a Golden Age of Satire?" *BBC News*, 10 Mar. 2017, www.bbc.com/news/entertainment-arts-39217855.

Behn, Aphra. "The Disappointment." 1680. *Oroonoko, The Rover, and Other Works*, edited by Janet Todd, Penguin Books, 2003, pp. 331–35.

Dowell, Ben. "*Private Eye* Hits Highest Circulation for More Than Twenty-Five Years." *The Guardian*, 16 Feb. 2012, www.theguardian.com/media/2012/feb/16/private-eye-circulation-25-years.
Edgeworth, Maria. "An Essay on the Noble Science of Self-Justification." 1795. *A Celebration of Women Writers*, digital.library.upenn.edu/women/edgeworth/ladies/ladies.html#letter-4. Accessed 8 Dec. 2019.
Fabricant, Carole, editor. *A Modest Proposal and Other Writings*. Penguin Books, 2009.
Marshall, Ashley. *The Practice of Satire in England, 1658–1770*. Johns Hopkins UP, 2013.
Swift, Jonathan. "A Modest Proposal." 1729. Fabricant, pp. 230–39.
———. "A Proposal for the Universal Use of Irish Manufacture." 1720. Fabricant, pp. 130–37.
Wilmot, John. "Satyr on Charles II." 1673. *Jack Lynch*, jacklynch.net/Texts/charles2.html#9. Accessed 8 Dec. 2019.
Zurawik, David. "Maher, Baldwin, Oliver, Colbert: Political Satire Thrives in Trump Era." *The Baltimore Sun*, 18 Feb. 2019, www.baltimoresun.com/opinion/columnists/zurawik/bs-fe-zontv-maher-oliver-political-satire-20190218-story.html.

Deborah J. Knuth Klenck

The Sincerest—and Most Fun—Form of Flattery: Imitation as Analysis of Eighteenth-Century Comic Texts

An almost lost art, classical imitation can be reclaimed when we teach an almost lost segment of the British canon: eighteenth-century literature.[1] Creating an imitation, in a general British literature survey course or a more advanced period course, can help students appreciate and even play with rhetorical devices put to a comic purpose. Imitation can help students approach texts from a remote era with confidence and mastery.

In former decades, when I easily mustered a full roster for an intermediate course called Restoration and Eighteenth-Century Literature and Culture, I introduced imitation through a reading of Samuel Johnson's "London: A Poem" (1738), considering the Third Satire of Juvenal, the model (in Latin and in English), to enjoy the trick of Johnson's updated references to the spendthrift, scapegrace poet and soon-to-be exile Richard Savage.[2]

The contemporary undergraduate, however, is often unfamiliar with the rhetorical figures on which so much of this literature depends. I have developed a nine-page handlist of rhetorical terms divided into two sections, patterns and tropes, with recognizable illustrations of, for example, anaphora with alliteration ("No shirt, no shoes, no service" [ice-cream parlor sign]) or *reduplicatio* ("To die, to sleep. / To sleep, perchance to dream" [Shakespeare 3.1.66–67]). I hardly expect students to distinguish among all these devices, much less learn their names, but rather to page through the list to enhance their alertness to rhetorical style. Avoiding elaborate explanation, whether identifying historical or literary references or pointing out a chiasmus or an *epiphrase*, can increase students' comfort with early texts. And, besides, only a very good joke can hold up under annotation. Assigning an imitation leads students to discover and replicate rhetorical flourishes for themselves, empowering them to read more widely among eighteenth-century texts.

Of course, even with a comic writer like Jonathan Swift, one has to choose carefully. The deadpan wit of *A Tale of a Tub* may be too dry, though it certainly offers an ideal example of litotes: "Last Week I saw a Woman *flayed*, and you will hardly believe how much it altered her Person for the worse" (462). But one of Swift's birthday odes to Stella is a fun model of how to praise with faint damns:

> Stella this Day is thirty four,
> (We won't dispute a Year or more)
> However Stella, be not troubled,
> Although thy Size and Years are doubled.
> . . . .
> Oh, would it please the Gods to split
> Thy Beauty, Size, and Years, and Wit,
> No Age could furnish out a Pair
> Of Nymphs so gracefull, Wise and fair
> With half the Lustre of Your Eyes,
> With half thy Wit, thy Years and Size. ("On Stella's Birthday" 721–22)

Ted Scheinman fulfills the assignment, creating a tribute to his mother in Swiftian octosyllabics in couplet-stanzas; the last stanza ends with a very Augustan triplet:

> The finest mother e'er alive
> To help her children grow & thrive,
> To discipline but not deprive—
> Mumsy this day is fifty-five.
>
> A classy dame as e'er I saw,
> Who's read the oeuvre of Evelyn Waugh;
> She knows her wine, her scotch, her cheese—
> What's French, and what is Viennese.

> ....
> Our matriarch! Queen Bee of the hive,
> The youngest bee of fifty-five;
> (To rob Virgilian metaphor)
> The loving drones who her adore—
> Say, "Not a day past fifty-four!"

Jane Austen's *Juvenilia* offer short treats in prose, whether these are taught in a period course, a fiction survey, or an advanced Austen seminar. Dedicating to her cousin "A Collection of Letters," the thirteen-year-old novelist makes it easy to imitate the passage's sole rhetorical device, alliteration—and helpfully capitalizes the culprits:

> To Miss Cooper—
> Conscious of the Charming Character which in every Country, and every Clime in Christendom is Cried, Concerning you, With Caution and Care I Commend to your Charitable Criticism this Clever Collection of Curious Comments, which have been Carefully Culled, Collected and Classed by your Comical Cousin —The Author
> (Austen, "Collection" 190)

Slightly more sophisticated as a literary exercise is this dedication of "The Beautifull Cassandra" (a novel in twelve very short chapters) to Austen's sister, Cassandra:

> Madam:
> You are a Phoenix. Your taste is refined, your Sentiments are noble, & your Virtues innumerable. Your Person is lovely, your Figure, elegant, & your Form, magestic. Your manners are polished, your Conversation is rational & your appearance singular. . . .
> your most obedient humble Servant The Author.
> (Austen, "Beautifull Cassandra" 53)

The Latin term for this rhetorical figure is *enumeratio*—simply, "listing"—and the joke is embedding an apparently parallel but actually contradictory item in the list to taint all the rest. (True, students need to understand the meaning of "singular" to get, and imitate, the joke.) Austen herself learned from Alexander Pope's use of this device—for example, in his list of items on the thoughtless debutante Belinda's dressing table in *The Rape of the Lock*: "Puffs, Powders, Patches, Bibles, Billet-doux" (1.138). As students learn to imitate Austen, they see Austen imitating Pope: "There has been one infallible Pope in the World," Austen wrote to Cassandra in a letter dated 26 October 1813 (*Letters* 245). One benefit of having students imitate Austen's comical nonsense is to make the formidable mock-heroic of *The Rape of the Lock* less forbidding, as they consider, beyond parallel structure, why "Bibles" is in the plural.

Austen uses another trick of Pope's in "Jack and Alice," where a wealthy woman is described: "In Lady Williams every virtue met. She was a widow with a handsome Jointure and the remains of a very handsome face. Tho' Benevolent and Candid, she was Generous and sincere; Tho' Pious and Good, she was Religious and amiable, and Tho' Elegant and Agreable, she was Polished and Entertaining" (14). The false parallelism of a handsome jointure and a handsome face (requiring a definition of "jointure"), uses a kind of zeugma, placing the adjective "handsome" in two senses with disparate nouns, just as Pope's famous couplet treats the verb "to take," describing Queen Anne as presiding at Hampton Court Palace: "Here Thou Great *Anna*! whom three Realms obey / Dost sometimes Counsel take—and Sometimes *Tea*" (3.7–8). The absurd patterned phrases that follow the zeugma ("Tho' [this], [nonetheless that]") make a nice pairing because they are actual parallelisms—expressed as if they are contrasts.

An epistolary text I teach in fiction surveys or seminars is Frances Burney's *Evelina*. The refreshing naivete of the hapless, all-but-orphaned heroine who hyperbolically recounts to her guardian in the country her series of London faux pas (she calls them "disasters" [Burney 33]) resonates with undergraduates who are Evelina's age. For example, dancing at a ball with a nobleman, Evelina is accosted by a rejected partner who accuses her "of ill manners" (33):

> A confused idea now for the first time entered my head, of something I had heard of the rules of assemblies; but I was never at one before . . . and so giddy and heedless I was, that I had not once considered the impropriety of refusing one partner and afterwards accepting another. I was thunderstruck. (33)

> But, really, I think there ought to be a book, of the laws and customs *à-la-mode*, presented to all young people, upon their first introduction into public company. (83)

Students enjoy responding to the following prompt: "Write a letter in the manner of Burney, wherein you enter a new milieu (a summer job, perhaps, or a study abroad program), and confess some sort of social error, the result of your ignorance of local customs. You may invent an anecdote or tell a true story, but follow Burney's style." Students read and discuss one another's work, having fun with rhetoric.

For a 2019 seminar, Brianna Torres recounts a Burney-esque first date arranged on *Tinder*. As the young letter writer arrives at her table, a gentleman seats her:

> I asked if he would oblige me with a glass of water.
> He looked surprised and apologized, "I should have introduced myself earlier."
> I was absolutely speechless. How could I have confused him with a waiter? Certainly, he was very well dressed . . . unquestionably a man of refined manners and speech. He must have thought me most impertinent . . . an inexperienced simpleton!
> But, things are going well:
> I was quite impressed with his appreciation for the arts, and discovered that we shared a love of Cavalli's operas. I soon felt quite at ease with Hugh. . . . I was also soon growing to admire him. . . .
> I was quite uncertain as to whether he felt as I did. I then happened to recall an article from *Sparkle*,[3] titled "5 Signs That He Is Obviously into You." I could recall only four, and so I observed his physical gestures in the hope that they would reveal his interest. He was leaning close to me, so that he was sitting on the edge of his seat—*one*; he had *twice* straightened his tie—*two*; and had once fixed his hair—*three*! The fourth piece of advice, however, I was not sure how to interpret (and what was the fifth?).

Group analysis of these creations helps students find common ground with one another and with unfamiliar authors and literary styles that have become less alienating.

One of the more unwieldy texts in a fiction survey is Laurence Sterne's *Life and Opinions of Tristram Shandy*, but I keep it on the syllabus as an antinovel, a postmodern work avant la lettre—and a very funny book. Sterne can bewilder twenty-first-century students with his freewheeling—anarchic, even—meandering progress, ranging over space and time; his sprinkling of Greek epigraphs (in Greek); and his rich, self-conscious rhetoric. For example, in one of Tristram's autobiographical details—like many episodes in the novel, it takes place before his actual birth—while Mrs. Shandy is in excruciating labor pains upstairs, her husband and his brother smoke in the back parlor, discussing her preference for the skills of the local midwife versus the prestige of the visiting physician—the "man-midwife," one Dr. Slop:

> —My sister, mayhap, quoth my uncle *Toby*, does not choose to let a man come so near her ****. Make this dash, [Sterne interrupts]—'tis an Aposiopesis.—Take the dash away, and write Backside,—'tis Bawdy.—Scratch Backside out, and put in Cover'd-way [a term from Uncle Toby's hobbyhorse meaning "military fortification"]—'tis a Metaphor. (Sterne 114)

Inviting students to collaborate with Sterne breaks down their resistance. I present them with the following prompt: "Write an imitation in the manner of *Tristram Shandy* that adopts its form and diction very closely and updates all the references to the present day." Andrea Mignone Viehe-Naess takes the novel's opening as a model:

> I Wish either my father or my mother, or indeed both of them, as they were in duty both equally bound to it, had minded what they were about when they begot me; had they duly consider'd how much depended on what they were doing. . . . I am verily persuaded I should have made a quite different figure in the world, from that, in which the reader is likely to see me. (Sterne 1)

The student's imitation laments that her parents' public education has disadvantaged her—and that somehow this has also led her to choose a major that sounds embarrassing:

> I wish my parents had worked harder in high school, and perhaps put more effort into getting into an Ivy League college—they are both to blame for this lack of legacy, as both name City College as their alma mater; had they considered my future, my lack of claim to preferential admission, and taken action—I truly think that this would not only have made me a different, more successful person, but probably would have made my life a whole lot simpler. . . . If my parents had planned just a little, they would not be in the uncomfortable position of attempting to explain to all the neighbors that their beloved daughter is a geography major. But that is getting a little ahead of ourselves, and, without order, one is left wearing socks over his shoes.

For five pages, the student brings in such Sternian devices as scripting dialogue with the reader—"('Now Madame, I beg you neither to skip over nor to disregard this paragraph. What? You have skipped it already? This pains me greatly.')"—and dramatizing the miseries of daily life:

> 'Tis a pity cried my mother, returning from the supermarket, 'tis a pity she cried, putting a box of Cheerios in the cupboard as she spoke—that I had to answer she was a ********* major—the humiliation, the obligatory compliment, oh you must be so proud, must be a delight—when she's around you never need a map—

The two-paragraph conclusion reads as follows:

> It could be worse.
>   What's the capital of Montana? said my father.

Allison Walcott uses Sterne's methods to describe an extended family's annual gathering at their summer cottage. She uses footnotes to explain obscure, only-in-the-family references, including a parallel to the Shandy family scandal of Aunt Dinah, "who, about sixty years ago, was married and got with child by the coachman" (Sterne 73). A note on the elaborately drawn family tree entry, "Suzi— b. 1958," evokes the hapless Aunt Dinah:

> Suzi still waits to meet a proper suitor, or someone who meets her rather particular requirements for that position. In my drafts, I had devoted an entire chapter to her odyssey of courtship, or lack thereof, its ins, outs, ups, downs, and twirls. However, my editor came to the brilliant conclusion that said chapter was of no use. Much to his dismay, and perhaps much to your chagrin, I have included Suzi's chronicle d'amour in Αππενδιχ A ["Appendix A," attempted in Greek], leaving it as it was originally titled, CHAP. III.

After several pages, the author must stop, admitting the impossibility of her task: "To quote my father, 'It is easier to Nail Jell-O to a Tree than to try to explain anything to do with this family.'"

Working with Sterne's long text this way early in the reading (the assignment specifies that students do not need to finish the novel before attempting an imitation) makes the reading approachable and enjoyable, since students now feel as though they have a better command of Sterne's style. Sterne's sense of play becomes clear, even at noncomic moments like the sentimental episode of the death of LeFever. Such assignments can reclaim a century of literature as accessible subject matter while fostering delight in language and literary style—without killing any jokes in the process. Comedy, in short, can lead students to take the eighteenth century seriously.

Notes

1. In a recent review essay, the late James A. Winn refers to the "sad shrinkage of this once-proud field of study": "our departments [have] jettisoned period requirements and comprehensive examinations," "departing colleagues [have not been] replaced," and so on (163). In 2002 Stanley J. Solomon addressed this problem in "Parting from Dr. Johnson": "The eighteenth century, after all, ha[s] become increasingly an area of the esoteric and of generally out-of-fashion elegant writing; it ha[s] become historically obscure and . . . peripheral to the education even of English majors. . . . It ha[s] become unmodern" (130).

2. When I can fit it into the syllabus, I have also assigned Johnson's short biography of Savage, which the English painter Joshua Reynolds famously could not put down once he had opened it (Boswell 121).

3. *Sparkle* is a fictitious e-zine offering beauty tips and relationship advice.

Works Cited

Austen, Jane. "The Beautifull Cassandra." Austen, *Juvenilia*, pp. 53–56.
———. "A Collection of Letters." Austen, *Juvenilia*, pp. 190–214.
———. "Jack and Alice." Circa 1786. Austen, *Juvenilia*, pp. 13–32.
———. *Juvenilia*. Edited by Peter Sabor, Cambridge UP, 2006.
———. *Letters*. Edited by Dierdre Le Faye, 3rd ed., Oxford UP, 1995.
Boswell, James. *Life of Johnson*. Edited by R. W. Chapman, Oxford UP, 1953.
Burney, Frances. *Evelina*. 1778. Edited by Edward A. Bloom, Oxford UP, 1968.
Johnson, Samuel. "The Life of Mr. Richard Savage." 1744. *Lives of the Poets*, vol. 2, Oxford UP, 1952, pp. 93–183.
Pope, Alexander. *The Rape of the Lock: An Heroi-Comical Poem in Five Canto's*. 1712. Edited by John Butt, Yale UP, 1963.
Shakespeare, William. *Hamlet. The Norton Shakespeare*, edited by Stephen Greenblatt, 2nd ed., W. W. Norton, 2008.
Solomon, Stanley J. "Parting from Dr. Johnson." *Profession*, 2002, pp. 130–39.
Sterne, Laurence. *The Life and Opinions of Tristram Shandy, Gentleman*. Edited by Melvyn New and Joan New, vol. 1, UP of Florida, 1978.
Swift, Jonathan. "On Stella's Birthday." Circa 1718. *The Poems of Jonathan Swift*, edited by Harold Williams, vol. 2, Oxford UP, 1937, pp. 721–22.
———. *A Tale of a Tub*. 1704. *British Literature, 1640–1789: An Anthology*, edited by Robert Demaria, Jr., 3rd ed., Blackwell Publishing, 2008, pp. 457–527.
Winn, James A. Review of *The Oxford Handbook of British Poetry, 1660–1800*, edited by Jack Lynch. *Scriblerian*, vol. 51, no. 2, spring 2019, pp. 162–66.

Helena Gurfinkel

The Importance of Failing at Teaching
The Importance of Being Earnest

According to Kimberly J. Stern, "[T]here are few things that teach so well in the undergraduate classroom as Wilde texts" (140). Such has certainly not been my experience. Reading selection is crucial. *The Picture of Dorian Gray* is a bildungsroman that appeals to a young person navigating identity in college. The novel's gothic characteristics have also helped me get students interested. The appearance of Dorian Gray in the 2003 film *The League of Extraordinary Gentlemen* made him a more immediately comprehensible and less enigmatic character.

With their seeming simplicity of style and profoundly adult themes, Wilde's fairy tales, which I have also taught on two or three occasions, straddle the same boundary that young adult novels do today. For this reason, the tales have been popular among my students, though a few have commented on their unwelcome pessimism. Students marvel at the beauty of Wilde's *Ballad of Reading Gaol*. The straightforward moral stance and popular form make the poem enjoyable and memorable. Religious themes, particularly absolution and redemption, garner appreciation among the student body that I teach.

But when I teach Wilde's 1895 masterpiece, *The Importance of Being Earnest*, I fail perennially to infect students with my enthusiasm for the play.

This essay discusses the institutional contexts in which I teach *Earnest* as well as the classroom strategies I employ. It also explains, if not justifies, my failure as an homage to Wilde's resistance to conventional learning. It does so by using the theoretical paradigm of queer pedagogy anticipated by Wilde.

Institutional Contexts

My university is a midsize public institution that serves primarily the surrounding region. English faculty members teach both majors and general education courses; a few contribute to our graduate curriculum. Many of our students are first-generation college students, and many work while earning their degrees.

I have taught *Earnest* in a variety of courses. Most recently, I used it as an example of a comedy in Introduction to Literature, a large, general education elective. While generally astute and interested in literature, students were either unable or reluctant to understand the plot twists. The reaction of students in another course, titled An Introduction to Literary Study, has been similar. The course is an introduction to the English major and minor and is a requirement of both. Unlike Introduction to Literature, it aims to teach analytical and critical approaches to literature specific to the English major, from the practices of close reading to a smattering of theoretical approaches for beginners. In this course, too, students have trouble following the plot and considering the thematics of gender and class.

The Importance of Being Modern: Oscar Wilde and Henry James is an upper-level seminar that gives advanced seniors and some graduate students a comparative overview of the two writers. In this course, a strategic biographical approach helps students navigate the primary texts. In small discussion-based master's courses that focus on late Victorian British literature and culture, some students may recognize the virtuoso humor and plotting of *Earnest*, but most dismiss them as superficial—that is, they take Wilde's definition of the play (in its subtitle) as "A Trivial Comedy for Serious People" at face value.

Pedagogical Strategies

I begin by discussing my more efficacious classroom strategies. Since Wilde's paradoxical style and the relative complexity of the play's plot tend to puzzle students, a biographical approach serves to untangle the confusion

(Gurfinkel). Melissa Knox notes that "biography is a particularly fruitful method" for making Wilde's oeuvre accessible to students, adding that "Wilde's work is an important entry point to his life, while for many other writers it is the other way around" (108). When discussing the double lives of John Worthing and Algernon Moncrieff, the hapless heroes of the play, or the sexually suggestive concept of "Bunburying" (Wilde, *Importance* 672), it is worth pointing out that Wilde, at the time when he was writing the play, was cohabiting, virtually openly, with Lord Alfred Douglas, thereby dangerously resisting the conventions of heterosexual married life. Inserting biography certainly clarifies central thematic concerns for students. It helps them engage with what Sos Eltis calls "Wilde's ubiquitous attacks on puritanism and the danger of a narrowly absolute morality" (101), rethink the traditional heterosexual marriage plot of New Comedy, and ponder the ways in which the play subverts it.

In some upper-level courses, such discussion enables me to delve into the origins of the marriage plot in Greek New Comedy, the contemporary Hollywood iterations of this plot, and its cultural rather than natural antecedents.

Related to the facts of Wilde's biography are the issues of feminism and gender roles. In all courses, I briefly introduce visuals pertaining to the new woman. I mention Wilde's feminism, his support of women artists, and his editorship—and renaming—of *The Woman's World*. Conversations about feminism and gender roles are exciting to students because of the excellent work of our women's studies program and certainly also because of the abiding presence of these issues in public conversations and popular culture. I regularly assign papers on gender and power in *Earnest* and am often able to elicit complex insights into gender role reversals cleverly served up by the play.

Sociopolitical and biographical approaches are familiar to students, while the more abstract philosophical ideas that the play introduces are often difficult to comprehend. I start any discussion with Wilde's "Phrases and Philosophies for the Use of the Young" and the preface to *The Picture of Dorian Gray*. Appealing to students' sense of rebelliousness, these aphorisms initially sow confusion but then lead to a variety of realizations about identity, the goals of art and artistic practices, and a young person's relationship to authority, including that of a teacher. Those students who absorb the paradoxes enthusiastically find *Earnest* a congenial experience.

The questions of identity and its elusive and constructed quality, as portrayed in the play, speak to Wilde's paradoxes. The confusion of names and the arbitrariness of bloodlines and family ties can inspire students to discuss how identity is formed in, and by, their contemporary society. Feeding into the discussion of identity formation is a conversation about the uses of social media. I ask students to imagine Cecily Cardew's *Facebook* page, on which she can easily turn relationships that are figments of her imagination into (virtual) reality. Similarly, social media would greatly enhance the adventure of Bunburying by enabling Jack and Algernon to assume false (or real?) identities and locations. The second time I taught the play, I asked students to invent such social media accounts and to post on behalf of the play's characters. The deployment of social media brings home to students Wilde's sophisticated play of signification and selfhood. It may also defamiliarize the experience of marriage and courtship, because today, relationships frequently play themselves out online and become dependent on the follower definitions rather than on a stable, predetermined truth or reality.

Pedagogical Contrariness

I have identified two potentially productive obstacles to teaching *Earnest*. Students find the play problematic in two ways: to them, it is elitist and teaches no moral lesson, at least not in the way they are accustomed to. A biographical approach portrays Wilde as a fighter for social progress: a gay rights icon, a protofeminist, a defender of Irish independence, an author of thoughtful and original reflections on class, poverty, and social justice. However, the adventures of aristocrats fail to cohere, in the minds of first-generation college students burdened with unrelenting debt, into a clear statement on the imperfections of society. Likewise, no moral lesson appears at the end of the play: the characters remain "trivial." Wilde's refusal of the high moral tone, though ostensibly appealing to young audiences, actually alienates them. The teacher's task, then, is to explain that wit as well as resistance to moral messaging are effective means of social critique. Paradoxically, students' puzzlement with the play is precisely the positive pedagogical outcome.

Stern ascribes to Wilde "a pedagogical style that—in its resistance to utility, certitude, and intellectual stasis—both evokes and clarifies the philosophical investments of the Aesthetic Movement" (129). "[R]esistance to utility [and] certitude" characterize not only what Stern calls "aesthetic pedagogy" but also queer pedagogy.[1] Linda Dowling calls the homoerotic pedagogy that Wilde experienced at Oxford "the Socratic eros" and "a pure form of intellectual . . . regeneration" (80). Today's queer pedagogy retains the ethos of liberalism and puts an even greater emphasis on resisting conventional ways of knowing.

Jes Battis describes queer pedagogy as "a kind of productive resistance, a savage joy" (xxii). Kevin Ohi views it as "increasing lucidity about pedagogical bafflement and betrayal—about, in some ways, the obscurity of insight, realization, and learning" (154). Lee Edelman argues that "queerness... maintains a persistently negative link to the logic of education. Like poetry in W. H. Auden's well-known phrase, queerness makes *nothing* happen; it *incises* that nothing in reality with an acid's caustic bite" (125). Wilde's unteachable play prods the instructor to adapt the radical pedagogy of teaching nothing or, at least, of not striving to produce the usual learning outcomes and skills grounded in rules and epistemological certainty. The goal is to liberate students' creativity and thought instead of shortchanging or inhibiting it. Not getting *Earnest* may just be the queerest, and the best, result.

The play itself is an exercise in failed pedagogy, highlighting the triumph of experience over cramming. Teachers probably identify with Miss Prism's earnest attempts to instruct Cecily: "Your German grammar is on the table. . . . We will repeat yesterday's lesson. . . . Cecily, you will read your *Political Economy* in my absence. The chapter on the Fall of the Rupee you may omit. It is somewhat too sensational" (Wilde, *Importance* 684–86). Cecily, however, prefers her own highly subjective diary that creates, rather than records, experience by inventing dates, events, identities, and relationships: "You need hardly remind me of that, Ernest. I remember only too well that I was forced to write the letters for you" (695). We should not balk at Cecily's eagerness to invent.

Instead, we should approach teaching *Earnest* with the confident insouciance of Lady Bracknell. Her conversation with Jack Worthing about his prospective marriage to her daughter, Gwendolen, includes the following pedagogical gems: "I have always been of opinion that a man who desires to get married should know either everything or nothing. Which do you know?" (Wilde, *Importance* 677). After Jack confesses to knowing nothing, his future mother-in-law opines, "I am pleased to hear that. I do not approve of anything that tampers with natural ignorance. Ignorance is like a delicate, exotic fruit; touch it and the bloom is gone. . . . Fortunately, in England . . . education produces no effect whatsoever. If it did, it would prove a serious danger to the upper classes" (677–78). Lady Bracknell's tirade illustrates Wilde's consistent critique of the rigid Victorian class hierarchy. But there is another way to look at her pedagogy: instead of worrying, as Miss Prism does, that Cecily learns nothing, Lady Bracknell rejoices that Jack knows nothing. If students do not learn that the play is about a specific historic event, social movement, or genre but instead continue to puzzle out the matters of identity or paradox, we may have failed with respect to top-down learning outcomes or high-school-style moral lessons. But we may have succeeded in the only way it is possible to succeed with *Earnest*.

Pedagogical Suggestions

The pedagogical necessity to fail at teaching *Earnest* with joy and conviction is something of a theoretical idea. What are the practical classroom suggestions? First, I would not dispense with short lectures and visuals explaining the sociohistorical background of the play. Through those, students can learn about the crucial issues of class, gender, sexuality, and education in late Victorian England. They can draw parallels between their own society and Wilde's and discover similarities or differences.

The play's focus on gender provides fertile ground for discussion. Students are usually interested in discussing the reversal of gender roles in the play, whereby the presumably quiet and submissive Victorian women are socially powerful and are in charge of assigning identities, while the male characters ultimately submit to the shackles of heterosexual marriage and class hierarchy. This conversation may lead students to ponder contemporary changes in gender roles.

Introducing visual materials normally helps students comprehend the sociohistorical underpinnings of a nineteenth-century text. However, I know of no cinematic text that would be helpful in this instance. Anthony Asquith's 1952 film, though brilliant, is far too distant from today's college students, while Oliver Parker's 2002 film, though visually more appealing, strays too far from the original (*Importance* [Asquith]; *Importance* [Parker]). However, if a class can attend a theatrical production of the play, it may come alive to students in a way that is not possible on the screen. Several years ago, I took a section of majors and minors to see a successful student production. Seeing a diverse group of peers performing the play drew the class closer to it and its ostensibly snobbish themes. A stage production may also help students follow the plot. Here I would also reiterate the potential benefits of a social media assignment that would allow students to consider the notion of a socially constructed identity and the power of an individual to construct their own identity.

As the first classroom activity after students have finished reading the play, simple plot summaries can be productive. Open-ended in-class or take-home assignments will also get both undergraduate and graduate students thinking without the need to seek definitive answers. Prompts may be as simple as the following: What confuses you the most about the play, and why? What draws you to the play, and what puts you off? Is the play flippant and light, or do you see tragedy or sadness behind the comedy? Does the play speak to your life in any way? Such questions hold no expectations. As students express their feelings and ideas, they may come up with an intellectual or affective thread that leads to their own productive misunderstanding. A generation of risk-averse and financially burdened students may join their teachers, and even Oscar Wilde himself, in allowing for a creative void when it comes to education. As I continue to teach the play, I hope to keep failing.

Note

1. A strong link exists between queerness and aestheticism not only philosophically but also in terms of the participation of queer and gender nonconforming artists in the Aesthetic movement.

Works Cited

Battis, Jes. "Homofiles: Desire, Praxis and Pedagogy." *Theory, Sexuality, and Graduate Studies*, edited by Battis, Lexington Books, 2011, pp. vii–xxiv.
Dowling, Linda. *Hellenism and Homosexuality in Victorian Oxford*. Cornell UP, 1997.
Edelman, Lee. "Learning Nothing: *Bad Education*." *Differences*, vol. 28, no. 1, 2017, pp. 124–73.
Eltis, Sos. "An Introductory Approach to Teaching Wilde's Comedies." Smith, pp. 100–07.
Gurfinkel, Helena. "Biography Is the New Queer: Teaching Oscar Wilde and Henry James." *Teaching LGBTQ Literatures: Concepts, Methods, Curricula*, edited by Will Banks and John Pruitt, Peter Lang, 2018, pp. 85–98.
The Importance of Being Earnest. Directed by Anthony Asquith, Javelin Films, 1952.
The Importance of Being Earnest. Directed by Oliver Parker, Lionsgate, 2002.
Knox, Melissa. "A Method for Using Biography in the Teaching of Oscar Wilde's Comedies." Smith, pp. 108–16.
Ohi, Kevin. *Henry James and the Queerness of Style*. U of Minnesota P, 2011.
Smith, Philip E., II, editor. *Approaches to Teaching the Works of Oscar Wilde*. Modern Language Association of America, 2008.

Stern, Kimberly J. "At Wit's End: Oscar Wilde's Aesthetic Pedagogy." *Nineteenth-Century Studies*, vol. 28, no. 1, 2018, pp. 127–45.
Wilde, Oscar. *The Ballad of Reading Gaol. Collected Works of Oscar Wilde*, Wordsworth Editions, 1997, pp. 891–909.
———. *The Importance of Being Earnest*. Wilde, *Collected Works*, pp. 663–716.
———. "The Phrases and Philosophies for the Use of the Young." *Oscar Wilde: Plays, Prose and Poems*, Black Cat, 1989, pp. 418–19.
———. *The Picture of Dorian Gray*. Wilde, *Collected Works*, pp. 1–154.

David Ritchie

How to Laugh for the Future

One might argue that today any comedy in a classroom should be preceded by a trigger warning, for comedy has a close association with woe. Web pages are devoted to Robin Williams, the pain behind the smile. No need to multiply examples. Why, in these fraught times, consider comedy in the classroom at all? Maybe we'd all be better off with something as harmless as . . . whatever in literature, or in the world, is harmless.

But laughter enlivens a space. I'd argue that it can be invaluable in many ways as an aid to learning, but it must be kind laughter. In today's classrooms we respect and value difference. Anyone who has tried to paint a portrait will explain that the process reveals not only the subject but us, humans, for we are skulls beneath a skin. The difference between a beaming smile and a shy one? Very, very small rearrangements of value, tone, and line. How to accommodate difference and comedy in the same space? My thesis is that to make progress we need mistakes to be acknowledged, and we need to treat one another more decently. And we must smile and laugh.

Who am I to write this? Someone who took up painting to learn seeing and writing for the theater in order to deepen my understanding of history. I write comedies and paint with bold colors. As a historian I am fluent in tragedy, but when I wrote for the stage about the First World War, and painted it, there was some joy mixed in. We humans are a rotten lot, blind as a skull sometimes, but we have jaws that allow us to laugh.

What does "kind laughter" mean? The Italian Pulcinella and the British puppet Punch have long noses and a long history of amusing audiences. Short noses have been funny too. Evelyn Waugh wrote of Millicent Blade's nose, "[I]t was not a nose to appeal to painters, for it was far too small and quite without shape, a mere dab of putty without apparent bone structure; a nose which made it impossible for its wearer to be haughty or imposing or astute" (30). But humor about noses in today's classroom? No. Appearances are not funny. (I wonder how I'd handle Malvolio's cross-gartering.)

A small sample of other worries. In a play about Winston Churchill and Dwight D. Eisenhower spending a day together in old age, I had Churchill duck behind a screen to answer a call of nature. Eisenhower was tasked with pouring champagne, Churchill's favorite Pol Roger. Churchill shouts across, "I don't suppose you could pour . . . somehow loudly?" The audience laughed, but now I wonder, Was this reinforcing stereotypes of elderly people?

When Alexander McCall Smith's characters refer to themselves as "traditionally built," should we think of this as body affirmation, or as disguised body-shaming (3)? One more example: the British comedian Jen Ives dressed in mountaineering gear to lead a journey up "Peak Trans" (Marshall). She compared trans women to spiders, "hairy beings who set traps and are generally more scared of you than you are of us" (qtd. in Marshall). Transgender people and cisgender people may experience Ives's joke differently.

To restate the obvious: humor is risky. So what do I propose? When deciding whether I want to use a text in class—and here I define text to include performances—in the past I have asked if we were going to be laughing with or laughing at. This was never a clear divide. We laugh at Malvolio and the Imaginary Invalid. But do we laugh at or with Walter Mitty, or C. Northcote Parkinson's people deciding whether a new bicycle shed is a worthy investment? Are people laughing at or with the hapless Mr. Bean?

It may be that my distinction is no longer helpful. So now what? We should consider what is foreign, beginning with that lovely line of Laurence Sterne at the outset of *A Sentimental Journey*: "'They order,' said I, 'this matter better in France.'"

L. P. Hartley's career was splendidly strange. Named not exactly after but with a nod to the father of Virginia Woolf (who was Leslie Stephen), Leslie Poles Hartley was a Leaf Scholar at Harrow School. "He studied leaves?" you ask. No, the scholarship was named after a banker, classical scholar, and psychical researcher (try finding that combination in a biographical entry today), Sir Walter Leaf.[1]

Hartley, however, is who we have in view here. After being conscripted out of Balliol College in 1916, he did not see active service in the First World War. The reason was a weak heart. He edited the *Oxford Outlook*; published some poetry, essays, criticism, and short stories; and then in 1925 he achieved neither fame nor fortune by writing a novella, *Simonetta Perkins*, which dramatized changes of mind about sexuality. Hartley then wrote and rewrote his second novel over two decades before it was published under the title *The Shrimp and the Anemone*. If this were the whole story we might know Hartley only through Virginia Woolf's diary, as "a dull fat man" (Tóibín vii), or by cutting comments recorded in Colm Tóibín's fine introduction to the New York Review Books edition of *The Go-Between*. But in 1952 Hartley began that novel, and it was published only five months later to great acclaim. There have since been two movies. The book opens with the now famous line, "The past is a foreign country; they do things differently there" (Hartley 17).

Hartley's line could be taken as encouragement to laugh at people rather than with them. I repeat, this is not what I encourage. When we smile over how strange the past is, how like a foreign country it is, we do harm in the classroom if we try to separate ourselves from those "foreigners," those who lived before us. Among its other purposes, humor can be used in the classroom to reinforce sensitivity to nuance and to broaden our sense of complexity. We should laugh because we are open to difference, not to separate ourselves from otherness.

I grew up in the past. My views were formed by radio, television, and schooling in the suburbs of London. I listened to *I'm Sorry I'll Read That Again* and *The Goon Show*; I watched *The Goodies*, *Monty Python*, and *Not the Nine O'Clock News*. I studied comedy with great care and attention, in the sure and certain knowledge that one day I'd either do stand-up or be a dairy farmer (we vacationed on a dairy farm). All was not sweetness and light—at school there was, of course, prejudice.

But I did not study nationalist history, parodied in *1066 and All That* (Sellar and Yeatman). Because we were becoming Europeans, for the International Baccalaureate we studied double foreignness—the past of foreigners, with a few British people wandering among them. I read and tried to understand Japanese cabinet documents as evidence of how the Greater East Asia Co-Prosperity Sphere came to be. Later, during a year abroad from the University of Sussex, I interviewed veterans of the French Resistance. They joked about combat: "It wasn't cabbages they were throwing at us."

People were funny, by which I mean the bus conductor, and the woman in the greengrocer who warned you not to squeeze the fruit. Banter everywhere. If you were slow to leave the soccer field when substituted, there'd be a voice saying, "I've seen milk go off quicker than that."

Yes, when you open the *Penguin Book of Modern Humour* from that era you find a bunch of white men and V. S. Naipaul. Absolutely wrong. What we need to recover, I argue, is not the content of that era but maybe some of the tone.

It won't be easy, laughing for the future. On a transatlantic flight I stared at the little icon of a plane crossing the ocean and remembered teaching a different class, one on the history of humor. My syllabus laid out a path from Shakespeare to the present. At one point we read nineteenth-century newspapers, the real McCoy, bought for cheap on *eBay*. Students learned that American newspapers published wit. From the *Saturday Evening Post* of 22 January 1859: "What is the difference between a seamstress and a groom? One mends the tear, while the other tends the mare" ("Conundrum").

My memory is that students couldn't see how this example was in any way funny. Too foreign. Too much the past. I sometimes find myself in the same spot. On a different plane I had tried to read Kingsley Amis's *Lucky Jim*. My edition began with an introductory essay by David Lodge. Because I gave the book away I can now only paraphrase, but it was absolutely clear that Lodge judged Amis the funniest of writers and that he found in this novel inspiration for his own campus novels. I like Lodge. And Malcom Bradbury. But I did not enjoy Jane Smiley, and Kingsley Amis raised not even a smile. Thus, you can show anyone what the past found funny and how humor worked, but all of us at one time or another will side with Queen Victoria: "We are not amused" (Fullerton).

So? On yet another plane, I found my brain saying, "Dying is easy; comedy is hard," and wondered why. I think I'd seen on a monitor in the airport that Clive James had died. I'd tried his prose on students, with poor results. I wondered as I buckled up whether his poems would work. Were they funny? I pulled from my backpack the recently acquired *Collected Poems* and opened at random to the following passage:

> Where do bus vandals get their diamond pens
> That fill each upstairs window with a cloud
> Of shuffled etchings? Patience does them proud.
> Think of Spinoza when he ground a lens. (James 235)

What could I teach from that? To think hard about the concept of the thesis statement. Here the author begins with an interesting question, indicates a position he is likely to take, gestures toward the evidence but says absolutely nothing about what he intends to prove or how he is going to compare and contrast. Let the students then object that the opening of a poem is not like the opening of an essay and we could be off on a useful journey.

Now, though, I'd say something about voice and tone. James was enjoying the pleasure of a moan: "Where *do* bus vandals get their diamond pens"? The poem carries over to a second page. When I reached the finish, I was already thinking I'd ask students not to turn the page quickly. We could pause to hazard or guess what James would say. Where might bus vandals carry us?

After a truncated history of innovative painting technique and of daubs in unusual locations, we get the following lines: ". . . All those initials on the glass / Remind you, as you clutch your Freedom Pass, / It's a long journey from the wilderness" (James 236). Surely students might smile with James at the idea of sitting in a bus or a plane, which restricts your own motion and allows you, in possession of a ticket, or "Freedom Pass," to arrive somewhere new both physically and intellectually? Then I'd have to explain how attitudes toward wilderness have changed. But the humor comes from the contrast between the highfalutin vocabulary—Churchill and others suffering "wilderness years"—and you or me sitting on a bus, looking at scratched glass and thinking on tensions between foreign behavior and familiar circumstance.

So how to distinguish good, tonally warm banter? Tough call. "Yes," he said in class, "generally we are persuaded by the weight of evidence, but Henry VIII's fifth wife would be forgiven for thinking, towards the end there, that four data points sufficed." I get that the drawback is compression and expectation of shared understandings. Eddie Izzard, on imperialism: "Do you have a flag? No flag, no country" (*Dress to Kill* 22:00). Funny, but only when you know what she's talking about.

So where does this leave us? Maybe encouraging listening yet more closely? "It is a short hole, and a full mashie will take you nicely on to the green, providing you can carry the river that frolics just beyond the tee and seems to plead with you to throw it a ball to play with" (Wodehouse, "Rodney" 266–67). Too foreign for today's students, I think. But this might work: "Into the face of the young man who sat on the terrace of the Hotel *Magnifique* at Cannes there had crept a look of furtive shame, the shifty hangdog look which announces that an Englishman is about to speak French" (Wodehouse, *Luck* 3). I have had success with P. G. Wodehouse's short story "Jeeves and the Greasy Bird." At age eighty-four Wodehouse was not in what he would call "mid-season form" ("Woman" 44), but in this story Wodehouse perfectly illustrates what happens when metaphors are jammed together like patrons of the subway: "I should imagine that it has often been said of Bertram Wooster that when he sets his hand to the plough he does not readily sheathe the sword" ("Jeeves" 27); "I suppose I've become so used to having Jeeves wave his magic wand and knock the stuffing out of the stickiest crises that I expect him to produce something brilliant from the hat every time" (49); "'Heaven help the tarpon that tries to pit its feeble cunning against you Jeeves,' I said. 'Its efforts will be bootless'" (55). And one for the road: "Normally the old relative is as genial a soul as ever downed a veal cutlet, but she's apt to get hot under the collar when thwarted, and in the course of the recent meal, as we have seen, I had been compelled to thwart her like a ton of bricks" (19–20). Though mixing metaphors is not, I would argue, as clearly and evidently funny as it was when these passages were written, the words have not lost all power to amuse, and they demonstrate what not to do.

How to know when something's working? At the end of my freshman writing class, I have experimented with several exit exercises. We came up with describing the class in metaphorical terms: "It was like being a frog in warming water," said one student. "It was like an estuary, lots of branches," said another. I think I'd describe these as a kind of bantering, indicative of relaxed but attentive learning. We tried drawing students' experiences of the class. Holding up his response, one student said (I'm paraphrasing), "I'm not funny and I don't know how to be funny, so I drew all the reasons why I'm late for class. Here's me forgetting my keys, and then my text, and then my cane." The class laughed *with* him, and I believe he saw at that moment how wrong his assessment was; he was capable of being funny, which is, I'd argue, a nice discovery at the end of the first semester of college.

My father used to say, "Il a des idées au dessus de sa gare," which he thought translated as "He has ideas above his station." It doesn't. But it's true that I do have such ideas; I am ambitious for humanity. Firesign Theatre's fourth comedy record was titled *I Think We're All Bozos on This Bus*. In my view we're all foreigners on this bus. And, so, we must risk laughter.

Note

1. To the contemporary eye, Leaf's career was as fantastic as that of Edward Bulwer-Lytton. No, Bulwer-Lytton did not just write the sentence that gave rise to the bad writing competition, but it's absolutely the case that he turned down an offer to be king of Greece.

Works Cited

"Conundrum." *The Saturday Evening Post*, 22 Jan. 1859, p. 8.
Dress to Kill. Directed by Lawrence Jordan, Epitaph, 2002. DVD.
Fullerton, Huw. "Did Queen Victoria Really Say, 'We Are Not Amused?'" *Radio Times*, 4 July 2018, www.radiotimes.com/news/2018-07-04/did-queen-victoria-really-say-we-are-not-amused/.
Hartley, L. P. *The Go-Between*. New York Review Books, 2002.
James, Clive. "Diamond Pens of the Bus Vandals." *Collected Poems, 1958–2015*, by James, Liveright, 2016, pp. 235–36.
Marshall, Alex. "Britain's Transgender Stand-Ups Find Comedy in a Hostile Climate." *The New York Times*, 26 Feb. 2021, www.nytimes.com/2021/02/26/arts/transgender-comedy-uk.html.
McCall Smith, Alexander. *Tea Time for the Traditionally Built*. Pantheon Books, 2009.
Sellar, W. C., and R. J. Yeatman. *1066 and All That: A Memorable History of England—Comprising All the Parts You Can Remember including One Hundred and Three Good Things, Five Bad Kings, and Two Genuine Dates*. Dutton, 1931.
Sterne, Laurence. *A Sentimental Journey through France and Italy*. 1768. *Project Gutenberg*, gutenberg.org/ebooks/804.
Tóibín, Colm. Introduction. Hartley, pp. v–xiii.
Waugh, Evelyn. Work Suspended *and Other Stories*. Penguin Books, 1951.
Wodehouse, P. G. *The Golf Omnibus*. Simon and Schuster, 1973.
———. "Jeeves and the Greasy Bird." *Plum Pie*, by Wodehouse, Simon and Schuster, 1966, pp. 9–55.
———. *The Luck of the Bodkins*. Triangle Books, 1938.
———. "Rodney Fails to Qualify." Wodehouse, *Golf Omnibus*, pp. 255–71.
———. "A Woman Is Only a Woman." Wodehouse, *Golf Omnibus*, pp. 37–50.

Part III

Resources

General

Berlant, Lauren, and Sianne Ngai, editors. *Comedy, an Issue*. Special issue of *Critical Inquiry*, vol. 43, no. 2, winter 2017, www.journals.uchicago.edu/toc/ci/2017/43/2.

> This special issue of *Critical Inquiry* is a challenging, heady collection of essays. Berlant and Ngai's introduction, "Comedy Has Issues," is especially useful in its discussion of how comedy can occasion aesthetic judgments and how comedy is not reducible to commercial entertainment even when it is obviously a commodity.

Bevis, Matthew. *Comedy: A Very Short Introduction*. Oxford UP, 2013.

> This brief but lively introduction is well suited to a class focused on comedy, introducing common theories of comedy and some history of the development of comedy. Students in the United States may be unfamiliar with examples drawn from British popular culture, but they should have no problem understanding the larger concepts they illustrate.

Boyle, Kirk, editor. *The Rhetoric of Humor*. Bedford / St. Martin's, 2017.

> Organized around Kenneth Burke's pentad, this reader introduces students to classic and contemporary arguments about comedy as well as comic arguments.

Carr, Jimmy, and Lucy Greeves. *Only Joking: What's So Funny about Making People Laugh?* Gotham Books, 2006.

> Carr and Greeves take a lighthearted and accessible approach to exploring humor theories and how comedy works in social settings, including a vast array of jokes along the way. Students in the United States may be unfamiliar with references to British popular culture.

Diogenes, Marvin, editor. *Laughing Matters*. Pearson Longman, 2009.

> This accessible reader offers a variety of theoretical essays on comedy alongside historical and contemporary examples.

Goebel, Bruce A. *Humor Writing: Activities for the English Classroom*. National Council of Teachers of English, 2011.

> This resource contains many student-friendly definitions and examples to help students new to the study of the comic get the basics. Many of the activities are workable not just in a K–12 classroom but also in a college classroom.

Greenberg, Jonathan. *The Cambridge Introduction to Satire*. Cambridge UP, 2019.

This overview of satire provides an efficient history of satire as a genre and a mode. Greenberg does an especially good job of weaving together literary history and the history of criticism.

Hokenson, Jan Walsh. *The Idea of Comedy: History, Theory, Critique*. Fairleigh Dickinson UP, 2006.

A comprehensive survey of comedy history and theory with special attention to the social functions of comedy.

Weitz, Eric. *The Cambridge Introduction to Comedy*. Cambridge UP, 2009.

This is an excellent, clearly structured introductory survey of both the theory and practice of comedy. Written from a performance perspective, it not only addresses the cultural uses of the genre and its characteristic thematic concerns but also, more importantly, attends to comedy's formal features and the way these are used to engage with the audience.

Theory

Attardo, Salvatore, and Victor Raskin. *The General Theory of Verbal Humor*. Mouton de Gruyter, 1993.

Among the premiere studies of humor theory, this book provides an analysis of the linguistic and contextual properties of the joke molecule, introducing incongruity as the foundational element for the construction of humor.

Critchley, Simon. *On Humour*. Routledge, 2002.

Critchley playfully introduces humor theories, social functions of humor, and connections between comedy and the metaphysical.

Ermida, Isabel. *The Language of Comic Narratives: Humor Construction in Short Stories*. Mouton de Gruyter, 2008.

This formative book presents an analysis of how the metatexts of a comic narrative are embedded in literary theory.

Gruner, Charles R. *The Game of Humor: A Comprehensive Theory of Why We Laugh*. Transaction Publishers, 1997.

Gruner examines playful aspects of humor, arguing that it is a game with winners and losers.

McGowan, Todd. *Only a Joke Can Save Us: A Theory of Comedy*. Northwestern UP, 2017.

This clear, logical, neat argument draws on many theories of comedy to attempt a new universalizing theory. McGowan considers connections between comedy and tragedy, pathos, and philosophy.

McGraw, A. Peter, and Caleb Warren. "Benign Violations: Making Immoral Behavior Funny." *Psychological Science*, vol. 21, no. 8, 2010, pp. 1141–49, https://doi.org/10.1177/0956797610376073.
    McGraw and Warren's article is a brief but cogent explanation of the benign violation theory.

McGraw, Peter, and Joel Warner. *The Humor Code: A Global Search for What Makes Things Funny*. Simon and Schuster, 2015.
    The first chapter of McGraw and Warner's book (1–15) contains an explanation of the benign violation theory aimed at a popular audience. Pairing McGraw and Warren's article with this book chapter can serve as an exercise in teaching students how to read a scholarly article and discussing the influence of audience and purpose on style and substance.

O'Shannon, Dan. *What Are You Laughing At? A Comprehensive Guide to the Comedic Event*. Bloomsbury, 2012.
    This highly accessible examination of elements contributing to a joke's funniness considers many reception factors, joke triggers, and enhancers.

Romanska, Magda, and Alan Ackerman, editors. *Reader in Comedy: An Anthology of Theory and Criticism*. Bloomsbury, 2017.
    Selections are brief but to the point; introductory material is thorough.

Shakespeare

Evans, Bertrand. *Shakespeare's Comedies*. 1960. Oxford UP, 1967.
    Evans's comprehensive study of Shakespeare's comedies presents insightful close readings based on the observation that comic effect is the result of divergent levels of informedness on the part of characters and audience. What matters most in these plays, according to Evans, is the arrangement and release of information, not their manifest content.

Gilbert, Miriam. "Teaching Shakespeare through Performance." *Shakespeare Quarterly*, vol. 35, no. 5, 1984, pp. 601–08.
    This article cogently explains the pedagogical ends to which in-class performance can be put. As Gilbert writes, "Performance-based teaching arises out of the desire to find something that students will both want and have to do in order to understand the play. Performance makes students close readers and exact speakers, and it does so without actually calling their attention to those ends. Aiming

at coherence, they usually achieve detail, specificity, even power" (603–04).

Lamb, Julian. "Sense and Sententiousness: Wittgenstein, Milton, Shakespeare." *Wittgenstein Reading*, edited by Wolfgang Huemer et al., De Gruyter, 2013, pp. 55–73.
    Lamb describes how expressions that appealed simultaneously to the ear and mind were useful to writers like Shakespeare. Lamb's essay is instructive because it delineates how comedic writing served authors who wrote outside the bounds of what was traditionally considered the genre of comedy.

Comic Strips and Comic Books

Cole, Jean Lee. *How the Other Half Laughs: The Comic Sensibility in American Culture*. UP of Mississippi, 2020.
    This recent entry into this scholarly tradition meticulously traces ethnic and immigrant cartoons to their origins on the vaudeville stage and in illustrated weeklies and, later, on the editorial pages and Sunday supplements of the turn-of-the-century yellow press and on the early silver screen.

Linneman, William R. "Immigrant Stereotypes, 1880–1900." *Studies in American Humor*, vol. 1, Apr. 1974, pp. 28–39.
    The fact that Linneman's essay appeared in the inaugural issue of *Studies in American Humor* indicates the centrality of ethnic parody and caricature in the American humor canon. Though his was a very early contribution to the scholarly inquiry into immigrant cartoons, many of his insights still hold.

McCloud, Scott. *Reinventing Comics: The Evolution of an Art Form*. HarperCollins Publishers, 2000.

———. *Understanding Comics: The Invisible Art*. HarperCollins Publishers, 1993.
    McCloud's texts use the genre to explore the creative process of making comics. McCloud explores language, symbols, how readers read comics, and much more. McCloud's texts will appeal to a broader audience, not just to fans of comics.

Bev Hogue

Afterword: Teaching Comedy during COVID-19

This collection was conceived well before the advent of COVID-19, before anyone knew how quickly our time-tested teaching practices could be challenged, disrupted, or utterly overturned. My teaching philosophy has long been based on principles of improvisation: structure, collaboration, assessment, adaptation. Like stand-up comics, teachers establish a structure for the learning experience, collaborate with students in making learning happen, assess the impact of the experience as it is happening, and adapt methods in light of changing situations. The demands of teaching during the pandemic certainly tested my improvisation skills, challenging me to adapt teaching methods in unfamiliar and sometimes uncomfortable ways. But as I look back over these essays now, I wonder how the pandemic affected the use of comedy in the classroom. Do dark times make comedy seem too frivolous for academic attention, or does comedy become even more essential as the darkness deepens?

Long before COVID-19, I asked a group of first-year honors students to answer a similar question. At the end of a semester devoted to studying comedy in theory and practice, we read Joseph Meeker's essay "The Comic Mode," which argues that comedy is "the closest art has come to describing man as an adaptive animal" (168) and that it therefore offers "a strategy for living" required for anyone eager to survive in a rapidly changing environment (169). In class, students debated whether comedy is a fringe benefit of human culture or a necessity for survival. After a lively debate supported by examples from their reading, one student made the question more personal: "How about you, Dr. Hogue? Has comedy helped you survive this semester?"

It was a complicated question. I'd started the semester with a full head of hair but lost it all by the third week and spent the rest of the semester covering my bald head with a succession of colorful scarves; repeated rounds of radiation and chemotherapy sometimes left me too weak to stand in front of my students. Sometimes I monitored online class discussions while attached to an IV in the local hospital's chemotherapy center, seeking distraction in my students' insightful explorations of comedy. I taught them how comedy can function as the glue to hold social groups together, and they put that lesson into practice as they bonded together to keep the class functioning while I was sicker than I'd ever been. I had suffered a dangerous allergic reaction during my first round of chemotherapy, but the nurses had laid out rescue drugs beforehand so I could recover quickly; chemotherapy may have helped my body survive, but my comedy class served as a rescue drug for my spirit. But that's just me. Can comedy remain relevant when the entire planet needs rescue drugs?

In the pandemic-infused fall of 2020, I taught a class called Concepts of Comedy that led students on a journey through a wide range of classic and contemporary comedy texts, with essential side trips into theory. We ended the semester with a novel none of my students had previously read: *A Horse Walks into a Bar*, by David Grossman. Set at a comedy club at an Israeli resort city, the novel recounts a stand-up comedian's final performance; readers view the act through the uncomfortable perspective of a curmudgeonly judge who resists laughter and finds comedy frivolous. The awkward performance is punctuated by physical comedy that combines pain and laughter, and it eventually moves into even darker territory as the comedian tries to transform traumatic experiences into jokes. In class discussions, students wrangled with challenging questions: Why does Holocaust humor exist? Does laughing at bullies legitimize bullying? When is pain funny—and why?

As we worked through the novel, I encouraged students to keep track of the many comparisons Grossman uses to help us conceptualize the functions of comedy in human cultures. For instance, in *A Horse Walks into a*

Bar, the comedian is described as "disrobing" (42), walking a tightrope (27), or selling out his loved ones (10), while the audience is a bunch of "idiots" (3), a judge and jury (10), or a family (172). The performance is portrayed as a "game" (172), a battle (34), and a "contract" (30), and the experience produces fuel (52), mirror (18), or "miracle" (58). The comedian offers the "temptation to look into another man's hell" (82) and transforms the audience into both "household members of his soul" and "hostages" (57). The joke that provides the title for the novel—"A horse walks into a bar"—is introduced at a particularly painful moment in the narrative (140), but the jokester never reaches the punch line, so the performance remains eternally incomplete; nevertheless, by the end of the book, the judge realizes that the suffering comedian's power lies in his "passing a flame from one candle to another" (177), transforming suffering into comedy to make connections among struggling human beings.

The final paper in the class asked students to choose one of Grossman's metaphors, analyze how it functioned in the novel and what it suggested about the nature of comedy, and explain whether it applied to a previous text we had read for the class. Reading and writing about a suffering comedian's attempt to improvise his way toward meaning, students grappled with the relationship between comedy and tragedy and began articulating their own philosophy of comedy, a task well suited to the COVID-19 context.

Meeker would say that the comic mode equips us to adapt and survive, and after seeing how many people reached for comedy to help them through the long pandemic lockdowns, I am inclined to agree. In the end we are all engaged in the game, the battle, the improvisation of teaching, and comedy is a natural concomitant to that experience. Like the comedian in *A Horse Walks into a Bar*, we meet our students in a dark place full of discomfort and uncertainty, collaborate with them to create meaning in the darkness, assess the impact of our act even while it's in progress, and adapt to the challenges posed by changing situations. The essays in this volume show us dozens of different ways of achieving these goals, which are even more important when a disaster like COVID-19 disrupts our usual methods. However difficult teaching during a pandemic may be, it has shown us that in the dark times we need comedy the most, when teachers, like comics, must improvise the best possible methods for "passing a flame from one candle to another" (Grossman 177).

Works Cited

Grossman, David. *A Horse Walks into a Bar.* Translated by Jessica Cohen, Vintage Books, 2017.

Meeker, Joseph. "The Comic Mode." *The Ecocriticism Reader: Landmarks in Literary Ecology*, edited by Cheryll Glotfelty and Harold Fromm, U of Georgia P, 1996, pp. 155–69.

Notes on Contributors

Laura Biesiadecki is a PhD candidate in English at Temple University and teaches courses in composition and gender and sexuality at the University of the Arts. Her research examines domesticity and the concepts of house and home in modernist fiction.

Charles Edward Bowie is associate professor of philosophy and religious studies and chair of philosophy and religion at Tennessee State University. As a teacher, he is passionate about using popular culture to make abstract subjects accessible and fun.

Christopher Burlingame works as a writing consultant and study skills specialist at Mount Aloysius College. He earned his PhD from Indiana University of Pennsylvania, his MFA from Chatham University, and his BA from Juniata College. In addition to pedagogy, his research interests include transgressive fiction and adaptation.

Stephen Casmier is associate professor of English at Saint Louis University. He teaches introductory literature courses as well as undergraduate- and graduate-level courses in African American literature. His current research explores the ties between contemporary African American literature and the countercultural movements of the 1960s.

Jared Champion is assistant professor in the Department of Liberal Studies at Mercer University. His research centers primarily on masculinity and humor and has appeared in the *Journal of Popular Culture, Popular Culture Studies Journal*, and *The Journal of Men, Masculinities, and Spirituality*. As a teacher, he takes great pride in applying a writing-intensive approach that builds students' confidence.

Miriam Chirico is professor of English at Eastern Connecticut State University. She has published articles on twentieth-century playwrights such as Eugene O'Neill, G. B. Shaw, Wendy Wasserstein, and John Leguizamo. Most recently she is the author of *The Theatre of Christopher Durang* and coeditor of *How to Teach a Play*. She is a board member of the Comparative Drama Conference.

Peter Conolly-Smith is associate professor at Queens College, City University of New York, where he teaches American history. His areas of specialization include representations of ethnicity and race. A multiple award-winning instructor, he received his PhD in American studies from Yale University. He is the author of *Translating America: An Ethnic Press Visualizes Popular American Culture* (2004).

Jeffrey M. Cordell works for national K–8 literacy products in Houghton Mifflin Harcourt's supplemental and intervention solutions division. He is also a professional theater artist, an educator, a personal coach, and an equity, inclusion, and diversity consultant.

Aaron Duplantier is a member of the teaching faculty in the English, modern languages, and cultural studies department at Nicholls State University. He is the author of *Authenticity and How We Fake It: Belief and Subjectivity in Reality TV, Facebook and YouTube* and has written extensively on pop culture and new media.

Megan M. Echevarría, professor of Spanish and film media studies at the University of Rhode Island, earned her PhD at the University of North Carolina, Chapel Hill. She publishes primarily on Hispanic literature and film, and her research frequently demonstrates her keen interest in interdisciplinarity, interculturality, and pedagogy. Her edited volume, *Rehumanizing the Language Curriculum* (2023), demonstrates the critical place of literary studies in twenty-first-century language curricula.

Mayy ElHayawi is associate professor of English literature at Ain Shams University. She was a postdoctoral Fulbright Scholar at Stanford University and the leader of the Fulbright Humanities Circle in Egypt. Her areas of research include diaspora literature, gender studies, medical humanities, and media studies.

Andy Felt has studied, performed, taught, and produced Shakespeare in locations as varied as Los Angeles, Redlands, London, New Brunswick, Cape Cod, and Orlando. He holds a BA from California State University, San Bernardino, and an MFA from Ohio University. Currently he is associate professor at Marietta College and the artistic director of the Theatre at Marietta College.

Christopher B. Field is associate professor of English at Tennessee State University. He coedited *"I'm Just a Comic Book Boy": Essays on the Intersection of Comics and Punk* (2019) and cowrote *Tell Me a Story: Using Narratives to Break Down Barriers in Composition Courses* (2017).

Lorna Fitzsimmons is professor of humanities at California State University, Dominguez Hills. She specializes in interdisciplinary humanities, including health, cognitive, and environmental.

Jay Friesen holds a PhD in cultural studies from the University of Alberta, where he presently works as an instructor and a partnership coordinator for community service learning. His interests lie in the intersection of comedy, community engagement, and, of course, teaching.

Jeffrey Galbraith is associate professor of English at Wheaton College, Illinois. He writes on satire and controversy in eighteenth-century England, focusing on the relations among literature, religion, and the secular. He has published on print culture, the rhetoric of slavery, post-Restoration drama, John Dryden, Daniel Defoe, and Jonathan Swift. His current project explores how authors engaged with, and responded to, the criticism of religion in the early Enlightenment.

Shelly A. Galliah has previously taught courses in professional and technical communication, composition, science fiction, literature, and popular culture. Her current interests are the pedagogical uses of popular culture and science fiction and comedic science communication. She currently works in communications and marketing for the Michigan Tech Global Campus.

Paul Benedict Grant is associate professor of English at Memorial University. His essays on humor and pedagogy have appeared in the MLA series Approaches to Teaching and in his coedited collection *Carver across the Curriculum: Interdisciplinary Approaches to Teaching the Fiction and Poetry of Raymond Carver* (2011).

Helena Gurfinkel is professor of English at Southern Illinois University, Edwardsville. She is the editor of *PLL: Papers on Language and Literature* and the author of *Outlaw Fathers in Victorian and Modern British Literature: Queering Patriarchy*. She is currently at work on a monograph on the Soviet film and television adaptations of the works of Oscar Wilde.

Vivian Nun Halloran is professor of English and associate dean for diversity and inclusion in the College of Arts and Sciences at Indiana University, Bloomington. She is the author of *The Immigrant Kitchen: Food, Ethnicity, and Diaspora* (2016) and *Exhibiting Slavery: The Caribbean Postmodern Novel as Museum* (2016).

Aaron R. Hanlon is associate professor of English at Colby College. His first book is *A World of Disorderly Notions: Quixote and the Logic of Exceptionalism* (2019). He also writes for broader audiences at *The Washington Post*, *The New York Times*, and elsewhere.

Bev Hogue is McCoy Professor of English at Marietta College, where she incorporates comedy into many writing and literature classes. Her work has appeared in such journals as *Modern Fiction Studies*, *MELUS*, *ISLE*, and *Pedagogy*.

Joy Katzmarzik studied English and history at Johannes Gutenberg University in Mainz, Germany, where her PhD thesis focused on American newspaper comic strips as an art form. She completed her practical teacher training at a German high school in 2020 and currently teaches English and history in Essen, Germany, at a secondary school for students who are deaf and hearing-impaired. She has been working as a freelance illustrator since 2011.

Eric Kennedy is visiting assistant professor of English at Hastings College. He holds a PhD in English from Louisiana State University. His scholarship focuses on sociocultural representations of the lower classes in twentieth- and twenty-first-century American literature and film.

Deborah J. Knuth Klenck taught satire, poetry, and fiction of the long eighteenth century for forty-two years at Colgate University, both on campus and as part of study-group semesters in London. Now professor emerita of English, she has written on Alexander Pope, Samuel Johnson, Barbara Pym, and especially Jane Austen.

Jess Landis is associate professor at Franklin Pierce University. She teaches English, writing, and first-year seminars. She is also an instructor in the university's Women, Gender, and Leadership Program. Her work has appeared in journals such as *Medieval and Renaissance Drama in England* and the *Journal of the Wooden O*.

Jade Lennon is a 2020 graduate of Louisiana State University.

Janice McIntire-Strasburg retired as associate professor of American literature at Saint Louis University in 2022. She is past executive director of the American Humor Studies Association. She coauthored *Mark Twain at the Buffalo Express* with Joseph B. McCullough and has published articles and book chapters about Mark Twain and various American humor subjects.

Samantha A. Morgan-Curtis, associate professor of English and women's studies at Tennessee State University, has published and presented on topics in British literature, pedagogy, popular culture, and gender theory, including the 2003 comic book limited series Marvel 1602, which takes Marvel characters to 1602 England.

Anja Müller-Wood is professor of English literature and culture at Johannes Gutenberg University Mainz. The author of *Angela Carter: Identity Constructed/Deconstructed* (1997) and *The Theatre of Civilized Excess: New Perspectives on Jacobean Tragedy* (2007), she is also coeditor of several essay collections and the open access *International Journal of Literary Linguistics*.

Richard Obenauf earned his MA and PhD at Loyola University Chicago. His research centers on tolerance and intolerance, censorship, political and religious heresy, and the history of ideas. Since 2010 he has taught interdisciplinary courses on literature, history, and politics in the Honors College at the University of New Mexico.

Iñaki Pérez-Ibáñez is assistant professor of Spanish and teacher education at the University of Rhode Island. He holds a PhD in Spanish from the University of Navarre and two master's degrees (one in education and one in computer science) from the University of Rhode Island. He has published four critical editions, one edited volume, and over thirty peer-reviewed articles and book chapters. In his scholarship he focuses primarily on Spanish Golden Age literature, interculturality, and teaching methodologies.

Meenakshi Ponnuswami is associate professor of English at Bucknell University, where she teaches modern drama and ethnic comedy. Her recent publications have focused on British Muslim playwrights and Alice Childress's drama theory. She is currently working on British Asian comedy and a collection of South Asian American plays.

Tiffany Potter is professor of teaching in the Department of English at the University of British Columbia. She publishes extensively in eighteenth-century studies and in pedagogy: she is the editor of *Approaches to Teaching the Works of Eliza Haywood* (2020) and the Broadview Press edition of Aphra Behn's *Oroonoko* (2020). She was awarded Canada's 3M National Teaching Prize in 2020.

Mary Ann Rishel has taught first-year writing seminars and humorous writing for over forty years, with special interest in humor theory and the scholarship of teaching and learning. She is professor emerita in the humanities at Ithaca College and professor (retired) at the Weill Cornell Medical College in Qatar.

David Ritchie, professor of history at Pacific Northwest College of Art until his retirement in 2021, is also a poet and a playwright. He is working on a book about the cultural history of weapons, a novel, and a collection of essays.

Lisa Smith is assistant professor of teaching of English at Pepperdine University, where she teaches early American literature and composition, focusing on gender, spirituality, and comics. She has published a monograph on newspapers during the First Great Awakening and a book on spiritual passion and has presented at Comic-Con International.

Ameer Sohrawardy is a lecturer in the English department at Ocean County College. He has published essays on *Julius Caesar* in *The English Journal*, on *The Comedy of Errors* in *Native Shakespeares: Indigenous Appropriations on a Global Stage*, and on George Sandys and the Anthropocene in *Early Modern Culture*.

Kimberly Tolson teaches English at Lewis-Clark State College. Her publications have appeared in *Pacific View Newsletter*, *Sonora Review*, *San Antonio Review*, *Solstice Literary Magazine*, and *100 Word Story*. She also fosters educational growth through board games on her personal *YouTube* channel.

Mariann J. VanDevere received her joint doctorates in English and media studies from Vanderbilt University. She also holds an MFA in creative writing (fiction) from Rutgers University. In addition to teaching writing courses at both her alma maters, Mariann served as a Fulbright English Teaching

Assistant at the University of the Witwatersrand in Johannesburg, South Africa, in 2012. While at Vanderbilt, Mariann engaged her creative and comedic side by founding The Comedy Collective, a sketch comedy group made up of undergraduate and graduate students of color. Currently, she works as a developmental editor and uses humor to help her clients build the skills and confidence needed to reach their writing goals.

Michelle D. Wise is associate professor of English at Tennessee State University. Her research interests include film studies, gothic studies, children's literature, popular culture studies, comic and graphic novels, and gender studies. She has presented and published on comic and graphic novels and on film.

James Zeigler is associate professor of English at the University of Oklahoma. He is the author of *Red Scare Racism and Cold War Black Radicalism* (2015) and coeditor of the journal *Genre*, which is published by Duke University Press on behalf of the University of Oklahoma's Department of English.